Anthropological Papers
Museum of Anthropology, University of Michigan
No. 81

The Bridgeport Township Site

Archaeological Investigation at 20SA620, Saginaw County, Michigan

Edited by
John M. O'Shea
and
Michael Shott

Ann Arbor
1990

Printed in the
United States of America

ISBN 0-915703-19-X

Cover design by Marty Somberg

Library of Congress Cataloging-in-Publication Data

The Bridgeport township site : archaeological investigation at 20SA620, Saginaw County, Michigan / edited by John M. O'Shea and Michael Shott.
p. cm. — (Anthropological papers ; no. 81)
Includes bibliographical references.
ISBN 0-915703-19-x
1. Bridgeport Township Site (Mich.) 2. Indians of North America—Michigan—Saginaw County—Antiquities. 3. Saginaw County (Mich.)—Antiquities. I. Shott, Michael. II. Series: Anthropological papers (University of Michigan. Museum of Anthropology) ; no. 81.
E78.B74 1989
977.4'46—dc20 89-48109
CIP

Contents

List of Tables

List of Figures

List of Plates

1
Introduction

John M. O'Shea
Museum of Anthropology, University of Michigan

The Bridgeport Township site (20SA620) is located in the northeast quarter of section 17 and the adjoining northwest quarter of section 16 of Bridgeport Charter Township (T11N, R5E) in Saginaw County, Michigan. The site is situated on a low sandy knoll approximately 850 meters north of the Cass River, at an elevation of 589 feet, or 182 meters, above mean sea level (a.m.s.l.). The core of the site was an area roughly 150 by 110 m in extent on the knoll, although archaeological materials in varying densities were visible on the surface over an area of several acres.

Although archaeological materials had been recovered from the vicinity for some time by local collectors, plans for the improvement of the Bridgeport Township Wastewater Treatment Plant brought about the first professional examination and reporting of the site. An archaeological salvage excavation was conducted at the site by the University of Michigan Museum of Anthropology during May and June of 1985 in advance of the site's final destruction as part of construction activities. This report represents the completion of data recovery activities for the site.

PREVIOUS INVESTIGATIONS

The initial documentation of the site was conducted by Fel Brunett, then of the Saginaw Archaeological Commission (Brunett 1982, 1983). Brunett's work at the site was preceded by amateur investigations in the site vicinity, by Michael J. Neering (see Brunett 1983) and Lloyd Bowen, both of Saginaw. Brunett's investigation of 20SA620 consisted of a brief surface reconnaissance and the excavation of 21 backhoe trenches (roughly 5 m long and from 0.5 to 1.0 m in depth), eight 1 m profile cuts and three 1 by 2 m test units. The location of the various test units and the general character of surface densities reported by Brunett are shown in Figure 1.1. These tests revealed a dark, organic soil layer that ranged from 0.5 to 1.0 m in thickness and contained quantities of cultural material. The base of this dark zone formed an uneven contact with the sterile yellow sands beneath it and suggested the existence of cultural features extending down into the lower sterile horizon.

An impressive range of cultural materials was reported by Brunett, which included ceramics from the Early, Middle and Late Woodland periods, and a lithic assemblage containing projectile points, drills, scrapers, cores and a drilled slate object. Equally impressive, however, were the organic, particularly plant, remains that were reported to include squash and wild cucumber seeds (but see Chapter 10), as well as bone representing turtle, fish, and white-tailed deer (see also Chapter 9). From these materials it was argued that the site deposits were the result of occupation during several time periods including Early, Middle and early Late Woodland.

The overall distribution and density of cultural materials at the site was characterized by Brunett as a generalized scatter of materials over an area roughly 150 m by 110 m (excluding any portion of the site that extended beyond the property to be affected by improvements to the wastewater treatment facility). Within the northeastern portion of this large scatter, a dense concentration of cultural material, roughly 50 by 50 m in area (Fig. 1.1), was recognized. Brunett also noted that a portion of the site had already been disturbed by construction and that topsoil containing quantities of cultural materials was to be found in several dirt piles on the site of the treatment plant.

Based on Brunett's investigation, Martha Bigelow, the director of the Bureau of History of the Michigan Department of State and State Historic Preservation Officer, in consultation with State Archaeologist John R. Halsey, recommended the site for inclusion on the National Register of Historic Places on the 13th of April, 1984. The site was determined eligible for inclusion on the National Register by the Department of the Interior on September 9, 1984. Since the construction plans for the wastewater treatment plant improvements left no alternative to the total destruction of the archaeological site, a data recovery plan for the site was formulated. This plan, based on the results of Brunett's testing, was prepared by myself, in consultation with Dr. Halsey. The original plan sought to focus research at the site on two basic themes: (1) to view the dynamics of the immediate post-Nipissing occupation of the Shiawassee embayment area, contrasting the relatively well known Late Archaic pattern of exploitation with the less well known Early Woodland pattern; and (2) to document the spread of tropical cultigens into the Saginaw region during the Woodland period. Two kinds of data recovery were critical to achieving these goals: the extensive excavation of large contiguous blocks in order to separate the distinct components

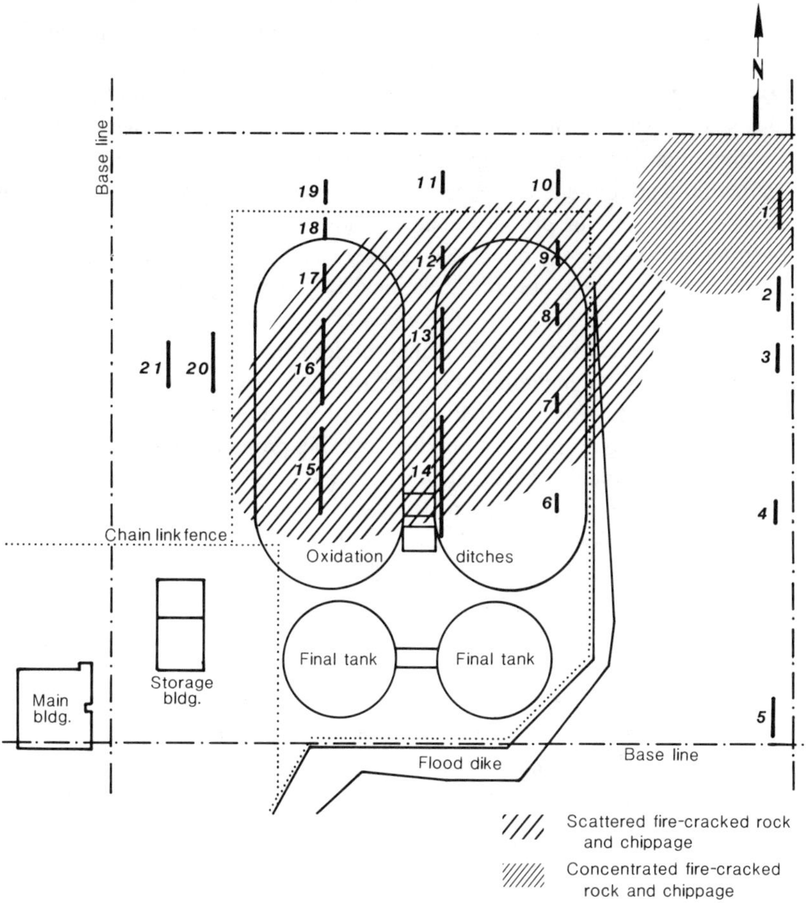

Figure 1.1 The location of test units and the characterization of surface densities at 20SA620 as reported by Brunett (1983).

present at the site, and the application of microrecovery techniques in order to collect the small and fragile plant and animal remains that would be crucial to documenting seasonality and subsistence change. The plan called for a two-stage investigation of the site: an extensive phase, where sample test units would be distributed over the entire area of surface scatter reported by Brunett to assess the overall distribution of activities and periods represented at the site, followed by an intensive phase in which a 10 by 10 m block in the area of dense concentration would be excavated to recover evidence of fine spatial structure. The data recovery plan was submitted to Bridgeport Charter Township and to the Environmental Impact Section of the Environmental Protection Agency on September 4, 1984.

Unfortunately, prior to the completion of the National Register nomination process, two events occurred which materially altered and damaged 20SA620. The first was the construction of twin oxidation ditches for the wastewater treatment plant expansion. This construction destroyed irrevocably three-quarters of the original site area as identified by Brunett. This destruction was limited, however, to the area of generalized scatter and did not affect the zone of primary concentration. It remains unclear when this construction was begun, but it seems likely that it was undertaken prior to the Township's application for a National Register eligibility determination for the site.

The second event was the accidental bulldozing of a large portion of the remaining site area, including the zone of maximum surface concentration noted by Brunett. This occurred on the 11th of July, 1984, and left intact only a narrow strip of the site along the township property line. At the request of the Environmental Protection Agency, an investigation of the circumstances surrounding the site destruction was conducted by the departmental consulting archaeologist of the Department of the Interior. The results of that investigation have not, to date, been made public.

As a result of these substantial modifications to 20SA620, the data recovery plan, which called for extensive area excavation to detect significant spatial separation of activities and components on the site, was no longer viable. Instead, the remaining site area was excavated *in toto*. As Figure 1.2 illustrates, this resulted in the excavation of a strip some 31 m long and 1 to 4 m wide. Clearly, the kinds of research problems that could be addressed on a site remnant of this type were severely limited. Instead, the problem became to salvage all of the site that still remained.

Although most of the potential for isolating spatially discrete loci of cultural activity at the site had been eliminated, the site still offered potential for the stratigraphic separation of distinct site components and for the recovery of intact features which could provide a view of changing site activities through time, and a context for the recovery of carbonized plant and animal materials. There was also the possibility that the distinct occupational components might exhibit some separation over the long north-south axis of the site. Despite the magnitude of destruction at 20SA620, there was still the potential to address many of the questions originally set out in the data recovery plan. The ability to answer these questions, however, depended on specific characteristics of the site deposit, which would only be known once excavation had begun.

A determination of the eastward extent of the site beyond the property owned by the township was beyond the scope of the revised excavation plan and remains unknown. The knoll on which the site is located continues some 12 m east of that property line. Although Brunett mentioned the possibility of the site continuing in this area, he made no direct assessment of the

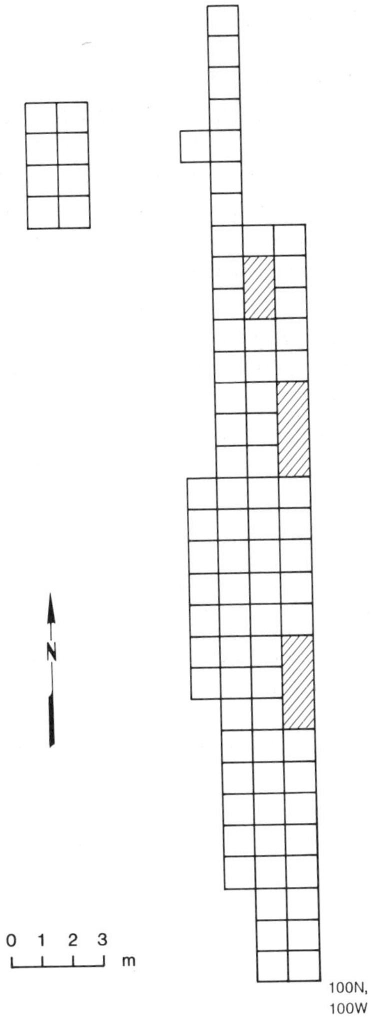

Figure 1.2 Plan of UMMA excavation at 20SA620.

possibility. During the University of Michigan excavations at 20SA620 permission was received to excavate two 1 by 1 m test squares in this area (see Chapter 5). These tests confirm that the occupation did continue in this area, but also strongly suggest that the focus of occupation at the site was in the area destroyed by construction.

NARRATIVE OF ACTIVITIES

A contract for archaeological data recovery at the site of 20SA620 was awarded to the University of Michigan Museum of Anthropology on the 14th of May, 1985. Fieldwork began on May 22 and continued for a period of six weeks. Preliminaries at the site included the precise demarcation of the township property line, the definition of the remaining site surface (which encompassed an area roughly 90 m^2) and the testing of areas disturbed by earthmoving in an effort to locate deep features that might survive intact within this disturbed zone. The results of shovel skimming in these areas were entirely negative and revealed either the basal sterile sand layer and the underlying clay of the ancient lake bottom (see Chapter 6) or evidence of filling and leveling.

The techniques of excavation, recovery and analysis at the site are described in Chapter 4. During the six-week period of excavation, geomorphological testing was conducted by William Farrand of the University of Michigan Department of Geology and Museum of Anthropology (Chapter 6). A survey of existing amateur collections from the 20SA620 site locality was also completed in collaboration with the Saginaw Chapter of the Michigan Archaeological Society.

During the course of fieldwork, laboratory facilities were provided by the director of the Saginaw Valley Historical Commission, Charles Hoover. Once fieldwork was completed, excavated materials were transported to the Great Lakes Division of the Museum of Anthropology for sorting and analysis. With the exception of the botanical remains, which were analyzed by Kathryn Egan of Michigan State University and the carbon-14 dates, all analysis was conducted at the Museum of Anthropology of the University of Michigan.

2
History of Saginaw Valley Research

Michael Shott
University of Northern Iowa

The history of archaeological exploration in the Saginaw Valley is long and distinguished, befitting an area which "contains the greatest concentration of archaeological sites in the State of Michigan" (Peebles 1978:84). Perhaps the earliest archaeological exploration of the region was McCormick's 1833–34 journey on the Cass and Flint rivers (McCormick 1881) in which he reported a large number of sites, many of which were subsequently destroyed before systematic archaeological investigation could be carried out (Shott and Welch 1984:2). Most were situated on the Flint River, but McCormick does supply an account of an aboriginal earthwork enclosure, 20SA123, in Bridgeport Township.

The first systematic archaeological research conducted in the Saginaw Valley was Harlan Smith's effort, carried out largely in conjunction with the St. Louis Exhibition. Smith, a Saginaw native, studied extant collections (substantial collections had been amassed even by that time) and conducted surveys of the area. His was the first published work on Saginaw archaeology in a major anthropological journal (Smith 1901). But Smith's efforts were preliminary in nature and he soon turned his attention to other regions. It remained for Fred Dustin to undertake the first systematic documentation of the scale of the Saginaw Valley archaeological record, a contribution which rightfully earned him the sobriquet of founder of archaeology in the region (Peebles 1978:86).

Dustin, a founding member of the Michigan Archaeological Society, carefully and patiently conducted survey work in all parts of the basin. Using a unique recording system later adopted by proteges such as Ralph Stroebel, Walter Schmidt and Arthur Walser, Dustin recorded dozens of sites and attempted some of the first syntheses of the region's prehistory (Dustin 1915, 1930; Fitting 1968). He employed a set of cultural and chronological systematics which are largely outmoded today, but his contribution was enormous; primarily through Dustin's efforts, Saginaw's impressive archaeological legacy was documented. Dustin also was instrumental in organizing a network of local workers to continue his efforts in the Saginaw Valley. This part of his legacy remains in the form of an active avocational organization and a continued association with universities in the state, notably the University of Michigan.

Partly at the strong urging of the local archaeological community (I. Butterfield, personal communication) major survey and excavation projects were launched by the University of Michigan in the late 1950s and continued well into the following decade. Peebles (1978) has chronicled these efforts. Chief among these was undoubtedly the excavation of the Schultz site (20SA2) in the early 1960s. Schultz, situated where the Tittabawassee, Shiawassee, Flint and Cass rivers converge to form the Saginaw River, witnessed occupation throughout the Woodland period, although the Early and Late Woodland components are most important. Since its excavation, Schultz has figured prominently in reconstructions of regional prehistory and prehistoric cultural organization (Bigony 1970; Cleland 1966; Fitting 1972; Ozker 1982; Peebles 1978), although Lovis and Ozker both argue that at least its Early Woodland occupation was no more than seasonal and may not have served as a central focus for the settlement system. Schultz and the nearby Green Point site (20SA1) yielded the first evidence for plant cultivation in the Great Lakes region (Ozker 1982:39–42; Wright 1964:21). The Schultz site continues to play an important role in interpretations of Woodland occupation of the Saginaw Valley.

The Kantzler site (20BY30) in Bay City also was excavated in the 1960s (Crumley 1973). It yielded major Middle and Late Woodland components.

The University of Michigan continued research during the 1960s on other Woodland sites (Bigony 1970) as well as a series of important Archaic sites. Although the Archaic period is not germane to this report, excavations at Schmidt (Fairchild 1977; Harrison 1966), Andrews (Papworth 1967), Hart (Wright and Morlan 1964) and Feeheley (Taggart n.d.) deserve mention. Taggart's (1967) synthesis of Late Archaic settlement dynamics served as a model for a long period of time and remains viable in most respects (Keene 1981; Lovis 1984). Michigan State University entered the Saginaw archaeological scene at that time with work at the important Fletcher site (Brashler 1978; Mainfort 1979).

During the 1960s, local individuals continued to make major contributions to the area's archaeological record. Donald Foster worked, among other places, at the Leach site (20SA202; Taggart 1981). Most importantly, however, Arthur Graves, with assistance from University of Michigan crews and other Michigan Archaeological Society members, excavated the Bussinger site (20SA194) the Bugai site (20SA215; Halsey 1976), and the Tyra site (20SA29). Data recovered from these notable Woodland habitation and burial sites have made important contributions to our understanding of the period.

During the 1970s, a number of projects of less ambitious scope were conducted in the Saginaw Valley. Fitting (1975a:xiv-xxvi) has summarized many of these, but several deserve special mention. Keene (1981) produced a major synthesis of Late Archaic adaptations in the area for his dissertation at the University of Michigan. The Saginaw Archaeological Commission (SAC) was formed during the decade as well. Staffed by Felice Brunett, SAC carried out numerous contract projects as well as documentary surveys of several townships in the county. Perhaps its most noteworthy project was the excavation of the Solms site on the Tittabawassee River, where a series of Woodland occupation floors was sealed by successive alluvial lenses. Solms yielded a substantial assemblage, especially of ceramics. In secure stratigraphic context, the assemblage could furnish at least part of a master sequence for the region. Its potential is enormous, but to date Solms remains largely neglected.

Several noteworthy projects have been conducted in recent years. In 1983, Michigan State University conducted excavations at the Weber I site (20SA581) in Frankenmuth Township (Lovis 1983). Located at what was the mouth of the Cass River during the Nipissing stage, Weber I yielded a rare *in situ* Middle Archaic component as well as Late Archaic and Late Woodland Wayne Tradition occupations. Lovis continued major efforts in the Saginaw Valley in 1984, working on the Third Street Bridge project in Bay City (Lovis 1986). Located adjacent to the Fletcher site, he discovered Late Archaic through Late Woodland occupations along a series of terraces formed by the Saginaw River during successive post-Nipissing stages in the Huron basin. Together with the Kantzler and Fletcher sites, this work documents the heavy aboriginal settlement of the lower reaches of the Saginaw Valley. In 1984, a survey of tremendously important and archaeologically complex portions of the Flint and Cass rivers was carried out (Dorwin 1985). The survey did not cover 20SA620 or the adjacent area. Unfortunately, the conduct and documentation of the survey was seriously deficient and little can be gleaned from the results. Definitive survey and analysis of sites located on the margins of these major streams must await future investigations.

3
Paleoecology of the Bridgeport Area

Kathryn C. Egan
The Museum, Michigan State University

Site 20SA620 is located within the lower basin of the Saginaw Valley, of Michigan, on an Algoma age terrace on the north side of the Cass River. Because archaeological evidence indicates that the site was not occupied until after the drop from the Nipissing to the Algoma Lake stage, around 3200 b.p., paleoecological reconstruction will focus on the post-Nipissing period, outlining the context to which the prehistoric occupants of the site adapted.

Saginaw Bay borders the Saginaw drainage basin to the east. To the north, west and south the region is bordered by beach terraces produced by Lake Saginaw and other pre- and postglacial high water levels. These terraces and moraines provide moderate relief and circumscribe the Cass, Shiawassee, and Tittabawassee rivers which drain into the Saginaw River and from there into Saginaw Bay. The interior of the drainage basin has relatively level lacustrine deposits broken by a crescent of end moraines running parallel to the bay. The dendritic river network which drains the region gives it a highly dissected character. Further, extensive wetlands are present due to the limited topographic relief and poorly drained glacial and lacustrine soils.

The environment of the Saginaw Valley region is structured by several factors including: glacial and postglacial events; geology; the network of rivers draining through the Saginaw River (Fig. 3.1); climate; and its location within the transition zone between the Carolinian and Canadian biotic provinces (Dice 1943; Potzger 1948; C. Cleland 1966; Curtis 1978). In combination, these factors define a unique ecosystem called the Saginaw District (Albert, Denton and Barnes 1986:18).

Located within the tension zone between the Carolinian and Canadian biotic provinces, the region supports northern, southern and transitional biotic communities. These communities occur in a patchy configuration. Fluctuations in lake level caused periodic flooding of the region throughout prehistory and further influenced the distribution of these communities. The

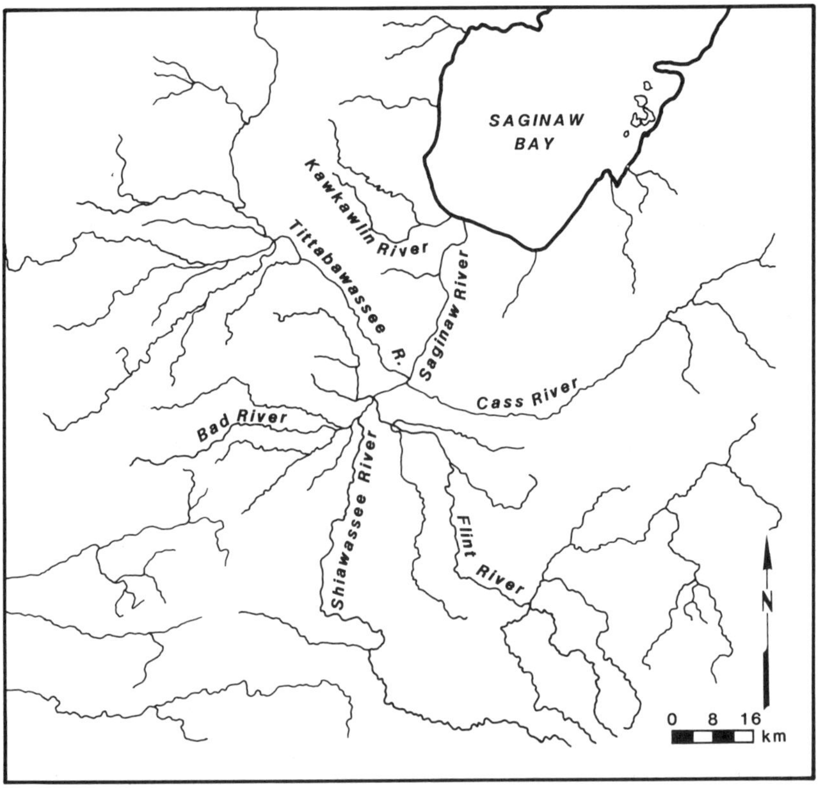

Figure 3.1. River systems draining the Saginaw Valley.

environment, therefore, provided a rich array of resources to the prehistoric inhabitants of the region (Yarnell 1964; C. Cleland 1966; Keene 1981), yet presented logistical problems due to uneven distribution of resources (Lovis 1985; Egan 1988).

GEOLOGY AND PHYSIOGRAPHY

The geology and physiography of the study area are strongly related to its glacial and postglacial history (Dorr and Eschman 1971). Until around 14,000 b.p., this region was covered by the Saginaw lobe of the Wisconsinan stage glacial advance. By about 13,800 b.p. the Saginaw lobe had retreated from the basin. Glacial meltwater collected in the Saginaw region forming Lake Saginaw, which drained south and west to Lake Chicago. Continued recession of the Saginaw lobe resulted in the creation of the Port Huron moraine and a second recessional moraine at Bay City. The size of Lake Saginaw continued to increase.

Subsequent to the establishment of the Saginaw Basin, the region was alternately inundated and drained by a series of postglacial lake stages. These long-term fluctuations in the Huron Basin elevations were the result of continued glacial retreat, isostatic rebound, and incision of new drainage outlets.

Lakes Saginaw and Chicago combined in the Lake Algonquin stage (605 ft/184 m, a.m.s.l.), when the basins of Lakes Huron and Michigan were free of ice (ca. 11,000 b.p.). Subsequent to this, low outlets, exposed by crustal depression to the north and continued glacial retreat, initiated the drainage of Lake Algonquin to the Lake Stanley stage (158 ft/48 m, a.m.s.l.) in the Huron Basin. Drainage to the Lake Stanley stage was accomplished by about 9500 b.p. Continued crustal warping, increased the level of the outlets and thus the elevation of waters in the Huron Basin to the Nipissing Great Lakes stage by 4700–4500 b.p. (Monaghan, Faye and Lovis 1986). At this time the Saginaw drainage system began to approximate its current configuration. Later closure of northern drainage outlets shifted outflow to the south (Nipissing II), and continued outlet incision allowed for drainage of the Nipissing high water levels. Water elevations briefly stabilized at the Algoma stage (595 ft/181 m, a.m.s.l.) approximately 3200 b.p. Modern lake level elevations (580 ft/177 m, a.m.s.l.) were established around 2600 or 2500 b.p. with continued drainage of the area (Speth 1972; see also, Lovis 1986 for detailed description of postglacial events).

Situated between 600 and 597 ft a.m.s.l., the 20SA620 site would have been exposed for occupation between the Lake Algonquin and Nipissing Great Lakes stages. There is, however, no evidence for human occupation at this time. During the Nipissing stage the site would have been inundated, and not re-exposed until recession of the Nipissing to the Algoma stage (see Chapter 6). Earliest evidence for occupation of the site is associated with the Terminal Archaic period, which ends around 2500 b.p. in the Saginaw Valley region, after the Nipissing recession.

Post-Algoma events strongly influenced the environment, affecting the distribution of wetlands and locations of stream channels. Recession of the Algoma stage to modern elevations (580 ft) resulted in continued ponding of water between the moraines at Saginaw and Bay City, creating extensive marshes and swamps. Upstream, the remnant Shiawassee Bay created during the Nipissing high water stage, remained a poorly drained wetland. Near 20SA620 there is a slough formed by a remnant stream channel abutting the Cass River. This channel may have been established during the Algoma stage and developed into a slough as lake levels dropped to their modern elevation.

Evidence suggests that subsequent to the drop from Algoma levels there were several short periods of high water in the Huron Basin and Bay City area (Speth 1972; Larsen 1985; Lovis 1989; see also Chapter 6). These

Figure 3.2. Topography of 20SA620 and its environs.

fluctuations have been correlated with changing patterns of temperature and precipitation (Larsen 1985). One such flood event is documented by Speth (1972) at the Schultz site (20SA2) at the confluence of the Saginaw and Cass rivers.

The Saginaw drainage basin is flat, interrupted occasionally by low ridges, sand dunes and moraines. Most of the interior of the region is clay lake plain.

Extensive glacial drainageways dissect it. The majority of the glacial drainageways are poorly drained and crosscut by excessively drained beach ridges. Low sand dunes have formed downwind of the drainageways; some are several miles long. A crescent of end moraines runs parallel to Saginaw Bay. Beach ridges and shallow depressions occur along the bay (Albert, Denton and Barnes 1986; see Chapter 6).

Site 20SA620 is situated on a sand dune within a till plain modified by water. The soils in the area are classified as members of the Tappan-Londo-Poseyville association, which are nearly level, poorly drained soils formed from loamy and sandy parent materials (USDA 1988). The geomorphological analysis in Chapter 6 of this volume details specific formation of the soils.

CLIMATE

The present climate of the Saginaw Valley is relatively mild due to the ameliorating effects of the lake. Average annual rainfall for the region is 28–32 inches and average annual snowfall is 50 inches. The maximum growing season is as long as 153 to 155 days. In Saginaw County, the average date for the last killing frost is May 5th and the average date for the first killing frost in autumn is October 7th. The growing season is comparable to that at the southern end of the state (Albert, Denton and Barnes 1986:18). This mild climate and long growing season are considered to have been sufficient for prehistoric agriculture (Yarnell 1964). Overall, the present climate in the Saginaw Valley is probably similar to the climate throughout the Woodland periods.

VEGETATION

Palynological sequences from several locales bordering the Saginaw Valley document the evolution of Holocene forest communities within this region. Following deglaciation of the region and until 8000 b.p. the area was forested first by spruce forest-tundra communities and then mixed pine and deciduous communities. By 8100 or 8000 b.p. an increasing diversity and abundance of hardwood species began to replace pine and by 7500 b.p. the Carolinian oak-hickory and Canadian pine-dominated biotic communities were established in central Michigan (Hushen et al. 1966). It was by this time that the ecotone between the Carolinian and Canadian biotic provinces was established with forest communities comparable to modern communities. Fluctuations in pollen frequencies of pine and hardwood species suggest that climatic changes resulted in vegetational shifts within the transition zone in this region (Gilliam, Kapp and Bogue 1967; McMurray et al. 1978). The northern portion of the Saginaw Basin lies within the tension zone, as currently defined, and the 20SA620 site is located just south of it. The floristic composition of the region was therefore strongly influenced by its location relative to the ecotone and variations in its composition.

Albert, Denton and Barnes (1986:18) have defined the Saginaw drainage basin as the "Saginaw District," a distinct ecosystem delimited by a unique set of geologic, climatic and biotic characteristics. Their reconstruction of the vegetation prior to logging indicates that communities containing a mix of southern and northern taxa occurred throughout the Saginaw District. Poorly drained clay, such as the lake-plain soils, supported forests with hemlock, white pine, burr oak, swamp white oak, red ash, and American elm, while beech-sugar maple forests grew in moderately well drained clay soils. Beach ridges originally supported white pine, red pine, black oak and white oak. Hemlock, northern white cedar, tamarack, red maple, trembling aspen and other swamp species grew in wetter depressions and pin oak was found in poorly drained mineral soils. On the narrow bands of fine-textured end moraines, beech-maple forest communities grew.

According to Veatch's (1959) reconstruction of the presettlement vegetation on the basis of soil type and the General Land Office (GLO) survey records, 20SA620 was situated within a white pine forest with some southern deciduous species. Southern, northern, and transitional, mesic and wet site forest and marsh communities occurred within 20 km of the site during the presettlement era. The highly mixed character of the presettlement vegetation is a consequence of the Saginaw Valley's position in the ecotone between the Carolinian-Canadian biotic provinces.

The GLO records of a 5 km area surrounding the site indicate that a diverse range of taxa grew around the site. Pine is present as well as a mix of other northern taxa, including beech (*Fagus grandifolia*), aspen (*Populus* spp.), and tamarack (*Larix laricina*). Southern taxa include butternut (*Juglans cinerea*), white oak (*Quercus alba*), black oak (*Quercus velutina*), hickory (*Carya* spp.), elm (*Ulmus* spp.), hackberry (*Celtis occidentalis*), ironwood (*Ostrya virginiana*), and hornbeam (*Carpinus caroliniana*); and transitional taxa include maple (*Acer* spp.), lynn (*Tilia americana*), ash (*Fraxinus* spp.), red oak (*Quercus rubra*), and willow (*Salix* spp.). There are three general types of forest communities represented: dry-mesic, mesic, and swamp.

According to the GLO records (1821) the area within a 1.5 km radius of the site contained a limited range of tree species, characteristic of dry-mesic sites during the presettlement era (Table 3.1). All taxa occur in relatively low densities and there is no apparent dominance of any single forest type (i.e., northern, southern or transitional).

The GLO records also note the presence of a swamp less than one mile north of the site and a marsh abutting the river on the south side where the current slough is located. Unfortunately the GLO records do not specifically describe

TABLE 3.1
Frequencies of Species Reported in the GLO Records within 1.5 km of 20SA620

Taxa	Counts
Ash/*Fraxinus* spp.	2
Beech/*Fagus grandifolia*	6
Butternut/*Juglans cinerea*	2
Elm/*Ulmus* spp.	2
Hickory/*Carya* spp.	2
Hornbeam/*Carpinus caroliniana*	2
Lynn/*Tilia americana*	4
Maple/*Acer* spp.	4
Pine/*Pinus* spp.	2
Tamarack/*Larix laricina*	2
White oak/*Quercus alba*	3

the vegetative communities occurring in these habitats. Comparable sites in Wisconsin (Curtis 1978) suggest, however, that the swamp probably contained a high diversity of woody and herbaceous northern and southern species. The specific composition of any swamp community is dependent on the pH of the water. Marshes characteristically have a low species diversity but are frequently dominated by grasses and economically useful taxa such as cattail (*Typha* sp.) and arrowhead (*Sagittaria* sp.).

Currently, the river margins in the Saginaw Valley support several varieties of fruit-bearing shrubs, including blackberry (*Rubus* spp.), grape (*Vitis* spp.) and hawthorn (*Crataegus* spp.). Archaeobotanical assemblages throughout the valley indicate that these resources were available and regularly exploited throughout prehistory (Yarnell 1964; Egan 1988; see also Chapter 10 of this volume).

FAUNA

A high diversity of economically important faunal species occurs in the Saginaw Valley. Mammals characteristic of forest and aquatic habitats in both the Carolinian and Canadian biotic provinces are present. Historically, 77 percent of the northern coniferous forest mammal species, 87 percent of southern deciduous forest mammal species, all of the inter-biome species, and 71 percent of Great Plains grasslands species found in Michigan were present in the Saginaw Valley (Baker 1983). Many of these taxa are represented in Woodland assemblages from the Saginaw Valley (Table 3.2) and testify to the diversity of species available.

TABLE 3.2
Identified Vertebrate Taxa from Woodland Sites in the Saginaw Valley, Michigan

	20SA2[a]	20BY79[b]	20BY28[c]	20BY30[d]
MAMMALS				
Muskrat	X		X	X
Deer	X	X	X	X
Beaver	X		X	X
Raccoon	X	X	X	
Elk	X		X	X
Bear	X		X	X
Dog	X			X
Dog/wolf			X	
Otter	X		X	
Meadow vole	X			
Mink	X			
Porcupine	X			
Fisher	X			
Woodchuck	X			
Rabbit				X
Squirrel				X
Wolf	X			X
Fox				X
Coyote				X
Marten	X			
Skunk	X			
Bobcat	X		X	
Pine vole	X			
Bog lemming	X			
Shrew			X	
Chipmunk			X	
TURTLES				
Soft-shell turtle	X			
Snapping turtle	X			X
Blanding's turtle	X			X
Map turtle	X			
Painted turtle	X	X		X
Pond slider	X			
Hidden-necked turtle		X		
BIRDS				
Duck	X			X
Swan				X
Blue-winged teal	X			
Merganer	X			X
Common mallard	X			
American bittern	X			
Crow	X			
Sandhill crane	X			X
Great blue heron	X			
Turkey	X			
Common loon	X			
Common snipe	X			

3.2 continued

	20SA2[a]	20BY79[b]	20BY28[c]	20BY30[d]
Canada goose	X			
Passenger pigeon	X			X
Scaup			X	X
Scoter				X
Redhead			X	
Grebe			X	X
Bald eagle				X
Owl				X
FISH				
Walleye	X	X	X	X
Drum	X		X	X
Sturgeon	X		X	X
Gar	X			X
Bullhead	X			
Channel catfish	X			
Bowfin	X		X	X
Catfish	X		X	X
Northern pike	X			X
Pike			X	
Largemouth bass	X			
Perch	X	X	X	X
Sucker	X		X	X
Lake trout	X			X
Largemouth bass				X
Smallmouth bass	X			
Black bass		X		
Crappie		X		
Sunfish			X	X
Sauger				X
Burbot				X

[a]Cleland 1966:94–96.
[b]Franz 1986.
[c]Lovis et al. 1989.
[d]Crumley 1973:200–214.

As noted above, the aquatic characteristics of the Saginaw Valley varied throughout the Algoma and post-Algoma periods when 20SA620 was occupied. For example, aquatic habitats changed in their configurations and would have supported different fish species. Currently, a wide range of species characteristic of lakes, rivers and shallow slow-moving waters such as marshes can be found in the Saginaw Valley (see C. Cleland 1966; Keene 1981). Anadromous species such as lake sturgeon and sucker are also present and seasonally abundant in riverine contexts. Archaeological evidence indicates that Woodland populations in the Saginaw Valley exploited many of these taxa (Table 3.2).

A variety of turtles common to both terrestrial and aquatic habitats are also represented in the Saginaw Valley. Archaeological remains from Woodland period sites in the Saginaw Valley indicate that a variety of species of turtle were exploited prehistorically (Table 3.2).

Finally, the Saginaw Valley is located within a minor flyway and seasonally attracts migratory waterfowl. Although densities vary by species, they can be considered an important resource within this area (Table 3.2; Keene 1981). Passenger pigeon (*Ectopistes migratorius*) was seasonally abundant throughout Michigan in early historic times and prehistorically as well. This species traveled in extremely large flocks, sometimes over a billion, and would have been a valuable resource to the prehistoric occupants of the Saginaw Valley and 20SA620 (Table 3.2; Keene 1981; C. Cleland 1966).

CONCLUSION

Throughout the time that 20SA620 was occupied, the paleoecology of the Saginaw Valley was similar to that observed historically. Located on the margin between the Carolinian and Canadian biotic provinces the Saginaw Valley supports a high diversity of plant and animal species. Further, the dendritic network of river systems, lack of elevational relief and poor drainage of many of the soil types within the valley resulted in vast expanses of wetland habitats. A diverse range of taxa from several biotic communities occur in the valley; these communities are patchy and disjunct in their distribution. Densities of resources are lower in this region than in either the Carolinian or Canadian biotic provinces because of the patchy nature of the environment. Therefore, yields from any forest taxa are low compared to southern or northern locales. The diversity and abundance of wetland and riverine resources within the valley would, however, offset the low productivity of these forest species. Further, the river network would provide easy access to a variety of resource zones and act as a buffer against local level fluctuations in resource productivity.

4
Excavation Procedures

Michael Shott
University of Northern Iowa

During the first three weeks of May, 1985, preparations were made for the fieldwork at 20SA620. Crew members were assembled, equipment was gathered, and arrangements were made with township officials for the use of township facilities on site. Schedules and protocol were discussed with the construction crew. We also spoke with members of the Saginaw Valley chapter of the Michigan Archaeological Society. Chapter President Richard Bisbing acted as a liaison with the local archaeological community. Arrangements were made through Mr. Bisbing to have a number of chapter members participate in the fieldwork. Several, notably Lloyd Bowen, approached us individually. Work with the chapter continued throughout the project, and a special meeting of the group was held on May 28, 1985, in Bridgeport. There, the project was discussed, further cooperation solicited, and contact established with local collectors.

An advance party consisting of John O'Shea, Paul Welch and myself arrived at 20SA620 on May 20, 1985. Conditions at the site were noted, and the area was examined for datum points suitable for the excavation, water sources, and the best location for the water screens. That visit also afforded us our first opportunity to meet with the township crew at the treatment plant site, and to inspect the on-site storage facilities available for project use. A brief reconnaissance of sections 17 and 18 of T11N, R5E was conducted courtesy of Bowen, who also showed us his collection from 20SA620.

The entire crew returned on May 22, and began clearing brush, establishing a baseline for the excavation, and assembling and installing water-screening equipment. Several trenches were excavated at the base of what appeared to be the remaining intact portions of 20SA620 on township property. All of them exhibited profiles of laminated or mixed black and yellow sand lying unconformably upon gray clay.

Inspection of these profiles made it clear that the bulldozer had penetrated the entire sand deposit to at least the top of the underlying clay. Loose sediment from the margins of the bulldozed area then had washed down onto the exposed floor of the bulldozed area.

EXCAVATION PROCEDURES

Inspection of the construction plans for the expanded treatment facility revealed that the elevation of the rim of the aeration tanks was 184.14 m/604.0 ft a.m.s.l. Since the tanks already were in place, that elevation served as an ideal arbitrary datum level, and was employed in this fashion during the excavation. All arbitrary level designations, therefore, are in meters below 184.14 m. A transit station then was established, and located on the construction plans by plotting its location relative to the boundary marker at the northeast corner of the township property.

In view of the limited intact area on township property, it was important to excavate all of it or as much as possible. Therefore, we decided to establish the north-south baseline for the excavation directly on the property line. Unfortunately, it was impossible to place that line by shooting directly south from the boundary marker, since several large trees blocked the line of sight. The line, however, had been marked further south by stakes which were used to establish the baseline from the south. Since the line dividing undisturbed areas from bulldozed areas did not precisely parallel the property line, the remaining intact deposit in fact formed an extremely long and acute triangle (Fig. 4.1). The southern edge of the excavation block coincided with the southernmost extent of intact deposits at the site. The area immediately south was visibly altered (Fig. 4.1), as described below. The property line at the southern edge of the excavation block was arbitrarily designated 100N/100W, and all other excavation units were numbered relative to that point. It bears emphasizing, however, that units were designated by the coordinate values of their southwest corners. Therefore, the unit located in the southeast corner of the excavation block was unit 100N/101W.

While these efforts were being made, two shallow depressions were observed which crossed the property line and excavation baseline at a slight angle. Each measured approximately 2 m in width and a minimum of several m in length. The depressions, however, terminated abruptly at the margin of the area bulldozed. Given their dimensions and locations, it was thought the depressions must represent the backfilled remains of two of the trenches which Brunett (1982) excavated at 20SA620. They may be his units 2 and 3 (1982: Map 2). Figure 1.1 shows that the two units occupy most of the apparently undisturbed strip of deposit south of the excavation block. This means that most of that wedge-shaped zone also was previously disturbed. No other vestiges of trenches excavated by Brunett were found.

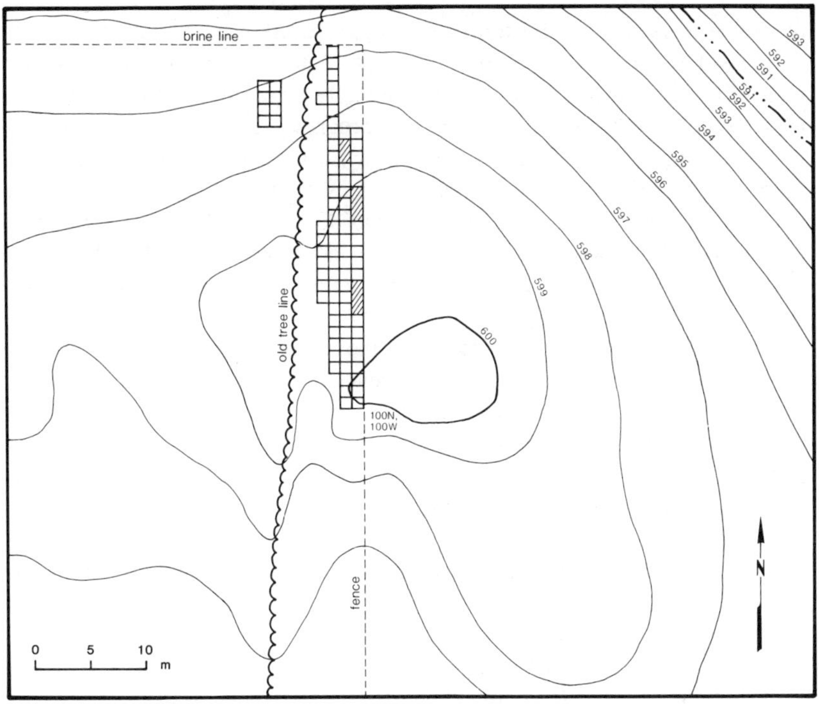

Figure 4.1. Plan of 1985 UMMA excavation overlaid on predisturbance topography.

After datum and baseline were established, the first task was to excavate two units from surface to the base of the deposit in order to determine the nature of the stratigraphy at 20SA620. These would serve as control units for the excavation. Units 104N/101W and 114N/101W were selected arbitrarily for this task, although the distance between the units was the deliberate result of our desire to examine the stratigraphy at two widely spaced locations. The units were troweled in arbitrary 10 cm levels. A stratigraphically homogeneous sediment was revealed from surface to a depth of 1.18 m below surface (2.64 m below datum). At that depth, the deposit graded to gray sand before terminating in yellow sand.

This sequence agrees substantially with results obtained by Brunett (1982, 1983). Technical descriptions of these and other sediment samples from 20SA620 are found in Chapter 6.

Following these measures, extensive excavation of the site was begun. Initially, it was conducted in arbitrary excavation levels of 10 cm thickness. In all cases, floors were excavated to level below datum (b.d.). Horizontal control was maintained by the 1 m grid staked out over the site, and vertical control was established by transit readings. Levels were numbered starting with level 1, at 1.2–1.3 m b.d. Since the surface elevation at 20SA620 generally was 1.5 m b.d., excavation actually began in level 4 or below in most units. In time, however, the slow progress of the excavation and the lack of changes in stratigraphy convinced us to continue the excavation in 20 cm arbitrary levels. The numbering of excavation levels, however, was not changed. Instead, each 20 cm level was denoted by the two 10 cm levels it included. Thus, subsequent levels were identified as "level 8–9" and so forth. Level numbers, basal depth below datum, and absolute elevation are shown in Table 4.1.

Initially, we also sought to excavate the entire remaining portion of the site by level, from south to north. However, sediment proved to be highly friable and prone to rapid drying upon exposure to sunlight. In some cases, water was sprayed on horizontal or vertical exposures to assist in observation and interpretation of sediments and features. Sediment friability, however, produced certain logistical problems. Extensive areas were left exposed at level while adjoining areas were being excavated. The exposed sediment dried out quickly and normal foot traffic was observed to slightly disturb the surface. For this reason, we shifted strategy; the site was not excavated by level from surface to base as a single spatial unit, but in three separate sections. When not undergoing excavation, each section was completely covered by plastic sheets to protect it from sunlight, rain and foot traffic.

At the start of each level, a new level sheet was begun. During excavation and at its completion, observations on the nature of sediments, the quantity and character of excavated artifacts, the presence of possible natural disturbances, and other pertinent qualities, were noted on these sheets.

Each excavation level of each unit also was assigned a minimum of two field specimen (FS) numbers. These served as catalog numbers in the field, and a running list of FS numbers was kept on site. For each level, one FS number was assigned to all artifacts recovered from the matrix, and the second was assigned to the eight-liter flotation sample. In addition, noteworthy artifacts encountered *in situ* were plotted in three dimensions and assigned unique FS numbers.

RECOVERY PROCEDURES

During the excavation of each square level, at least one 8-liter sample of soil was collected for flotation (see below), while the rest of the soil was screened. In an effort to maximize the recovery of small animal bone, water screening through 1/16″ mesh was employed as the standard mode of recovery. The water screen system consisted of three moveable screens resting on a fixed framework and two gasoline-powered pumps. The soil was washed

TABLE 4.1
Correspondence of Levels and Elevation

Level	Meters Below Datum at Base	Meters a.m.s.l.
1	1.3	182.84
2	1.4	182.74
3	1.5	182.64
4	1.6	182.54
5	1.7	182.44
6	1.8	182.34
7	1.9	182.24
8	2.0	182.14
9	2.1	182.04
10	2.2	181.94
11	2.3	181.84
12	2.4	181.74
13	2.5	181.64

through the screens using low pressure nozzles to minimize damage to fragile items. Once the soil was removed, the remaining materials were allowed to dry briefly on the screen and were then gently brushed on to a drying screen. Each sample sent to the water screen was accompanied by a plastic collection bag containing all provenience data for the sample and the assigned FS number written in indelible ink. Once dry, the sample was rough sorted, separating fire-cracked rock (FCR) from the rest of the recovered materials and discarding obviously modern organic material. The samples were then bagged and sealed for further processing: the FCR at the laboratory of the Saginaw County Historical Museum, and the rest at the Museum of Anthropology in Ann Arbor.

Logistically, the use of water screens posed few problems, excluding the occasional malfunction of the water pumps. Because of large quantities of recent organic matter in the samples, drying the samples took longer than expected; the organic matter clogged the fine mesh of the screens and absorbed water. In instances of very dense modern organics, as at the very surface of the site, and in the sloping and disturbed western margin of the site, soil was not water screened, but instead was dry screened through 1/4″ mesh.

The samples collected for flotation were initially placed in labelled trash bags with a second labelled bag inside. Sample volume was measured by the excavator at the time of collection. At the flotation station, a duplicate collection bag was made out with the additional notation of "heavy." The sample was then poured into a screen-bottomed bucket (1/16″ mesh) suspended in a large trash barrel full of water. A tea strainer was then swirled around in the screen-bottomed bucket, with the contents being emptied onto a square of tightly woven cotton cloth. This process was repeated until no further material was recovered. Any dirt clumps found were gently broken up by hand. On completion, the cloth containing the collected materials was gathered and closed with a twist-tie, and then pegged to a clothesline with the original plastic bag. The screen-bottomed bucket was then removed from the water, the residue rinsed clean, and emptied onto a second cloth. This cloth was then also closed up and pegged on the clothesline beside the light fraction, with the "heavy" plastic bag. The samples were allowed to dry, usually taking at least a day, and then the contents of the cloths were emptied into their respective plastic sample bags. Some of the larger twigs and roots were removed at this stage, but the samples were not systematically sorted. The cloths were double checked to make sure nothing adhered. The trash barrel was dumped and rinsed twice a day or after every eighth sample.

The flotation process retains all material which will not pass through a 1/16″ screen. The light fraction included most of the botanical material, charred or modern, though roots usually were also present in the heavy fraction. Some charred material typically was also recovered with the heavy fraction.

Cross-sample contamination was possible from two sources: (1) materials could be caught in the edges of the screen within the flotation bucket; and (2) some material that passed through the 1/16″ screen would float in the water, rising up through the screen into subsequent samples. Special care was taken to minimize the first contamination possibility, but little could be done about the second. Although no quantitative test was made, the degree of cross-sample contamination appeared very minor, and for materials greater than 1/16″ in size, it was trivial. Recovery of materials less than 1/16″ was certainly not complete, but again we have no basis for estimating the proportion of such smaller materials that were not recovered. Quantities of these small materials should be considered approximate, in contrast to the larger material which was recovered completely.

The laboratory processing of bulk materials recovered from 20SA620 differed depending on the nature of the material. Fire-cracked rock recovered from the water screen was separated on the drying screens. The FCR was then shipped to the laboratory of the Saginaw County Historical Museum where it was size sorted (greater than and less than 16 mm), counted and weighed. Other materials were bagged and transported to the Museum of Anthropology for further processing. All bulk samples, both from flotation and the water screen were initially coarse-sorted by eye to separate the basic categories of material (ceramics, lithic material, FCR, bone, charcoal, daub, and modern organic matter) in preparation for detailed analysis. The further processing of these materials is described in Chapters 6 through 11.

A recent bovid burial was encountered in units between 100N and 103N.

Upon reaching the base of level 7, it was apparent that the burial probably extended the entire depth of the deposit. Accordingly, excavation was abandoned in those units. With this exception, the main section of the excavation block, between 100–129N and 101–103W was found to consist largely of sediments not visibly disturbed by natural or recent human agents. As subsequent discussion will show, however, a significant degree of disturbance can be inferred from the character and distribution of archaeological remains at 20SA620. Figure 4.2 is a profile of the 100W line between 100–122N (baulks around large tree stumps between 108–111N and 116–119N mean that the profile is along the 101W line between those points). The profile map at the end of this volume shows that the deposit lenses out gradually to the north. At the northern extreme of the main block, however, in unit 129N/101W, excavation immediately revealed trench fill, probably associated with one of the at least two pipeline excavations which disturbed 20SA620. east of control unit 104N/101W. Unit 104N/91W (Fig. 4.2) was excavated in arbitrary 20 cm levels using a local datum. However, we were able to determine the elevation of the southwest corner of unit 104N/81W (Fig. 4.3) before commencing its removal. By coincidence, that elevation is 1.60 m b.d., which corresponds to the base of level 4. The unit then was excavated in arbitrary 20 cm levels using the site datum. Both units were excavated chiefly to compare the depth and nature of the deposit exposed in them to that of the main excavation block. Sediment samples obtained from them are compared to other samples from 20SA620 in Chapter 6.

TREATMENT OF FEATURES

Generally, features were recognized in plan as excavation proceeded in a unit. They were sometimes distinctly recognizable, but more often appeared as a subtle difference in color or texture of the matrix. When a feature was identified, excavation ceased in the unit, and a set of standard procedures was implemented. First, FS numbers were obtained for flotation samples, as well as artifacts from each section of the feature. A preliminary plan of the feature was drawn, noting its soil color and texture, configuration, and the location of possible disturbances such as tree roots or rodent burrows. Photographs of the feature in plan view were taken. The feature then was sectioned on its longitudinal axis, or on a north-south line if it was approximately circular in plan. One-quarter or one-half of the feature then was removed by hand. Although distinct lenses of feature fill were sought in all cases, none was found. An eight-liter flotation sample was taken from this section. Exposed profiles then were inspected, drawn, and, in most cases, photographed. Remaining sections of the feature were then excavated by hand. Sediment recovered from all sections of the feature matrix was water-proc-

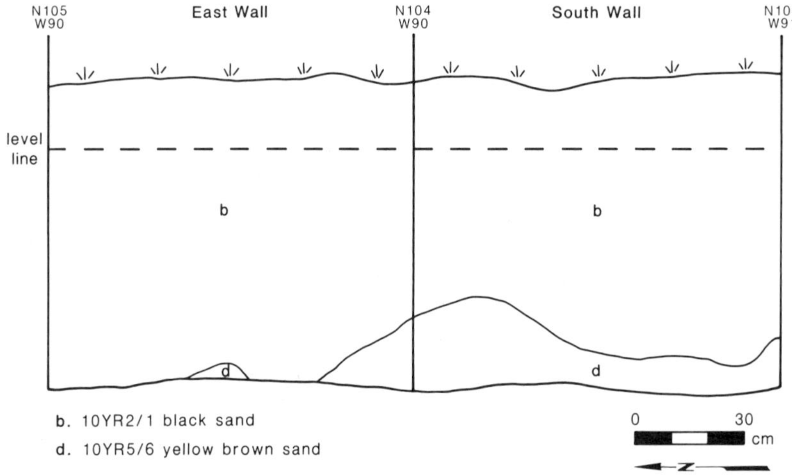

b. 10YR2/1 black sand

d. 10YR5/6 yellow brown sand

Figure 4.2. Stratigraphic profiles, square 104N/91W.

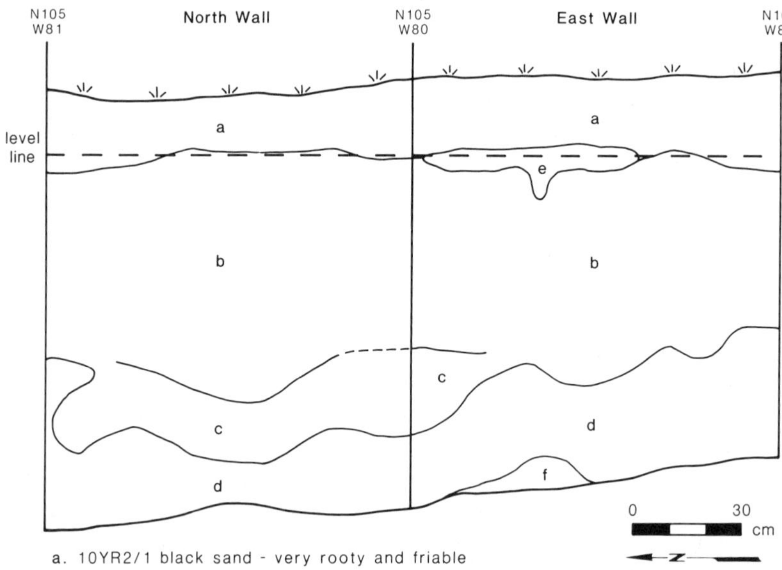

a. 10YR2/1 black sand - very rooty and friable

b. 10YR2/1 black sand - less rooty, less friable

c. 10YR3/3 dark brown

d. 10YR5/6 yellow brown sand

e. mixed 10YR2/1 and 10YR6/6 sand

f. 10YR4/6 dark yellow brown sand

Figure 4.3. Stratigraphic profiles, square 104N/81W.

essed using standard techniques as described previously. Artifacts in or near the feature were plotted in place.

Upon excavation and close inspection, a number of features defined and recorded proved to be natural disturbances, such as rodent burrows. Only 11 demonstrable features were identified at 20SA620, a surprisingly small total in view of Brunett's (1982, 1983) observations (see Chapter 2), and a somewhat disappointing one in view of our expectations. Moreover, upon excavation only five proved to be of probable prehistoric cultural origin. Only one, feature 4, was found in the vertical center of the deposit; all others were located at the base of the occupational zone, as were most natural features.

In general, features discovered at the base of the occupational zone at 20SA620 were identified not because of color or texture differences which they exhibited in comparison to surrounding matrix, but because they extended into the underlying yellow sand. In view of this, it is probable that features at higher levels within the occupational zone escaped detection because they could not be distinguished from surrounding matrix. However, geological analysis (Chapter 6) suggests that frequent, intensive occupation of 20SA620 produced extensive reworking of sediments at the site. Under such circumstances, it is likely that some features which may have formed were disturbed and effectively destroyed during the occupational period of the site. In addition, it is worth noting that the majority of the features which Brunett (1982, 1983) recognized were observed at the base of the occupational zone, a finding which agrees closely with the excavation results. Since Brunett only was able to view a single profile of each possible feature, it is possible that some that he recorded were natural disturbances similar to those found during the excavation.

5
Site Description

Michael Shott
University of Northern Iowa

RADIOCARBON CHRONOLOGY

A radiocarbon chronology for the cultural occupation of 20SA620 was a major goal of the investigation. Unfortunately, the charcoal assemblages from the features proved insufficient for conventional chronometric dating techniques and the absence of diagnostic objects from the features and the degree of postoccupational disturbance of the site rendered accelerator mass spectrometry inadvisable. Under these circumstances, the only option considered was to submit charcoal samples from individual excavation units. Material collected by excavation level within the units could be treated as a stratigraphic column in this fashion. For this purpose, charcoal samples from control units 107N/101W and 117N/102W were selected for radiocarbon assay. In addition, since the charcoal assemblages from the 10 cm levels of each unit were small, to get a sample of sufficient size it was necessary to pool samples in level 4–5 and in level 6–7.

No individual charcoal specimens were assayed in this manner, since charcoal from 20SA620 was almost uniformly small. Instead, samples submitted for assay were pooled, consisting of specimens grouped together by level.

In addition to charcoal recovered from the 1985 excavation, a specimen excavated from a Late Woodland feature by Lloyd Bowen was assayed. Identified as oak (*Quercus* sp.; see Chapter 10), the specimen weighed 5.0 g. The feature context and its contents are discussed at length in Chapter 10.

Results of the radiocarbon assay are shown in Table 5.1. In general, the assays are internally consistent, ranging from a late prehistoric date in level 4–5 to a Late Archaic date in level 10–11. One, however, B-16263 from level 10–11 of unit 117N/102W, does not agree with the others. In view of the myriad disturbance processes which operated at 20SA620, a single

TABLE 5.1
Radiocarbon Dates from 20SA620

Unit N	Unit W	Level	Sample No.	^{14}C Age	Calendar Age	Interpretation
107	101	4-5	B-16259	390 ± 60	1560 a.d.	Acceptable
107	101	6-7	B-16260	2820 ± 140	870 b.c.	Acceptable
117	102	8-9	B-16262	3350 ± 60	1360 b.c.	Acceptable
107	101	10-11	B-16261	3510 ± 80	1560 b.c.	Acceptable
117	102	10-11	B-16263	3090 ± 90	1140 b.c.	Unacceptable
Bowen				880 ± 80	1070 a.d.	Acceptable

^{14}C ages were calculated using the 5560 half-life and were corrected.

anomalous date among six should occasion no surprise. Whatever the cause, B-16263 is treated as an anomaly, and is not considered further. This leaves the four remaining assays to form a consistent stratigraphic sequence for the site.

Plotting the values against excavation level reveals the curve depicted in Figure 5.1. Assuming the dates are correct, the curve may be considered as a rough sedimentation rate curve for 20SA620, with a high initial rate tapering off gradually. This pattern is consistent with an eolian origin for the deposit in which the site rests, as will be discussed in Chapter 6. Figure 5.1 also plots artifacts whose three-dimensional coordinates were measured, and Table 5.2 lists the artifacts. The artifacts are diagnostic, and their age can be established independently within reasonable limits. True to the general rather than precise accuracy of the chronological sequence, exact agreement between inferred age and the ^{14}C curve is not obtained. Instead, some piece-plotted artifacts in upper levels are very close to the curve, while others diverge. Significantly, the earliest piece-plotted diagnostic is fairly close to the curve. The evidence gleaned from this exercise is fairly encouraging, since it displays some degree of conformity to the chronological curve.

The Bowen Feature assay of 880 b.p. is completely consistent with the artifact assemblage from the feature. The several artifact classes are treated in detail in subsequent chapters. In combination, the Bowen Feature evidence indicates a Late Woodland assignment for the feature.

TABLE 5.2
Piece-plotted Diagnostic Artifacts

FS	N	W	Depth	Description
100	111	101	1.56	Riviere Ware sherd
456	110	101	1.63	Shiawassee(?) rim sherd
4	114	101	1.74	Mackinac rim sherd
388	102	102	1.77	Wayne rim sherd
372	103	101	1.79	Wayne rim sherd
618	110	102	2.11	Satchell biface

FS = Field Specimen, depth is in m below datum.

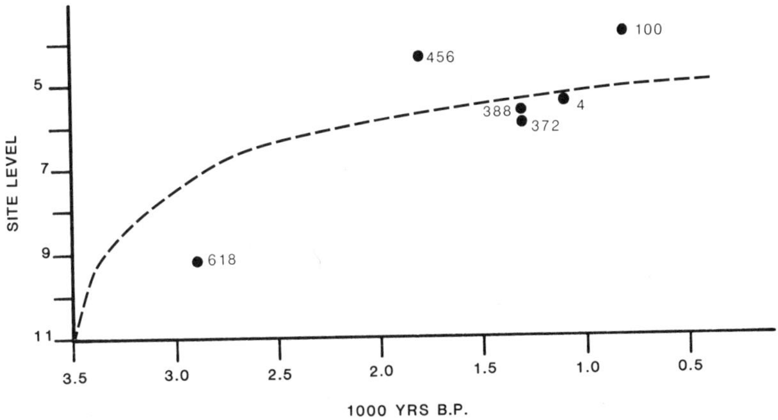

Figure 5.1. Correspondence between radiocarbon age, level and diagnostic artifacts.

FEATURE DESCRIPTIONS

Feature 4

Feature 4 was encountered in level 5 of unit 110N/102W (Fig. 5.2*a* and *b*). This is one of the highest elevations at 20SA620, and the feature was discovered 1.58 m below datum (b.d.) there. It appeared as a distinct band of oxidized sand (5YR3/4) forming an irregular, roughly circular basin (Fig. 5.2*a*). The zone of oxidized sand was interspersed with FCR and a large cord-wrapped body sherd (FS 377).

Feature 4 was exposed on the edge of a baulk formed to avoid a large tree stump (Fig. 5.2*b*). The section exposed in unit 110N/102W was recorded and excavated as a unit. It measured five liters in volume and was treated as a

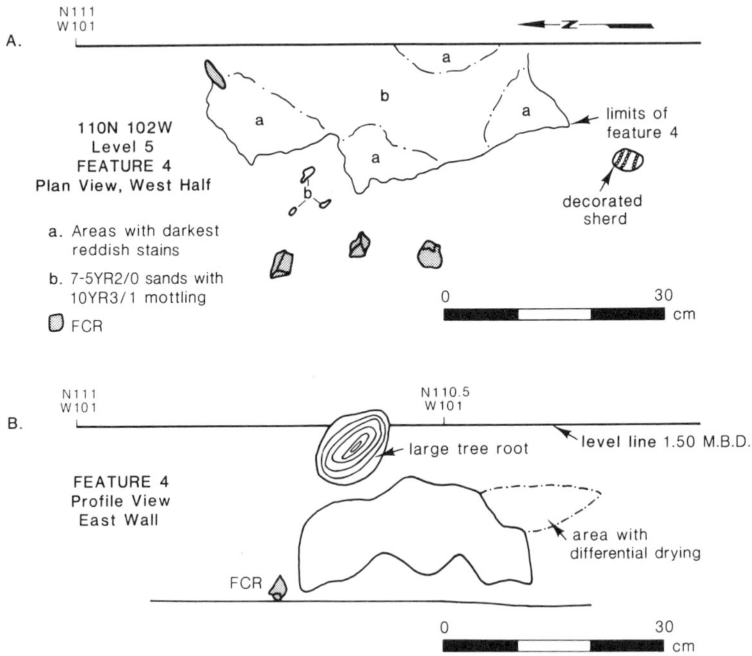

Figure 5.2. Plan and profile view of feature 4.

flotation sample. The profile exposed in the wall between 101W and 102W then was inspected and drawn. Unit 110N/101W was largely occupied by the stump and could not be excavated in its entirety without the risk of extensive slumping and loss of sediment on the adjacent property. Therefore, the remaining section of the feature was reached by opening the western half of unit 110N/101W, and excavating it to the level of the feature. The unit was excavated no further after the remaining feature section was removed.

That effort, however, exposed the remainder of the feature, and with it a large piece of charcoal situated near the feature but outside of it. That section was excavated as a unit, and an additional flotation sample was processed as well. Unfortunately, analysis determined that this sample bore uncarbonized material and vestiges of cut marks which clearly indicated that it was a post-occupational intrusion, probably a fence post (Chapter 10).

Feature 4 is approximately 30 cm in longitudinal axis and 25 cm in transverse section (Fig. 5.2*a*). Its depth is approximately 16 cm. The base of the feature was 1.74 m b.d.

Viewed in profile, the margins of feature 4 are not visible, suggesting that post-occupational disturbance has obliterated them. The feature exhibits an irregular base as well, probably the result of similar processes. Feature 4 was unique among features at 20SA620 in the clearly defined zone of oxidized sand it exhibited. In large measure, this attribute probably accounted for its discovery, since it was the only indisputably cultural feature not found at the base of the occupational zone.

Feature 4 is interpreted as a hearth. The oxidation probably was the result of intense temperature attained in the course of some activity involving fire. The absence of zones of oxidized soil within the feature fill itself, as opposed to its margins, suggest a single episode of use (Ozker 1982:143).

Associated cultural material includes the aforementioned body sherd, as well as a rim sherd of early Late Woodland affinity (see Chapter 8).

Feature 6

This roughly circular feature was encountered in level 11 of unit 112N/103W. Plan view is shown in Figure 5.3*a*; unfortunately, the east half of the feature was removed before the plan was drawn. It measured 28 cm east to west, and 27 cm north to south. When recognized, the feature extended 5 cm in depth (Fig. 5.3*b*). Its base was 2 m b.d.

Feature 6 was relatively well defined in both horizontal and vertical plan. No natural disturbances were apparent. Feature fill was a homogeneous black sand (10YR2/1), while surrounding matrix was lighter in color (10YR5/8). The entire five-liter volume of feature 6 was removed and processed as a flotation sample.

Unfortunately, cultural material was almost nonexistent in feature 6. This renders it difficult to determine its age and cultural affiliation. Nevertheless, its depth strongly suggests an Early Woodland placement for the feature. Its shallow basin form indicates that feature 6 probably was a hearth or small storage pit.

Feature 7

Feature 7 was encountered in level 11 of unit 113N/101W. It is located at the juncture of the black and yellow sand zones, and appeared in plan view as a semicircular zone of black sand (7.5YR2/0) rimmed by gray brown sand (10YR3/2). Situated at the base of the 20SA620 deposit and along both the east wall of the excavation block and the property line, only part of the feature was accessible and could be removed (Fig. 5.4*a* and *b*). All of that section was excavated and processed as a flotation sample, measuring 25 liters in volume. In profile, feature 7 is a fairly steep-sided basin with a flat bottom (Fig. 5.4*b*). The base of the feature was heavily mottled, and was found at 2.34 m b.d.

The longitudinal axis of feature 7 measured 90 cm and the exposed section was 40 cm in maximum width perpendicular to that axis. The feature, when recognized, was approximately 20 cm in depth. No internal stratigraphy or

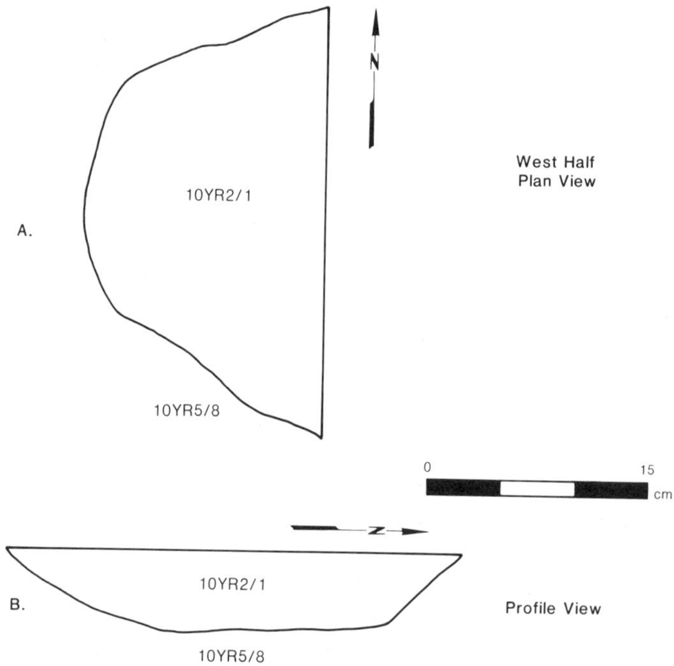

Figure 5.3. Plan and profile view of feature 6.

discrete fill lenses were observed. However, the margins of the feature exhibited a vague reddening, possibly the result of oxidation (Fig. 5.4*a*).

No diagnostic artifacts were found in or near feature 7. The overall assemblage of cultural material from the feature is relatively modest. Feature 7 was a basin-shaped pit, probably a storage pit judging from its profile. However, the previously mentioned reddened margins suggest that high temperatures may have been reached in the feature. If so, it may also have served briefly as a hearth or oven.

Feature 10

Feature 10 is a possible cultural deposit found in level 11 of unit 118N/103W. Roughly circular, it measured 40 cm in diameter (Fig. 5.5). The feature was approximately 10 cm in depth, but the base could not be defined owing to the extensive krotovina visible in profile. Base of the feature was approximately 2.35 m b.d.

In plan view, feature 10 consisted chiefly of a zone of black sand (7.5YR2/0). Zones of brown and gray sand, representing rodent burrows, rimmed this matrix, and probably intruded into it. Feature 10 was heavily disturbed by

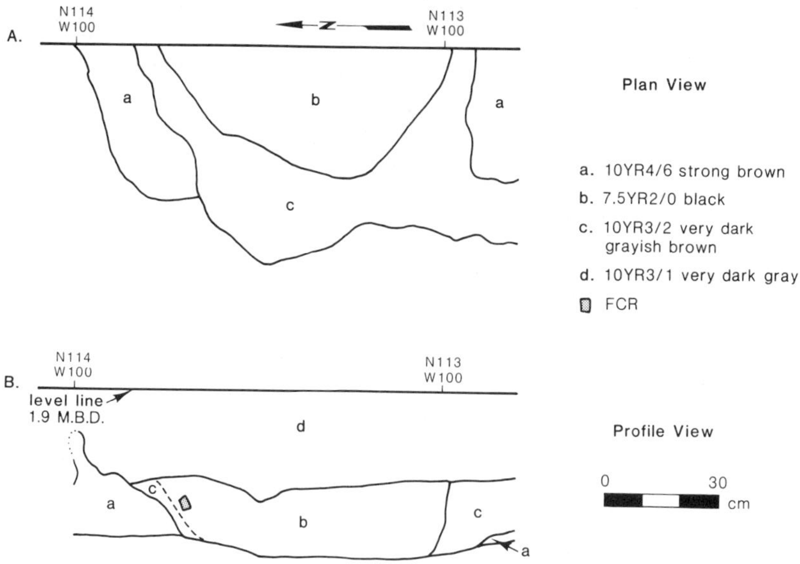

Figure 5.4. Plan and profile view of feature 7.

natural agents. The black sand matrix of the feature was removed and replaced in places with underlying yellow sand, suggesting the action of burrowing mammals. No distinct cultural strata or lenses were evident in profile.

A four-liter flotation sample was obtained from the west half of the feature. The remainder of that section as well as the entire east half was water-screened.

The artifact content of feature 10 is modest, to say the least. No diagnostic cultural material was found in the feature. Once again, however, the feature's vertical position argues for an Early Woodland placement.

It is possible that feature 10 is a natural feature. However, the matrix of black sand was homogeneous where undisturbed by krotovina, and it is treated here as a cultural feature.

Bowen Feature

A feature was discovered and excavated at 20SA620 over 10 years ago by Lloyd Bowen of the Michigan Archaeological Society. As subsequent chapters will show, Bowen has amassed a sizable collection of artifacts from the site, and the study of his collection was an important adjunct to the investigation. Bowen made available to us a sketch map of the site along with a set of notes, which together describe and document the circumstances

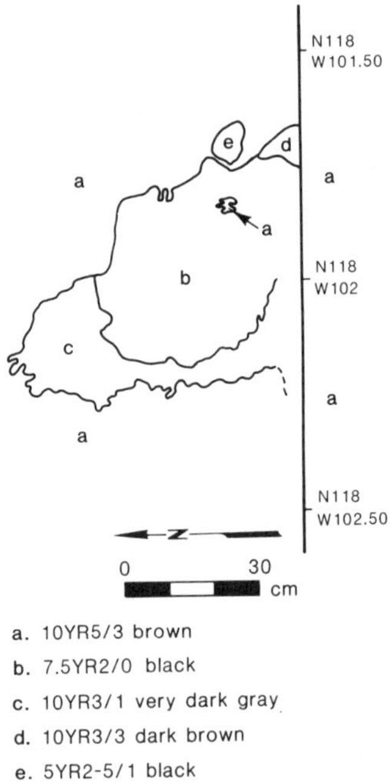

Figure 5.5. Plan view of feature 10.

of the feature's discovery, as well as the discovery of several noteworthy artifacts.

The feature was discovered after the excavation of the first of several pipelines along the northern margin of the township property. The first was a brine line excavated by the Dailey (later Vlasic) Pickle Company. When the pipeline trench was refilled, trees were planted to mark the line. This forced a change in direction of plowing over the site area, from the north-south pattern originally followed to a perpendicular east-west one. In Bowen's judgment, this change was responsible for exposing the feature. It appeared on the ground surface as a relatively dense concentration of fish bone. Bowen carefully measured the distance to the feature from a fencepost along the east margin of the property. Unfortunately, that and all other posts had been removed by the time the 1985 excavation began. Obviously, the original ground surface was altered by that point as well, with the result that the precise location of the feature could not be determined. Bowen places it within approximately 15 m of the excavation block.

Bowen excavated the feature by first removing the plow zone. He exposed the feature in plan at the base of the plow zone, and found that it was roughly circular and measured 16 inches in diameter. He then excavated the western half of the feature matrix and wet-screened the contents. The feature was found to measure 15 inches in depth below the base of the plow zone. Bowen noted that the feature matrix appeared to consist more of fish bone and other cultural remains than of sediment. Furthermore, some of the sediment was white or grey, and may have been ash. Dry volume of the excavated section of the feature was approximately 18 quarts. Contents then were dried and sorted. With commendable foresight, Bowen left half of the feature *in situ*; unfortunately, it was destroyed before our excavation could begin. Nevertheless, the existing half of the feature was an invaluable addition to the feature assemblage from 20SA620.

DISCUSSION OF FEATURES

As noted previously, none of the features excavated at 20SA620 exhibited distinct lenses of fill or otherwise showed evidence of multiple use or fill episodes. Most were relatively shallow basins; no deep, straight-sided storage pits were found. These observations are consistent with the pattern found at the Schultz site (20SA2; Ozker 1982:143). Features there, however, apparently had greater artifact contents (Ozker 1982: Table 14), although they probably were incorporated into fill incidentally (1982:144).

No post molds were found at 20SA620, although several anomalies that proved to be rodent burrows were sectioned and examined in the hope that they were post molds. A number of post molds were found at Schultz, although only a few were excavated (Ozker 1982:147–49). This suggests either that post molds were absent at 20SA620 because it was a briefly occupied camp at which there was no need to erect substantial structures, or that post molds that may have existed there were eradicated by the agents of disturbance previously discussed.

Certainly, post molds would be extremely difficult to detect in disturbed earth. It is impossible to speculate on the probability of existing post molds being destroyed. The proposition that, due to brief occupation, there were no post molds can be evaluated to some degree, though. Ozker (1982:163–65) felt that the Schultz site, or at least the Early Woodland portion, consisted of brief seasonal occupations not unlike what is postulated for 20SA620. This furnishes no basis for distinguishing between the sites in their length or nature of occupation. In addition, Yellen (1977) ethnographically records post molds on hunter-gatherer sites in Africa occupied for very brief periods, generally on the order of several days. It is unlikely, therefore, that post molds are confined to permanent or semipermanent settlements, and that they may have been excavated even at short-term campsites. In view of this, their absence at 20SA620 cannot be explained as a by-product of the presumably brief occupations of the site. Instead, some functional interpretation must account for it.

The limited spatial distribution of the features (features 4, 6, 7 and 10 were located between 110N and 119N) suggests two further observations: that features were produced at the site more often in the Early Woodland than in later periods, and that they were confined to certain areas of the site. That is, a measure of spatial structure is apparent in the Early Woodland occupation. It would be unwise, however, to place a great deal of confidence in these observations. On the one hand, features may have been produced in later occupations, but subsequently eradicated by intensive occupation, in the manner suggested in Chapter 6. Thus, the observed paucity of later features may be simply a by-product of occupational intensity. On the other hand, a significant portion of the excavation block south of 110N was disturbed, and features which may have existed there, destroyed. In short, the complex series of occupational and postoccupational disturbances to 20SA620, and the insults it has received from several quarters, prevent us from attaching a great deal of significance to the observed distribution of features at the site.

The vertical distribution of features cannot be used alone to infer the presence of distinct occupation floors (see Chapter 11). While it is true that most features were found near the base of the occupational zone, their paucity at higher elevations can be at least partly explained by intensity of occupation and the constant reworking of the deposits. Moreover, if the sediments at 20SA620 accumulated at an essentially constant rate, the site's surface would have risen gradually with time. Each successive occupation, therefore, would occur on a new and slightly higher surface than the previous one. Under these circumstances, distinct occupation floors would not be formed.

Finally, the feature data can be used to compare 20SA620 to other sites with respect to the character and intensity of Early Woodland occupation. This exercise employs data from the Early Woodland level at the Schultz site and the Dawson Creek site in Ontario (Jackson 1986). Feature density, at least within a period, may be considered a rough measure of occupational intensity of a site. Differences in Early Woodland occupational intensity between 20SA620 and the Schultz site are not evident in the data provided by pit features. Table 5.3 shows that very similar densities characterize the Early Woodland components at the sites. In making this comparison, only features 6, 7 and 10 from 20SA620 were considered definite Early Woodland features. The area figure for 20SA620 was obtained by subtracting the six partly excavated units between 100–102N from the total of 62 m^2, since those units were not excavated to a depth sufficient to reach Early Woodland levels. Ozker (1982:140) reports 30 pit features from Schultz. It should be emphasized here that only pit features were included in the Schultz site totals, post molds and artifact concentrations being omitted because they are not comparable phenomena. Including the latter, in particular, would substantially increase the Schultz total, since 14 were noted at the site (Ozker 1982:150). The low value at Dawson Creek may be explained by the possibility that Early Woodland occupation there was confined to an area smaller than that excavated, since the excavation block also contained later Woodland material.

Using comparable data, Table 5.3 shows that no major difference characterizes Bridgeport and Schultz in feature density. If that is taken as a measure of occupational intensity, therefore, we cannot conclude that the Schultz site and 20SA620 were occupied at different degrees of intensity.

Table 5.3 also compares metric attributes of presumed Early Woodland features at 20SA620 to the other sites. Feature volume at Dawson Creek is significantly greater than the 20SA620 value (t = -3.74, df = 6, p = .01), while a similar but somewhat less definitive result is obtained in comparing the feature axis at Schultz with this site (t = -1.28, df = 22, p = .21). Thus, despite the impressive feature density at 20SA620, the population of features appears to consist of smaller units. However, this conclusion, too, is qualified if the partial recovery of features owing to visibility and recognition problems at 20SA620 is recalled. Furthermore, differences in feature populations between 20SA2 and 20SA620 are less pronounced than might be expected, especially since the former generally is considered a major Early Woodland settlement. Early Woodland settlement systems in the Saginaw Valley may be more complex than believed.

HUMAN REMAINS FROM 20SA620

In addition to the other materials recovered from 20SA620, six fragments of human bone and six loose teeth were encountered. The assemblage of human remains is summarized in Table 5.4.

Human remains were confined to the southern portion of the excavated area of the site, occurring in units 106N/102W, 107N/102W, 107N/103W and 108N/103W, between levels 6 and 11. The presence of human bone in the slumped portion of unit 107N/103W, including the largest intact fragment from 20SA620, raises the possibility that the greater part of the burial may have been destroyed when the site was bulldozed prior to excavation.

The material recovered appears to be attributable to a person over forty years old. Tooth size and mandibular morphology are of a range characteristic of females, although the remains are far too fragmentary for this to be more than a tenuous suggestion. All of the teeth present are heavily worn, but none presented evidence of caries or other dental pathology. The degree of wear and the absence of caries suggest a foraging diet, rather than the starchier diet characteristic of later Late Woodland farmers.

TABLE 5.4
Human Remains from 20SA620

Unit	Level	Element	Comments
106N/102W	6	cranial fragments (2)	probably frontal, adult
107N/103W	10–11	medial phalange	
		mandibular body	fragment only
		lower premolars (2)	age 40+ based on tooth wear[a]
		lower canines (2)	age 40+ based on tooth wear[a]
		lower molar	root only
107N/102W	6	cranial fragment	probably parietal
108N/103W	8–9 (in slump)	left mandible	Broken posteriorly at the coronoid process, anteriorly at the distal root of the M1. Two teeth—M2 and M3—survive. Age 40–45 based on tooth wear.
		right lower molar	M3

[a]Tooth age-wear assessments following Lovejoy 1985.

TABLE 5.3
Early Woodland Features and Feature Density at 20SA620 and 20SA2

Site	No. of Features	Area Excavated (m^2)	Feature Density (per m^2)	Mean Feature Volume (l)	Mean Feature Axis (cm)
20SA2	30	494	.061		92.8
20SA620	3	56	.054	15.0	52.7
Dawson Cr.	6	384	.016	85.3	

The area in which the remains were found was disturbed by the root system of a large tree (which in fact hindered excavation of three units of the site grid) and by rodents. Given the multicomponent character of 20SA620, it is also possible that the burial was disturbed prehistorically by later human activity. In all likelihood, the human bone arrived in its discovered position as a result of these factors.

The absence of human bone from other areas of 20SA620 and the consistency of the osteological indicators of skeletal age, suggest an isolated burial episode rather than a formal cemetery. As excavation was limited by property boundaries, it was not possible to determine whether additional burials might exist further east on the knoll. Although this remains a possibility, it seems unlikely given the surface topography of the knoll and the small quantities of bone recovered.

No cultural material could be associated directly with the human remains. Two smoothed-over body sherds were recovered in the immediate vicinity of the bone, but given the uncertainty of the depositional context, the significance of this association is unclear. Although the sherds are nondiagnostic by themselves, if they were associated with the human remains, they would most likely date the burial to either the Middle Woodland or later Late Woodland periods and not to the main, early Late Woodland occupation of 20SA620 (see Chapter 8). Given this possible association, in combination with the absence of dental caries already noted, a Middle Woodland date is a tenuous, yet most probable, age for the burial.

6
Geological Observations on 20SA620

William R. Farrand
Department of Geological Sciences, University of Michigan

INTRODUCTION

Geological studies in conjunction with archaeological investigation in the Saginaw Valley began with Wright's (1972) work at the Schultz site (20SA2). There, and at nearby sites, geological analyses have proven valuable adjuncts to archaeological research, showing that these are river bottom sites whose depositional sequences involve a series of alluvial episodes. The interdigitation of occupational horizons and sterile lenses is a noteworthy property of these sites, especially 20SA2 (Wright 1972).

In contrast, the sediments of 20SA620 are not alluvial, although the site is situated on the floodplain of the Cass River. The Schmidt site (20SA192) (Fairchild 1977; Harrison 1966) more closely resembles 20SA620, since both consist of wind-transported sands. Nevertheless, Stein's (1974) analysis shows that Schmidt site sediments are composed of wind- and water-deposited sands associated with the Nipissing Great Lakes stage in the Huron Basin. In Stein's judgment, the Schmidt site sediments are shore and near-shore deposits formed by the waters of the Shiawassee embayment (1974). The morphology and elevation of 20SA620 render a similar origin for its sediments extremely unlikely, as the following discussion will show. Moreover, most of the cultural occupation at Schmidt is Archaic in age, although the precise dates of the several occupational episodes remain in doubt (Crane and Griffin 1968:77; Fairchild 1977: Table 1; Harrison 1966).

The following analysis provides a foundation for comparison of 20SA620 with other Saginaw Valley sites. As discussion will show, this analysis has important implications for the dates of site occupation and for the nature of the sedimentary matrix in which cultural deposits and material are encased.

The 20SA620 site is located along the section line between sections 16 and 17, T11N, R5E, Saginaw County, Michigan, about 850 m (2800 ft) north of the right bank of the Cass River. The Cass River originates near the northern tip of the "thumb" of Michigan, near Ubly, and flows southwestward, passing Cass City and Vassar to the Frankenmuth-Bridgeport area where it swings to the northwest and becomes tributary to the Shiawassee River just southwest of the city of Saginaw. Thus, the Cass River flows along the distal margin of the Port Huron moraine from Ubly to Saginaw.

The Port Huron moraine, although quite subdued, is the major topographic feature in the Saginaw-Bridgeport area. It trends northwest-southeast through Saginaw, being breached by the Saginaw River in the metropolitan area. Otherwise, it forms a low, but persistent barrier, that in times past created a broad lacustrine embayment of the ancestral stages of Lake Huron in the area that is now dry land southwest of the city of Saginaw (Farrand 1982). Such embayments existed at the times of Glacial Lake Algonquin (ca. 11,000 b.p.) and again during the Nipissing Great Lakes and Algoma phases (5000–3000 b.p.). At such times, 20SA620 would have been situated on or near the northeastern shore of a broad, shallow embayment that extended some 20 km (12 mi) to the southwest of the site. At Algonquin and Nipissing times, the site itself would have been slightly below lake level, although between those times and after the Nipissing phase the site area would have been habitable.

The site area sits just above the level of the Algoma shoreline and presumably would have been well situated for exploition of lacustrine resources when the Algoma phase embayment occupied the lowlands outside the Port Huron moraine, that is, some 4000–3000 years ago (Farrand 1988; Larsen 1985). After the Algoma phase, the lake waters gradually receded, accompanied by the mouthward extension of the Cass and other rivers across the former lake bottom and the drying of the lake floor sediments. The dried-out sediments were blown by the prevailing westerly winds to form the numerous low sand dunes that characterize much of the Saginaw lowlands. As a first approximation, site 20SA620 appears to be located on one of these low dunes.

I visited the site on June 6 and 7, 1985, and again briefly at the end of the same month. Examination of the local geomorphic setting of the site itself and the surrounding area was made in the company of the excavators. They also supplied detailed, large-scale topographic maps of the immediate area. Sediment samples were collected by the excavators during the course of the excavations and subsequently analyzed in the Quaternary Geology Laboratory at the University of Michigan under my direction.

LOCAL ENVIRONMENT, SOILS AND SEDIMENTOLOGY

Geomorphology

Site 20SA620 is located on a low knoll, along the section line. The summit of the knoll lies in the woods just east of the excavations and reaches an altitude just barely above 600 ft a.m.s.l. (Fig. 3.2). Moreover, the knoll is more or less bisected by a small ravine, about 40–50 m (130–160 ft) east of the section line, that carries water intermittently southward to the Cass River. The head of this ravine swings to the northwest, crossing the section line just north of the excavated area. The west end of the knoll has been artificially removed by bulldozing but, according to local reports, it extended only a few meters to the west of the section line in its original state.

South of the site the land surface has also been modified somewhat in the course of the development of the area, although not excessively so. The surface slopes gently southward to the right bank of the Cass River, which is a low-cut bank 2–3 m above the present water level of the Cass River. Dark brown silt loam alluvium exposed in the cut bank was sampled for comparison with sediments found in the excavation area.

Along the right bank of the Cass River, just upstream in section 16, are two sloughs that are apparently lateral channels of the Cass (Fig. 3.2). Presumably they are flooded at times of high water, and they contained residual, stagnant ponds at the time of our visit. Behind these sloughs and parallel to the course of the river is a bluff, the base of which is close to 595 ft a.m.s.l. This presumably is the Algoma shoreline. Although this bluff does not exist in the immediate area of the site, the site sits at an altitude equivalent to the top of the Algoma bluff, and thus would have been on dry land overlooking the lake at Algoma time. On the other hand, a distinct break in slope that seems to represent the Nipissing phase shoreline occurs 600–700 m (0.4 mi) north of the site, that is, along the south side of Washington Road. Since the Nipissing shore is about 605 ft a.m.s.l., the site area would have been under at least 1.5 m (5 ft) of water during the Nipissing phase. The exact depth of water covering the site area during Nipissing time is uncertain because the dune sand accumulation in the site area is most likely post-Nipissing in age. This dune, thus, sits on the former floor of the Nipissing embayment and postdates the Nipissing phase.

The detailed engineering maps prepared in connection with the construction of the sewage treatment facility show the upper limit of the One Hundred Year Flood. This limit does not follow the local contours exactly, which suggests that the flood information was added to these maps from independent information, and was not mapped locally. (The source of this flood information is not specified.) Site 20SA620 actually sits below the upper limit of the One Hundred Year Flood shown on these maps. Presumably, then, the site area would have been subject to occasional flooding during the millennium following the drainage of the Algoma embayment.

The land surface west and northwest of the site area, that is, the former floor of the Nipissing embayment, has only very low relief, with slight undulations of some .3 to .5 m (1 to 1.5 ft) amplitude. The soils of the slight rises are bright-colored and sandy, while the soils of the swales are dark-colored and floored with somewhat finer sediments. As is the case for 20SA620, the crests of these low rises lie commonly within one foot above or below 600 ft a.m.s.l.

Soils

The fields on this surface (west and northwest of the site) were inspected and tested with a soil auger. Fortunately at this time the crops had hardly begun to emerge and visibility was excellent. Special attention was given to the fence rows because they appeared to be the sites of local accumulation of windblown sand, perhaps presenting an analog to sand accumulation in the area of the excavations. Actually, there were no fences present, simply strips of uncultivated land marked by brushy vegetation and small trees. These fence rows stand in relief (.5–1.0 m) above the surface of the adjacent fields and are conspicuously sandy relative to the soils in the fields. They appear to be modern eolian accumulations, presumably associated with plowing disturbance of the fields. While fence-row sand is dirty pale yellow with abundant roots and other recognizable organic materials, it is nothing like the very dark gray to black, organic-rich sand of the knoll at 20SA620, or of the Vogelaar site discussed below.

The soils in the cultivated fields are mostly silty and loamy, apparently belonging to the Kibbie, Pella and perhaps Barry soil series. The classification of the soils of the fence rows is uncertain. They cover areas too small to be mapped separately on soil surveys. Many of them can perhaps be mapped as Wixom or Arenac, although the latter name is no longer valid in this area of southern Michigan, according to the most recent soil classification chart (Mokma and Stroesenreuther 1982). Where they are deeper, they may be Kingsville, or if well drained, the Rubicon, Mesic Variant.

The Saginaw County Soil Survey is not very helpful in this regard because it consists of the old 1933 soil survey, with a number of older, discontinued names, superimposed on an aerial photographic base. This involved expanding the former survey published at 1:62,500 to a much larger scale, without increasing commensurately the amount of detail mapped. These new survey sheets show broad areas of fine sandy loams or silt loams, largely Kibbie and Pella series, but no individualized areas of well-sorted sands such as those occurring in the area of 20SA620.

ANALYSIS

Geological analysis of sediments at 20SA620 was undertaken for several reasons. The first and most general was to provide a basic description of the character of sediments at the site for interpretive and comparative purposes. In addition, however, analysis was designed to determine the origins of the deposit in which the site occurs, since this in conjunction with the regional geomorphological sequence would furnish bracketing dates for site occupation. Finally, the depth and apparently homogeneous nature of the sediments, despite considerable evidence of cultural variability, demanded explanation. We sought to determine if distinct stratigraphic units could be identified by analysis, even though none was evident in the field.

Samples were collected and analyses conducted with these questions in mind. In the course of excavation at 20SA620, the homogeneity of the sediments was puzzling. Inspection of the area surrounding the site, as discussed in detail below, failed to provide evidence of similar deposits. However, D. B. Simons of the Michigan Archaeological Society indicated to us that 20SA620 resembled the Vogelaar site (20SA133), situated approximately 19 km (12 mi) to the southwest in this respect. Vogelaar was visited on June 28, 1985. The length of the site was traversed and abundant cultural material was observed on the surface. None of this cultural material was collected, but a sediment sample was secured for analysis. That analysis is described in the following report of geological research at 20SA620.

Site Sediments

Grain-size analysis by sieving and determination of organic carbon by loss-on-ignition were performed on three series of sediment samples along an east-west transect from the main excavation area eastward into the woods. This transect lies along grid line 104N, and the samples come from one-meter squares at 101W (in the main excavation area), 91W and 81W, the latter two squares being in the woods, 10 and 20 m (33–66 ft) east of the main excavations.

No obvious soil horizonation, other than the root mat in the top part of the profile, nor archaeological features were visible within the upper 0.75 to 1.0 m of the excavated profiles, which showed essentially uniform, very dark gray to black sand. In the lower part of the profiles, the color changed abruptly to pale yellow along an irregular boundary, but the nature of the sandy sediment was otherwise essentially the same as above. Along this lower contact there was commonly a horizon of light gray sand, about 0.1 cm thick, interrupted at places by dark yellowish brown stains. The light gray horizon might be referred to as an E soil horizon, although the unusually great thickness of the overlying black A horizon makes such a designation dubious. Some of the dark yellowish brown stains were considered to be features during the course of the excavations, but it must also be considered that they could be natural products of pedoturbation, especially in light of the observation that few of them had any unusual concentration of associated anthropogenic debris. At the very bottom of the excavated squares the sand tended to become somewhat finer, more compact and sticky. Samples were collected from the arbitrary excavation levels, beginning with level 4 or 5 (in different trenches), that is, below the zone of intense root growth.

Sediment samples for geological analysis were collected from control units excavated at the site. In those units, the standard 8-liter sediment sample was divided; only half was processed at the flotation tank, while the other was retained for analysis. Samples were stored on site in Bridgeport Township facilities until field work was completed, when they were returned to Ann Arbor for analysis.

The sediment analyses are presented in tabular form in Tables 6.1 and 6.2, and the grain-size distributions for the various units are shown in Figures 6.1, 6.2 and 6.3. The miscellaneous samples include the alluvium from the bank of the Cass River (mentioned earlier), silty clay that underlies the dune sand at the site, and sand from the Vogelaar site. As shown clearly in the histograms, the sands from the site are all very similar regardless of their depth or organic carbon content. They are well-sorted sands with a modal size between 0.25 and 0.125 mm (2–3 phi) and slightly positively skewed, that is, somewhat enriched in finer grains relative to the mode. This grain-size distribution is perfectly consistent with an interpretation of eolian origin. As mentioned in the preceding paragraph, the sands tend to become finer at the base of the excavations, about one meter or so below the present surface. This is exemplified by sample FS 680 from .85-.9 m depth in square 104N/91W (Table 6.1), which is a loamy sand whereas all the overlying sediment is classified simply as "sand" in U.S. Department of Agriculture soil texture terminology. The Vogelaar site sample is also a well-sorted, eolian sand essentially identical with that of the 20SA620 site.

An auger hole roughly five meters west of the excavations penetrated at least 0.7 m of pale yellowish gray, very plastic silty clay ("auger sample" in Table 6.1 and Figure 6.3). In this area the original overlying sand had been removed by bulldozing, exposing the silty clay, which is apparently a lacustrine sediment that extends throughout the local area and under the dune sands of the site. Presumably it was deposited in the shallow offshore areas of the embayment in Nipissing times.

The riverbank alluvium (Fig. 6.3) is clearly quite a different sediment from either the eolian sand or silty clay of the site area. More than 75% of its grain-size distribution is smaller than 0.0625 mm (4 phi), classifying it as a silt loam. Presumably, it represents modern flood loam deposited on the present-day floodplain of the Cass River. Its high organic carbon content

(6.16%) reflects the incorporation of organic debris from the floodplain during flood events.

DISCUSSION AND SUMMARY

Whereas the morphology of the 20SA620 site suggests that of a low sand dune that accumulated on the drained lake floor of an embayment of the Nipissing phase of ancestral Saginaw Bay, the sediment profile is quite different from that usually encountered in such dune sands. In terms of soil classification, this profile does not match that of any soil series described by the Soil Conservation Service. The black A horizon is far too thick. For such a thick profile in a moderately well drained setting there is hardly any textural or structural development in the underlying horizons.

The working hypothesis that the sand accumulation in the site area was the result of wind deflation of black topsoil from adjacent fields as a result of cultivation in historic times proved untenable for two reasons. First, other eolian accumulations that appear to be genuine wind-row deposits between modern fields are neither as thick nor by any means as dark colored as the sediments in 20SA620. Secondly, the presence of prehistoric artifacts throughout the black sands argues against the interpretation of their deposition during the past two centuries of agricultural activity. Moreover, the configuration of the black sand deposit in the site area is not consistent with a fence row origin. It is not a linear accumulation, but extends well eastward, as shown by the two test pits (104N/91W and 104N/81W), into the adjacent wood lot that appears never to have been under cultivation in historic times.

Further indications concerning the origin of the site sediments come from comparisons with the Vogelaar site. Vogelaar is located 18.8 km (11.7 mi) southwest of 20SA620 on the opposite (SW) shore of the former Nipissing embayment, 600–605 ft a.m.s.l. It sits on a northwest-to-southeast trending sand ridge that appears to be a Nipissing beach ridge topped by dune sand. A shallow pit dug into the crest of this ridge revealed a sediment very similar to that at 20SA620, as well as abundant fire-cracked rocks and some artifacts. A sample of this sand looks identical to that from 20SA620 in grain-size distribution, color and organic content (Table 6.1; Fig. 6.3).

Papworth (n.d.:2) describes the stratigraphy at Vogelaar thus:

> . . . a black, silty topsoil overlies a reddish sand which loses its color, fading gradually into light grey as water is reached and beneath this sand is a grey compact clay with some sand content.

Although this description does not agree in all respects with the 20SA620 stratigraphy, it is clear from the 1985 visit and from notes and profiles taken

TABLE 6.1
Absolute Weights of 20SA620 Samples

Unit	Level	Phi Scale Sieve Ranges[a]				
		<4	4 to 3	3 to 2	2 to 1	1 to 0
104N/101W	4	11.6	35.9	118.7	14.8	1.2
	5	11.7	44.6	112.6	13.8	1.3
	6	9.3	33.2	122.1	14.6	1.4
	7	6.4	46.1	95.7	11.8	1.2
	8	3.2	29.5	101.4	6.9	0.5
	9	3.0	40.4	94.4	5.6	0.4
	10	2.4	43.9	86.8	3.5	0.2
104N/81W	5+6	15.4	29.5	75.2	7.1	1.0
	7+8	13.1	30.6	78.5	7.5	1.1
	9+10	10.3	29.1	73.2	6.8	1.0
	11+12 black sand	8.4	33.6	86.7	7.5	1.0
	11+12 yellow sand	3.8	44.2	91.7	3.3	0.2
	13+14	2.5	27.9	107.8	5.2	<0.1
	15+16	2.1	24.7	105.1	6.7	0.1
104N/91W	FS 671	7.8	26.5	97.3	10.6	0.8
	FS 680	41.8	20.4	78.4	22.4	2.8
Vogelaar soil sample		7.0	37.2	78.1	12.8	0.8
Cass River bank sample		83.5	24.9	1.9	0.1	0.1
20SA620 auger sample		124.6	0.6	0.5	0.5	0.2

[a]The phi size scale is a logarithmic transformation of the grain size in millimeters: phi = $-\log_2 d$, where d = grain diameter in mm.

during Papworth's expedition to Vogelaar that a black sand (not silt, as Papworth (n.d.) describes it) zone extends well below the plow zone there. It is not as thick as the similar zone at 20SA620, but its origin as an anthropogenic zone is probable, given its similarity in composition to the sediments of 20SA620.

Therefore, the presence of artifacts, the unusually thick deposit of black sand unlike any local soils, and the known occurrence of similar relations at other archaeological sites in the area all point to a strong anthropogenic influence during the accumulation of this sand deposit at 20SA620. It seems unlikely that the entire knoll of dune sand resulted from human activity, but it suggests that human activity was relatively intense here during or soon following the dune accumulation. The dune is presumably of post-Nipissing, pre-Algoma age, and it could have been a focus for human activities while the Algoma Lake phase existed in this embayment. It would have been situated just above the Algoma shoreline and would have provided a relatively high point of dry soils favorable for a camp or an exploitation outpost. Even in post-Algoma times, the dry soil conditions of the site area would have been favorable to human activities relative to the marshy conditions that would have existed between the sandy knoll and the banks of the Cass River.

Phi Scale Sieve Ranges [a]					Total Weight (g)
0 to −1	−1 to −2	−2 to −3	−3 to −4	−4 to −5	
0.6	0.4	–	5.0	–	182.8
0.5	0.3	0.4	–	–	184.5
0.4	0.3	–	–	–	181.0
0.3	0.5	–	–	–	161.5
0.2	0.2	–	–	–	141.7
0.1	0.2	–	–	–	143.9
0.1	<0.1	–	–	–	136.9
0.4	0.2	–	1.6	–	128.6
0.4	0.1	0.2	–	–	131.2
0.5	0.7	0.4	1.6	14.5	120.9
0.3	0.4	–	–	–	137.5
<0.1	<0.1	0.3	–	–	143.2
–	–	–	–	–	143.4
–	–	–	–	–	138.7
0.2	0.3	–	1.3	–	143.2
0.9	0.8	1.4	10.4	–	166.7
0.3	0.2	–	–	–	136.2
–	–	–	–	–	110.5
0.1	–	–	–	–	126.5

Finally, the character of the sediments in the site can perhaps be best explained by a combination of ash and charcoal from hearths, soil disturbance by human traffic across the area, the original dry, sandy nature of the parent material, and wind. The abundance of fire-cracked rock in the site attests to fires and human activities. The fact that the fire-cracked rocks, artifacts and bone fragments are rather widely dispersed throughout the deposit, rather than being clustered into discernible features, suggests that disturbance was common. Simply walking across such dry, loose sand will cause some of it to be kicked up and moved around, and if there is little or no vegetation to stabilize the surface, the wind will also blow the loose sand and ashes around. Of course, the digging of pits by humans or burrowing by animals will contribute to the process of homogenization of the deposit. Unfortunately, the heavy black color of the upper meter or so of the sand has rendered the recognition of such features very difficult.

The formation of site 20SA620, thus, appears to have resulted from human activities on the surface of a post-Nipissing sand dune. The thick black sandy sediment at the site, and at other archaeological sites in the area, is unlike any natural soils locally and, along with the presence of artifacts, argues

TABLE 6.2
Granulometric Weight Percentages for the Sand Fractions of 20SA620 and Related Samples

Unit	Level	Phi Scale Sieve Ranges						Wt % Carbon
		< 4	4 to 3	3 to 2	2 to 1	1 to 0	0 to −1	
104N/101W	4	6.35	19.64	64.93	8.10	.00	.33	2.87
	5	6.34	24.17	61.03	7.48	.70	.27	2.84
	6	5.14	18.34	67.46	8.07	.77	.22	2.45
	7	3.95	28.46	59.07	7.28	.74	.19	2.32
	8	2.26	20.82	71.56	4.87	.35	.14	.85
	9	2.08	28.08	65.60	3.89	.28	.07	1.08
	10	1.75	32.07	63.40	2.56	.15	.07	.65
104N/81W	5 + 6	11.98	22.94	58.48	5.52	.78	.31	6.64
	7 + 8	9.98	23.32	59.83	5.72	.84	.30	4.26
	9 + 10	8.52	24.07	60.55	5.62	.83	.41	3.50
	11 + 12 black sand	6.11	24.44	63.05	5.45	.73	.22	2.27
	11 + 12 yellow sand	2.65	30.87	64.03	2.30	.14	< .10	1.00
	13 + 14	1.74	19.46	75.17	3.63	< .10	.00	.71
	15 + 16	1.51	17.81	75.78	4.83	.07	.00	.67
104N/91W	69-84 cm depth	5.45	18.51	67.95	7.40	.56	.14	.87
	FS 680 85-95 cm depth	25.07	12.24	47.03	13.44	1.68	.54	1.46
Vogelaar soil sample		5.14	27.31	57.34	9.40	.59	.22	2.44
Cass River bank sample		75.57	22.53	1.72	.09	.09	.00	6.16
20SA620 auger sample		98.58	.47	.40	.40	.16	.08	6.09

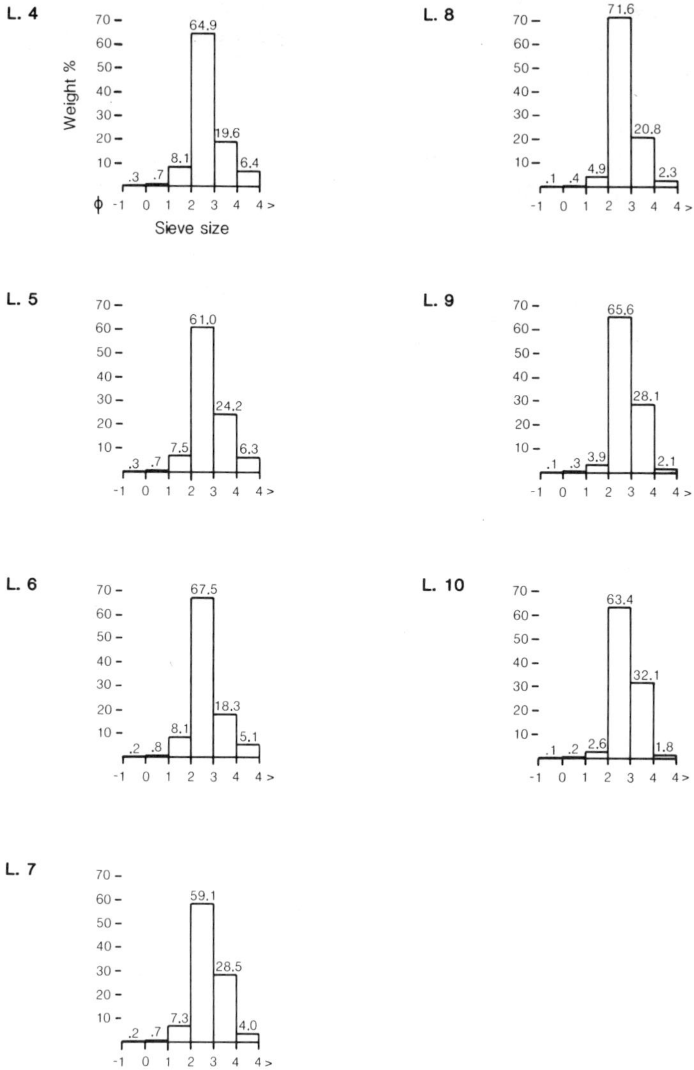

Figure 6.1. Grain-size distribution, square 104N/101W.

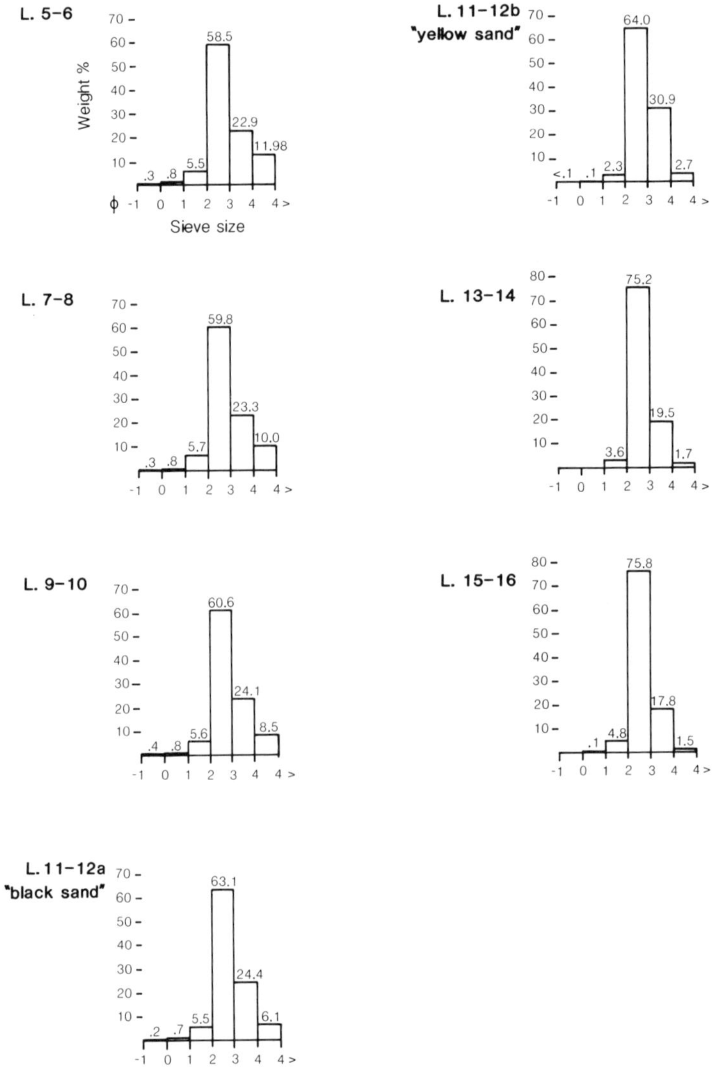

Figure 6.2. Grain-size distribution, square 104N/81W.

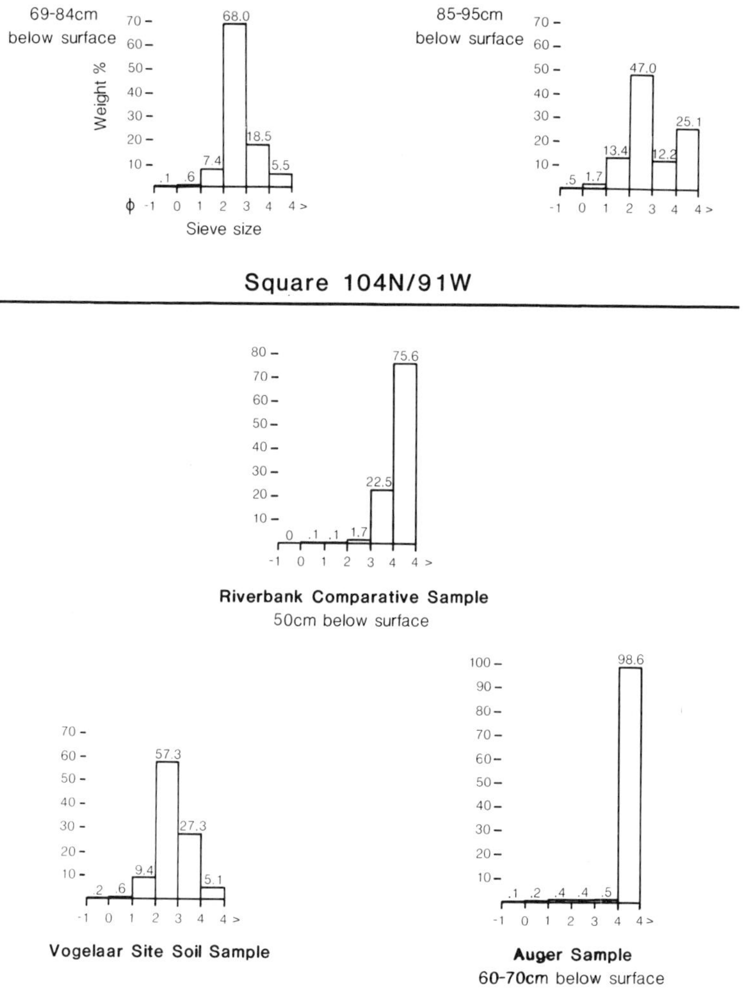

Figure 6.3. Grain-size distributions, miscellaneous samples.

strongly for anthropogenic influence following the initial dune accumulation. At Algoma time, the dune overlooked a broad, shallow lacustrine embayment, and the site would have been well situated for the exploitation of various resources. Even later, the site would have been favored for its relatively high position and dry soil.

7
Lithic Analysis

Michael Shott
University of Northern Iowa

This chapter will examine three categories of the stone tool assemblage from 20SA620: chipped stone tools and other tools; lithic debris; and fire-cracked rock. Chipped stone tools are divided into several widely recognized classes including bifaces, unifaces and cores. No functional classification of the tool assemblage is attempted. Instead, salient properties of the tools—morphology, metric attributes, wear patterns and composition, to name several—are compared to items recovered from other sites in the Saginaw Valley and elsewhere in the Great Lakes and Midwest. Chronological and stylistic affinities can be charted in this fashion, and the nature of the successive occupations of 20SA620 can be placed in a broader context.

STONE TOOLS

Bifaces

Late Archaic. Several specimens identified as Satchell bifaces were recovered from 20SA620. The Satchell type is distinguished by its long, stemmed lanceolate form and by its composition. Satchell implements are usually composed of a siliceous material that was called *argillite* in the past. Recently, the term *graywacke* has been favored; Kenyon (1980) pointed out that "argillite" is petrologically inaccurate. Here, the more general term *metasediments* is used for this siliceous material.

Metric attributes of the small 20SA620 Satchell biface assemblage are presented in Table 7.1, and the mean value for the 20SA620 assemblage is compared to other, typologically kindred, assemblages in Table 7.2. Note that one biface is formed by the refitting of two fragments, FS 505 and FS 618

TABLE 7.1
Attributes of Satchell Bifaces from 20SA620

FS	Unit		Level	Length (mm)	Width (mm)	Thick-ness (mm)	Stem Length (mm)	Mate-rial	Condi-tion
	N	W							
505[a]	107	101	7						
618[a]	110	102	10	103.6	25.7	10.7	22.4	MS	whole
86	107	102	4		22.8	9.7	14.8	MS	proximal
334	107	101	5		20.7	8.5		MS	distal

MS = metasediment
[a]Conjoined specimen; numbers refer to conjoined specimen.

TABLE 7.2
Mean Metric Attributes of Satchell Assemblages

Site	Length (mm)	Width (mm)	Thick-ness (mm)	Stem Length (mm)	Source
20SA620	103.6	23.1	9.6	18.6	—
Davidson	60.7	44.6	9.6	16.7	Kenyon 1980a
Sissung	61.4	36.9	11.2		Kenyon 1980b
Ausable		33.8	10.9		Kenyon 1980b
Pinegrove	42.2	26.0			Simons 1979
Warner Sch.		20.5			unpublished

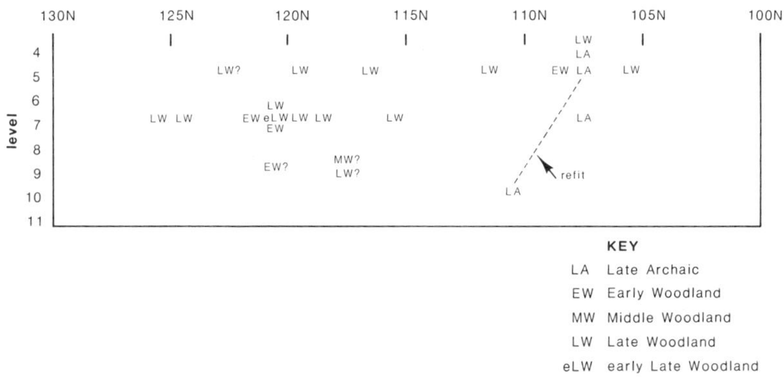

Figure 7.1. Composite profile distribution of diagnostic bifaces.

(Plate 7.1*a*), and that the reconstructed implement is exceptionally long. FS 86, a proximal fragment, is shown in Plate 7.1*b*.

One uniface composed of metasediments also was found at 20SA620 (Plate 7.5*i*). The working assumption is made here that all artifacts composed of metasediments are of Satchell affinity.

Originally, Satchell occupation in the Great Lakes region was thought to date to the Paleo-Indian to Early Archaic transition. This placement was made on strictly typological grounds, by equating the Satchell type with Plano industries of the West (Peske 1963). Since that time, however, it has become evident both by the position of Satchell implements in stratigraphic sequences (Roosa 1966) and on chronometric grounds that Satchell occupation was Late Archaic in age. Satchell sites in Michigan (Simons 1972), Ontario (Kenyon 1980) and Ohio (Stothers 1982) have produced carbon-14 dates falling between 3000 and 4000 b.p.

Ironically, Satchell tools from 20SA620 are not confined to the base of the

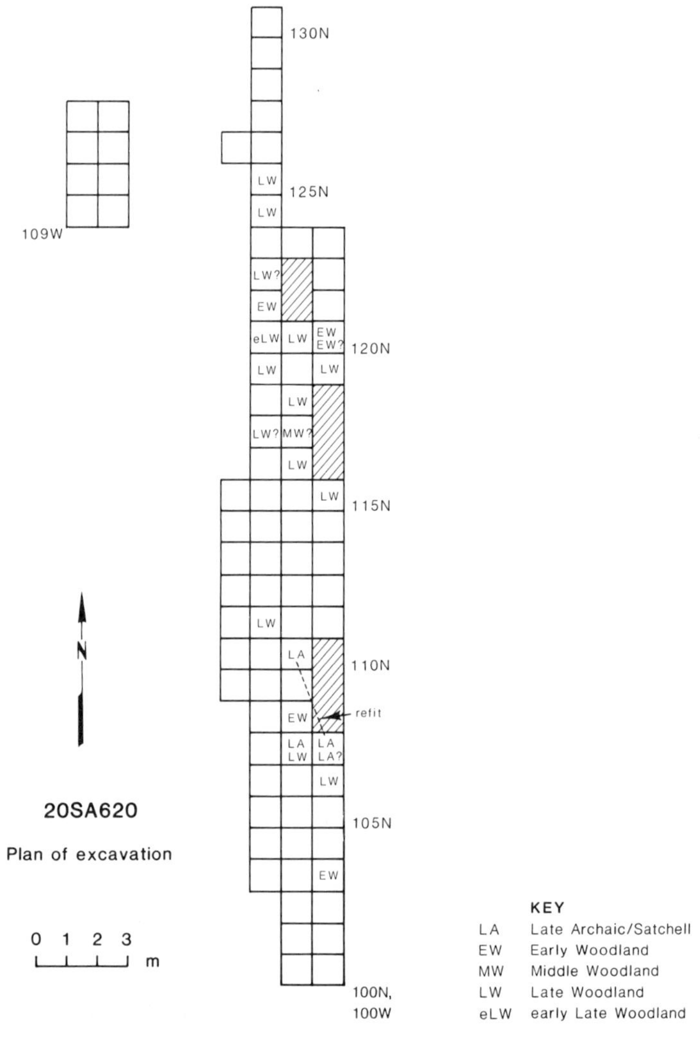

Figure 7.2. Composite plan distribution of diagnostic bifaces.

deposit. On the contrary, most are situated in upper excavation levels near the modern ground surface (Fig. 7.1). Only FS 618—one fragment of the reconstructed biface—is found at the base of the deposit. The other piece of the tool was found in level 7 of an adjacent unit, an occurrence which obviously indicates postoccupation disturbance at the site. Since most Satchell implements are adjacent to a recent bovid burial (Figs 7.1 and 7.2), it is entirely possible that they were redeposited when the burial pit was

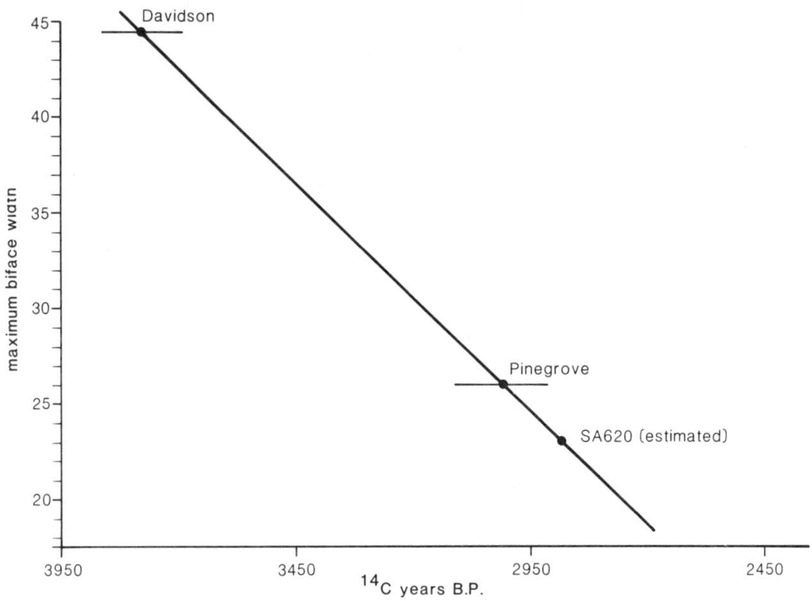

Figure 7.3. Maximum shoulder width of Satchell bifaces vs. site age.

excavated. Alternatively, natural agents such as burrowing rodents may have displaced them.

Although generally out of primary context, Satchell bifaces from 20SA620 can be employed to estimate the date of first occupation of the site. This can be accomplished by calculating their mean shoulder width and comparing it to a highly provisional relationship which expresses that quantity as a function of time. Mean shoulder width of the 20SA620 Satchell biface assemblage is 23.1 mm. Two other Satchell assemblages, whose dates of occupation are known, can be compared to this figure (Table 7.2). Kenyon (1980:20–21) suggests that shoulder width can be treated as a function of time. Figure 7.3 is a graphic depiction of the relationship; placing the 20SA620 assemblage on the line defined by the other sites according to its mean shoulder width yields the estimate of 2980 b.p. for the Satchell occupation there.

The perils of this exercise are self-evident. As a rough estimate of initial occupation, however, it has produced a perfectly reasonable figure. Placing the Nipissing fall in the Huron Basin at approximately 3200 b.p. (Eschman and Karrow 1985; Larsen 1985), this allows over three centuries to elapse before 20SA620 was occupied. However, Monaghan et al. (1986) date the Nipissing fall to 2900 b.p. based on dated sediments at the Weber I site (20SA581) in Frankenmuth. Their fixing of the event leaves little time before

TABLE 7.3
Metric Attributes of Kramer Bifaces from 20SA620

FS	Unit		Level	Length (mm)	Width (mm)	Thick-ness (mm)	Stem Length (mm)	Mate-rial	Condition
	N	W							
795	120	101	7		22.4	8.1	15.8	BP	proximal
349	108	102	5		17.7	7.2	8.2	BP	proximal
20SA2				52.1	24.5	8.4	15.8		

BP = Bayport chert

Plate 7.1. Satchell bifaces:
a. conjoined FS 505/618 *b*. FS 86

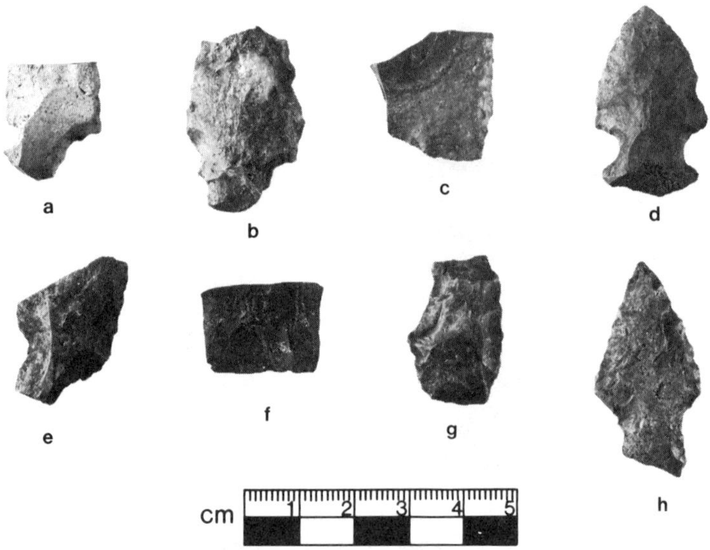

Plate 7.2. Stemmed bifaces:

a. FS 577	*e*. FS 804
b. FS 745	*f*. FS 795
c. FS 693	*g*. FS 349
d. FS 593	*h*. FS 800

Plate 7.3. Probable Late Woodland and other notched bifaces:
a. FS 202 *c*. FS 806
b. FS 264 *d*. FS 778

Plate 7.4. Late Woodland biface:

a. FS 317	*e*. FS 662
b. FS 652	*f*. FS 742
c. FS 330	*g*. FS 792
d. FS 291	*h*. FS 599
	i. FS 786

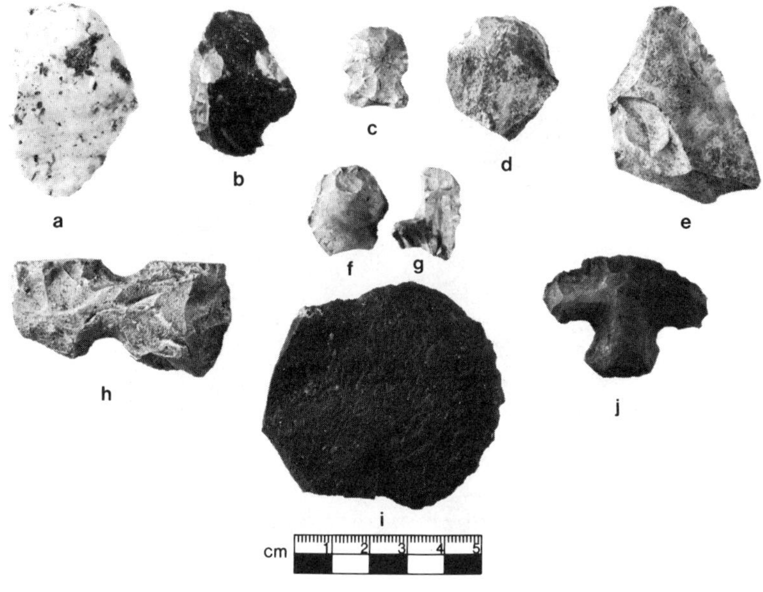

Plate 7.5. Unifaces and utilized flakes:

a. FS 605
b. FS 743
c. FS 745
d. FS 778
e. FS 778
f. FS 830
g. FS 830
h. FS 864
i. FS 339
j. FS 104

Plate 7.6. Miscellaneous lithic specimens:
a. FS 577 *c*. FS 495
b. FS 637 *d*. FS 620

Satchell occupation and, if accurate, makes that occupation virtually instantaneous once the lake retreat exposed previously inundated land surfaces.

Early Woodland. Two proximal fragments of Kramer bifaces (Munson 1971; Ozker 1982) were found at 20SA620. The Kramer biface, which is diagnostic of the Early Woodland form in the Great Lakes region, is described in some detail by Ozker (1982:92), who stresses not only the straight stem and ovate blade morphology on original specimens, but abrasion of basal margins as well.

One Kramer biface, FS 349, found in level 5 of unit 108N/102W, does not fit Ozker's description especially well, since it features unabraded basal margins. However, the tool is reworked, exhibiting a pronounced shoulder on one margin (Plate 7.2g) above which the blade margin is heavily indented. The opposite margin features large primary facets and steep edge angles, which indicate heavy use and resharpening. It is likely, therefore, that the specimen was reworked. In fact, the narrow blade suggests either heavy use as a cutting implement on both margins, or that it was used as a drill. Unfortunately, the distal element is missing. It is worth noting, however, that Kramer bifaces from the nearby Schultz site exhibit considerable variability in blade morphology, while retaining similar basal elements (Ozker 1982: Fig. 37).

The other Kramer specimen, FS 795, was recovered in level 7 of unit 120N/101W. Although only a stem fragment (Plate 7.2*f*), and possibly an incomplete one at that, the implement is of classic Kramer form and manufacture, as best can be determined from its fragmentary state. Basal margins are ground, and the base itself is lightly ground.

Both specimens are composed of Bayport chert. Metric attributes are presented in Table 7.3, which gives mean values from the Schultz site Kramer assemblage for comparison. It is interesting to note that the latter values consistently exceed the attributes of the 20SA620 specimens. If, as possibly occurs on the Satchell bifaces, shoulder width declines with time (Kenyon 1980:21), then Kramer occupation of 20SA620 is somewhat later than at the Schultz site.

Both in Illinois and in the Saginaw Valley, Kramer occupation is well-dated to the first millennium B.C. (Munson 1971; Ozker 1982). In these areas, Kramer bifaces are associated with Early Woodland ceramics of Marion or Schultz Thick affinity. At the Schultz site, Kramer bifaces and Schultz Thick ceramics were found in Depositional Unit 4, from which carbon-14 assays of 2480±150 b.p. and 2490±130 b.p. were obtained (Ozker 1982:25). A similar date, perhaps slightly more recent assuming Kenyon's (1980) observation is correct, may be inferred for the Kramer occupation of 20SA620. Kramer bifaces have been found elsewhere in the Saginaw Valley, notably at the Butterfield site (Wobst 1968: Pl. VII, H) in Bay County.

Level 7 of unit 121N/103W yielded a stemmed biface, FS 800, of Bayport chert (Plate 7.2*h*). The stem is narrow and unground, and the base has been snapped off. A second fracture removed one shoulder of the specimen. Despite numerous resharpening facets, which indicate heavy use, the blade retains a symmetrical form. Heat treatment is apparent from a reddened oxidized zone on the tool (Ozker 1976b).

This specimen probably is a Schultz Stemmed biface. Ozker describes this biface type as:

> unlike the Kramer point in the absence of grinding, instead the tang lateral and basal edges tend to be straight, chipped, and even. The tang width tends to be slightly greater than the length, and the whole point is smaller than the Kramer . . . [1982:96]

Several Schultz Stemmed bifaces were found at the Schultz site (Ozker 1982: Fig. 38). All were made of Bayport chert, and one exhibits evidence of heating.

Table 7.4 shows very close agreement in metric attributes between FS 800 and the Schultz specimens. It also includes a biface recovered from the early Late Woodland level of the Weber I site (Robertson 1989: Fig. 10D). Although that specimen resembles FS 800 in outline form, metric attributes are not similar. An Early Woodland placement for FS 800 is supported by available data.

A somewhat more problematic specimen is FS 804 (Plate 7.2*e*), which was located in level 9 of unit 120N/101W. The item, composed of Bayport chert, is a medial fragment. It exhibits heavy resharpening on one margin and virtually none on the opposite one, which suggests use as a knife. It is straight stemmed so far as can be determined. Base and shoulders of FS 804 were formed by massive primary flaking, and one face of the base is occupied by a single facet which extends onto the blade before terminating in a hinge fracture. The tool is similar to a specimen found in the Early Woodland levels at the Schultz site (Ozker 1982: Fig. 39, Cat #69663). Table 7.5 shows close agreement between the tools in width; the Schultz specimen, however, is considerably thicker. On the strength of the overall resemblance, FS 804 is assigned to the Early Woodland period.

Figure 7.1 shows that the small Early Woodland diagnostic assemblage from 20SA620 is largely confined to lower levels of the site. However, one specimen—FS 349, a Kramer proximal fragment—was recovered from level 5 of unit 108N/102W, at the disturbed south end of the excavation block. Like similarly situated Satchell implements, FS 349 probably is from a secondary context. In addition, several Early and Late Woodland diagnostic tools are found in the same level in a small concentration near 120N (Figs. 7.1, 7.2). Clearly, disturbance or a point of contact between occupational hori-

TABLE 7.4
Comparative Metric Data for FS 800

	Length (mm)	Width (mm)	Thick-ness (mm)	Stem Length (mm)	Source
FS 800	38.5	19.8	5.7	12.5	—
Schultz Stemmed	39.0	22.0	7.5	14.0	Ozker 1982: Fig.38
Expanding Stem	40.0	22.0	7.2	13.5	Ozker 1982: Fig.38
	24.7	16.4	5.2		Robertson 1984: Fig.10D

TABLE 7.5
Comparative Metric Data for FS 804

Specimen	Width (mm)	Thickness (mm)
FS 804	20.0	7.4
69663	19.0	10.

zons is indicated. The disturbed character of some of the 20SA620 deposit makes it impossible to distinguish these alternatives.

Middle Woodland. Definitive evidence of Middle Woodland occupation is absent in the lithic assemblage of 20SA620. This is not especially surprising in view of the paucity of Middle Woodland material in the Saginaw Valley. These occurrences include major occupations at the Schultz site (Fitting 1972), the Kantzler site (Crumley 1973), and the Bussinger site (Halsey 1976), along with limited evidence from other Saginaw Valley sites (Halsey 1976; Lovis 1979). Interestingly, Lovis (1985) notes a pattern at Fletcher, situated near the Kantzler site, which resembles the evidence from 20SA620: comparatively abundant Early Woodland and especially Late Woodland remains, with a much lower frequency of Middle Woodland material.

A possible Middle Woodland biface, FS 693, was found in level 9 of unit 117N/102W (Plate 7.2*c*). Composed of what is visually identified as Flint Ridge chert from eastern Ohio (Luedtke 1976:230), the specimen is a small medial fragment of a biface. It has been reworked and reduced in bipolar fashion with flakes struck from what were originally the tool margins. The specimen's condition makes typological identification impossible. Figure 7.1 shows that it was found at a depth consistent with *in situ* Middle Woodland placement at the site. However, possible Early and Late Woodland diagnostic tools were recovered from the same excavation level in nearby units. Since the specimen is reworked, it is placed in a distinct tool class, which will be discussed later; metric attributes are listed in Table 7.20.

Another specimen, FS 593, found in disturbed context on the margin of the excavation, may also be of Middle Woodland affinity (Plate 7.2*d*). The biface is made of Bayport chert and features a deep red hue on one face, possibly from exposure to heat (Ozker 1976b). It is intact, and of broad side-notched or expanding stem form. Light abrasion is found on the stem margins, but does not extend to the base. The tool is plano-convex in transverse section and bears a remnant of the original flake platform on the base. This biface is similar to expanding stem bifaces from Schultz, illustrated by Fitting (1972: Fig. 62). Its metric attributes closely agree with mean values for the Schultz site specimens (Table 7.6). Fitting (1972: Table 59) indicates that 44 percent of items of this form were found in Middle Woodland levels at Schultz, while 22 percent occurred in Late Woodland provenience. A Middle Woodland assignment of FS 593 is statistically most likely. The assignment is supported by White (1968: #7 in Fig. 56), whose Gibson biface type resembles the 20SA620 specimen.

Late Woodland. Late Woodland diagnostic bifaces are abundant at 20SA620. A Bayport biface, FS 778 (Plate 7.3*d*), with a poorly formed expanding stem was recovered in level 7 of unit 120N/103W (Fig. 7.1). The stem and base are unground. The specimen is asymmetrical in outline form and irregular in transverse section; these properties may be by-products of the heavy use and resharpening. Both tool margins are steeply angled and bear numerous resharpening facets. One is reworked past the original tool shoulder. A slightly off-center remnant of the original tool surface is present on one face, and is isolated by the extensive faceting produced by resharpening.

It is difficult to classify FS 778. Its metric attributes are compared in Table 5.7 to those of a Late Woodland biface assemblage from the Stadelmeyer site (Bigony 1970:150) and a Middle Woodland biface from the Birch Run Road site (Clark 1979:44, #79–7). It resembles more closely the Late Woodland specimen. In addition, it appears to be similar to other Late Woodland specimens from the Schultz site (Fitting 1972: Fig. 63D) and Foster site (Bigony 1970: Plate XVII, B), although metric attributes are not presented in those cases. Significantly, however, the Naugle site has produced somewhat similar forms in both Late Archaic and Late Woodland provenience (Ozker 1976a: Figs. 4 and 5). Finally, Brunett (1981: Fig. 9) illustrates a similar specimen associated with Wayne Tradition ceramics at 20MD367. A tentative Late Woodland placement is made for FS 778.

Level 7 of unit 111N/104W yielded a large side-notched biface, FS 806, of probable Late Woodland affinity (Plate 7.3*c*). The specimen is a proximal fragment of Bayport chert. Notches and base are formed by large primary facets and are unground. It bears evidence of extensive use and wear. The blade probably tapered sharply toward the distal end, as resharpening reduced specimen width and produced nearly concave tool margins. The blade is beveled, and the margins exhibit heavy step fracture attrition on opposing faces. Use as a heavy duty cutting implement is indicated.

Metric attributes of FS 806 are shown in Table 7.8. Fitting (1972: Fig. 63D, Table 50) illustrates similar tools from Late Woodland contexts at Schultz, and mean values for those tools are included in Table 7.8 as well. Although the tool is similar in form to Middle Woodland Snyders bifaces, the table shows that specimen width values differ sharply when FS 806 is compared to a Snyders assemblage from the Illinois River valley (White 1968:Table XIV), and a biface from the Birch Run Road site (Clark 1979:

TABLE 7.6
Comparative Metric Data for FS 593

	Length (mm)	Width (mm)	Thick-ness (mm)	Stem Length (mm)	Source
FS 593	34.5	20.7	6.8	11.1	—
20SA2	32.5	20.3	7.8		Fitting 1972: Fig.62

TABLE 7.7
Comparative Metric Data for FS 778

FS	Length (mm)	Width (mm)	Thick-ness (mm)	Stem Length (mm)	Source
FS 778	38.1	17.3	9.7	12.2	—
Stadelmeyer	53.	19.	6.	15.	Bigony 1970:150
Birch Run		23.	6.	9.	Clark 1979:44

TABLE 7.8
Comparative Metric Data for FS 806

	Length (mm)	Width (mm)	Thick-ness (mm)	Stem Length (mm)	Source
FS 806		34.1	10.8	16.8	—
20SA2		33.5	10.8		Fitting 1972: Table 50
Ill. Val.	69.1	54.5		15.5	White 1968: Table 14
Birch Run	37.	18.0	9.5	8.0	Clark 1979:44

#78–24). A Late Woodland placement seems more appropriate for the specimen from 20SA620.

A small side-notched tool, FS 599, was found in level 5 of unit 111N/103W (Plate 7.4*h*). Composed of Bayport chert, it is an intact specimen formed by minimal retouching of a thin flake. The ventral surface of the original flake is retained nearly unmodified, and ripples are clearly evident there. Only the tool margins on that surface are faceted. It is excurvate in longitudinal section. Small, well-defined notches are located well above the base. This specimen strongly resembles the Raccoon Side-notched biface form. First defined by Mayer-Oakes (1955:84, Fig. 34), the form is well known in the Ohio River Valley. Chronological range of the type is not well established, but Carskadden and Morton (1974:Table 2) place the Raccoon Side-notched form between early Late Woodland Jack's Reef and later triangular forms.

Thus, bifaces of this form and manufacture generally may be considered Late Woodland in Michigan. Beld (1985: Plate 7) recovered several at the Conservation Park site (20GR33) in Gratiot County, and Roosa also found similar specimens at the Warner School site (20GS6) in Genesee County. Although the latter site was disturbed, the items there are of probable Late Woodland age (Roosa 1966:30). Fitting (1972: Fig. 58A) illustrates similar specimens of Late Woodland affinity from Schultz. Unfortunately, he does not present metric data on the specimens. However, Clark (1979: #45, #79–14) recovered two similar bifaces at the Birch Run Road site which he assigns a Middle Woodland placement. Metric attributes of these various bifaces are shown in Table 7.9; general agreement is found between FS 599 and the other specimens, with only specimen thickness differing sharply. The 6.1 mm value for FS 599 is unusually thin for a biface, although the Birch Run Road specimens are even thinner. In addition, Clark (1979) reports that similar tools have been recovered from Middle Woodland levels at Gratiot County's Kanitz site. Possibly, the Raccoon Side-notched biface form spans the Middle and Late Woodland periods in the Saginaw Valley. The 20SA620 specimen is provisionally assigned to the Late Woodland period.

A typical Late Woodland "bird point," FS 786, was found in level 7 of unit 119N/101W (Plate 7.4*i*). Composed of Bayport chert, the specimen has an expanding stem. Base and stem margins are heavily abraded. Although FS 786 may indeed have been used as an arrow point for small game, it bears evidence of other use. Both margins have numerous small resharpening and use facets. The transverse section is nearly plano-convex, and marginal faceting is more common on the convex face, although by no means confined to it. Several resharpening flakes were struck from near the tip, which is blunt rather than pointed. The tip is not fractured. The specimen may be assigned to the Late Woodland occupation at 20SA620, although it is not similar in metric attributes to Fitting's Small Expanding Stem type (1972: Fig. 62, Table 47; Table 7.10). The Butterfield site has yielded similar specimens in Late Woodland context (Wobst 1968:Plate V, J and K; Plate VI, I-K). Once more, it is intriguing to note note the resemblance of a Late Woodland form to earlier types. Table 7.10 also presents metric data for a tool from the Terminal Archaic horizon at Weber I (Robertson 1989: Fig. 10C). Metric attributes are similar to those of FS 786. Despite this finding, FS 786 is considered a Late Woodland form here, although the possibility that it is Late Archaic must be considered (Lovis and Robertson 1989:218).

Triangular bifaces are more common in southeastern Michigan sites than in the Saginaw Valley (Krakker 1983). A modest assemblage was recovered from the Butterfield site (Wobst 1968:Plate V, A-E, Plate VI, P and Q) and from the Schultz site (Fitting 1972: Fig. 58). Yet triangular bifaces, which

TABLE 7.9
Comparative Metric Attributes for FS 599

	Length (mm)	Width (mm)	Thick-ness (mm)	Stem Length (mm)	Source
FS 599	26.2	14.7	6.1	7.1	—
Birch Run	24.	15.	3.5	7.0	Clark 1979:45

TABLE 7.10
Comparative Metric Attributes for FS 786

	Length (mm)	Width (mm)	Thick-ness (mm)	Stem Length (mm)	Source
FS 786	24.0	16.7	5.5	7.0	—
20SA2	32.5	20.3	7.8		Fitting 1972: Table 47
Weber I	27.2	18.4	6.3		Robertson 1984: Fig.10C

are considered diagnostic of the Late Woodland period, are the single most common biface type at 20SA620. Seven triangular bifaces were found at the site (Plate 7.4*a-g*). An eighth specimen, FS 86, is a corner fragment of a triangular biface. Metric attributes of the triangular biface assemblage are shown in Table 7.11 (although FS 86 is included in the table, it was not included in the calculation of mean values for the assemblage).

Krakker (1983:410) notes a gradual decline through time in mean base width of triangular bifaces in southeastern Michigan. Table 7.12 summarizes relevant data from that area and adjacent Ontario (see also Fox 1980). Plotting base width against excavation level in the 20SA620 assemblage suggests that a similar pattern characterizes Saginaw Valley Late Woodland industries as well (Fig. 7.4). Mason (1986: Table 14.1) presents data from the Rock Island site in Wisconsin that demonstrates a similar trend, although the absolute chronological and metric values in that case differ substantially.

Metric data on Late Woodland triangular bifaces can be used to estimate the date of the Late Woodland occupation of the site. The body of data compiled by Fox (1980:11), Krakker (1983:452), and Stothers (1977:62) serves as the basis for this effort (Table 7.12). Although several sites are radiocarbon dated, the age of others is only estimated. Dates shown in Table 7.12 are approximate. Figure 7.5 plots mean base width of triangular biface assemblages against sites on an ordinal chronological scale. A steady trend through time of reduction in base width is apparent in the data. It is interest-

TABLE 7.11
Metric Attributes of Triangular Bifaces from 20SA620

FS	Unit N	Unit W	Level	Length (mm)	Width (mm)	Thickness (mm)	Material	Condition
317	106	101	5	(14.9)[a]	16.2	2.1	BP	proximal
86	107	102	4			2.6	BP	proximal
652	115	101	7	(19.1)	19.7	4.7	BP	proximal
330	116	102	5	(20.7)	20.0	4.5	BP	proximal
662	117	103	9	47.9	30.7	4.8	BP	whole
291	119	103	5	26.5	19.1	2.2	BP	whole
792	120	102	7	34.0	14.4	5.5	BP	whole
742	125	103	7	20.8	18.6	3.5	BP	whole

BP = Bayport chert

[a]Estimated from nearly intact dimensions.

TABLE 7.12
Chronological Trends in Base Width in Triangular Biface Assemblages

Site	Age (A.D.)	Mean Base Width	Source
Cayuga	795	24.0	Stothers 1977
20SA620		19.8	—
Porteus	1050	18.5	Stothers 1977
Younge	1200	18.9	Krakker 1983
Huron R.	1350	17.4	Krakker 1983
Slack-Caswell	pre-1500	14.8	Fox 1980
Weiser	1500	14.8	Fox 1980
Lawson	1510	14.9	Fox 1980
Draper	1500+	16.0	Fox 1980

SOURCE: Krakker and Shott 1984: Table 12.

ing to note a reversal in the trend in the sixteenth century, although the evidence is too limited to place a great deal of confidence in it. Nevertheless, a similar reversal of the general trend apparently occurred elsewhere in Ontario (Fitzgerald 1982:177, Table 35).

If 20SA620 conforms to the general trend, its mean Late Woodland age is bracketed by the 795 ± 132 a.d. date from the Cayuga Lake site and the 1050 ± 70 a.d. date from the Porteus site.[1] The mean value for the 20SA620

[1]The most recent of three dates obtained from that site (Stothers 1977:63).

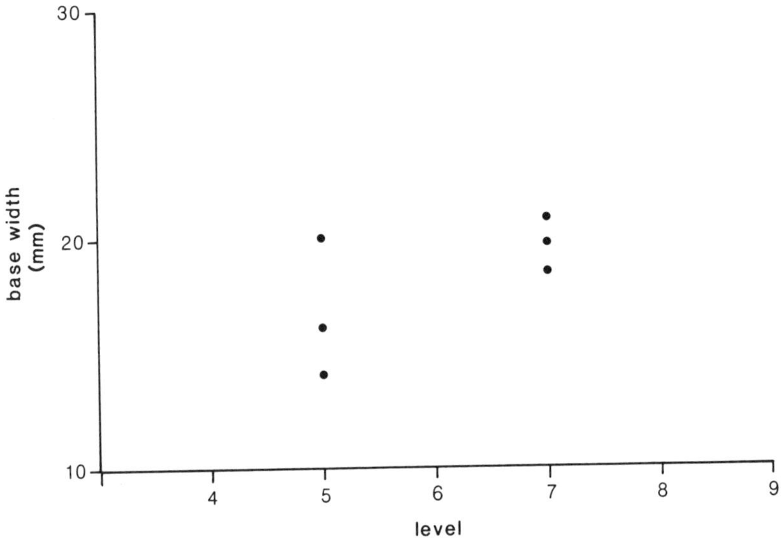

Figure 7.4. Base width of triangular bifaces vs. level.

assemblage is closer to the Porteus date, suggesting that the occupation was likelier to have occurred at the recent end of the bracketed period.

Again these findings should be interpreted with caution. It would be preferable to employ data only from Saginaw Valley sites in such an exercise, but available chronological and assemblage data are inadequate for the task. The results are best viewed as provisional. They are, nevertheless, in agreement with data from the ceramic analysis, discussed in Chapter 8.

A second line of reasoning concerning chronological trends in Late Woodland biface assemblages is supported by the data. Luedtke (1978) noted patterns in the percentage frequency of different biface types by subperiod within the Late Woodland period. Specifically, the data she compiled show a steady increase with time in the relative frequency of triangular bifaces, largely at the expense of corner-notched biface forms. Levanna and Madison types are common among the former, Jack's Reef (Ritchie 1961:26) among the latter. Along the same chronological axis, a decrease of lesser magnitude in side-notched forms is evident, while stemmed bifaces exhibit a slight increase (Luedtke 1978:7).

Luedtke's data include Late Woodland assemblages from the Saginaw Valley, notably the Schultz site. It is reasonable, therefore, to compare the percentage composition of the 20SA620 Late Woodland lithic assemblage with these data. Table 7.13 shows that comparison, with the values for 20SA620 listed against aggregate values for each of the four subperiods. It

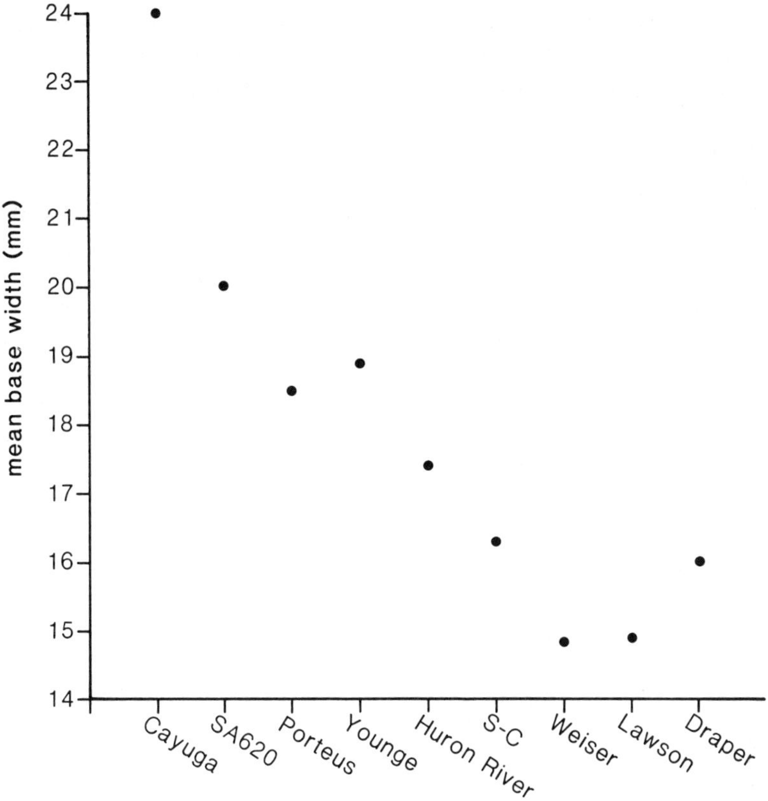

Figure 7.5. Chronological trend in the mean base width of Late Woodland triangular bifaces.

TABLE 7.13
Percentage Composition of Biface Types in Late Woodland Assemblages Studied by Luedtke (1978)

Period	Corner-notched	Side-notched	Stemmed	Triangular
1	42.3	13.5	18.9	24.3
2	2.6	26.3	23.7	47.4
3	5.6	16.9	20.6	56.8
4	1.8	6.2	26.5	65.5
20SA620	0.0	9.1	18.2	72.7

must be noted here that the side-notched form to which she refers is distinctly different from the 20SA620 specimen: "Side-notched points are notched well up the side of the blade and as a result the base of the point is as wide or wider than the blade" (1978:6). Such a description does not fit FS 806, although FS 599 clearly should be included in the class.

Table 7.13 indicates that the 20SA620 Late Woodland lithic assemblage most closely resembles Luedtke's subperiod 4. Therefore, the composition of that assemblage suggests that the Late Woodland occupation of 20SA620 occurred late within that period. Unfortunately, Luedtke does not provide bracketing dates for the subperiods she defines. In an earlier study, however, she indicates that subperiod 1 predates A.D. 1000, and subperiod 4 postdates that figure. Subperiods 2 and 3 include sites from chronological ranges which straddle the A.D. 1000 benchmark, but with the centers of their ranges predating and postdating the figure, respectively (Luedtke 1976:321). If Luedtke's dates are accurate, the data indicate that the Late Woodland occupation of 20SA620 postdates A.D. 1000, a finding which is consistent with other data.

Other Bifaces. Several fragmentary bifaces were found at 20SA620 which, owing to their condition, could not be assigned to established types (e.g., FS 745; Plate 7.2*b*). Metric and other attributes are presented in Table 7.14. Several specimens merit some discussion.

A proximal biface of Bayport chert, FS 577, is shown in Plate 7.2*a*. In addition to the blade, part of the base was fractured, and the fractured edge was then reworked. The specimen bears the largely unfaceted ventral surface of its flake blank. The flake bulb of percussion (Crabtree 1972) coincided with the fractured corner of the base, and may have been the reason it was removed if that removal was deliberate. Review of the Saginaw Valley literature yielded a single possible analog for FS 577, from the Bussinger site: Halsey (1976: Plate XII) calls it a Dustin biface, a Late Archaic biface in this region (Harrison 1968). Other than Halsey's "Dustin biface," which actually bears minimal resemblance to FS 577, there is no good analog for the specimen in the Saginaw Valley literature.

A heat-damaged medial fragment, FS 202, is possibly of Upper Mercer chert (Plate 7.3*a*), of which there are outcrops in eastern Ohio (Luedtke 1976). The specimen bears numerous large potlid fractures (see Crabtree and Butler 1969; Ozker 1976b), including one which effectively removed the base, and incipient cracks across both faces. Its condition precludes definitive assignment.

A Bayport biface of uncertain affinity FS 264 (Plate 7.3*b*) resembles Late Archaic Leach bifaces (Taggart 1981) and Middle Archaic tools found at Weber I (Robertson 1989: Fig. 19F, G). It also resembles Ritchie's (1961:19) Brewerton Side-notched type, also of Late Archaic age. However, Fitting (1972: Figs. 61, 63) illustrates similar implements from Woodland provenience at Schultz, and FS 264 also resembles Late Woodland bifaces

TABLE 7.14
Metric and Discrete Attributes of Nondiagnostic Bifaces from 20SA620

FS	Unit N	Unit W	Level	Length (mm)	Width (mm)	Thick-ness (mm)	Stem Length (mm)	Mate-rial	Condi-tion
153	104	102	4	42.3	23.0	9.2		BP	whole
240	122	103	4	24.5		7.6		BP	proximal
258					24.8	7.7		UN	medial
266	126	109	10		19.1	9.3	10.9	BP	proximal
393	110	103	6		18.0	6.6		BP	proximal
421	107	103	6	53.3	30.3	11.3		BP	distal
447	103	102	7	27.0	15.6	9.2		BP	distal
566	106	101	9	24.5	24.6	8.7		BP	proximal
631	115	103	7			3.7		UN	distal
632	111	101	7	19.0	15.0	5.4		BP	proximal
687	116	102	9		13.4	4.9		BP	distal
691	112	102	9		14.5	4.3		BP	medial
718	111	101	11			5.0		BP	distal
745	118	102	7	31.4	21.9	10.0	9.7	BP	proximal
745	118	102	7		12.8	5.0		BP	distal
789	116	102	12		9.9	2.5		BP	distal
806	111	104	7	35.9	34.1	10.8	16.8	BP	proximal
814	125	109	11	17.0	11.3	3.7		UN	medial
820	125	108	11			5.9		BP	distal
821	120	103	9		16.2	8.0		BP	distal
840	123	103	9		18.7	10.9		BP	proximal
852	120	101	11			5.5		BP	proximal
864	119	103	11	58.8	30.2	12.0		BP	whole
884						4.0		BP	proximal
888	127	108	13		7.2	5.3		FR?	distal

BP = Bayport UN = Unknown FR = Flint Ridge

from Raven Rocks rockshelter in southeastern Ohio (Prufer 1981: Fig. 4*a-c*). In view of its condition, no assignment of the specimen is attempted.

Finally, FS 888 is a distal fragment of a drill found in level 13 of unit 127N/108W (Fig. 7.1). The specimen has beveled edges. Although its fragmentary condition makes it impossible to classify it with certainty, FS 888's level provenience and raw material—probably Flint Ridge chert—argue for Early Woodland placement.

Unifaces

Eight unifaces and two fragments of unifaces were found at 20SA620. The metric and other attributes of measurable specimens are compiled in Table 7.15. Figures 7.1 and 7.2 depict the horizontal and vertical distribution of the specimens.

A metasedimentary uniface, FS 339, has been mentioned previously. It is a fairly large specimen which bears only light retouch along a single edge or margin. Brief use is suggested by these attributes.

Another uniface, FS 778, is formed on a large, thick percussion flake (Plate 7.5*d*). Its form is irregular, and the tool bears no evidence of having been hafted. Also recovered in the same unit and level was a large flake with unifacial faceting along its straight distal margin (Plate 7.5*e*). It too appears not to have been hafted.

A small uniface, FS 830, was found in level 9 of unit 124N/103W. It was formed on a small thick flake (Plate 7.5*f*). One lateral margin of the specimen retains a section of Bayport cortex; the opposite margin bears a small shallow notch. The bit was formed on the proximal end of the flake blank, which had a pronounced bulb of percussion. This has left the bit quite thick. The flake distal margin forms the butt of the specimen; apparently, it terminated normally as dorsal and ventral surfaces intersected, but was snapped deliberately above the point to form an abrupt butt. Therefore, the specimen evidently was modified for hafting.

The bit of FS 830 bears large, expanding primary facets, probably the result of freehand percussion. Superimposed upon them is an irregular series of small snap and scalar fractures (Keeley 1980:24–25) which indicate extensive use and resharpening. It is worth noting that the ventral surface of the bit has been modified by the removal of several facets. Technically, these facets make the specimen a biface rather than a uniface, but its morphology and functional attributes make it clear that it was designed and used as a unifacial scraping tool. Bifacial retouch on scrapers has been observed previously at Wolf Phase and other Late Woodland sites in southeastern Michigan (Krakker and Shott 1984:97). This specimen was recovered from level 9, and so probably dates to an earlier period. Table 7.16 shows that the specimen

TABLE 7.15
Metric Attributes of Unifaces from 20SA620

FS	Unit N	Unit W	Level	Length (mm)	Width (mm)	Thick-ness (mm)	Stem Length (mm)	Mate-rial
104	103	101		32.0	44.7	11.2	14.0	BP
339	117	102	5	61.6	62.2	11.7		MS
561	108	103	9	68.2	38.6	11.8		TM?
743	125	103	7	37.8	28.7	5.2		BP
745	118	102	7	20.8	17.7	7.3	8.6	BP
778	120	103	7	54.0	34.8	11.0		BP
778	120	103	7	28.6	29.1	12.5		BP
830	124	103	9	24.4	20.7	7.3		BP

BP = Bayport MS = metasediment TM = Ten Mile

TABLE 7.16
Comparative Metric Attributes for FS 830

	Length (mm)	Width (mm)	Thick-ness (mm)	Source
FS 830	24.4	20.7	7.3	—
20SA2	29.0	25.0	9.0	Fitting 1972: Table 54
20SA2	31.0	27.0	7.5	Ozker 1982: Appendix K[a]
20SA2	32.0	23.3	9.6	Ozker 1982: Appendix K[b]
Bussinger	34.2	29.9	7.5	Halsey 1976: Table 33

[a] "Hafted Type A"
[b] "Biface End Scraper"

is smaller than most hafted uniface types found at Saginaw Valley archaeological sites.

An obviously hafted uniface, FS 104 (Plate 7.5*j*), was found in surface provenience. It features a deliberately notched and chipped stem; its base is lightly abraded, either by design or as a result of working in the haft. The specimen bears pronounced and well-defined shoulders. Maximum thickness is just proximal of the bit, and the longitudinal section forms an offset triangle. Apparently, the original flake blank was even thicker, and its maximum thickness has been reduced by use and resharpening. The bit is heavily faceted, both with resharpening and wear facets. Viewed in plan, the bit edge is irregular, probably as a result of this heavy use and maintenance.

Unlike FS 830, the ventral surface bears no faceting. Review of the area literature reveals no apparent similar specimens, but the tool's surface provenience suggests a Late Woodland placement.

A small stemmed uniface, FS 745, was found in level 7 of unit 118N/102W (Plate 7.5*c*). Its stem is formed by shallow notches, and the base is slightly concave but unabraded. The stem, but not the bit, is bifacial. The bit appears to have been heavily utilized, judging from the extensive resharpening and wear facets it bears. It is rounded in plan view. Table 7.17 compares the metric attributes of FS 745 with mean values of similar specimens from the Schultz site (Fitting 1972:204, Table 54). The specimen from 20SA620 is significantly smaller in all dimensions, but is similar in form. Fitting (1972: Table 59) reports that the specimens were found in all levels at Schultz, but that most were of Early Woodland provenience. Ozker (1982: Fig. 40) illustrates an apparently very similar specimen from the Early Woodland levels at Schultz. These observations and its level provenience combine to suggest that FS 745 is Early Woodland in age.

Beld (1985:38) recovered two hafted unifaces at the Conservation Park site. Neither, however, resembles the 20SA620 specimens; one, in fact (20GR33–219, Plate 9), is a reworked Meadowood biface. The second is from a contiguous unit, so both probably are Early Woodland in age. This conclusion strengthens the Early Woodland assignment of FS 745.

Finally, a very curious specimen, FS 864, was recovered at 20SA620 (Plate 7.5*h*). In plan view, it is double-edged or double-bitted, and appears to be a small axe or chisel. Made of Bayport chert, the specimen was formed on a large flake. One margin is formed from either the remnants of a large platform or some other flat surface on the original blank. Large, wide notches on opposite margins separate the two bits. The notches are not abraded. The ventral surface of the flake blank is partially faceted; this tool, like several others, is technically a biface. The opposing bits bear little evidence of use or resharpening, and it is not clear if the specimen, after having been fashioned, was actually put to use. Search of the literature reveals no similar specimens. Its level provenience suggests Early Woodland affinity for FS 864.

Taggart (1981:4) reports the discovery of "dumbbell" scrapers at 20SA202, the Leach site on the Flint River. He indicates that they are bifacial, like FS 864. However, the Leach specimens are found in Late Archaic provenience. Their possible affinity to FS 864 is not established.

Utilized Flakes

Two utilized flakes were found at 20SA620: FS 605 (Plate 7.5*a*) was found in level 5 of unit 111N/102E, and FS 743 (Plate 7.5*b*) in level 7 of unit

TABLE 7.17
Comparative Metric Attributes for FS 745

	Length (mm)	Width (mm)	Thick- ness (mm)	Stem Length (mm)	Source
FS 745	20.8	17.7	7.3	8.6	
20SA2	29.0	25.0	9.0		Fitting 1972: Table 54
20SA2	31.0	27.0	7.5		Ozker 1982: Appendix K[a]

[a]"Hafted Type A"

125N/103E. Both tools bear evidence of use and/or retouch on one flake margin, but lack the bit and butt attributes of formal unifaces.

Bipolar Cores

This core type is among the most common artifact classes found at prehistoric sites in the Great Lakes region. Binford and Quimby (1963:283) describe bipolar cores as having

> two opposed striking platforms or zones of percussion. These two zones are directly opposite each other, with the cleavage faces on both sides of the core converging on both zones of percussion.

The origin and function of bipolar cores has been the subject of some controversy. The two opposing arguments cannot be extensively reviewed here, but one considers bipolar cores functional objects in their own right. Thus, Taggart (1967) classifies bipolar cores as wedges, presumably used in splintering wood and bone. Binford and Quimby (1963) argue, instead, that the objects are spent by-products of bipolar reduction of small cores, often broken or exhausted tools. Flenniken (1979) and Hayden (1980) support this argument on experimental grounds. The only known ethnographic sources that can account for the production of these objects (e.g. Masao 1983; White 1969) cite bipolar lithic reduction as the process responsible for their production. In this study, they will be considered the exhausted remnants of bipolar reduction.

Twenty-five bipolar cores were found at 20SA620. Metric attributes of the assemblage are presented in Table 7.18. For comparative purposes, similar attributes of other archaeological and ethnographic assemblages are listed in Table 7.19. Reasonably close convergence in values is apparent in most cases, which supports the inference that the objects are in fact bipolar cores.

TABLE 7.18
Metric Attributes of Bipolar Cores from 20SA620

FS	Unit N	Unit W	Level[a]	Length (mm)	Width (mm)	Thickness (mm)	Material
129	113	104		34.0	27.4	12.5	BP
146	114	104	4	40.1	24.9	7.6	BP
162	118	102	4	16.9	16.9	7.5	BP
191	100	101	4	19.2	16.3	6.7	BP
254	103	101	5	19.7	14.5	11.2	BP
334	107	101	5	29.0	16.8	8.6	BP
338				30.4	21.3	7.6	BP
431	109	102	6	17.1	13.1	3.9	BP
563	105	101	9	23.0	21.7	5.3	BP
575	104	91		22.1	21.7	6.9	BP
575	104	91		32.2	16.8	9.0	BP
583	108	102	9	31.1	18.8	6.2	BP
610	112	103	7	27.1	15.5	6.8	BP
626	117	103	7	28.5	19.1	8.3	BP
659	113	103	9	17.6	16.7	7.9	UN
660	111	101	9	17.6	16.7	7.9	BP
698	114	103	11	19.0	15.6	5.7	BP
768				23.4	18.1	5.9	BP
785	121	101	7	27.9	20.5	5.5	BP
792	120	102	7	28.9	27.5	11.4	BP
792	120	102	7	19.0	16.8	8.5	BP
830	124	103	9	27.1	21.1	9.6	BP
845	124	109	13	22.2	15.0	8.0	BP
866	114	104	7	28.7	22.1	14.1	BP
890	127	103	9	15.7	14.5	5.9	BP

BP = Bayport UN = unknown

[a]Level provenience is omitted in several instances, either because specimens were found on the surface or in disturbed context on the western margin of the excavation. In addition, unit 104N/91W was excavated using local levels, so the two specimens from that unit have separate level provenience.

It is not surprising to note that no bipolar cores are fashioned from metasediments; all are composed of Bayport or some other kind of chert. Possibly metasediments are suited to bipolar reduction. It is equally possible, however, that they are curated in a different manner than are objects made of siliceous stone (Goodyear 1982).

A special class of bipolar cores merits separate attention: finished tools—bifaces and unifaces—which, probably following a period of normal use, have been reduced in bipolar fashion. The result of this sequence of uses is a finished tool which bears evidence of stepping and crushing on opposing margins. Tools used in this manner may be considered recycled; after their normal use-life, they have been adapted for use as bipolar cores.

Both bifaces and unifaces from 20SA620 have been so recycled, although

TABLE 7.19
Mean Metric Attributes of Bipolar Core Assemblages

Assemblage	Length (mm)	Width (mm)	Thick-ness (mm)	*N*	Source
20SA620	24.7	18.9	7.9	25	—
20SC77	24.1	17.0	8.1	14	Krakker 1984
N. Mich.	31.5	23.1	14.8	49	Binford and Quimby 1963
New Guinea	20.0	28.0	10.0	43	White 1969
Experimental	23.8	21.9	11.1		Flenniken 1979

the former are more common. Table 7.20 compiles metric attributes for recycled tools, and Table 7.21 compares them to mean values of other bipolar cores from the site (i.e., those which do not bear evidence of previous use as a formal tool). It is clear upon inspection of Table 7.21 that cores fashioned from recycled tools are significantly smaller in all dimensions than their nonrecycled counterparts. This observation supports the judgment that these cores were were exhausted or abandoned tools which were then adapted for a second use.

Miscellaneous Specimens

Found in level 7 of unit 111N/103W, FS 620 is a cobble of shale or slate which has been chipped along almost its entire circumference (Plate 7.6*d*). Original cobble surface is retained, however, over most of the two faces of the object. Cleavage planes are visible in sections exposed by faceting, and a large crack runs partially through the specimen. Possibly FS 620 served as a wedge or hammer, but there is no evidence of wear or abrasion apart from the deliberate marginal chipping. Ozker (1982: Plate 45) illustrates several items which resemble FS 620, but their function is not identified. FS 620 measures 51.6 mm by 46.4 mm by 25.6 mm.

A fragment of a ground stone tool, FS 637, was found in level 7 of unit 116N/103W (Plate 7.6*b*). Made of igneous material, the fragment is a transverse section of a cylindrical object. The surface of the specimen has been deliberately ground. Possibly, it is a fragment of a maul or pick.

FS 577, recovered in unit 104N/91W, is a slate fragment (Plate 7.6*a*). It retains one apparently cut and ground margin; all other margins of this fragmentary specimen are fractures. Specimen width is 39.1 mm, and thickness is 6.0 mm. Two wide, shallow, roughly parallel grooves are found on one face. Both terminate abruptly at a fracture, and almost certainly extended

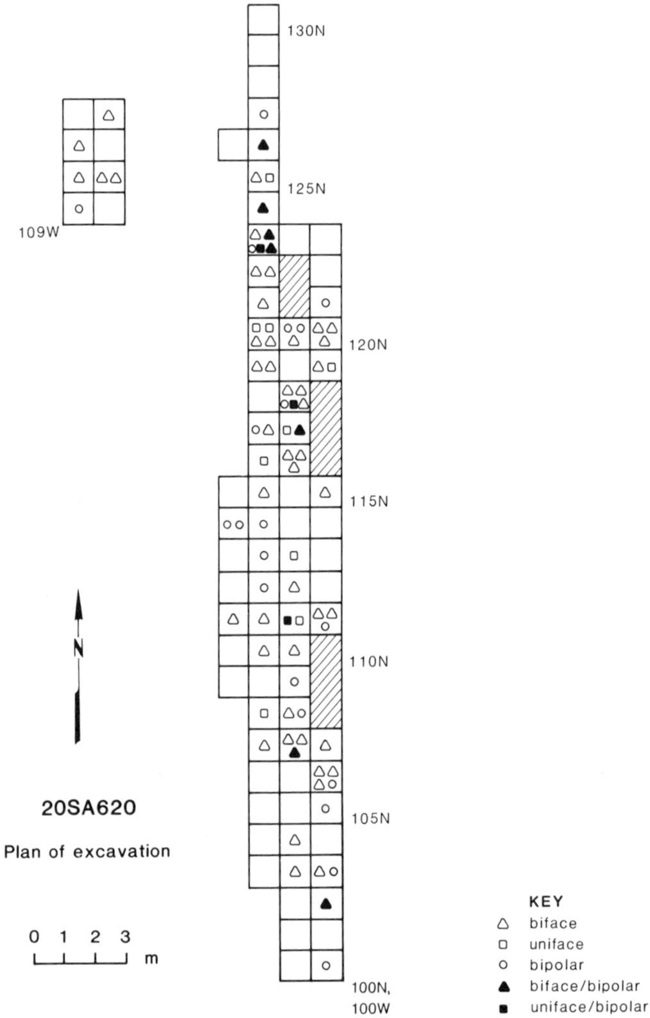

Figure 7.6. Composite plan distribution of cores.

further on the intact original specimen. The opposite face bears several shallower, less well-defined grooves which follow the same axis as those on the first face. The tool is an abrader of some sort. Abraders have been found previously at Saginaw Valley sites (Ozker 1982: Fig. 43), but they are generally composed of sandstone.

A fragment of red slate, FS 495, was recovered in level 7 of unit 196N/102W (Plate 7.6*c*). It probably is an unfinished gorget which may have been

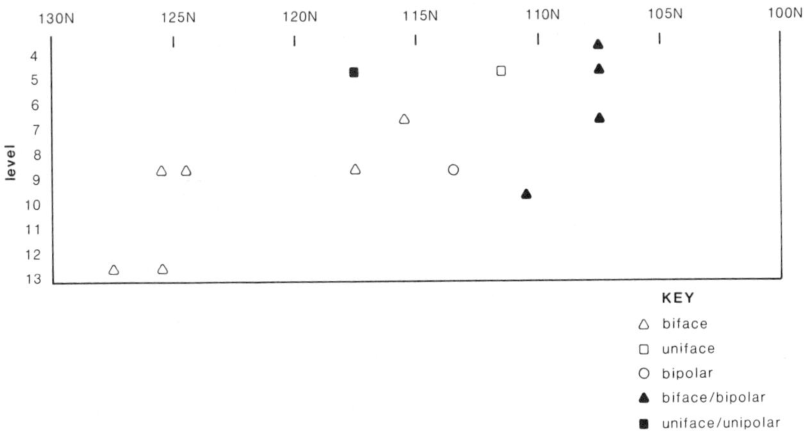

Figure 7.7. Composite profile distribution of cores.

TABLE 7.20
Metric Attributes of Tools Recycled as Bipolar Cores

FS	Unit N	Unit W	Level	Length (mm)	Width (mm)	Stem Length (mm)	Material	Type
85	111	102	4	20.0	18.6	6.0	BP	uniface
248	126	103	10	21.0	19.8	5.7	BP	biface
380	102	101	6	17.3	18.9	7.8	BP	biface
693	117	102	9		12.4	4.8	FR	biface
745	118	102	7		23.1	5.1	BP	uniface
748	124	103	7	26.1	15.9	8.8	BP	biface
763	123	103	7	18.4	12.8	7.8	BP	biface
830	124	103	9	22.8	17.6	7.8	UN	biface
837	125	108	13				UM	biface

BP = Bayport FR = Flint Ridge UN = Unknown UM = Upper Mercer

abandoned because it was broken. One face and margin are completely ground. The opposite margin is apparently a cleavage plane of the parent material. The opposite face is ground smooth, but it bears several broad, shallow facets struck from each margin after the face was ground. There is no evidence of a drillhole on the specimen. It measures 55.1 mm by 39.9 mm by 11.1 mm.

Recovered in level 4 of unit 121N/103W, FS 228, is a fragment of a ground stone celt. The specimen may be a flake or spall rather than a fragment of a tool. It bears grinding on only part of the dorsal surface, while the remainder

TABLE 7.21
Mean Metric Attributes of Bipolar Cores and Recycled Tools

Class	Length (mm)	Width (mm)	Thick-ness (mm)	*N*
Bipolar cores	25.2	18.9	7.9	25
Recycled bifaces	22.4	16.9	7.2	7
Recycled unifaces	20.0	20.9	5.5	2
All	24.5	18.6	7.6	34

is faceted. Width of the item is 33.4 mm. Other dimensions are not complete and cannot be measured.

From level 7 of unit 120N/103W, FS 778 is a retouch or incidental flake struck from the bit of a celt. Its dorsal surface is highly polished, and the line of intersection between dorsal and ventral surfaces is the bit of the tool. This specimen indicates the use and resharpening of a ground stone celt at 20SA620.

LOCAL COLLECTIONS FROM 20SA620

The Saginaw Valley is renowned not only for its archaeological heritage, but for its tradition of responsible local scholarship as well. Today, Saginaw holds its place in the front rank of the Michigan Archaeological Society, and the local chapter, a charter member of the Society, continues to thrive. While Saginaw probably has more private archaeological collections than any other region of Michigan, many of these have only limited scientific value, since they are poorly catalogued. Often, their owners are reluctant to share the information which their collections embody, making them worthless. Other collections, however, are well-provenienced and quite valuable. During the UMMA investigation at 20SA620, we received assistance from several local MAS members, which have added measurably to our knowledge of the site and its occupational history.

Richard Bisbing, then Chapter president, made arrangements for UMMA archaeologists to examine a number of private collections from the Saginaw Valley. Invaluable information concerning 20SA620 was obtained from the collections of Michael Neering, Charles Hitsman, Keith Lutz, and especially Lloyd Bowen.[2] Discussion in this section will focus in large measure upon

[2]Lloyd Bowen has subsequently donated his collection from 20SA620 to the Museum of Anthropology.

the collections of these individuals.[3] Additional information on the Lutz collection was furnished by Margaret Holman of Michigan State University.

The private collections from 20SA620 were all examined and photographed. Discussions with the collectors elicited information concerning the distribution of artifacts across the site, the circumstances under which collections were made, and other pertinent details. Special attention was paid to the Bowen and Neering collections. Bowen supplied valuable information on the approximate location of some of his discoveries, and diagnostic specimens from both collections were measured.[4]

Table 7.22 summarizes data obtained on the frequency of various artifact classes in the several local collections from 20SA620. Data on metric and discrete attributes of diagnostic bifaces in the Bowen and Neering collections are shown in Table 7.23.

Apart from the selection in favor of retouched tools, it is immediately apparent that the local collections from 20SA620 differ typologically in important respects from the UMMA assemblage. Specifically, both the Bowen and Neering collections include several types of bifaces of Late Archaic or Early Woodland affinity that are absent in the UMMA assemblage. Table 7.24 depicts the differences in tabular form. Inspection of the table shows that the UMMA assemblage is dominated by Early and Late Woodland types. Although these are present as well in the private collections, the latter include possible Feeheley (Taggart n.d.) and definite Dustin, Durst, Meadowood and Turkey Tail forms.

Bowen's collection also includes several specimens composed of what is tentatively identified as Burlington chert from the Illinois Valley. These include a stemmed uniface, two biface fragments, a bipolar core, and lithic debris. Although the fragmentary condition of the tools makes it impossible to identify diagnostic forms, use of Burlington chert in Michigan typically is ascribed to the Middle Woodland period (Prahl 1970). No Burlington chert tools were recovered during the UMMA excavation of site. The Bowen Collection suggests more spatial variability across 20SA620 than is apparent in other data. Aside from illustrating the value of inspecting local collections, it also suggests a more extensive Middle Woodland occupation of unknown duration, centered somewhere to the west of the excavation block.

Other specimens from the Bowen collection merit consideration. Two stemmed unifaces are included in the collection; they resemble, at least in

[3]We would be remiss, however, if we failed to acknowledge the valuable information supplied by Gordon MacPhail, J. McNally, Gary Roenicke, Thomas Rondo, and especially Bernard Spencer. The collections of these persons are extensive and their careful examination, already underway, are proving highly informative. Since the collections are from other sites, however, they are beyond the scope of this report. Detailed treatment will be reserved for a later study.

[4]Parenthetically, Neering possesses a Dustin assemblage, evidently a cache, from adjacent 20SA351. It warrants separate treatment in its own right.

TABLE 7.22
Local Collections from 20SA620

Collection	Ceramics	Bifaces	Unifaces	Bipolar Cores	Debris	Other
Bowen	many	96	68	3	30+	2 celts, 1 gouge, 1 sandstone abrader, 3 cobbles,1 sandstone hoe(?) pipe stem,pipe bowl
Hitsman	0	5				
Lutz	0	6	1		59	
Neering	10	12	3	15	2	celt bit, gorget fragment

general form, FS 104 and FS 745. Bowen's collection also includes a series of large and small unifaces, and a series of unifaces fashioned from exotic cherts. Among the latter are two unifaces of Upper Mercer chert and one each composed of Western Onondaga chert and Indiana hornstone. The sources of these cherts are in southwestern Ontario and southern Indiana (Luedtke 1976: Fig. 9).

Upper Mercer is usually found in Michigan assemblages of Paleo-Indian, Early Archaic and early Late Woodland affinity (Luedtke 1976:289). The nearby Bussinger site has yielded an extensive Upper Mercer assemblage in association with Wayne Tradition ceramics (Halsey 1976). Wayne Tradition occupation at 20SA620 is documented in the ceramic assemblage, but not otherwise by lithic artifacts. Thus, the Bowen collection furnishes complementary data to that obtained from the excavation.

Bowen and Neering both possess ground stone tools from 20SA620 (Table 7.20). The former collection includes an especially large celt which was found roughly 20 m south of the UMMA excavation block.

Finally, the Bowen collection also includes several nondiagnostic biface and uniface specimens, as well as a fragment of a ground stone celt, from property which adjoins the Township parcel to the east. That material, however, was not discovered on the ridge occupied by 20SA620, and so is not considered to be part of the site assemblage.

LITHIC DEBRIS

Lithic debris, or flakage, is almost always the most common class of lithic remains at archaeological sites. The study of flakage can reveal the nature of lithic reduction processes and the activities carried out at sites. Lithic debris has come to assume even greater importance with the recognition that tool curation and complex patterns of technological organization complicate the relationship between tools and prehistoric cultural behavior. Any conclusions about prehistoric cultural behavior based on only finished tools is apt to produce limited results. Debris, in contrast, can furnish a more complete and accurate indication of the activities which occurred at sites (Henry et al. 1976:61), at least those activities which involved the use of stone tools.

A variety of approaches to lithic debris analysis characterized previous archaeological studies in the Saginaw Valley, befitting the abundance and complexity of the archaeological record and the long history of research there. Most efforts identify certain flake attributes, such as lipped platforms, as diagnostic of specific reduction stages or techniques. Experimental studies, however, have demonstrated that attributes considered diagnostic of reduction stages or techniques are in fact produced under a variety of circumstances (Henry et al. 1976; Patterson and Sollberger 1978). Consequently,

TABLE 7.23
Attributes of Diagnostic Bifaces in Local Collections from 20SA620.

Condition[a]	Metric Attributes (mm) Length	Width	Thickness	Stem Length	Stem Width	Material[b]	Type
Neering Collection							
W	54.8	24.3	6.4	9.7	20.1	TM	Meadowood
P	27.7+	22.7	5.7	8.7	25.0	WO	Meadowood
P	15.0+	14.8+		10.0	14.8+	WO	Meadowood
Bowen Collection							
W	55.0	28.6	5.8	8.8	21.4	WO	Meadowood
W	56.2	22.1	5.6	8.9		WO	Meadowood
W	58.0	21.5	7.9	15.2	15.3	UN	Schultz[c]
W	35.8	20.4	8.2	12.4	16.2	UN	Schultz
W	32.6	18.8	9.6	11.1	15.5	BP	Schultz
W	52.9	22.1	10.2	14.8	13.2	BP	Dustin
P	40.0+	24.1	9.8	9.7	12.9	BP	Dustin
W	46.0	20.1	6.0	9.1	15.4	BP	Dustin
W	45.1	20.1	9.2	8.8	15.8	BP	Dustin
W	42.4	15.5	7.0	9.2	13.3	BP	Dustin
W	33.8	17.6	7.1	9.2		BP	Dustin
W	34.7	16.2	5.1	8.9	12.3	BP	Dustin
W	31.0	18.2	7.5	10.7	17.2	BP	Dustin
W	39.5	17.1	8.0	9.6	15.6	BP	Dustin
W	38.4	16.3	5.6	9.5	11.2	UN	Dustin

W	54.1	31.0	12.0	14.0	33.4	BP	Feeheley?
W	55.7	27.0	11.1	16.8	28.3	BP	Feeheley?
P	40.5+	33.0	9.6	10.8	21.6	BP	Feeheley?
W	38.0	26.2	8.8	12.8	27.8	BP	Feeheley?
W	61.7	23.5	9.9	15.0	27.7	BP	Feeheley?
P	29.9+	39.8	7.6	14.5	26.3	BP	Feeheley?
M	51.5+	37.4	7.4		25.2	NW	?
W	30.6	22.7	6.7			IH	Turkey Tail
W	32.7	25.1	7.0	15.3	17.9	BP	Kramer
W	25.4	14.1	6.5	7.3	16.8	WO	Raccoon
W	30.9	17.2	4.5	9.8	15.4	NW	Raccoon
W	24.2	15.8	5.3	7.3		BP	Raccoon
W	23.9	16.6	3.9			BP	Madison
W	21.0	13.1	2.9			BP	Madison
W	30.0	21.2	5.3			BP	Madison
W	33.2	16.2	8.2			BP	Madison
P	17.7+	14.0	5.2			BP	Madison

[a]W = whole P = proximal M = medial

[b]BP = Bayport NW = Norwood TM = Ten Mile WO = Western Onondaga IH = Indiana Hornstone UN = unknown

[c]Schultz Stemmed

TABLE 7.24
Diagnostic Bifaces by Collection from 20SA620

Type	Bowen	Neering	Hitsman	UMMA
Feeheley	x	–	x	–
Dustin	x	–	–	–
Satchell	x	x	–	x
Durst	–	x	–	–
Meadowood	x	x	–	–
Kramer	x	x	–	x
Schultz	x	–	–	x
Turkey Tail	x	–	–	–
Raccoon	x	–	–	x
Triangular	x	x	x	x

x = present – = absent

they cannot be used to establish the presence of those stages. Furthermore, these previous approaches viewed lithic reduction as a series of essentially discrete stages, rather than the continuous process it is. Methods capable of depicting variability in debris assemblages in continuous terms, therefore, merit close attention as well.

Another method used in most flakage studies is the time-consuming examination and classification of each specimen. These assemblages frequently number in the thousands of items, and in many cases the inspection of all specimens is highly impractical and yields few benefits. Some kind of probabilistic sampling may be a practical alternative, but archaeologists have been slower to apply it to debris assemblages than to other archaeological phenomena. Analytical techniques which are capable of faster and more economical treatment of specimens clearly warrant consideration.

For these theoretical and practical reasons, analysis of the 20SA620 debris assemblage was conducted by the processing of unit and level provenience lots. Each lot was sorted by size through a series of graded, phi-scale sieves with mesh sizes of 16, 8, and 4 mm, resulting in the production of four size classes per lot: >16 mm, >8 mm, >4 mm, and <4 mm.[5] These sieves effectively sort specimens by their medial axis (Farrand, personal communication).

Within each size class, a further sorting of Bayport specimens was carried

[5]In reality, the effective mesh size of sieves is the diagonal formed by each $n \times n$ square comprising it. Therefore, effective size classes used in this study are >22.6 mm, >11.3 mm, >5.6 mm, and <5.6 mm (e.g., 22.6 mm is the diagonal of a 16 × 16 mm square). For ease of presentation, the mesh size as described initially will be used.

TABLE 7.25
Lithic Debris by Excavation Level

Level[a]	Debris Type					% Non-Bayport
	Faceted	Flat	Broken	Non-Bayport	Total	
2	19	12	30	9	70	13
3	32	30	59	13	134	10
4	78	75	161	27	341	8
5	194	184	364	61	803	8
6	86	67	209	77	439	17
7	289	225	536	82	1132	7
8	13	8	22	5	48	10
9	175	123	360	111	769	14
10	13	10	19	6	48	12
11	140	90	217	75	522	14
12	4	3	6	3	16	19
13	15	12	21	5	53	9

[a]Low counts in levels 8 and 10 indicate only that those levels were combined with levels 9 and 11, respectively, in most units.

out. Because of their rarity, non-Bayport lithic flakes were not subdivided beyond the size-sorting stage. Flakes bearing platforms were distinguished from flakes lacking this attribute, and a distinction between faceted and flat platforms was made. This distinction separates specimens produced in the resharpening of bifaces from those produced in resharpening unifaces.

Measurements of this nature have proven highly effective in experimental studies (Henry et al. 1976; Patterson and Sollberger 1978; Stahle and Dunn 1982). In particular, Stahle and Dunn (1982) have used this method to compile cumulative distributions over a series of size classes. They successfully identified specimen distributions with distinct types of lithic reduction practices, and obtained close agreement with a family of theoretical frequency distributions (1982:88–90). Their approach provides a framework for evaluating the nature of specific empirical cumulative distributions and identifying the reduction practices which characterized the assemblages. The 20SA620 debris assemblage can be assessed in this manner.

Table 7.25 compiles data on flake types per excavation level at 20SA620. The percentage of non-Bayport chert lithic debris per level also is shown there. More detailed breakdown of the data, including counts by size class, is shown in Table 7.26. There, upper excavation levels have been aggregated to ensure comparison with lower levels, resulting in six level intervals.

Following Stahle and Dunn (1982), cumulative distributions by percentage were compiled for the faceted and flat platform components of the 20SA620 debris assemblage. Faceted platform flakes may be considered the by-product

TABLE 7.26
Lithic Debris by Category, Size Interval, and Level

Size Interval	Debris Category				
	Faceted	Flat	Broken	Non-Bayport	Total
Level 2-3					
16	0	2	3	2	7
8	23	17	36	10	86
4	26	16	48	10	100
< 4	2	7	2	0	11
Level 4-5					
16	6	10	7	7	30
8	104	103	154	38	399
4	158	143	340	41	682
< 4	4	3	25	0	33
Level 6-7					
16	17	26	15	13	71
8	175	115	289	81	660
4	182	151	422	63	818
< 4	1	0	19	2	22
Level 8-9					
16	3	10	6	8	27
8	72	52	111	47	282
4	110	65	254	60	489
< 4	3	4	11	1	19
Level 10-11					
16	4	5	4	2	15
8	62	44	81	32	219
4	80	50	140	45	315
< 4	7	1	11	2	21
Level 12-13					
16	0	0	1	0	1
8	11	4	7	3	25
4	7	11	19	4	41
< 4	1	0	0	1	2

of biface reduction and resharpening, and comparison of the distributions across excavation levels can furnish information on changing biface reduction practices at the site. Flat platform flakes indicate the reduction and resharpening of unifaces. Faceted platform flake cumulative distributions are displayed in Figure 7.8, which shows that only minor differences are found between levels. In effect, the cumulative distribution of biface reduction appears to be constant through time. Minor differences are also seen when flat platform flakes are considered. The two slightly anomalous distributions are found at opposite ends of the sequence. Not coincidentally, these also are the smallest samples, so sampling variability may account for them. At first glance, therefore, results of the analysis employing cumulative distributions are not especially informative.

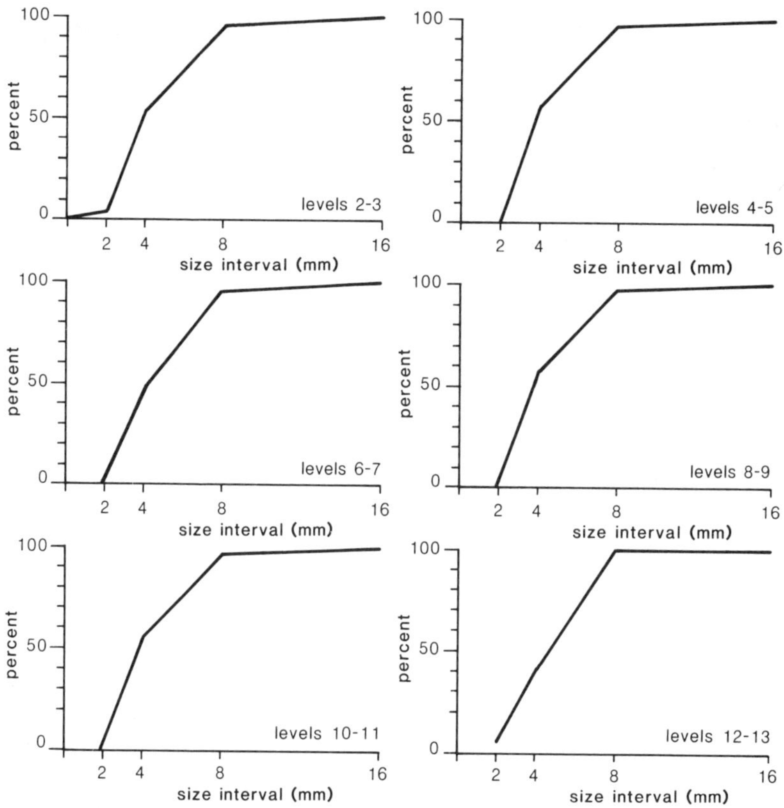

Figure 7.8. Size distribution of faceted platform flakes by level.

Differences do emerge, however, when data are aggregated further. Even here, however, only some differences are apparent. Figure 7.9 shows the cumulative distribution resulting from the combination of excavation levels 2 through 7, and 8 through 13. This roughly divides the Late Woodland from earlier occupations of 20SA620. Figure 7.9 shows that close similarities are still found between flat platform flake groups. In contrast, faceted platform flakes diverge, with the level 2–7 assemblage containing more specimens in the larger size classes than the level 8–13 assemblage. In effect, the upper level assemblage has more large specimens. This finding indicates a trend through time toward either larger tools, or toward more primary reduction at the site.

The chipped stone tool data provide no support for the first alternative. More primary reduction, therefore, must have occurred at 20SA620 during its occupation by Late Woodland populations. This trend can be explained

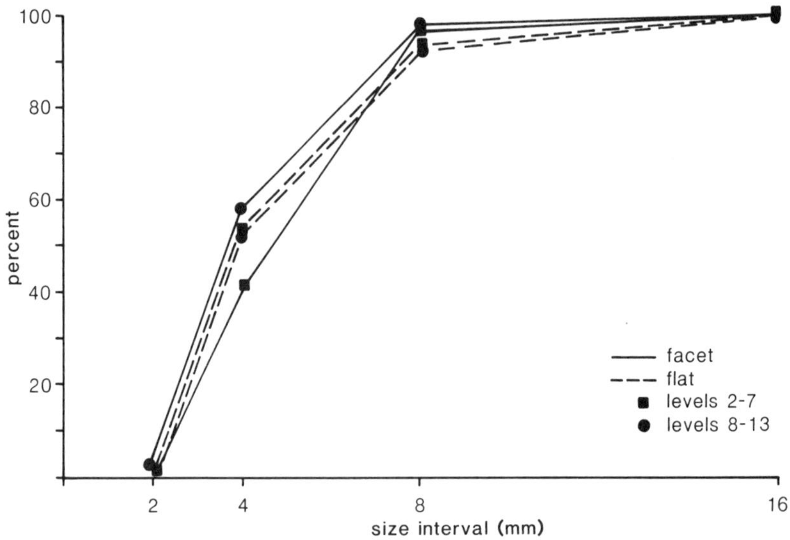

Figure 7.9. Size distribution of flat and faceted platform flakes.

in part by the postulated greater residential mobility of earlier groups in the Saginaw Valley. Greater mobility, and the use of a larger territory, would act to increase the rate of tool curation, which would promote in turn heavy use and resharpening of tools. These processes would tend to produce debris assemblages dominated by smaller specimens. Conversely, Late Woodland groups may have curated their lithic technology to a lesser degree, and may have engaged in on-site core reduction rather than segmenting their reduction sequence.

A pattern of greater residential mobility during the Early Woodland period also is consistent with other data provided by the debris assemblage. Aggregated excavation levels 2–7 are composed of 9 percent exotic raw material, while levels 8–13 have a comparable figure of 14 percent. This is a slight difference to be sure, but one consistent with greater residential mobility, and consequent greater access to exotic raw material during the Early Woodland period.

RAW MATERIAL UTILIZATION

Chipped Stone Tools

Patterns of raw material use are an important source of information on the organization of prehistoric societies. They can furnish information on the

TABLE 7.27
Raw Material Composition of the 20SA620 Lithic Assemblage

	Material					
	BP	MS	FR	UM	TM	UN
Bifaces						
Late Archaic	0	3	0	0	0	0
Early Woodland	3	0	0	0	0	0
Middle Woodland	1	0	0	0	0	0
Late Woodland	13	0	0	0	0	0
Other	21	1	1	0	0	3
Total	38	3	1	0	0	3
Other Tools						
Unifaces	7	1	0	0	0	2
Bipolar cores	24	0	0	0	0	1
Recycled tools	7	0	1	1	0	1
All Tools	107	4	3	2	0	8
%	86	3	2	2	0	6

[a]BP = Bayport MS = metasediment FR = Flint Ridge UM = Upper Mercer TM = Ten Mile UN = Unknown

scale of social systems, the nature of exchange relationships between systems and the organization of technologies (Luedtke 1976). The lithic assemblage from 20SA620 is dominated by the local Bayport chert, but small amounts of other materials also are present. In the following discussion, patterns of raw material utilization are considered, both in the finished tools and the debris components of the assemblage.

Table 7.27 shows that most tools from the site consist of Bayport chert. Of the non-Bayport bifaces, only metasediments (confined to the Satchell occupation) and some unidentified cherts account for more than a single specimen. Other classes of remains exhibit similar relative frequencies of Bayport and other materials, with minor differences that can be attributed to the small assemblage sizes. One aspect of the observed distribution merits brief attention. Table 7.27 indicates that tools recycled as bipolar cores—all but two of which are recycled bifaces—include one specimen each of Flint Ridge and Upper Mercer chert. These are high quality materials from eastern Ohio, and may be considered exotic to the Saginaw area. Since recycling represents an attempt to extend the functional life of a specimen, it is not surprising that specimens composed of exotic chert should be somewhat disproportionately represented in this class of remains. Obviously, assemblage sizes are extremely low and the finding must remain provisional, but it is consistent with the view that exotic materials at 20SA620 were more extensively used and curated than were local materials.

TABLE 7.28
Frequencies of Biface Types at Fletcher and 20SA620

Type	Fletcher		20SA620			
			UMMA		Combined	
	N	%	*N*	%	*N*	%
Bifurcate	1	.02	0	.00	0	.00
Satchell	0	.00	2	.11	5	.08
Feeheley	0	.00	0	.00	7	.12
Dustin	0	.00	0	.00	10	.17
Meadowood	7	.11	0	.00	5	.08
Durst[a]	9	.15	0	.00	1	.02
Kramer	3	.05	2	.11	4	.07
Adena	1	.02	0	.00	0	.00
Schultz	1	.02	1	.05	4	.07
Dickson	1	.02	0	.00	0	.00
Snyders	1	.02	0	.00	0	.00
other MW	0	.00	1	.05	1	.02
Exp. Stem	16	.25	3	.16	3	.05
Raccoon	3	.05	1	.05	4	.07
Jack's Reef	9	.15	0	.00	0	.00
Triangle	9	.15	9	.50	17	.28

[a]Combined Durst/Ace-of-Spades

Lithic Debris

Among non-Bayport lithic debris, certain specimens could be identified to raw material sources. Overall, 38 percent of the non-Bayport materials could be identified; metasediments and quartzite, neither of which is siliceous, are by far the most common. The range of lithic sources present is impressive, but the amounts in which they occur are extremely small.

For some materials, including Flint Ridge, Ten Mile Creek and Upper

TABLE 7.29
Relative Frequency of Period Diagnostics at Fletcher and 20SA620

Site	Late Archaic	Early Woodland	Middle Woodland	Late Woodland
Fletcher	.00	.35	.02	.61
20SA620	.37	.24	.00	.40

Mercer, more than enough tools were recovered to account for such small amounts of debris. That is, the tools could have been imported to the site, used and resharpened in some degree, and then discarded rather than curated upon periodic abandonment of 20SA620. This would have produced enough, probably more than enough, debris to account for the totals recovered. Others, such as Western Onondaga, Kettle Point, Norwood, Burlington and Indiana hornstone, are rare, if not absent altogether, among finished tools. The presence of even small amounts of debris from these sources, therefore, indicates some measure of tool curation, since no or too few tools were recovered at the site to account for the debris. When local collections are taken into consideration, however, this pattern is altered, since Western Onondaga, Burlington and Indiana Hornstone are represented there. This leaves only Norwood and Kettle Point completely unrepresented in the tool assemblage.

Quartzite is well represented in the debris assemblage, accounting for 23 percent of the specimens recovered. Yet not a single quartzite tool was found at 20SA620 during the excavation, and no specimens were noted in the local collections. Subject to all the provisos concerning limited samples at the sites, this pattern suggests that quartzite tools were being brought to 20SA620, used and resharpened there, and then carried on to the next settlement. In short, the pattern is one of high curation of quartzite tools. Quartzite is locally available across most of lower Michigan and it is not generally considered a high quality raw material, although it was highly efficient in certain applications. Curation of specimens composed of quartzite would not be expected, and these results are counterintuitive.

In fact, exotic cherts are often considered high quality and worthy of extensive curation. In such circumstances, we should expect to see few tools of exotic chert at Saginaw Valley sites, and some amount of debris. There should be more debris than the recovered tools could have generated as they were used and maintained, if this pattern holds. Yet precisely the opposite is found in the 20SA620 assemblage.

LITHIC ASSEMBLAGES AT 20SA620 AND FLETCHER

William Lovis (1985:163) has tabulated the frequency of various biface types from the Fletcher site in Bay City. Although Fletcher and 20SA620 differ in important respects in their ecological setting, both are stream margin occupations.

Table 7.28 compares the observed and relative frequencies of various biface types at Fletcher and 20SA620. For these purposes, the Durst and Ace-of-Spades classes were combined, as were Levanna and Madison types, into a single Late Woodland triangular biface class. None of the triangular bifaces from 20SA620, however, could be classified as a Levanna biface. For 20SA620, Table 7.28 includes figures for the excavated assemblage as well as for the combined assemblage consisting of the excavated items and the specimens in local collections.

It is immediately apparent upon inspection of Table 7.28 that significant differences characterize the two assemblages. Fletcher exhibits a higher frequency of later-period diagnostic tools, especially Late Woodland ones. Because it includes an Early Archaic bifurcate-base biface, it also features the longest span of occupation. Table 7.29 summarizes the diagnostic tools by major periods represented. Closer examination of Table 7.28 also reveals that the Early Woodland assemblages from the two sites differ chiefly in the strong representation of Durst/Ace-of-Spades bifaces at Fletcher and the virtual absence of this class at 20SA620. If the various biface classes represent distinct functional tool kits rather than stylistic modes, this finding suggests that a wider range of activities occurred at Fletcher. This would not be a surprising conclusion based on the overall character of the Fletcher assemblage, and Lovis's (1985) belief that Fletcher was occupied repeatedly for a variety of purposes. In similar fashion, the Late Woodland assemblage at Fletcher is more evenly divided among classes; 20SA620's is dominated by triangular bifaces. In this instance, the difference is at least partially temporal, since Jack's Reef bifaces are far more common in early Late Woodland Wayne Tradition occupations than in later ones (Halsey 1976; Luedtke 1978). Triangular bifaces, in contrast, are more common later.

SUMMARY

The Bridgeport Site was first occupied not long after the end of the Nipissing Great Lakes phase and was occupied intermittently through the Late Woodland period. Bifaces are the most common lithic class at this site, and bifaces of Late Archaic, Early Woodland, Late Woodland, and possibly Middle Woodland affinity are found in this assemblage. The most numerous diagnostic biface class is the Late Woodland, and several kinds of evidence suggest that the Late Woodland occupation of the site occurred largely after A.D. 1000.

The ceramic evidence (Chapter 8) and lithic evidence do not entirely agree with respect to the site's occupational history. Middle Woodland diagnostic ceramics apparently are more common than Early Woodland ones, while the opposite is true in the lithic assemblage. Use of the site by more than one kind of settlement system is indicated (see Ozker 1982:77).

Patterns in the size distribution of lithic debris also suggest changing practices through time. Distributions weighted toward larger size classes in upper levels of the deposit suggest changes in the local settlement system toward the logistic end of a residential-logistic continuum (see Binford 1980). If this suggestion is supported in future research, it strengthens the interpretation that this site was a special-purpose occupation, not a residential site like the Fletcher, during the Late Woodland period.

Bipolar cores are common elements of Late Woodland assemblages in Michigan (Binford and Quimby 1963), and this site is no exception to the pattern; slightly more than half of all bipolar cores at the site were found in upper levels. Recycling of tools as bipolar cores also occurred frequently. Greater bipolar reduction at the later stages of occupation at 20SA620 may partly account for the size distribution of lithic debris in upper levels. The lithic assemblage is dominated by Bayport chert and limited evidence indicates no difference of any kind between Woodland periods in the patterns of raw material use at the site.

Chronological trends in biface metric attributes have been used to estimate the age of several occupations at 20SA620. Although these data are limited and the results provisional, they provide one focus for future research that may help to place the site in an accurate context.

8
The Ceramic Assemblage

Claire McHale Milner
Museum of Anthropology, University of Michigan

INTRODUCTION

The Saginaw Valley has provided some of the most significant archaeological data for the southern half of the lower peninsula of Michigan. In particular, excavations at the Schultz site (20SA2) and a number of other sites—Kantzler (20BY30), Fletcher (20BY28), Frazer-Tyra (20SA9), Valley Sweets (20SA24), Stadelmeyer (20SA195), Mahoney (20SA193)—have established the rudiments of a ceramic chronology against which sites from the rest of the region and beyond are compared. The Saginaw Valley has yielded a rich archaeological data base for the entire Woodland sequence. As tabulated from the State of Michigan's Site Inventory, 97 Late Woodland, 29 Middle Woodland and 28 Early Woodland sites are recorded in Saginaw county alone, as well as 81 additional sites for which the period within the Woodland sequence has not been identified. Nearby counties such as Bay County have similarly heavy site densities.

Despite this rich data base, analyses of the Schultz site continue to dominate the interpretations of the Woodland period in this region. With the exception of Elizabeth Garland's recent work on Early Woodland components in the southwestern area of the state (1984), few Early Woodland occupations have received an in-depth analysis comparable to the Schultz site study by Doreen Ozker (1982). Garland's recent article (1986) stands as the only attempt to summarize the relationships and differences between the few Early Woodland components known in Michigan. During the Middle Woodland, the Schultz site is clearly the primary occupational focus within the Saginaw Valley as evidenced by intensity of occupation, and the presence of mounds and enclosures. However, we have yet to adequately explore the nature of the smaller-scale Middle Woodland occupations and the relationship of these sites to Schultz. In the Late Woodland, the Schultz site is no

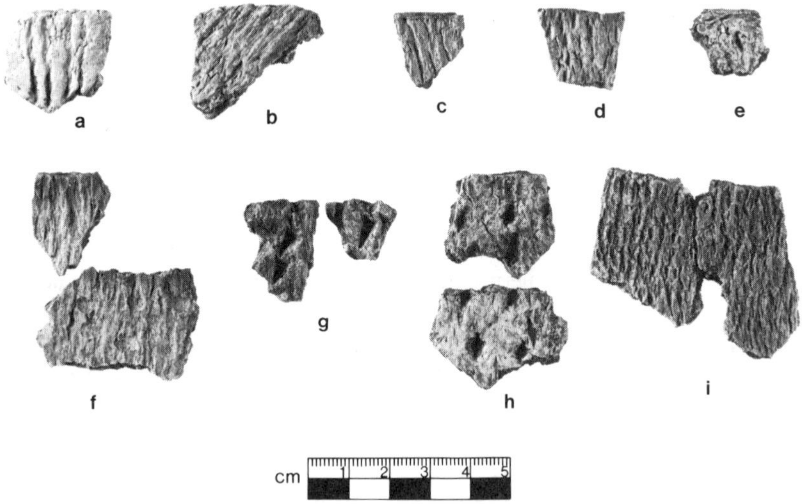

Plate 8.1. Early Late Woodland vessels:

a. Vessel 46	*e*. Vessel 50
b. Vessel 28	*f*. Vessel 9
c. Vessel 30	*g*. Vessel 31
d. Vessel 49	*h*. Decorated set 8
i. Vessel 10	

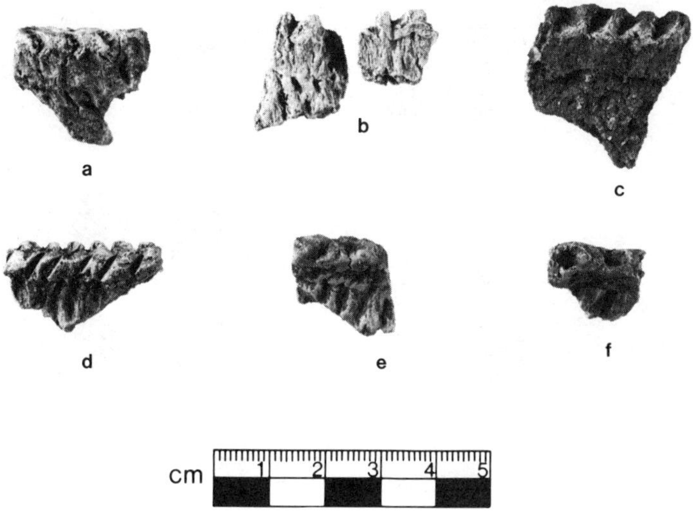

Plate 8.2. Early Late Woodland vessels:
a. Vessel 47 — *d*. Vessel 32
b. Vessel 26 — *e*. Vessel 23
c. Vessel 2 — *f*. Vessel 3

Plate 8.3. Exterior surface treatments:

a. Vessel 44	*d*. Vessel 41
b. Vessel 43	*e,f*. Vessel 59
c. Vessel 24	*g*. Vessel 14

Plate 8.4. Interior surface treatments:
a. Vessel 44 *d.* Vessel 41
b. Vessel 43 *e,f.* Vessel 59
c. Vessel 24 *g.* Vessel 14

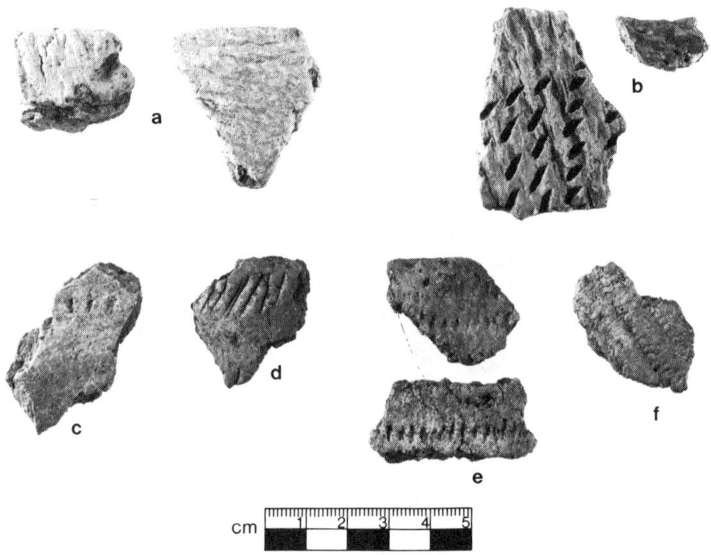

Plate 8.5. Characteristic decorations:

a. Early Woodland, vessel 63
b. Early Woodland, vessel 40
c. Late Woodland Younge Tradition, decorated set 1
d. Late Woodland Younge Tradition, vessel 63
e. Middle Woodland, vessel 64
f. Middle Woodland, vessel 69
g-i. Middle Woodland, vessel 27

Plate 8.6. Late Woodland vessel from the Bowen collection.

Plate 8.7. Vessels from the Bowen collection.

longer the occupational focus in the Late Woodland as it was in the Middle Woodland, but the differences between Late Woodland settlements require further elucidation (see Lovis 1985). Despite the changing role of this site in the subsistence-settlement systems of the Early, Middle and Late Woodland periods, the Schultz site dominates the interpretations of these periods, without the benefit of a fuller picture of adaptive systems operating at these times in the Saginaw Valley.

As many of the Saginaw Valley sites, excepting the Schultz site, are known only from surface collections or minimal subsurface testing, the chance to excavate an extensive area of a multicomponent Woodland site in the Saginaw Valley provides an opportunity to address problems concerning changing adaptations during the Woodland period. The Bridgeport Township site lies only four miles upriver from the Schultz site. The analysis of the archaeological assemblage from these excavations will provide further information on the temporal and cultural context of the Woodland periods in the Saginaw Valley.

The goals of the analysis of the ceramic assemblage from the Bridgeport site are: (1) to provide the chronological context for the Woodland period occupations at this site; (2) to examine the varying intensity of occupation during the different Woodland periods represented at the site; (3) to study the spatial distribution of temporally distinctive ceramics to isolate variation in the locus and intensity of components within the site;[1] and (4) to assess the chronological and cultural significance of this site in relationship to the known Woodland occupation of the Saginaw Valley.

METHODOLOGY

The methodology employed in this study was designed to focus on the spatial distribution of temporally distinctive vessels, through analysis of rim and body sherd attributes known to have temporal significance in the Saginaw Valley. The ceramic assemblage from 20SA620 was first sorted by provenience unit. Rim fragments and decorated sherds were isolated and served as the basis for the determination of the number of vessels present at the site. Undecorated body sherds were divided into those sherds with a maximum dimension greater than 2 cm or less than 2 cm. This division is based on the minimum sherd size for which determinations of surface treatments and other characteristics can reliably be made. Certain characteristics were observed on the small ceramic crumbs, but they were treated separately

[1]This goal is a particularly crucial one in light of the lack of visible stratigraphy at the site. Analysis of variability in the ceramic assemblage may be one of the few means by which any spatial separation of components can be ascertained.

from the larger body sherds because of the decreasing reliability of these observations.

Rim sherds were separated and evaluated visually in order to discover fits or similarities which demonstrate that fragments came from the same vessel. Proximity was used only as a secondary criterion to evaluate the plausibility of a particular relationship. (As will be seen, the few actual fits that were found exhibit a relatively high degree of dispersion of fragments from individual vessels, which casts doubt on the usefulness of proximity in defining affiliations.) Plates 8.1 through 8.7 are photographs of a sample of diagnostic rim and decorated sherds. The plate numbers for these sherds are listed in the appendix of vessel descriptions at the end of this volume.

Few body sherds could be associated unequivocally with particular vessels as defined on the basis of the rims because of the exfoliated, fragmentary nature of the assemblage. Because similar vessels were often found in close proximity to one another, body sherds could not readily be assigned to specific vessels. Therefore, effort was directed both toward the detailed description of rims and decorated fragments and the formal analysis of the body sherds in order to address the chronological questions posed for this assemblage. Each distinctive rim was counted as a vessel in a minimum-number-of-vessels count.

The rims and clearly associated decorated and body sherds were described by the same criteria as the unidentifiable body sherds: exterior and interior surface treatment, type of cord impressions, weight, thickness, paste and temper characteristics, and manufacturing indicators. In addition, rim and lip shape and thickness, number of fragments assigned to each vessel, and decoration on the interior and exterior of the rim and on the lip were recorded. The potential chronological significance of these criteria will be discussed separately for each vessel. Assessments of rim shape should be treated with caution. Many of the rims are very fragmentary and rim shape descriptions are therefore often tenuous at best. An asterisk has been placed after each rim shape description that is based on a very small section of rim.

Decorated sherds that could not be linked conclusively to a particular vessel were described separately. A description of the decorative features and a consideration of the probable placement of the sherd on the vessel was made. Then, the probable affiliation of the decorated sherds with particular vessels was evaluated on the basis of proximity and shared characteristics. If no affiliation could be reasonably demonstrated, the decorated sherd was counted as an additional vessel for a probable vessel count. Finally, fragments of miniature vessels and ceramic pipes were described separately.

The following characteristics were recorded on each large (i.e. greater than 2 cm) body sherd: provenience, weight, thickness (if both interior and exterior surfaces were present), interior and exterior surface treatments, the kind of cord impressions if present, evidence of coil manufacture, presence of residues, the presence of a modelled (or undulating) interior, and characteristics of paste and temper. The coding key for sherds greater than 2 cm is presented in Table 8.1.

Thickness has been noted as an important criterion for distinguishing between temporal phases during the Saginaw Valley Woodland, as well as Woodland phases throughout the Great Lakes-Midwest Riverine region. The Early Woodland period is characterized by thick sherds. Halsey (1976:160) claims that the thickness of late Early Woodland Shiawassee vessels from the Bussinger site ranges from 11 to 16 mm. Garland (1986:62) reports a comparable body sherd thickness average of 14.6 mm for late Early Woodland vessels from the Eidson site in southwestern Michigan. In addition, Crumley has noted a decrease in ware thickness from Early to Middle Woodland and the development of a bimodal distribution of body thicknesses that continues throughout the Middle Woodland. The two thickness modes that Crumley found at the Kantzler site are 6.0 to 6.9 mm and greater than 8 mm. The early Late Woodland, particularly in the southern portion of the Lower Peninsula, is characterized by very thin Wayne wares with a local variation called Saginaw Thin by Fischer. Fischer claims an average of 4.5 mm for the thickness of Saginaw Thin from the Schultz site (Fischer 1972:182). Thus, sherd thickness may be a significant indicator of temporal variation between site components.

However, sherd thickness, by itself, cannot resolve chronological questions. The trends that have been observed do not produce exclusive or nonoverlapping distributions, particularly when variability in thickness on any single vessel is considered: the lower walls and bases of Late Woodland vessels can be as thick as Early Woodland body sherds. Secondly, there appear to be periods (Middle Woodland and later Late Woodland) with higher variability in wall thickness within and between wares, which tends to obscure the distinctive differences between periods such as the Early Woodland and the early Late Woodland. Finally, the Saginaw Valley is not exclusively the repository of wares defined from the southeastern Michigan ceramic traditions. Vessels that appear to have affinities with ware types from more northerly and westerly localities may be present (Wobst 1968). Such vessels may not evidence the same general trends in ceramic technology and stylistic variability, and thus may further complicate the picture.

On the basis of previous observations concerning critical variation in paste and temper characteristics, six categories were defined and are presented in Table 8.1. Two small but distinctive categories were identified as analysis progressed: paste 5 sherds have a friable paste with medium to heavy temper initially identified as a distinctive category on the basis of vessel 14 in this ceramic assemblage; and paste 6 is characterized by a poorly consolidated laminar ware with very heavy temper density, for example, vessel 19 of this assemblage.

TABLE 8.1

Large Body Sherd Coding Key[a]

Catalog number
Provenience:
- North
- West
- Level

Weight (grams)
Thickness (millimeters)
Interior surface treatment:
- 0 – undetermined
- 1 – very smooth
- 2 – smooth with larger particles poking through
- 3 – rough (no smoothing or altering of interior; often found on sherds with very sandy paste or heavy grit temper density)
- 4 – brushed
- 5 – incised or striated (parallel lines crossing the entire interior surface, not randomly placed, isolated incised, or brushed lines)
- 6 – cord impressed

Exterior surface treatment:
- 0 – undetermined
- 1 – smooth
- 2 – smoothed-over cord impressed
- 3 – cord-impressed
- 4 – fabric-impressed
- 5 – smoothed and brushed
- 6 – cord-wrapped-object treated (stick or edge of cord-wrapped paddle leaving deeply ridged surface)

Cord type:
- 1 – fine ($<$ 3.5mm wide, applied with a tightly paddle)
- 2 – medium ($>$ 3.5mm, applied with a looser wrapped paddle)
- 3 – coarse (same thickness as medium cord, but a looser twisted cord)
- 4 – undetermined

Residue:
- 0 – absent
- 1 – present

Coil breaks:
- 0 – absent
- 1 – present

Paste types:
- 0 – determined
- 1 – hard, compact to laminar paste with light to medium density of grit temper
- 2 – sandy, coarse with medium to heavy density of grit temper
- 3 – siltier, chunky
- 4 – either 2 or 3, generally heavier density of temper
- 5 – friable with medium to heavy temper
- 6 – poorly consolidated laminar with very heavy temper density

Modelled interiors:
- 0 – absent
- 1 – present

[a]Code numbers refer to variable labels for data on file at the UMMA Great Lakes Range

These paste and temper characteristics are unfortunately not as temporally exclusive as initially hoped, for several reasons. They are difficult to discern given the high degree of erosion and exfoliation present in this assemblage. There is also a high degree of variation in these characteristics on any individual vessel and within any ware. Paste 1 primarily includes the early Late Woodland wares, although smaller body sherds of Middle and Late Woodland periods may be included. Paste 2 sherds encompass Early Woodland and coarser Middle Woodland wares, which may not be distinguishable by paste alone. Although initially defined as a mixed category, the distinctive Shiawassee ware sherds were generally included in the paste 4 category. In conjunction with other variables, paste and temper characteristics may help in sorting out the components at this site.

The observed interior surface treatments are presented in Table 8.1 and examples are illustrated in Plate 8.4. This variable may help to distinguish temporally different wares in the following ways. High incidences of wiping or brushing of the interior have been noted on wares from the Middle to Late Woodland transition, but not on the Middle Woodland Green Point ware nor on Late Woodland wares. At the Schultz site, Fischer (1972) defines a late Middle Woodland ware, Ruben Linear Cord-impressed, which has striated interiors, probably falling into the incised category as defined for this assemblage (Plate 8.4*a-d*). The cord-impressed category may also encompass Early Woodland wares that are often cord impressed on the interior (Garland 1986, Halsey 1976) (Plate 8.4*e-f*). This cord impressing may be difficult to distinguish from incising, because of the degree of erosion of this ceramic asemblage, noted particularly for the sandy Early Woodland wares.

Exterior surface treatments, presented in Table 8.1, provide an additional category with the potential for sorting out temporally distinct archaeological contexts. Smooth surfaces with no evidence of prior surface treatment typify Middle Woodland wares, such as Tittabawassee and Green Point. This shift to smooth surface treatment has been noted across much of the Eastern Woodlands during the Middle Woodland. This surface treatment, however, is also evident among later Late Woodland wares and, therefore, must be considered in conjunction with other characteristics in order to clarify temporal affiliation. An increase in smoothed-over cord impressions on vessel exteriors has been observed during the early Late Woodland and into later phases of the Late Woodland in Michigan and adjacent areas of Ontario (Lovis 1973:43–49; Stothers 1977:96). However, Fischer (1972) observes frequent smoothing over of cord impressions on Shiawassee ware vessels. It must also be noted that the degree of smoothing can vary considerably over the surface of any given vessel.

Cord impressions are further broken down into three categories, varying by cord thickness and spacing on the paddle (Table 8.1). Much variation is subsumed under these broad categories. However, these categories should, at the very least, differentiate the coarse loosely twisted cord used on Early Woodland vessels from the fine cord impressions that typify early Late Woodland assemblages.

Fabric impressions are often indicative of later Woodland phases. Brose (1966:18–19) noted such impressions at the Valley Sweets site, naming a new early Late Woodland Wayne ware type "Wayne Textile-marked." However, Halsey (1968:134) argues that textile marking appears on Riviere ware rather than Wayne ware vessels, thus placing the application of textile or fabric on vessel surfaces later in the Late Woodland period. Others have identified the Late Woodland application of fabric on vessels (Lovis and Davis 1986). Crumley (1973) finds that late Middle Woodland ceramic assemblages are characterized by an increase in the kinds of surface treatments, including the use of fabric.

No systematic study of variability in the use of and types of fabric over time has been done. This is in part due to the difficulty of consistently distinguishing fabric from regular cord impressions. Plasticene impressions of all large (greater than 2 cm) sherds and rim and decorated fragments from 20SA620 were taken in an attempt to identify the use of fabric. However, it became apparent that fabric can easily be misidentified as fine cord impressions in this assemblage. The fabric impressions identified in the Bridgeport assemblage are described in the analysis of exterior surface treatments.

Several other attributes have been recorded which may further clarify site components. Because the occurrence of these attributes could not be determined in many instances, only the presence, not absence, of these attributes can be considered meaningful. Coil breaks along sherd fractures were noted when present. Manufacture by the coil technique has been observed for Early and Middle Woodland wares, but not for Late Woodland wares. Thus, its presence is useful in making some broad temporal distinctions.

However, this characteristic is not always observable when the coiling technique was used, depending in part on the depositional context and postdepositional factors leading to further fragmentation of the ceramics. The relationship of coil breaks to thickness may be partly a function of the higher visibility of coil breaks on thicker sherds rather than an actual increase in the evidence for this kind of manufacture. Furthermore, from the evidence of small sherds alone, there are no distinctive attributes resulting from other manufacturing techniques, such as paddle-and-anvil, although this technique was probably used to construct the majority of the vessels at this site. Thus, the presence of coiling can point to the earlier periods, but its absence cannot necessarily be taken to indicate a later date.

Early Woodland wares tend to have undulating or modelled surfaces, particularly the interiors, because of the crude construction of the vessels. The presence of modelled interiors, in conjunction with other attributes, may point to Early Woodland affiliation. However, the observation of modelled interiors requires a sherd with a large enough interior surface so that this attribute is visible. If different wares at the site have different tendencies to fragment (for example, the fragile, thin early Late Woodland wares are probably not as resistant to fragmentation as the coarser, thicker earlier wares), our ability to observe this characteristic may be similarly skewed.

Finally, the presence of residues on the sherds was noted as an indicator of vessel function. However, the potential for differential preservation of residues, particularly for the earlier components that may have been subjected to longer and more intense postdepositional disturbances, limits functional inferences based on the presence or absence of such residues.

ASSEMBLAGE DESCRIPTION

The ceramic assemblage recovered from 20SA620 consists of 4,964 sherds, weighing a total of 5,682.8 g (Table 8.1a). Sherds that are less than 2 cm in size account for 74.2% of the assemblage by count and 36.7% by weight. Of these small sherds, only 10% have both interior and exterior surfaces intact, 76.2% have one surface and 13.8% have neither surface. It is clear from these counts that there is a high degree of pre- and postdepositional breakage of the ceramics from this site. The large sherds (greater than 2 cm) make up 22.6% of the assemblage by count and 55.7% by weight. These sherds also evidence a high degree of attrition. Less than half of the large sherds (46.5%) retain both surfaces, so that thicknesses could be recorded. The average weight of each sherd is 2.8 g, with a range of 0.3 to 32.6 g.

The rims and decorated sherds that provide a large degree of the temporal information for the site include 156 sherds or 7.6% of the assemblage by weight and 3.2% by count (Table 8.1a). From the analysis of these fragments, a minimum number of vessels (MNV) of 70 has been obtained, with a probable vessel count (PNV) of 80 based on the addition of the decorated sherds. The fragmentary nature of the assemblage is again demonstrated by the low average weight of 2.7 g for these temporally diagnostic sherds. Individual vessels are generally represented by only a single sherd, either a rim (for the MNV) or a decorated (added to the MNV for the PNV) sherd with a range from one to six sherds defining the vessels.

The temporal assignment of these vessels is presented in Table 8.2 and the attributes that characterize each vessel are given in the Appendix at the end of this volume. The vast majority of the vessels represented by the rim and decorated sherds are early Late Woodland (Plates 8.1 and 8.2). Most of the vessels fit into Wayne ware, a ware defined in the Saginaw region, but which shares strong similarities to other regions of Michigan and beyond (Brashler 1981; Brose 1966; Fitting 1968; Halsey 1976). A minority of these vessels

TABLE 8.1a
Ceramic Assemblage

	Wt (g)	*N*
Sherds < 2 cm	2084.1	3685
Sherds > 2 cm	3169.0	1123
Rims/decorated sherds	429.7	156
TOTAL	5682.8	4964

appear to have certain characteristics that may point to close affinities to wares in other regions, such as Allegan ware from southwest (Rogers 1972) and south-central Michigan and Mackinac ware defined in the Straits region (McPherron 1967). Several additional vessels have characteristics which place them at the end of the early Late Woodland, around A.D. 1000 (Plates 8.3*e-f*, 8.5*c-d*, 8.7). In addition, a few later vessels are present in this assemblage, although the precise cultural affiliations generally cannot be pinpointed on the basis of the available data.

The second most well represented temporal phase is the interim between late Middle Woodland and early Late Woodland, called the Transitional phase (Plate 8.3*a-d* and 8.4*a-d*). The assignment of vessels to this phase is tentative because of the lack of conclusive proof that this period existed as an archaeologically distinct entity. Several archaeologists (Fischer 1972; Holman 1984; Lovis and Davis 1986) have argued the existence of a distinguishable transitional phase, based on the blending of traits that define Middle and early Late Woodland wares.

Finally, a small number of vessels reflect Early (Plate 8.4*a-b*) and Middle Woodland (Plate 8.5*e-i*) occupations at the site. Both earlier Tittabawassee and later Green Point types are recognized. The earliest ceramics at the site date to the later Early Woodland, as reflected in the Shiawassee ware vessels recovered at the site.

Thickness

On the basis of previous observations about patterned variation in vessel thickness over time for Woodland ceramic assemblages, it was predicted that thickness would be a critical attribute for differentiating temporal components in the ceramic assemblage. Unfortunately, thickness could be measured on only 46.5% of the sample ($N = 522$) of the large sherds. A histogram of the thicknesses of the large sherds shows three clear modes (Fig. 8.1). However, the first mode (3.0–7.5 mm) encompasses a wide range of values that might obscure temporally distinct wares. With the thickness values that Fis-

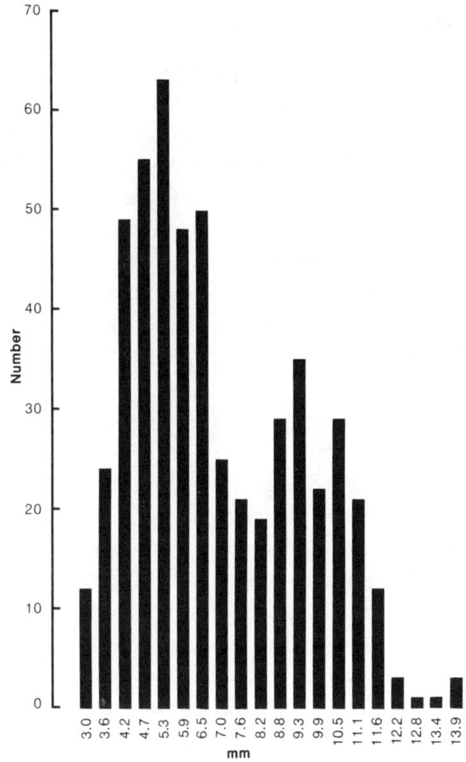

Figure 8.1. Thickness of large body sherds.

cher and Crumley observed in mind (see Methodology section), the first mode was subdivided at 5.0 mm in an attempt to isolate the distinctively thin early Late Woodland wares, reducing the temporal noise within the large first mode in the histogram.

The large body sherds from the Bridgeport site have a mean thickness of 7.2 mm with a minimum value of 3.0 and maximum of 14.5 mm. The distribution of the body sherds by the thickness categories is as follows (Table 8.2a). Category 2 contains the largest proportion of the sherds (41.4%) with 29.7% falling into category 3. A fifth of the assemblage (20.5%) is assigned to category 1, with only 8.4% assigned to the thickest category 4. The distribution of rim thicknesses roughly match the variability of thickness values for the body sherds. The thicknesses used for the vessels are, of course, not necessarily comparable to the body sherd data or to each other, considering the potential differences in vessel thickness in the vicinity of the rim.

Relationship of Thickness to Other Body Sherd Attributes

Utilizing these thickness categories, relationships between thickness and other body sherd characteristics were evaluated.[2]

Coil fractures tend to occur on sherds that are thicker than average (Table 8.2b). Sherds with coil breaks have a mean thickness of 9.5 mm. The majority of sherds with evidence of coil manufacture fall into the two thickest categories with only two sherds with coil breaks assigned to thickness category 1 and seven sherds to category 2.

Residue was observed primarily on thin wares ($\bar{x}$ = 6.1 mm), occurring on no body sherds with thicknesses greater than 11 mm. The majority (85.7%) of the 28 sherds with residue fall into thickness categories 1 and 2 (category 3: 14.3%).

Modelled interiors tend to occur on sherds over 8.7 mm thick. As a matter of fact, 70.2% of the 38 sherds fall into thickness categories 3 and 4. Only five body sherds with modelled interiors had thicknesses which fell into the thinnest category 1, and nine in category 2.

Thickness varies with exterior surface treatment in the following ways (Fig. 8.2, Table 8.3). Cord-impressed surfaces occur on relatively thin sherds ($\bar{x}$ = 5.8 mm). The mean thickness is lower than the mean thickness computed for the entire assemblage and is very close to the mean for paste 1 sherds ($\bar{x}$ = 5.5 mm). This is in contrast to sherds with smoothed-over cord-impressed exteriors, which on the average are thicker, but occur on sherds with a wide range of thicknesses. These relationships are clearly borne out by the histogram of thickness for types of exterior surface treatment as well as by the high percentage of cord-impressed sherds which fall into categories 1 and 2. In fact, 73.8% of the sherds in category 1 have cord-impressed exterior surfaces.

Smoothed-over surfaces occur on sherds with a mean thickness of 7.7 mm, very close to the overall mean thickness for the entire site. There is a large amount of variation in thickness for sherds with this type of surface treatment, reflected in Figure 8.2. Close to half of the smoothed-over sherds fall in category 2. However, more sherds than expected fall into categories 3 and 4 and fewer in the first category than expected. The histogram of thicknesses for this surface treatment reveals a bimodal distribution unlike the more tightly clustered pattern for cord-impressed exteriors.

The type of cord used to impress the exterior varies in patterned ways relative to the thickness of the body sherds. The finer cord is used on thinner wares and the coarse cord on thicker vessels, as the distribution of cord type

---

[2]Sherd counts for a particular variable may be different in different sections of this chapter due to the fact that some kinds of variables cannot be observed on some sherds: this alters the data set when two or more variables (e.g., surface treatment and coil breaks) are being considered at once.

TABLE 8.2
Vessels by Time Period and Ware Category

Period	Number			Vessel No.
Late Early Woodland:				
Shiawassee	3	(6)		34,37,63
			–	21*,40,54
Middle Woodland:				
Tittabawassee		(6)	–	1*,17*,25*,39*,27,58*
Green Point	2			64,69
Undetermined		(2)		55,d9
Late Middle Woodland/ Early Late Woodland:		(10)	–	14*,21*,29*,35,40*,41*,42*,24,43,44
Early Late Woodland:				
Wayne	15	(35)		2,4,7,8,9,10,26,28,32,33,46,49,52,61,67
			–	1*,5,6,12,15,16,22,25*,29*,36,41*,42*,47,53,58*,d12,d16,d2,d19,24
Late Wayne (ca. 1000)	2			20,45
Allegan-like	5			11,30,50,66,68
Mackinac-like	3			3,23,65
Riviere au Vase (ca.1000)	2	(3)		31,62
			–	d1
Late Late Woodland	1	(6)		59
			–	14*,17*,39*,18,13
Undetermined:	10			38,48,51,56,57,60,70,19,d4,d6,d14

*Vessels placed in two categories because of alternative temporal placements.
-Vessels tentatively assigned to time period/ware.
( )Maximum possible number of vessels assigned to phase (tentative plus securely assigned).

TABLE 8.2a
Distribution of Body Sherds by Thickness

Thickness	*N*	%
1 (3.0-4.9 mm)	107	20.5
2 (5.0-1.7 mm)	216	41.4
3 (7.5-10.9 mm)	155	29.7
4 (11.0-14.6 mm)	44	8.4
TOTAL	522	100.0

TABLE 8.2b
Distribution of Coil Fractures by Body Sherd Thickness

Thickness	Frequency of Coil Fractures	
	N	%
1	2	3.9
2	7	13.7
3	32	62.7
4	10	19.7
TOTAL	51	100.0

by thickness shows in Figure 8.3 and by the cross-tabulation of type of cord by the thickness categories (Table 8.4).

Smooth exteriors are found on sherds with an average thickness of 8.8 mm, higher than the average for the entire assemblage. The distribution of these sherds relative to the thickness categories shows that over half of the sherds fall into category 3 (66.7%) which encompasses thicknesses of 7.5 to 11 mm. Interestingly, the thickest body sherd recovered from this site (14.51 mm) has a smooth exterior.

Fabric-impressed sherds are very homogenous with respect to thickness. All of the fabric-impressed sherds fall into the first or second thickness categories, ranging between 4.5 and 7.5 mm ($\bar{x}$ = 6.2). This tight clustering of thickness values is emphasized by the low standard deviation (.83) for this set of sherds. Although none of the fabric-impressed sherds are as thin as some of the cord-impressed sherds, the maximum thickness (7.5 mm) is substantially less than the maximum value for any other kind of surface treatment.

The two remaining surface treatments were observed on very few sherds. The three sherds with cord-wrapped-object impressed exteriors for which thickness could be measured fall within a thickness range of 7.67–8.23 mm.

TABLE 8.3

Thickness of Large Body Sherds vs. Exterior Surface Treatment

Exterior Surface Treatment	Thickness of Large Body Sherds[a]				Total
	(1) 3.0–4.9	(2) 5.0–7.4	(3) 7.5–11.0	(4) 11.0–14.51	
Smooth	3 11.1 2.8	3 11.1 1.4	18 66.7 13.0	3 11.1 7.5	27 5.4
Smoothed-over cord-impressed	21 8.6 19.6	105 43.0 49.1	90 36.9 65.2	28 11.5 70.0	244 48.9
Cord-impressed	79 40.7 73.8	85 43.8 39.7	23 11.9 16.7	7 3.6 17.5	194 38.9
Fabric-impressed	3 15.0 2.8	17 85.0 7.9	0	0	20 4.0
Brushed	1 9.1 .9	4 36.4 1.9	4 36.4 2.9	2 18.2 5.0	11 2.2
Cord-wrapped oject	0	0	3 100.0 2.2	0	3 .6
Total	107 21.4	214 42.9	138 27.7	40 8.0	431

Cells include count/row %/column %.

[a]In millimeters.

The mean thickness for sherds with smoothed and brushed exteriors is 8.5 mm, very similar to those with smooth surfaces, but there is a wide range of thicknesses associated with this category.

With the exception of incised interiors, there is little clear or informative patterning in interior surface treatment that is independent of paste characteristics. Smooth interiors are seldom found on sherds in category 4. Of the sherds with rough interiors, more fall into category 3 and less in the thinner categories than is expected from the proportion of various thicknesses for the entire assemblage. These relationships may in part be a function of the relationship between paste and thickness. Paste 1 sherds tend to be thinner

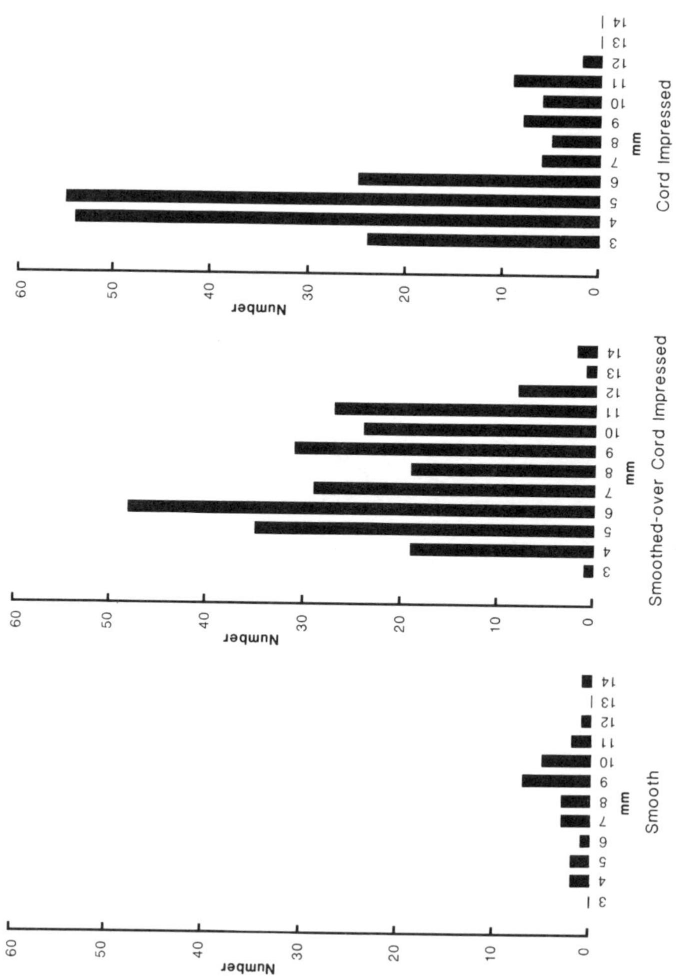

Figure 8.2. Thickness of large body sherds by exterior surface treatment.

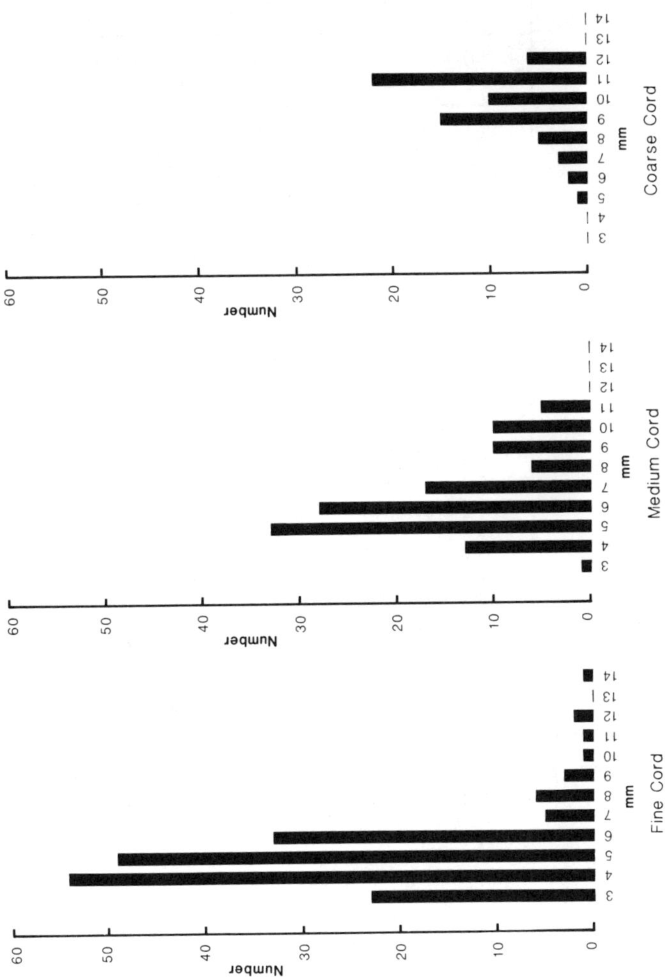

Figure 8.3. Thickness of large body sherds by cord type.

TABLE 8.4

Body Sherd Thickness vs. Cord Type

Cord Type	Body Sherd Thickness[a]				Total
	(1) 3.0–4.9	(2) 5.0–7.4	(3) 7.5–11.0	(4) 11.0–14.52	
Fine	77 43.3 77.8	86 48.3 46.2	11 6.2 9.9	4 2.2 11.4	178 41.3
Medium	16 13.0 16.2	73 59.3 39.2	31 25.2 27.9	3 2.4 8.6	123 28.5
Coarse	0	6 9.4 3.2	40 62.5 36.0	18 28.1 51.4	64 14.8
Undetermined	6 9.1 6.1	21 31.8 11.3	29 43.9 26.1	10 15.2 28.6	66 15.3
TOTAL	99 23.0	186 43.2	111 25.8	35 8.1	431

Cells include count/row %/column %.
[a]In millimeters.

and since they also tend to have smooth interiors, more thin sherds are found with smooth interiors. Similarly, paste 2 sherds tend to be thicker and have rough interiors. The majority of sherds with incised interiors fall into categories 2 and 3 ($N = 14$, 82.4%), and no incised sherds are less than 5 mm thick.

Paste

Paste 1 sherds make up the majority (62.8%) of the large body sherds (Table 8.4a). The second most numerous type is paste 2, a sandy coarse ware (23.0%). Pastes 3 and 4 are represented by only 3.7% and 6.6% of the assemblage respectively. Paste categories 5 and 6 amount to less than 4% of the sample.

The distribution of the vessels in terms of paste categories poses a significant contrast with the body sherd data (Table 8.4a). This contrast may be in part a function of the high degree of erosion and exfoliation in this assemblage, making it hard to categorize many of the large body sherds. Seventy-

TABLE 8.4a
Frequency of Paste Types

Paste	Body Sherds		Vessels	
	N	%	*N*	%
1	688	62.8	60	75.0
2	252	23.0	8	10.0
3	41	3.7	7	8.7
4	72	6.6	3	3.7
5	9	0.8	1	1.3
6	34	3.1	1	1.3
TOTAL	1096	100.0	80	100.0

TABLE 8.5
Thickness of Large Body Sherds by Paste Type

Paste Type	Thickness of Large Body Sherds[a]				Total
	(1) 3.0–4.9	(2) 5.0–7.4	(3) 7.5–11.0	(4) 11.0–14.51	
(1)	98	161	13	0	272
	36.0	59.2	4.8		
	91.6	74.5	8.4		52.1
(2)	4	25	110	40	179
	2.2	14.0	61.5	22.3	
	3.7	11.6	71.0	90.9	34.3
(3)	1	12	7	1	21
	4.8	57.1	33.3	4.8	
	.9	5.6	4.5	2.3	4.0
(4)	2	8	23	3	36
	5.6	22.2	63.9	8.3	
	1.9	3.7	14.8	6.8	6.9
(5)	0	2	1	0	3
		66.7	33.3		
		.9	.6		.6
(6)	2	80	1	0	11
	18.2	72.7	9.1		
	1.9	3.7	.6		2.1
Total	107	216	155	44	522
	20.5	41.4	29.7	8.4	

Chi square = 328.22; Cramer's Phi = .4578; cells include count/row %/column %

[a]In millimeters.

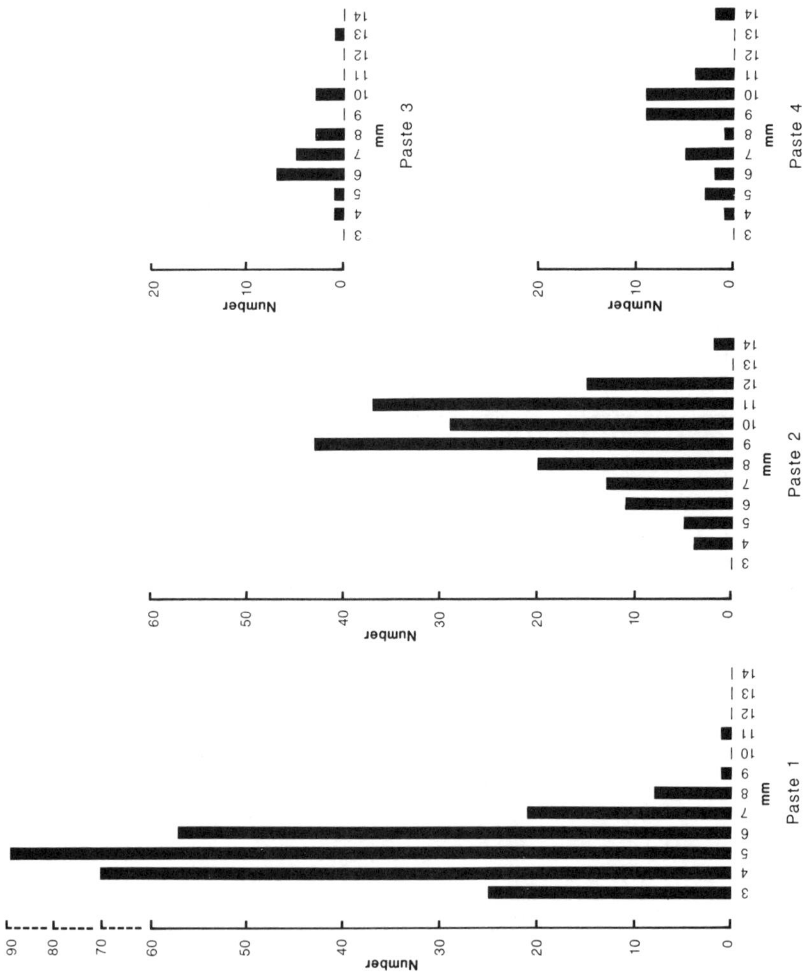

Figure 8.4. Thickness of body sherds by paste type.

five percent of the vessels are categorized as paste 1 in contrast to 62.8% of the body sherds. Proportionately fewer vessels are included in the paste 2 category than the body sherds. Only seven vessels belong to paste 3, and three to paste 4. As mentioned above, pastes 5 and 6 are associated with two specific vessels, 14 and 19, respectively. The narrow definition of these vessels is demonstrated by the low percentages of body sherds of these paste types present in the ceramic assemblage.

Relationship of Paste to Thickness

As suggested above, the pastes and thicknesses of the body sherds in this assemblage and the relationship between these two variables potentially provide the most useful information for the separation of temporally distinct components at the site (Table 8.5, Fig. 8.4). Histograms and mean thickness for each paste type reveal clear differences between paste types along this variable.

Paste 1 sherds have a mean thickness of 5.5 mm, well below the mean for the entire assemblage (7.2 mm). The histogram of thickness values for this category, as well as the relatively low standard deviation (1.2), reveal a high degree of clustering of thicknesses for this paste type. In terms of the previously defined thickness categories, 95.2% of the sherds defined as paste 1 fall into the first two thickness categories; that is, they are less than 7.5 mm thick. None fall into the thickest category. Furthermore, 91.6% of sherds with thickness values below 5 mm are paste 1 sherds.

In contrast, paste 2 sherds have a higher mean (9.4 mm) than the mean of the entire assemblage and of paste 1 sherds. Thicknesses of paste 2 sherds are slightly less clustered (SD = 1.9) than paste 1 sherds, as the histogram in Figure 8.4 illustrates. However, 83.8% of paste 2 sherds have thicknesses greater than 7.5 mm. Furthermore, 71% of category 3 and 90.9% of category 4 are made up of paste 2 sherds.

Less can be said about the remaining paste categories because of small sample sizes. Paste 3 sherds have thickness values that cluster toward the middle of the range of thickness values for this ceramic assemblage, falling into thickness categories 2 and 3. The distribution of thicknesses for this paste type approximates most closely the proportions of thicknesses present in the assemblage as a whole, and its mean thickness (7.6 mm) closely approximates the mean thickness of the entire assemblage as well. Thickness measurements for paste 4 sherds are more variable than for other paste types (SD = 2.2). However, there is a tendency toward thicker sherds with a mean value of 9.0 mm. The distribution relative to the thickness categories reflects this tendency as 72.2% of the paste 4 sherds fall into categories 3 and 4.

Only three body sherds with thickness measurements are classified as paste 5 sherds. All have thicknesses that fall between 5 and 11 mm, with a mean of 7.7 mm. Vessel 14, which is characterized by this paste type, has a thickness of 8.43 mm. Only eleven body sherds with thickness measurements are assigned to paste 6. The mean thickness for this paste type is 5.8 mm.

The strength of the relationship between types of paste and the thickness of body sherds is confirmed to some degree by the chi-square test and a test of the strength of the chi-square, Cramer's phi. The chi-square for paste by thickness is 328.22. To adjust for sample size, a Cramer's phi of .4578 was calculated, demonstrating a relatively strong association between these two body sherd attributes ($df = 15$).

The cultural significance of the thickness and paste attributes is suggested by the association of these attributes in large body sherds. The tendency for paste 1 sherds to be thin suggests an early Late Woodland affiliation. Paste 2 sherds tend to be thicker, pointing to the earlier Early and/or Middle Woodland time periods, based on previous observations of these characteristics. As predicted, paste 3 and 4 appear to be catch-all categories, as the variability in thickness values related to these paste types suggests. Paste 4 primarily includes thicker sherds, as expected if it encompasses Shiawassee ware.

The variable of thickness serves to differentiate vessels for some but not all time periods. With one exception (vessel 55), all the typed vessels that fall into thickness category 1 appear to be of early Late Woodland origin. The second category is heavily dominated by early Late Woodland vessels, with several possible late Middle Woodland/early Late Woodland vessels, one late Late Woodland and one Middle Woodland vessel also present. Category 3 contains the widest variety with no type predominating. Middle Woodland, Younge phase, transitional late Middle/ early Late Woodland and possibly Shiawassee vessels are found in this category. Finally, only four vessels have thicknesses over 11 mm (category 4) and all but one are late Early Woodland Shiawassee vessels. The fourth may belong to the transitional late Middle/early Late Woodland phase.

To summarize, category 1 includes the thin early Late Woodland wares, such as Wayne and Saginaw Thin, and category 4 contains the thick Early Woodland wares. Other wares, such as the Middle Woodland Tittabawassee and Green Point wares, and many of the late Late Woodland ceramics are distributed more broadly, but the majority fall into the second and third categories. Although thickness can by no means simply assign a body sherd to a time period, there are strong trends in thickness values over time which, in conjunction with other sherd attributes, may aid in the separation and comparison of historically significant components.

The Relationship of Paste to Other Body Sherd Attributes

The association of other body sherd attributes with paste categories provides some corroborating evidence for the chronological and cultural significance of these paste categories. In particular, the patterning of attributes such as coil breaks, modelled interiors, residue, thickness and exterior surface treatment relative to paste characteristics, provides some potentially informative data with which to assess the chronological context of the site.

The majority of 61 coil breaks occur on paste 2 sherds (57.4%). An additional 21.3% are of paste 4 and 6.6% appear on paste 3 sherds. Only 13.1% are found on paste 1 sherds, although this category comprises the majority of body sherds at the site. Only one paste 4 sherd had a coil break.

Of 38 examples, residues appear predominantly on paste 1 sherds (76.3%). The remaining examples are found on pastes 2 (7.9%), 4 (10.5%) and 5 (5.3%).

Pastes 2 (58.9%) and 4 (14.3%) account for the majority of 56 recorded modelled interiors, although a relatively high proportion are also recorded on paste 1 sherds (23.2%). Only two body sherds with modelled interiors fall into paste categories 3 and 6.

Interior surface treatment appears to be, to a large degree, a function of paste. The sandier, coarser paste 2 sherds tend to have rough to slightly smoothed interiors (98.2%). Nearly half of both paste 3 (46.2%) and 4 (42.1%) sherds have smooth interiors, a function of the higher amount of silt in the paste. Paste 1 sherds generally have very smooth to smooth interior surfaces (68.9%), due probably to its finer, more compact quality. The category of brushing is problematic, due to potential alteration of brushing evidence from both postdepositional and post-recovery processes. It is clear that paste 1 sherds are brushed more often than sherds of other paste types (119, or 60.7%, of brushed sherds are paste 1). The category of incising shows strong patterning relative to paste. Although incising occurs on only 18 sherds, 72.2% of these sherds were categorized as paste 2.

Exterior surface treatments vary systematically with paste type (Table 8.6). About half of the sherds with cord-impressed exteriors that have been subsequently smoothed are categorized as paste 1 types. One-third of smoothed-over cord-impressed sherds are paste 2 sherds; an additional 10.9% are placed in paste categories 3 and 4. Cord-impressed exteriors are more often found on paste 1 sherds (80.9%) than on sherds of all other paste categories combined. Fewer sherds of the other paste categories have this exterior surface treatment than would be expected from the proportions of such sherds in the ceramic assemblage. There are proportionately more sherds of paste 1 with this surface treatment than for smoothed-over cord-impressed sherds. These relationships are further supported by the fact that the majority of paste 2 sherds (63.4%) have smoothed-over surfaces while

TABLE 8.6
Paste Type vs. Exterior Surface Treatment

Exterior Surface Treatment	Paste Type						Total
	(1)	(2)	(3)	(4)	(5)	(6)	
Smooth	9 20.5 1.7	21 47.7 10.4	6 13.6 18.8	5 11.4 11.1	1 2.3 33.3	2 4.5 7.1	44 5.2
Smoothed-over	224 54.1 42.3	128 30.9 63.4	19 4.6 59.4	26 6.3 57.8	0	17 4.1 60.7	414 49.3
Cord-impressed	266 80.9 50.2	43 13.1 21.3	5 1.5 15.6	9 2.7 20.0	0	6 1.8 21.4	329 39.2
Fabric-impressed	28 84.8 5.32	1 3.0 .5	0	3 9.1 6.7	1 3.0 33.3	0	33 3.9
Brushed	2 13.3 .4	7 46.7 3.5	0	2 13.3 4.4	1 6.7 33.3	3 20.0 10.7	15 1.8
Cord-wrapped cord	1 20.0 .2	2 40.0 1.0	2 40.0 6.3	0	0	0	5 .6
TOTAL	530 63.1	202 24.0	32 3.8	45 5.4	3 .4	28 3.3	840

Cells include count/row %/column %

only 21.3% are cord impressed. In contrast, paste 1 sherds are split more equally between smoothed-over (42.3%) and cord-impressed (50.2%) surface treatments.

The type of cord used also varies in patterned ways with paste type. Nearly all of the fine cord-impressed sherds fall into the paste 1 category (90.6%), and nearly all of the coarse cord-impressed sherds belong to the paste 2 category (90.6%).

Smooth exteriors with no evidence of prior surface treatment occur predominantly on paste 2 sherds (47.7%). The second most common paste type with smooth exteriors is paste 1 (20.5%) with a few paste 3 (13.6%) and 4 (11.4%) sherds also treated in this manner. Interestingly, pastes 2, 3 and 4 have proportionately more smooth surfaces than expected from the proportion of these surface treatments in the entire sample, in contrast to the under-representation of this surface treatment on paste 1 sherds (1.7%). A clear majority (84.9%) of fabric-impressed surfaces are found on paste 1 sherds, with a few sherds of pastes 2 and 4 similarly treated. Little can be said about smoothed and brushed, and cord-wrapped-object surface treatments, because of the minor occurrences of these treatments in this assemblage.

Pastes 5 and 6 have the following distribution relative to surface treatment. Paste 5 sherds are found with smooth, fabric-impressed, and smoothed and brushed exteriors. The exteriors of paste 6 sherds range from smooth and smoothed and brushed to cord-impressed and smoothed-over treatments. This variability casts doubt on the assertion that these paste types represent single vessel types. It is possible that either a variety of exterior surface treatments were used on single vessels, or that the fragmentation of body sherds limits our ability to consistently distinguish surface treatments.

The distribution of temporally defined vessels by paste type accentuates some of the problems in a simplistic chronological interpretation of body sherds based on paste attributes alone. Vessels that have been classified as possible late Late Woodland vessels are lumped in paste 1 with early Late Woodland vessels. Initially, it was thought that paste 2 would isolate primarily the coarse Early Woodland wares. However, vessels described as having sandy, coarse paste appear to include a mixture of early Middle Woodland Tittabawassee (vessels 27, 39, 48, 55) and Early Woodland (vessels 40, 37, 54, 21) types. Two of the three vessels attributed to paste 4 are Shiawassee types (vessels 34 and 63); 38 has an undetermined chronological affiliation. It is clear that it is difficult to differentiate late Early Woodland and early Middle Woodland body sherds, without close attention to thickness and temper characteristics. Finally, paste category 3 subsumes the majority of what are considered to be transitional late Middle Woodland/early Late Woodland vessels (24, 35, 42, 43, 44) and two clearly late Middle Woodland Green Point (64, D.9) vessels.

Coil Manufacture

It has been suggested that the presence of coil breaks provides one means to distinguish temporal components at the site. However, only eight vessels from this site have evidence of coil manufacture. Only 61 large sherds (5.4%) and 24 (0.7%) of the small sherds carried evidence of coil manufacture.

Of the vessels with coil fractures, three are typical of late Early Woodland Shiawassee ware (34, 37 and 63). One is a Middle Woodland Green Point vessel (64) and one appears to be an early Middle Woodland Tittabawassee vessel (27). Two vessels may belong to the ill-defined Transitional period (21, 35). No temporal affiliation has been assigned to the remaining vessel, although it apparently is not Late Woodland in age. One decorated sherd with a coil break appears to be a fragment of a Shiawassee vessel, but was not counted as an additional vessel, because of its possible relationship to vessels 37 or 63.

The association of coil breaks with particular attributes on the large body sherds reinforces the association of coil manufacture with a limited portion of the Woodland time span based on the rim data. Coil breaks are found most frequently on paste 2 sherds, the paste type defined as a coarse sandy ware for which a late Early Woodland to Middle Woodland affiliation is suggested. Nearly a quarter of the coil breaks are observed on paste 4 sherds which, on the basis of the defining characteristics and the distribution of vessel types by paste, are predominantly interpreted as Shiawassee ware. As the vessel evidence indicates, coil manufacture may continue into the Transitional phase. The presence of several coil fractures on paste 3 sherds may lend additional support to this conclusion. Eight sherds with coil breaks are designated paste 1 sherds, which is not surprising since paste 1 is the most broadly defined paste category.

Coil breaks also appear predominantly on thicker body sherds. If this is not merely a function of differential visibility (see Methodology section above), it may provide further evidence of the earlier Woodland components at the site. The majority of coil breaks are found on category 3 sherds (7.5–11 mm). This range of thicknesses closely matches the thickness range cited by Crumley (1973) for Middle Woodland sherds. An additional ten sherds with coil breaks fit into category 4 which matches the range of thicknesses observed for Shiawassee wares by Halsey (1976).

Of the eight vessels with evidence of coil manufacture, three fit in thickness category 4, three in category 3, one in category 2, and two vessels could not be measured. All but one of these vessels are Early or Middle Woodland in age.

A patterned relationship between coil breaks and exterior surface treatment may exist. For 75.5% of 58 coil-fractured sherds, the exterior surface is treated with smoothed-over cord impressions and 14.3% have completely smooth surfaces. An additional 14 sherds are so smoothed over that the type of cord used to impress the exterior cannot be determined. Coil breaks appear on sherds with a wide range of interior surface treatments, covering the gamut from smooth to rough, brushed and incised.

Residue

The presence of residue on sherds is one of the few direct indicators of use. This assemblage contains a very small amount of residue. None of the rim and decorated fragments upon which individual vessels were identified have residue on any surface. Only 38 large sherds (3.4%) and 55 small sherds (1.5%) have residue accretions. Lovis and Davis (1986) note a similar lack of residues on Middle and Late Woodland sites in the Bay City area (20BY77 and 20BY79). This paucity may suggest that vessels at the site were used primarily as storage containers rather than for cooking.

Although we are dealing with an extremely small sample, association of residue with other body sherd attributes that may have temporal significance was explored to evaluate any functional differences between components. Only one sherd with a coil break has residue on it. The majority of the large body sherds with residue are thin and belong to paste 1. The majority of these sherds have smooth or brushed interiors; none have incised interiors and only two have modelled interiors. Over half of the sherds with residue have cord-impressed exteriors (54.5%), not suprising since paste 1 sherds tend to have cord-impressed exteriors. Although the rim sherd evidence does not allow a direct assignment of vessels with residue to any particular time period, residue is found predominantly on body sherds from early Late Woodland vessels, as indicated by the associated body sherd characteristics.

Modelled Interior

An undulating or modelled interior is present on 56 large sherds. Modelled interiors tend to occur on thicker sherds. Most of these sherds are classified as paste 2, although they also occur with some frequency on paste 1 sherds. As expected, this form of interior treatment is related to a wide range of interior surface treatments, ranging from smooth to rough and brushed. Finally, modelled interiors are found predominantly on sherds with smoothed-over cord impressions (54.3%) on the exterior and, secondly, on cord-impressed sherds (32.6%).

As suggested in the Methodology section, the presence of modelled interiors may be an indicator of late Early Woodland vessel manufacture. Three vessels have modelled interiors; two are classified as Shiawassee ware (37, 63) and one is a probable Middle Woodland vessel (64). Of the three vessels with modelled interiors, one (37) has a rim thickness of 5.44 mm and the second (63), 12.87 mm. Although the thickness of vessel 37 seems anomalously thin, rim thickness may not be comparable to body sherd thickness, particularly when the small size of the rim that represents vessel 37 is considered. The observation of modelled interiors on thicker sherds, the majority of which have a coarse, sandy paste, provides some additional confirmation of the presence of this characteristic on late Early Woodland vessels. However, this attribute is also recorded on some of the larger paste 1 sherds, perhaps fragments of the lower portions of later Woodland vessels. This sherd attribute is only useful as a chronological indicator in conjunction with other observations.

Exterior Surface Treatment

Smoothed-over cord impressions are present on nearly half of the large sherds with cord impressions present on 39.2%. Therefore, some kind of cord impression is visible on 88.4% of the assemblage (Table 8.7). In this assemblage, the majority of the body sherds and vessels are impressed with fine cord, while relatively few body sherds and vessels are impressed with coarse cord (Table 8.7a). About a third of the body sherds and vessels are impressed with medium cord. The smoothed-over cord impression category encompasses a great deal of variation in degree of smoothing and, therefore, is probably not a particularly useful category with which to evaluate changes in smoothing over time. This is particularly true because variability of smoothing on a single pot is probable. However, for 23.9% (N = 96) of the smoothed-over cord-impressed sherds, the kind of cord impressions could not be determined, and therefore, represent heavy smoothing. A small number of smooth surfaces with no hint of prior surface treatments were recovered (N = 44, 5.2%) with an additional small sample of sherds that were visibly smoothed by brushing. Two additional surface treatments were observed in low frequencies: fabric impressed and cord-wrapped object impressed. Those small sherds with observable exteriors reflect the same general breakdown of surface treatments as the large sherds (Table 8.7).

The variability of exterior surface treatment on the vessels presents an interesting contrast with the body sherd data (see Plate 8.3). This is, in part, a function of differential treatment of rim areas, which are often smoothed during the process of decoration. Cord impressions are slightly less frequent and fabric impressions are proportionately more frequent on rims than on body sherds. This disparity is probably due to our inability to consistently differentiate fabric impressions, particularly the fine variety, from fine cord impressions on relatively small body sherds (Table 8.7).

Exterior surface treatment shows some interesting patterning relative to other body sherd attributes, such as cord type, coil breaks, and modelled interiors. There is little difference in the type of cord found on sherds for which the exterior surface has or has not been smoothed over after cord marking. The majority of body and rim sherds in both categories are impressed with fine cord. However, there are slightly more body sherds with smoothed-over surfaces that are marked with coarse cord and fewer with fine cord than on those not smoothed (Table 8.7b).

Seventy-five percent of the 49 sherds evidencing coil manufacture have smoothed-over exteriors. Seven sherds with smooth exteriors have coil fractures. In contrast, there are only two sherds with coil breaks and cord-impressed exteriors. Only one sherd with a fabric-impressed exterior and two with brushed surfaces (4.1%) are recorded as having coil fractures.

Fifty-four percent of the 25 modelled interiors appear on sherds with

TABLE 8.7
Exterior Surface Treatment

	Exterior Surface Treatment					
	Smooth	Smoothed-over	Cord-impressed	Fabric-impressed	Cord-wrapped Object	Brushed
Number of large body sherds	44	414	330	33	5	15
%	5.2	49.2	39.2	5.2	0.5	1.8
Number of small body sherds	74	622	748	54	0	12
%	4.9	41.2	49.5	3.6	0	0.8
Number of vessels	6	37	22	7	1	0
%	8.2	50.7	30.1	9.6	1.4	0

TABLE 8.7a
Frequency of Cord Types

Cord	Body Sherds		Vessels	
	N	%	*N*	%
1 Fine	340	54.0	49	60.9
2 Medium	205	32.5	25	29.4
3 Coarse	85	13.5	5	9.7
TOTAL	630	100.0	79	100.0

TABLE 8.7b
Variation of Cord Type by Exterior Surface Treatment

Cord	Smoothed		Not Smoothed	
	N	%	*N*	%
1 Fine	29	8.9	193	59.4
3 Coarse	56	18.4	147	48.2

smoothed-over cord-impressed exteriors. Fifteen sherds with cord-impressed exteriors and five with completely smooth exteriors have modelled interiors. No sherds with fabric-impressed or cord-wrapped-object exteriors show evidence of modelling.

Residue is distributed differentially with respect to surface treatment. Only five sherds with smoothed-over exteriors and five with fabric-impressed exteriors have residue on them. Residue appears on only five sherds with smooth or brushed exteriors. Interestingly, about half of the sherds with residue ($N = 18$) have cord-impressed exteriors.

Thirty-three fabric-impressed sherds were recovered. Two different types of fabric are found in this assemblage: (1) a medium cord weft crossing a very thin, single strand of fiber ($N = 27$); and (2) a heavier fabric with medium cords for both warp and weft ($N = 6$). These two types of fabric are not differentiated for the body sherds. Only 54 (1.5%) small sherds with clear evidence of fabric impressions were recorded, but this small number is a function of our inability to differentiate fabric from fine cord impressions on such small sherds. These fabric-impressed sherds represent very discrete types at this site, as reflected by strong patterning with respect to other body sherd attributes.

Only five sherds were treated with a cord-wrapped object on the exterior.

The characteristics of and spatial distribution of these body sherds suggests that these sherds are portions of only three vessels. Two sherds were located in the vicinity of vessel 27, a Middle Woodland vessel. Since they share paste characteristics (paste 2) and exterior treatment, they are probably fragments of this vessel. A third sherd of paste 1 was found much farther south (102N/102W) and therefore, probably belongs to another vessel. It is located in an area where numerous minimum vessels have been identified. The two remaining sherds with cord-wrapped-object treated exteriors were recovered from a unit distant from the main excavation block (104N/91W), and have been categorized as paste 3.

Drawing on the expected and observed relationships between different kinds of exterior surface treatments and other sherd attributes, several observations about the chronological importance of some of the exterior surface treatments can be made. Fabric and cord impressions tend to occur on thin paste 1 sherds and generally indicate early Late Woodland deposits. The corresponding lack of coil breaks and modelled interiors on ceramics with these types of exterior treatments lends some support to this conclusion (keeping in mind the danger of interpreting the absence of these attributes). However, some of the fabric-impressed vessels at this site may belong to the slightly earlier Transitional phase. Also, Crumley (1973) has identified the use of fabric during the Middle Woodland at the Kantzler site. Therefore, fabric-impressed sherds cannot be automatically assigned to the early Late Woodland.

The attribute of smoothed-over cord impressions does not pattern as neatly against either paste or thickness attributes. The large number of early Late Woodland vessels with some degree of smoothing of the cord impressions further restricts the usefulness of this attribute as a temporal indicator. Despite this problem, it is of chronological interest that the majority of coil breaks and modelled interiors occur on sherds with this type of surface treatment. Smooth exteriors on the vessels at this site point to either Middle or later Late Woodland affiliation. The body sherd attributes of paste, thickness, coil breaks and modelled interiors fit this temporal mixing. Other exterior surface treatments occur too infrequently to assign any temporal significance.

Finally, the type of cord appears to be a significant temporal marker, as suggested by the distribution of cord type on the chronologically defined vessels and by the association of cord type with other body sherd attributes. Fine cord is predominantly used on thin, paste 1 sherds and therefore, points to a probable Late Woodland, particularly early Late Woodland assignment for these sherds. In contrast, coarse cord covaries strongly with paste 2 and high thickness values, pointing to an Early Woodland component.

Interior Surface Treatment

This attribute is one of the least informative attributes coded in this study, in part because of the degree of surface erosion present in the assemblage. It also appears that interior surfaces received little attention from the vessel manufacturers. Smooth, smooth with some grit particles poking through, and brushed are the three predominant interior surface treatments on sherds at this site. Of those sherds with observable interiors, fewer than 10 percent have either very rough-textured, cord-impressed, or incised interiors. Observations of interior surfaces on the small sherd sample can provide little additional information, because of the decreasing accuracy of such observations on such small surfaces (Plate 8.4.)

Interior surface treatments on the rims are present in roughly the same proportion as the body sherds. However, more incised or striated interiors were identified on the vessels than on the body sherds, probably because this interior treatment may be restricted to the vicinity of the rim. There are also slightly more smooth and fewer rough interiors on the vessels, perhaps again a function of differential treatment of rim areas on vessels (Table 8.8).

Interior surface treatment displays only a minor degree of patterning relative to exterior surface treatment. The coarser the cord, the more rough-textured is the interior, and the finer the cord on the exterior, the smoother the interior. This trend is probably a function of the paste types upon which various types of cord impressions are used. The two sherds with cord impressions on the interior are both impressed with fine cord on the exterior surface. Sherds with fabric-impressed exteriors tend to have smooth or brushed interiors (N = 15, 79%). Smooth, smoothed-over and smoothed and brushed exteriors have no obvious patterning in terms of the kinds of interior treatments. Nearly half (48.2%) of the 94 sherds with cord-impressed exteriors have smooth interiors with the remainder of the sample split between moderately smoothed (N = 43, 22.1%) and brushed (N = 47, 24.1%).

It appears that, with the exception of incised interiors, the condition of the interior surface treatment is to a large extent determined by paste characteristics. All the sherds with incised or striated interiors have cord-impressed or smoothed-over cord-impressed exteriors. They tend to be thicker sherds and fit the paste 2 category. Interestingly, 84.6% (N = 11) of those sherds with incised interiors are marked on the exterior with coarse cord. These combinations of attributes fit descriptions of Early Woodland wares (Halsey 1976). However, the use of striations has also been noted on late Middle Woodland/early Late Woodland vessels.

Summary

The formal analysis of the ceramic assemblage from the Bridgeport Township site provides the data with which to address the first goal of this study,

TABLE 8.8
Interior Surface Treatment

	Interior Surface Treatment					
	Smooth	Less Smooth	Rough	Brushed	Incised	Cord-impressed
Number of large body sherds	279	174	52	199	18	2
%	38.5	24	7.2	27.5	2.5	0.2
Number of small body sherds	1121	454	38	168	10	0
%	62.6	25.3	2.1	9.4	0.6	0
Number of vessels	28	12	3	12	5	1
%	45.9	19.7	4.9	19.7	8.2	1.6

the chronological context for the Woodland occupations at this site. Although the proportions of vessels assigned to each time period should be accepted cautiously because of the highly fragmentary nature of the assemblage, it is still clear that the early Late Woodland component contributes the largest amount of the ceramics to this site, with earlier and later Woodland phases represented by markedly smaller amounts. The earliest Woodland phase is the late Early Woodland, as represented by a few Shiawassee ware vessels. Both early and later Middle Woodland vessel types, with similarities to Tittabawassee and Green Point wares as defined at the Schultz site, are found. Evidence points to a slightly later (and perhaps more intense) occupation during the late Middle Woodland/early Late Woodland, as represented by the second highest number of vessels at the site. After the main early Late Woodland occupation, the site is again occupied during the Late Woodland, as a few vessels with affinities primarily to the south of the Saginaw Valley indicate.

The formal analysis of particular ceramic attributes provides some corroborating evidence for the various occupations at the site. Such information is garnered from the patterned covariation of attributes with potential chronological significance and the relative proportions of attributes within the assemblage. The distribution of the thickness values of body sherds points to a preponderance of later wares, particularly early Late Woodland which are known to be thinner than wares from other Woodland periods. The thicknesses of the temporally defined vessels at the site tend to confirm this observation. Thickness has proven to be useful in differentiating the classic Wayne or Saginaw thin variants of early Late Woodland wares from the thick Shiawassee wares, but the intermediate range of values encompasses wares from the entire Woodland sequence represented at the site.

Patterning between the thickness and paste attributes may have additional chronological significance. Paste 1 sherds tend to be thin, whereas the other paste categories (2–4) include sherds that are thicker, but also encompass a wider variety of thickness values. It appears therefore that thin paste 1 sherds are from predominantly early Late Woodland vessels, a conclusion corroborated by the vessel data. The few late Late Woodland vessels also generally fall into these categories, although it is doubted that this time period has contributed much to the ceramic assemblage because of the minimal number of vessels assigned to this later period.

In contrast, paste 2 and 4 sherds are markedly thicker and, when cord impressed, tend to have coarse cord marks. According to the vessel assignments, such vessels are generally of either Early or Middle Woodland age. Prior expectations about the covariation of paste, thickness and cord type during these periods tend to be confirmed. The silty paste 3 category proved to be less diagnostic than expected, but with interesting consequences. Ceramics from this category are not characterized by distinctive sherd thickness values. But in terms of the temporally diagnostic vessels, paste 3 encompasses primarily Middle Woodland and slightly later Transitional vessels. The possibility of a homogenous set of vessels with a mix of Middle and early Late Woodland traits was not a prior expectation of this study.

In addition, two minor paste categories, 5 and 6, are found at the site. Variation within these categories in terms of their relationship to other attributes and the small sample size, as well as the difficulty in conclusively assigning an age to the related diagnostic fragments, limits any chronological inferences on the basis of these paste types.

The covariation of these two pastes with other body sherd attributes adds some support to the above chronological interpretations. Evidence of coiling is found on only a few Early and Middle Woodland vessels and two possible Transitional vessels. As expected from the temporal inferences based on paste and thickness attributes, coil breaks are found most frequently on paste 2 sherds and on thicker sherds. Thus, the relationship of coil fractures to other attributes reinforces the association of coil manufacture with a limited portion of the Woodland time span. However, it is interesting to note that coil manufacturing may continue to be employed as late as the Transitional phase. Similar to coil breaks, modelled interiors are found predominantly on the thicker paste 2 sherds, suggesting that this attribute does appear on vessels from the earlier portion of the Woodland sequence.

The variability of interior and exterior surface treatments also shows some interesting patterning. With one exception, interior surface treatment appears to be primarily a function of paste type. Incised or striated interiors tend to occur on thick, paste 2 sherds with coarse cord-impressed exteriors. The co-occurrence of such attributes initially suggests a late Early Woodland affiliation. However, the presence of Transitional vessels at the site with wiped or striated interiors, as seen on the vessels, may account for some of this variation on body sherds (Plate 8.4*a-d*).

The variation of exterior surface treatment relative to other attributes reveals trends that can provide information for separating different cultural components. Cord impressions without subsequent smoothing tend to be found on thinner, paste 1 sherds, indicating a probable early Late Woodland affiliation. Some additional support for the chronological significance of this attribute is found in the lack of coil breaks and modelled interiors on sherds with cord-impressed exterior surfaces. Additionally, the majority of body sherds with fine cord impressions are thin, paste 1 sherds, again pointing to a temporal affiliation later in the Woodland sequence. Fabric-impressed sherds are a very homogeneous set which are thin, have paste 1 characteristics, and lack coil breaks and modelled interiors, thus suggesting an early Late Woodland age or later. Those few sherds with fabric-impressed exteriors that do not have these other characteristics may come from Middle Woodland vessels, since the use of this treatment has been previously observed for this earlier time period (Crumley 1973). The majority of sherds with cord-wrapped-object treated exteriors belong to one Middle Woodland vessel.

The most frequent surface treatment present at the site, smoothed-over cord impressions, does not pattern neatly relative to other attributes. Although smoothed-over cord-impressed sherds tend to be thicker paste 2 sherds, and account for the majority of coil breaks and modelled interiors, this category of surface treatment is more variable than cord impression. This is also reflected in the presence of this treatment on vessels of every Woodland period at the site. Thus, previously accepted statements about the chronological implications of smoothed-over cord impressions cannot be simplistically applied to distinguish temporal components in sites which include deposits from Early to Late Woodland, without regard to other body sherd attributes. Sherds with smooth exteriors are also rather variable in terms of other attributes. When the temporally distinctive vessels and other attributes are considered, it appears that many of these sherds are probably vessels from either Middle or later Late Woodland occupations.

The presence of residue is the only sherd attribute of direct functional significance that was recorded at the site. The minor amount that was observed on body sherds and the lack of any residue on the rims and decorated fragments limits chronological/functional inferences. However, it should be noted that residue is primarily found on thin, cord-impressed, paste 1 sherds.

This observation provides evidence for the use of ceramic vessels for cooking during at least the early Late Woodland. The absence of residue, however, does not negate the possibility that a vessel was used in this context.

SPATIAL ANALYSIS

Distribution of Vessels

Individual vessels are defined primarily on the basis of very few diagnostic fragments, either portions of rims or decorated body sherds, and few undecorated body sherds could be related to particular vessels. However, vessels that are defined on the basis of more than one sherd (20 vessels and 6 decorated sets) provide information about the degree of dispersion of individual vessels, and thus, the degree of disturbance and mixing of the archaeological deposits in general.[3] What cannot be readily determined in all cases is the source of the dispersion, such as the impact of subsequent occupations at the site or rodent and root activity.

Of the 20 vessels which are defined by more than one fragment, 14 are distributed in more than 1 unit. A series of maps were constructed (Figs. 8.5*a*, 8.6) to show the distribution of vessel fragments that occur in more than one unit and/or level. Fragments of nine of these vessels are located horizontally within 3 m of each other and therefore do not reflect a high degree of dispersion of individual vessels. Portions of the remaining vessels are found from 4 to 9 m apart. Three of these more dispersed vessels (3, 14, 19) are located in the southern end of the main excavation block. This sector of the site is the most intensive area of ceramic deposition, possibly reflecting a great deal of reoccupation or activities which may have resulted in the destruction and dispersal of vessels. It is also in proximity to the modern burial of the cow which has caused mixing of the deposits (see Chapter 5).

The spatial distribution of vessel 27 reflects an interesting pattern. The movement of fragments of this vessel may be due to postdepositional downslope movement of artifacts. Four fragments of this vessel were recovered on the higher portion of the site in level 6–7; a fifth fragment was found 7 m away and 30 cm deeper (Fig. 8.6). Vessel 32 was dispersed across 7 m but in the same level (Fig. 8.5). Of the vessels whose fragments occurred in more than one arbitrary (l0 cm) level, twelve occurred within 20 to 40 cm of each other. The exceptions, separated by over 40 cm, are also two of the vessels with a large degree of horizontal dispersal of fragments (14, 19).

---

[3]The dispersion of decorated sherds relative to the vessels of which they may be a fragment is not considered because the degree of proximity was a criterion for making the tentative association between vessels and decorated sherds.

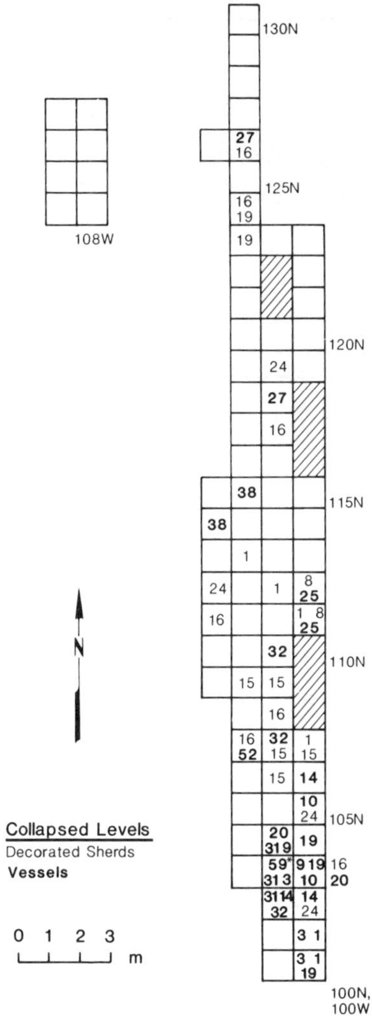

Figure 8.5. Decorated sherds and vessels—all levels.

Because these two vessels were so unique in terms of paste and temper characteristics, body sherds that appeared to be related were sorted out from the assemblage and coded as separate paste categories (vessel 14 corresponds to paste 5, vessel 19 to paste 6). Although no actual fits were discovered, nine body sherds and four diagnostic fragments were assigned to paste 5. Thirty-two body sherds and three diagnostic fragments were assigned to paste 6. In both cases, the majority of associated sherds were found clustered in

Vessels

Levels														
1–3						19		25						
4–5	1	3			14	19	20	25		31	32			59
6–7		3	9	10	14	19	20		27	31		38	52	
8–9			9	10								38	52	
10–11									27					

Decorated Sherds*

Levels						
1–3	1					
4–5	1	8	15	16	19	24
6–7	1		15	16		24
8–9				16	19	
10–11						

*Not necessarily the same vessel

Figure 8.6. Decorated sherds and vessels—all transects.

the southern part of the site, between 100N and 108N for paste 5 (92.3%) and 100N to 109N (88.6%) for paste 6. The outlying sherds may have been incorrectly assigned to these vessels, considering the fragmentary nature of the sherds.

Of the seven decorated sherd sets (which may or may not represent additional vessels), sets 15, 16 and 24 probably do not represent single vessels, so the distribution of the sherds cannot provide information about dispersal patterns. Decorated set 19 includes two diagnostic sherds which fit together. They were recovered from the same unit but were vertically separated by 40 to 50 cm. Considering the minuscule size of the fragment found at the deeper provenience, a number of postdepositional processes might account for this movement. Finally, decorated set 1, which includes four sherds, had a greater degree of dispersal, over 6 m horizontally and and 60 cm vertically.

Any conclusions about the degree of mixing and dispersal at this site made on the basis of the distribution of vessel fragments must be viewed with extreme caution for several reasons. First, in general, body sherds generally are not assigned to a specific vessel, and thus only spatial dispersal or clustering using the very small sample of diagnostic fragments has been considered.

Secondly, there are very few actual fits between vessel fragments (vessels 14 and 31) found in more than 1 unit, despite efforts to discover such fits. Claims of relationships between diagnostic sherds were made conservatively to increase confidence in matches between isolated specimens.

Distribution of Body Sherds

The body sherds are clearly concentrated in four 10 cm levels. Level 4–5 contains 33.4% of the large body sherds, and 42% were recovered from level 6–7. Few large sherds (4.1%) were recovered in the uppermost level of the deposits (level 2–3). Because of the uneven ground surface, only the southern higher portion of the site had excavation units extending into arbitrary level 2–3. By level 8–9, the deposits began to thin out, with only 15.5% of the ceramics recovered from this level. In levels 10–11 and 12–13, ceramic deposits were scarce (5.1%). The 108W and 109W tier of units were placed on a piece of low-lying ground and thus only yielded ceramics from levels 10 to 13 (Table 8.9).

Ceramic Clusters

The nature of spatial patterning at the Bridgeport site can also be inferred from the density distributions of the body sherds by weight (Figs. 8.7 and 8.8).[4] The plan views and profiles of ceramic densities reveal discrete concentrations of ceramic deposition with a decrease in density away from these concentrations. In level 2–3, a tight cluster of large body sherds is found from 112 to 114N/101W, which marks a concentration that increases in density in level 4–5 and extends somewhat laterally, with only remnants of the cluster visible in levels 6–7 (cluster 2). A second, more marked cluster is defined by density contours in level 4–5 in the southernmost portion of the block, from 100N to 108N (cluster 1). Two clusters within this southern concentration are suggested by the contours and may represent discrete events of ceramic deposition. However, the relatively small samples of pottery in these clusters and their proximity to each other prevent the separation of these clusters analytically. The cluster centering at 104 to 105N/101W extends into level 8–9, with only small amounts of ceramics recovered in this area by level 10–11.

A third major locus of ceramics (cluster 3) is visible on the density maps concentrated primarily from 113 to 117N/102 to 103W, with a sharp drop-off to the south of these units and a less marked drop-off to the north. Given the high ceramic densities to the north in 118–121W/101–103N, a second cluster

[4]The density distributions of the small sherds were plotted separately and were found to essentially match those of the large sherds with a few exceptions. Therefore, only the maps of large sherd distributions are illustrated. Disparities between these large and small body sherd distributions are considered further in Chapter 11.

TABLE 8.9
Spatial Distribution of Large Body Sherds

Clusters	Levels						Total
	2-3	4-5	6-7	8-9	10-11	12-13	
(1)	21 4.1 48.8	229 44.3 64.7	177 34.2 39.7	86 16.6 52.4	4 .8 8.0	0	517 48.7
(2)	17 10.4 39.5	78 47.6 22.0	49 29.9 11.0	11 6.7 6.7	9 5.5 18.0	0	164 15.5
(3)	5 1.5 11.7	44 12.8 12.5	213 62.1 47.7	52 15.2 31.8	27 7.9 54.0	2 .6 50.0	343 32.3
(4)	0	3 8.1 .8	7 18.9 1.6	15 40.5 9.1	10 27.0 20.0	2 5.4 50.0	37 3.5
TOTAL	43 4.1	354 33.4	446 42.0	164 15.5	50 4.7	4 .4	1061

Cells include count/row %/column %.

in that area may be present. This is also implied by the slightly higher densities of ceramics in the 118 to 121N spot which begins at a higher elevation (level 4–5) than the cluster immediately to the south. But this second concentration is obscured by the (possibly earlier) very marked concentration to the south. Therefore, two separate clusters could not be distinguished analytically. There is little indication of the cluster centered at 115N above level 6–7. This cluster thins out with depth in the lower levels (8–9 and 10–11). Finally, the units to the north of 121N have a low density of both large and small sherds from levels 4 to 13 with no evidence of clustering. (This area is lumped together with the 108–109W block of units which lie at the same north proveniences and is labelled cluster 4 for ease of analysis, although it does not in reality form a cluster.) The sherd densities seem to shift slightly from south to north with depth, as would be expected if the deposits were on a slope. The distribution of fragments from vessel 27 also suggests the downslope distribution of artifacts.

These clusters, partitioned on the basis of a visual assessment of the density contour maps of body sherd weights, also differ in the amount of pottery in each cluster. Cluster 1 encompasses 48.7% of the large body sherds and cluster 3 contains 32.3% of the large body sherds. Cluster 2 only

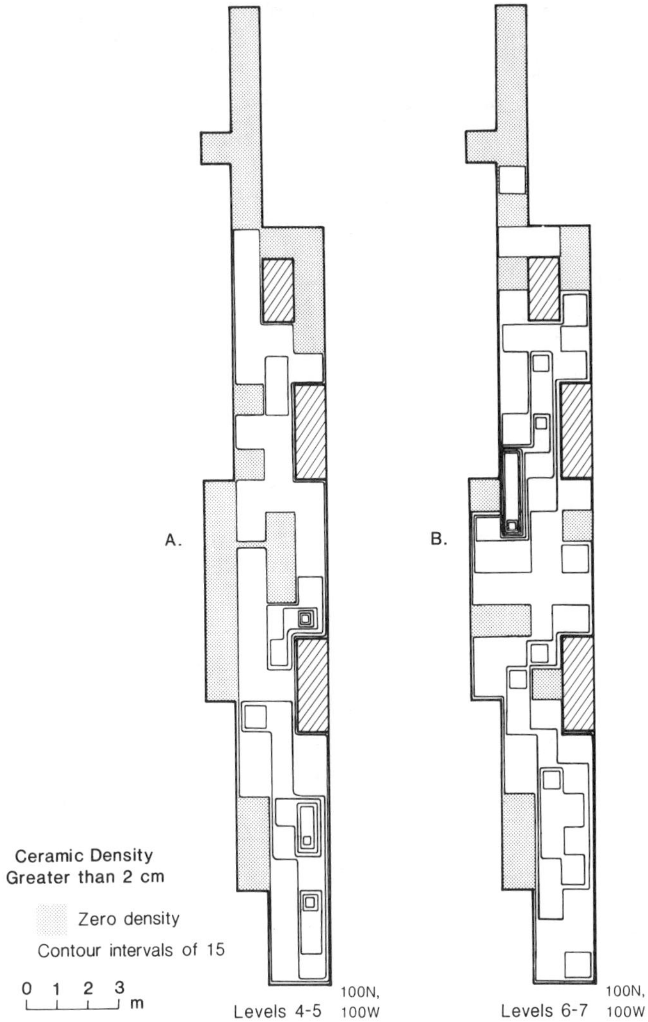

Figure 8.7. Ceramic density of large body sherds—levels 4–5, 6–7.

has 15.5% of the large sherds and the remaining 3.5% fall into the leftover fourth category.

However, as summarized above, the density of sherds varies by level. More large sherds are concentrated in cluster 1 than in any other cluster in levels 2–5 and 8–9, but the main focus of ceramic deposition shifts to cluster 3 in level 6–7 (47.8% in cluster 3, 39.7% in cluster 1). Similar to cluster 1, more cluster 2 sherds are found in levels 4–5 and 6–7 than in other levels.

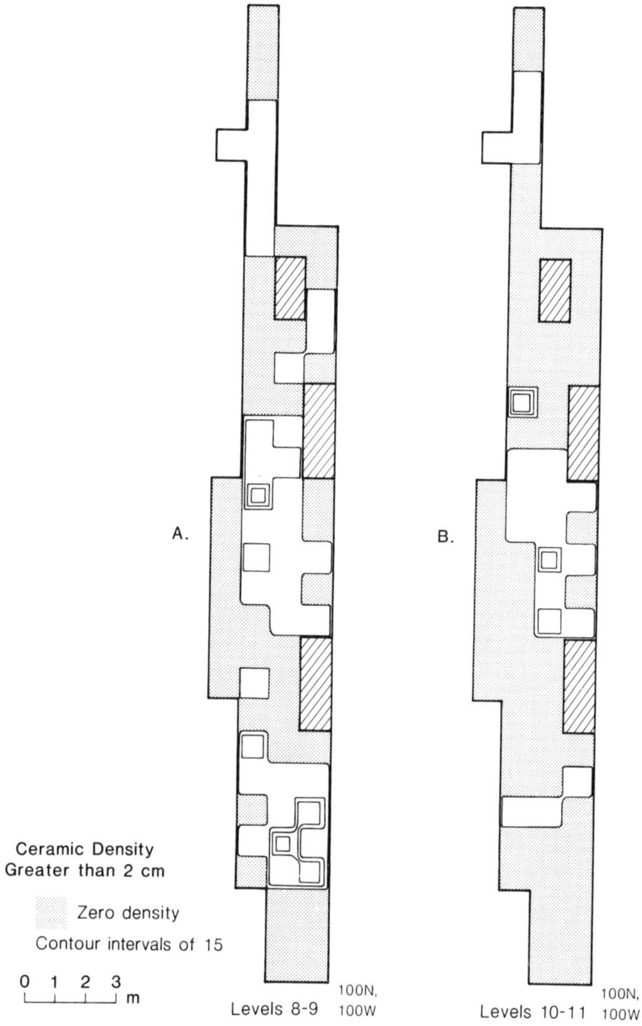

Figure 8.8. Ceramic density of large body sherds—levels 8–9, 10–11.

Although there are generally few sherds recovered from levels 10–11 and 12–13, they are primarily concentrated in clusters 3 and 4, again suggesting a sloping ground surface as I have mentioned above (Table 8.9).

We can tentatively postulate, on the basis of the different elevations of these clusters, that cluster 1 may represent a later occupation than cluster 3. Cluster 2 may be of an intermediate age between cluster 1 and 3. This interpretation, of course, would require a better understanding of prehistoric land surfaces and processes of site formation. There is no evidence from these spatial patterns, however, that temporally discrete components can be distinguished at this site on the basis of the ceramic assemblage. In fact, despite the evidence of clusters, the broad distribution of sherds between these clusters across the site, the high concentration of the ceramic deposits within only 40 cm of the site, and independent evidence of disturbances by roots, rodents and modern activities all suggest that discrete components should not be expected. Rather, a high degree of mixing and overlapping of components within the undifferentiated geological context would be expected.

Chronological Significance of Vessel Distributions

The primary sources of data for assessing the chronological contexts at the Bridgeport site are the distribution of vessels and other diagnostic artifacts.[5] The temporal assignment of these artifacts are represented by the designated symbols in Figures 8.5*b*, 8.9 and 8.10. At first glance, it appears as though there is little patterning of these chronologically informative artifacts. When level and cluster are considered, some patterning is suggested. As expected, the ceramic assemblage does not indicate discrete components but overlapping and shifting foci of occupation.

Although only seven diagnostic vessels and decorated sherd sets were recovered from level 2–3 (Fig. 8.9), they cover a wide spectrum of time periods, from Middle to Late Woodland. No Early Woodland vessels were found in this level. The two possible Middle Woodland vessels alternatively may be of Late Woodland age. The remaining vessels appear to be early Late Woodland up to the later phase of the early Late Woodland, as represented by collared Wayne and Riviere au Vase specimens. Although many of the temporal assignments of vessels in this level are tentative and it is a small sample upon which to base chronological inferences, this level can probably be assigned to the later phases represented at this site. There is too small a sample to consider any differences between clusters in this level. It should be stated that levels 2–3 and 4–5 encompass materials from the modern ground surface at the site, and therefore, mixing of components would not be unexpected due to historic activities in the area.

At level 4–5 (Fig. 8.10 *left*), several of the ceramic clusters have emerged. The main concentration of pottery falls into the southern portion of the site, cluster 1. Of those vessels and decorated sherds for which temporal assignments were made, the majority in cluster 1 are early Late Woodland. Also present in relatively high numbers are late Late Woodland vessels. Thus, the

[5]Several vessels recovered from slumps and profile scrapings are not used in this discussion due to lack of tight provenience, including vessels 45, 51, and 53, parts of vessels 14 and 59; and decorated sets 5, 12, 13, 23, 25 and 26.

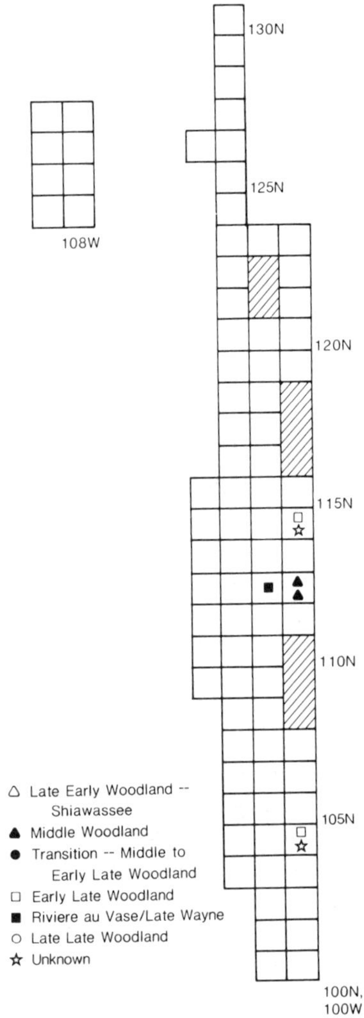

Figure 8.9. Distribution of ceramics, level 2–3.

majority of vessels in cluster 1 indicate a late age for cluster 1. The exceptions include several vessels which may be late Late Woodland or transitional Middle/Late Woodland in age. One late Early Woodland vessel (54) and three possible Middle Woodland vessels were also recovered from this cluster. It is interesting that with the exception of the Early Woodland vessel, none of the other pre-early Late Woodland vessels have definite temporal assignments and may in fact fall into the later phases.

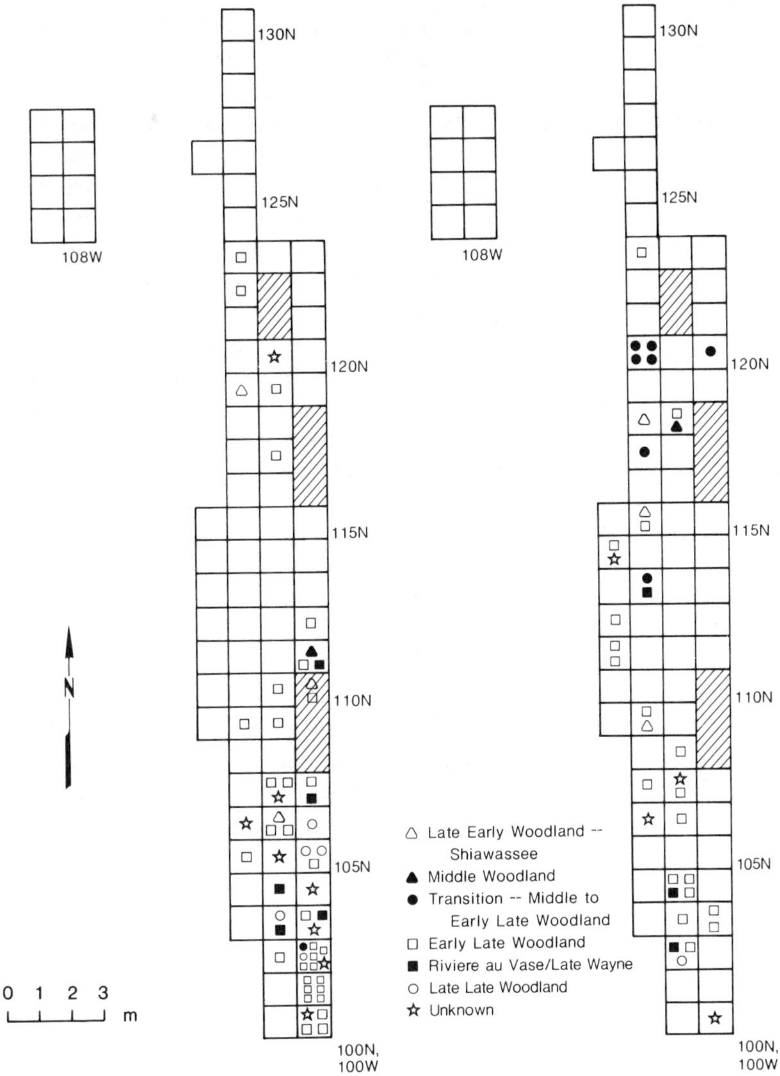

Figure 8.10. Distribution of ceramics. *Left*, level 4–5. *Right*, level 6–7.

Cluster 2 contains the second highest pottery concentration in level 4–5. Similar to cluster 1, it has predominantly early Late Woodland vessels. One vessel is either an early Late Woodland or a Middle Woodland vessel. A second may be from an Early Woodland or Transitional phase occupation. Again, the potential chronological anomalies are uncertain. Only the top of cluster 3 appears in this level. It contains several early Late Woodland and one late Early Woodland vessel. Finally, the area north of cluster 3, designated cluster 4, yielded only two early Late Woodland vessels. These distributions suggest that cluster 1 and 2 in this level are predominantly early Late Woodland in age, with a significant later Late Woodland occupation adding to the ceramic deposits in the south end of the main excavation block.

In level 6–7 (Fig. 8.10*right*), despite slight decreases in the number of sherds in clusters 1 and 2, there is an overall increase in ceramic density, due to the markedly increased densities in cluster 3. Cluster 1 continues to contain predominantly early Late Woodland vessels with one vessel of later Late Woodland or Transitional age. Similarly, cluster 2 has early Late Woodland vessels with one Early Woodland vessel. Cluster 3 is dominated in this level by Transitional phase vessels, although there are also vessels of Early Woodland, Middle Woodland and early Late Woodland age. It would appear that the high concentration of pottery in this portion of the site is the result of an early Late Woodland occupation overlying an earlier, concentrated Transitional phase occupation. Also appearing in this 20 cm level is evidence for less intense, earlier occupations during the Middle and Early Woodland periods.

These observations provide evidence for a shift in the spatial focus of the occupations. Transitional to early Late Woodland materials are concentrated in the southern portion of the site, while the less intensive Early and Middle Woodland occupations occurred in the northern portion. The overlapping of occupations from these numerous periods, as well as the concentration of a Transitional phase occupation, may account for the high pottery density of cluster 3 in this level. Little can be said about cluster 4 in terms of diagnostic vessels, since only one vessel, of early Late Woodland affiliation, was identifed from cluster 4 in level 6–7.

Level 8–9 contains much less pottery across the entire site (Fig. 8.11*left*). Cluster 1 continues to be predominantly early Late Woodland, with one Middle Woodland vessel present. Cluster 2 has only one vessel, also of early Late Woodland affiliation. Unlike cluster 1, which represents six 10-cm levels, the majority of cluster 3 ceramics were recovered within two levels. Only one early Late Woodland vessel was recovered from the cluster 3 area in level 8–9. The northern set of units, cluster 4, contained more diagnostic sherds in this level than in any other (reinforcing the sloping-surface interpretation for this area). These vessels are of early Late Woodland and Middle Woodland affiliation.

Little can be said for level 10–11 (Fig. 8.11*right*). Only three diagnostic vessels were recovered from this level. Interestingly, two are definitely assigned to the Middle Woodland time period and one belongs to either the Middle Woodland or Transitional occupations. No diagnostic ceramics were recovered from level 12–13.

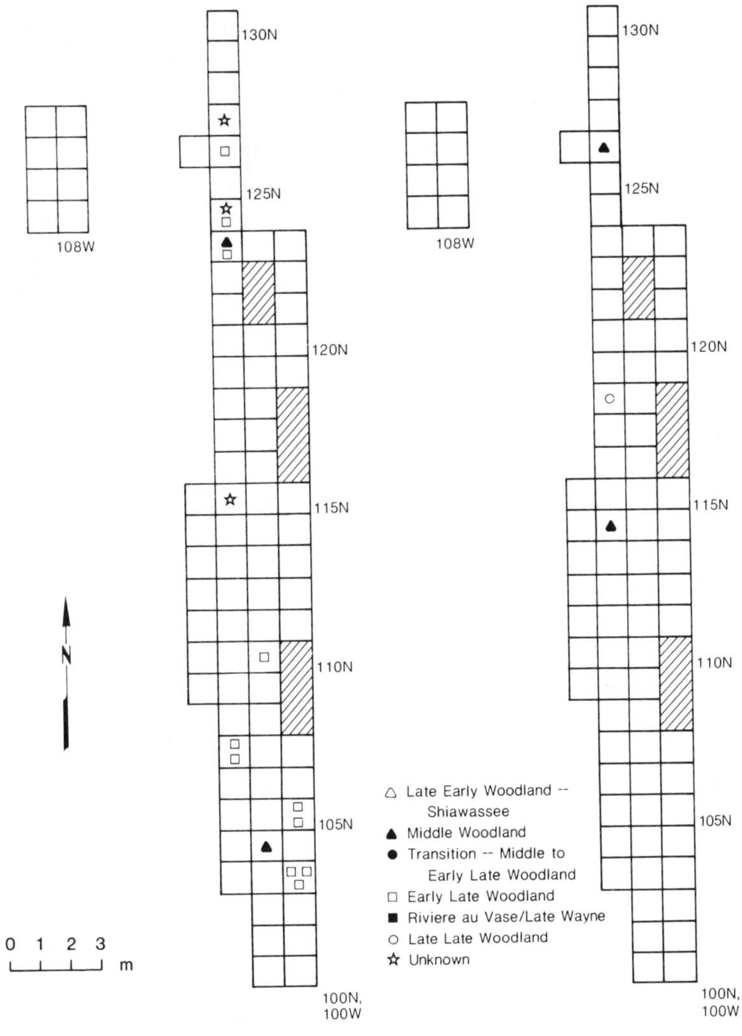

Figure 8.11. Distribution of ceramics. *Left*, level 8–9. *Right*, level 10–11.

Distribution of Body Sherd Attributes by Level

Drawing on the analysis of the large body sherds, as well as previous observations about temporal trends in particular vessel attributes, the distribution of body sherd attributes lends some support to the model of spatial patterning of components developed from the distribution of diagnostic sherds. First, variation in body sherd attributes by level across the entire site

TABLE 8.10
Thickness of Large Body Sherds by Level

Levels	Thickness of Large Body Sherds[a]				Total
	(1) 3.0-4.9	(2) 5.0-7.4	(3) 7.5-11.0	(4) 11.0-14.51	
2-3	3 20.0 3.0	5 33.3 2.4	7 46.7 4.8	0	15 3.0
4-5	44 34.4 44.4	67 52.3 32.7	15 11.7 10.2	2 1.6 4.8	128 26.0
6-7	37 15.5 37.4	95 39.9 46.3	80 33.6 54.4	26 10.9 61.9	238 48.3
8-9	12 14.6 12.1	28 34.1 13.7	32 39.0 21.8	10 12.2 23.8	82 16.6
10-11	2 7.7 2.0	10 38.5 4.9	11 42.3 7.5	3 11.5 7.1	26 5.3
12-13	1 25.0 1.0	0	2 50.0 1.4	1 25.0 2.4	4 .8
Total	99 20.1	205 41.6	147 29.8	42 8.5	493

Cells include count/row %/column %.
[a]In millimeters.

will be considered. The spatial distributions of attributes by level reflect some patterning. However, arraying these body sherd attributes by level alone may yield rather spurious results, since there may have been lateral shifts in occupation as well as variation in prehistoric ground surfaces that lump temporally distinct occupations in the same levels. Therefore, the samples will also be broken down by level and by the clusters visible in the sherd weight density maps, as outlined above.

In the formal analysis, paste and thickness demonstrated internal patterning and patterning relative to other body sherd attributes. Previous analyses on variability in ceramic wares over time have inferred possible cultural-historical meaning from such patterning. Thus, these attributes provide an

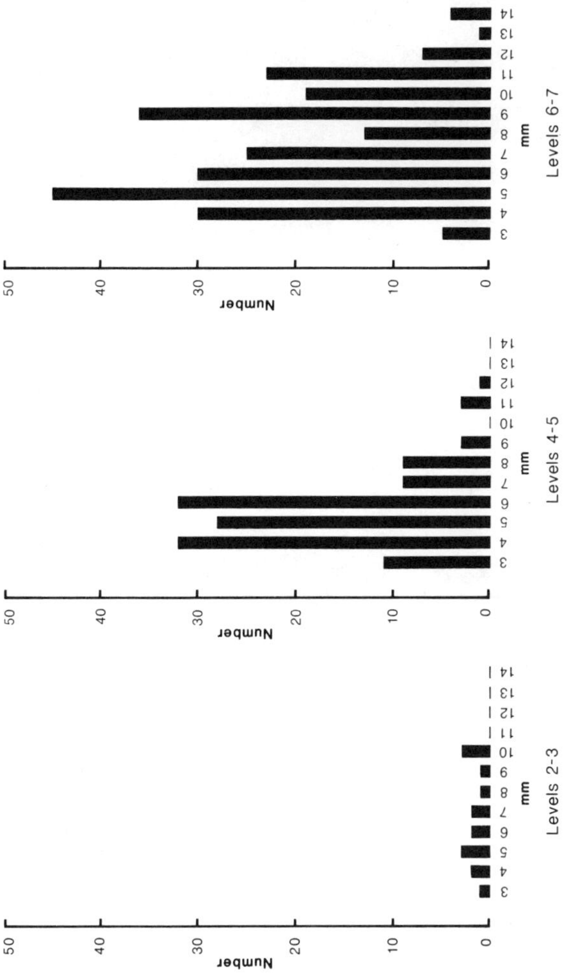

Figure 8.12. Thickness of large body sherds by level (2–3, 4–5, 6- 7).

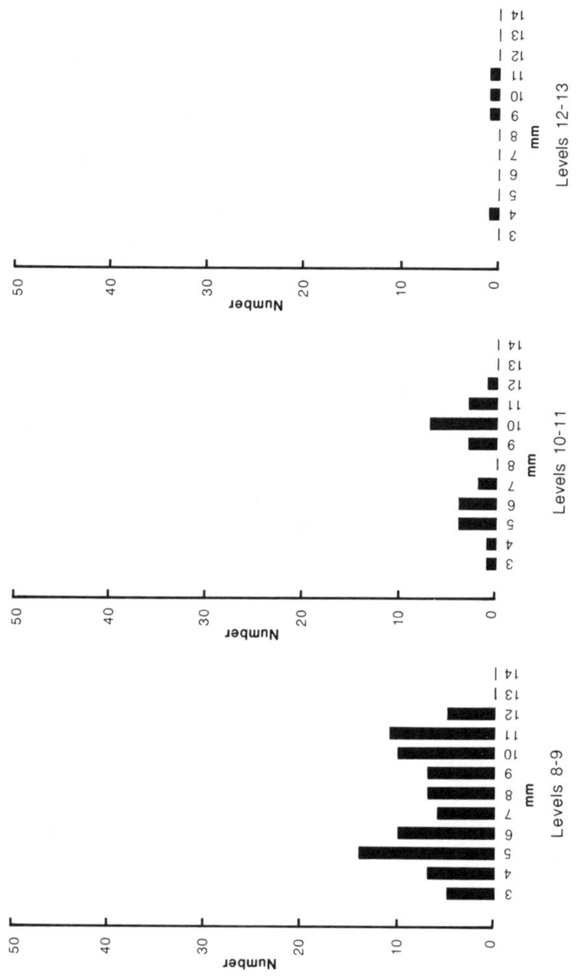

Figure 8.13. Thickness of large body sherds by level (8–9, 10–11, 12–13).

additional source of data with which to evaluate a number of temporal hypotheses.

Table 8.10 and Figures 8.12 and 8.13 present the distributions of large body sherd thickness by level, using histograms and the categories previously constructed from the thickness histogram for the entire ceramic assemblage. Although there are a small number of sherds on which thickness could be measured in level 2–3, these sherds tend to be thin with a mean thickness of 6.96 mm. The predominance of thinner sherds continues in level 4–5 ($\bar{x}$ = 5.88 mm). There is also less variation in thickness within these levels, as the standard deviation (1.68) and histogram demonstrates. As a matter of fact, 86.7% of the sherds in level 4–5 are less than 7.5 mm thick.

The range and variability of sherd thickness changes markedly in level 6–7. Nearly half of the sherds in this level are thicker than 7.5 mm. The mean sherd thickness increases from level 4–5 to 6–7 ($\bar{x}$ = 7.6 mm). However, the thickness categories obscure the bimodality of thickness values and the wide range of variability visible in the histogram for these levels, as well as the higher standard deviation (2.5). The variability may be due to the fact that the ceramics are lumped horizontally between clusters and/or that most of the ceramic deposition for all time periods occurred within this 20 cm level. (Splitting the level by cluster may resolve this issue.) Thus, the real break in the sherd thickness attribute appears between levels 4–5 and 6–7.

The variation in sherds found in level 8–9 parallels, to a large degree, the variability in level 6–7. The mean (7.8 mm) and standard deviation (2.6) are similar in levels 6–7 and 8–9, and the histogram reflects, although to a lesser degree, the bimodality of sherd thickness in level 6–7. Very few sherds were recovered from levels 10–11 and 12–13. However, similar to the previous levels, there is some indication of a continuing bimodality of thickness values, although there is an overall increase in the thickness of the body sherds (level 10–11: $\bar{x}$ = 8.3 mm; level 12–13: $\bar{x}$ = 8.7 mm).

Spatial shifts in the make-up of the ceramic assemblage by paste types parallel the shifts observed for thickness (Table 8.11). Levels 2–3 and 4–5 are dominated by paste 1 sherds. With the general increase in the number of sherds in level 4–5, there is an increase in all other paste categories. The majority of paste 5 (55.6%) and paste 6 (56.3%) sherds occur in level 4–5, with no sherds of these paste types recovered from levels 8 through 13. Although paste 1 contributes the majority of sherds in all levels, there is a definite decrease in the proportion of paste 1 sherds in level 6–7, primarily due to an increase in paste 2 sherds. Also, more paste 3 and 4 sherds occur in level 6–7 than in any other level. The proportion of paste types in level 8–9 generally matches the proportions in level 6–7, although there is a slight unexpected increase in the proportion of paste 1 sherds and a decrease in paste 2 sherds. Paste 1 and 2 sherds dominate level 10–11, with proportionately more paste 2 sherds in this level than in any other level (discounting level 12–13, since there are only five sherds with recorded paste information from this level) (Table 8.11).

The distributions of coil breaks and modelled interiors are nearly identical to, and coincide with the changes noted in, the distribution of paste and thickness with depth. Over half of the sherds with coil breaks (55.6%) and those with modelled interiors (54.9%) were found in level 6–7. Fewer sherds with these two characteristics occur in the overlying levels and more in the underlying levels than expected on the basis of the density of ceramics by level. In other words, there is a slight increase in the presence of coil breaks and modelled interiors with depth, independent of ceramic densities. Again, the marked change in the deposits occurs at level 6–7. In contrast, sherds with residue are more evenly distributed in levels 4 to 9 with none in levels 10 to 13.

The distributions of types of interior and exterior surface treatments reveal little patterning by level at the Bridgeport site. The majority of each type of exterior surface treatment is found in the dense level 6–7, and in roughly the same proportions in all levels. Interior surface treatments are patterned by depth in the same way that the exterior surface treatments are, with one exception. No sherds with incised or striated interiors were recovered above level 6.

Distribution of Body Sherd Attributes by Cluster

Consideration of changes in the thickness of body sherds by level alone reveals some changes with depth, but also suggests the possibility of lateral differences within levels, particularly within level 6–7. This inference is confirmed to some degree by displaying the thickness values of body sherds by cluster, without additionally splitting the sample by level (Fig. 8.14, Table 8.12). The histogram for cluster 1 reveals a marked unimodal distribution toward the thinner values ($\bar{x}$ = 5.9; SD = 1.7). The composition of the clusters by thickness categories shows that 86.8% of sherds in cluster 1 are less than 7.5 mm thick. These results fit the observation, based on the frequency distribution of diagnostic vessels: that cluster 1 is dominated throughout all levels by thin early Late Woodland ceramics with constant but minor occurrences of vessels from other time periods.

Similar to cluster 1, cluster 2 is dominated by early Late Woodland vessels, although there is proportionately more mixing of components in this cluster than in cluster 1. The histogram and standard deviation (SD = 2.9) for cluster 2 reflect a broader distribution of thickness values, with a slight tendency toward medium-thin vessels ($\bar{x}$ = 7.4 mm). However, it is difficult to infer meaning from this weak patterning, due to the small sample size of cluster 2. Various combinations of provenience units were tried, such as placing cluster 2 with cluster 1 or 3, but it was found that the contrast

TABLE 8.11
Paste Type by Level

Level	Paste Type (1)	(2)	(3)	(4)	(5)	(6)	Total
2-3	31	2	0	3	1	6	43
	72.1	4.7		7.0	2.3	14.1	
	4.7	.9		4.3	11.1	18.8	4.2
4-5	264	32	10	13	5	18	342
	77.2	9.4	2.9	3.8	1.5	5.3	
	40.4	13.6	27.0	18.8	55.6	56.3	33.0
6-7	233	139	21	31	3	8	435
	53.6	32.0	4.8	7.1	.7	1.8	
	35.7	59.1	56.8	44.9	33.3	25.0	42.0
8-9	100	43	5	15	0	0	163
	61.3	26.4	3.1	9.2			
	15.3	18.3	13.5	21.7			15.7
10-11	24	17	1	6	0	0	48
	50.0	35.4	2.1	12.5			
	3.7	7.2	2.7	8.7			4.6
12-13	1	2	0	1	0	0	4
	25.0	50.0		25.0			
	.2	.9		1.4			.4
Total	653	235	37	69	9	32	1035
	63.1	22.7	3.6	6.7	.9	3.1	

Cells include count/row %/column %

between cluster 1 and 3 became more marked in terms of attributes such as paste by treating cluster 2 as a separate entity. It is also clear that cluster 2 has a different, more concentrated distribution of sherd densities by level than either cluster 1 or 3. From these lines of evidence, it does appear that cluster 2 should be treated separately, despite its small size relative to clusters 1 and 3.

The histogram of thickness values for cluster 3 is particularly informative in view of its numerous components. The histogram shows a clear bimodal distribution of thickness values and a relatively high standard deviation (SD = 2.3) reflects this large range of variability. The proportion of values by thickness categories also differentiates cluster 3 from the other clusters. Whereas most sherds from cluster 1 fall into either thickness category 1 or 2, the majority of sherds in cluster 3 fall into categories 2 and 3 ($\bar{x}$ = 8.5 mm). Thus, the bimodality found for sherd thickness in level 4 across the

TABLE 8.12
Thickness of Large Body Sherds by Cluster

Cluster	Thickness of Large Body Sherds[a]				Total
	(1) 3.0–4.9	(2) 5.0–7.4	(3) 7.5–11.0	(4) 11.0–14.51	
(1)	74 34.7 71.8	111 52.1 53.9	26 12.2 17.4	2 .9 4.8	213 42.6
(2)	11 21.6 10.7	17 33.3 8.3	17 33.3 11.4	6 11.8 14.3	51 10.2
(3)	13 6.1 12.6	67 31.6 32.5	98 46.2 65.8	34 16.0 81.0	212 42.4
(4)	5 20.8 4.9	11 45.8 5.3	8 33.3 5.4	0	24 4.8
Total	103 20.6	206 41.2	149 29.8	42 8.4	500

Cells include count/row %/column %
[a]In millimeters.

entire site is replicated in cluster 3, which tends to confirm the interpretation of overlying multiple components for cluster 3, based on diagnostic sherd distributions. Finally, cluster 4, although containing relatively few sherds, contains thinner sherds ($\bar{x}$ = 6.9 mm) in contrast to neighboring cluster 3. In fact, no sherds greater than 10.7 mm thick were recovered from cluster 4.

The distribution of thickness values for sherds by cluster and level was also considered, although such splitting reduces the sample sizes to such a degree that any inferences based on the distributions are rather suspect. Because of these declining sample sizes, observations are reported only for the denser levels, 4 through 9. Changes in the distribution of thicknesses by level in cluster 3 do tend to support the interpretation of multiple components which all converge at, and thus result in, cluster 3. There is a trend of decreasing thickness from levels 4 through 9 (Table 8.13). In level 4–5, 66.7% of the sherds are less than 7.5 mm thick, whereas in level 6–7, only 39.2%, and by level 8–9, only 24.3%, are less than 7.5 mm thick. This trend is in stark contrast to cluster 1 where most of the sherds are less than 7.5 mm thick, despite changes in depth. An increase in vessel thickness between

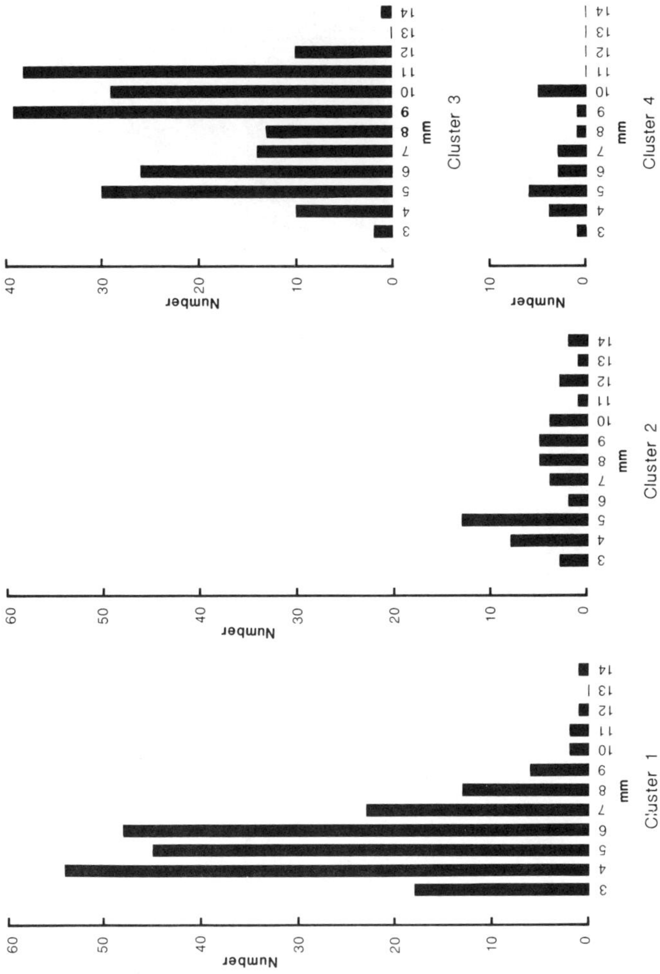

Figure 8.14. Thickness of large body sherds by cluster.

TABLE 8.13
Thickness of Large Body Sherds by Level and Cluster

Level	Cluster	Thickness of Large Body Sherds[a]			
		(1) 3.0-4.9	(2) 5.0-7.4	(3) 7.5-11.0	(4) 11.0-14.51
Level 4-5:	(1)	36 40.9 81.8	46 52.3 68.7	6 6.8 40.0	0
	(2)	6 33.3 13.6	8 44.4 11.9	4 22.2 26.7	0
	(3)	1 4.8 2.3	13 61.9 19.4	5 23.8 33.3	2 9.5 100.0
	(4)	1 100.0 2.3	0	0	0
Level 6-7:	(1)	24 32.3 64.9	41 54.7 43.2	9 12.0 11.3	1 1.3 3.8
	(2)	3 15.0 8.1	6 30.0 6.3	5 25.0 6.3	6 30.0 23.1
	(3)	10 7.1 27.0	45 32.1 47.4	66 47.1 82.5	19 13.6 73.1
	(4)	0	3 100.0 3.2	0	0
Level 8-9:	(1)	8 22.9 66.7	18 51.4 64.3	8 22.9 25.0	1 2.9 10.0
	(2)	0	1 33.3 3.6	2 66.7 6.3	0
	(3)	2 6.1 16.7	6 18.2 21.4	16 48.5 50.0	9 27.3 90.0
	(4)	2 18.2 16.7	3 27.3 10.7	6 54.5 18.8	0

Cells include count/row %/column %

[a]In millimeters.

levels 4–5 and 6–7 for cluster 1 can be easily accounted for by the fact that level 6–7 contains by far the main concentration of ceramics for the entire site and thus should contain the most mixing of components.

Paste types are also differentially distributed between clusters (Table 8.14). Regardless of level, paste 1 sherds heavily dominate the ceramic assemblages in cluster 1 and 2. Also, the majority of paste 6 sherds are located in cluster 1. In contrast, cluster 3 has significantly fewer paste 1 sherds and more paste 2 sherds than in other clusters. In fact, 66.9% of paste 2 sherds occur in cluster 3, and nearly half of both paste 3 and 4 sherds are found in cluster 3. Almost half of the sherds in cluster 4 are paste 1 sherds with proportionately high representations of paste 2 and 4 sherds, and no paste 5 and 6 sherds.

Splitting the sample by level and cluster reveals additional patterning (Table 8.15). Cluster 1 is dominated by paste 1 sherds throughout all levels, starting at 90.5% in level 2–3 and ranging from 75% to 80% in the remaining levels. Similarly, the majority of sherds in cluster 2 and 3 in level 4–5 are paste 1 sherds. (Little can be said about paste types in level 2–3, because of the small sherd sample.) In level 6–7, the make-up of the cluster 3 ceramics changes, with about half of the sherds assigned to paste 2. Proportionately fewer paste 1 sherds are present in this cluster (30.3%) than in any other cluster for this level. Also, more paste 2, 3 and 4 sherds are found in cluster 3 than in any other cluster for this level. This distribution of paste types in cluster 3 continues through level 8–9. In level 10–11, the contrast between cluster 1 and 3 continues, although the sample size limits the significance of these observations.

The spatial distributions of coil breaks, modelled interiors and residue also manifest some interesting patterning. Over half of both coil breaks (55.6%, N = 30) and modelled interiors (54.9%, N = 28) are found in level 6–7. Cluster 3 yielded the majority of sherds with coil breaks (63%, N = 34), with the remaining coil-broken sherds split among the other clusters. The majority of the coil breaks (64.4%) from cluster 3 occur in level 6–7, although this is most likely a function of the high ceramic densities in the level. As has been seen in the discussion of changes in attribute distributions by level, modelled interiors closely track the distribution of coil breaks, with 63.5% (N = 33) occurring in cluster 3. No sherds with modelled interiors occur in cluster 2 and only one was found in cluster 4. Interestingly, the 18 (34.6%) sherds with modelled interiors found in cluster 1 are distributed throughout most levels with no patterning by depth. In contrast, sherds with modelled interiors recovered from cluster 3 occur primarily in level 6–7 (66.7%). Unlike the distribution of coil breaks and modelled interiors, the occurrence of residue on body sherds is concentrated in cluster 1 (75.7%, N = 28), the majority occurring in levels 4 through 9.

Types of exterior surface treatment display little spatial patterning when

TABLE 8.14
Paste Type by Cluster

Cluster	Paste Type (1)	(2)	(3)	(4)	(5)	(6)	Total
(1)	402 77.6 60.5	47 9.1 19.7	16 3.1 43.2	19 3.7 27.5	7 1.4 77.8	27 5.2 81.8	518 49.3
(2)	115 71.9 17.3	21 13.1 8.8	5 3.1 13.5	13 8.1 18.8	1 .6 11.1	5 3.1 15.2	160 15.2
(3)	129 38.4 19.4	160 47.6 66.9	15 4.5 40.5	30 8.9 43.5	1 .3 11.1	1 .3 3.0	336 32.0
(4)	18 48.6 2.7	11 29.7 4.6	1 2.7 2.7	7 18.9 10.1	0	0	37 3.5
Total	664 63.2	239 22.7	37 3.5	69 6.6	9 .9	33 3.1	1051

Cells include count/row %/column %

plotted out by cluster (without further breaking up the sample by level). The distribution of fabric-impressed sherds reflects an anomalous, restricted spatial distribution, with 60.6% ($N = 20$) of fabric-impressed sherds found in cluster 1 and a further 24.2% ($N = 8$) in cluster 2. An additional spatial anomaly is the proportionately higher representation of heavily smoothed-over cord-impressed sherds in cluster 4 than in other clusters. When levels are taken into consideration, there is a slight tendency in levels 6–7 and 8–9 for more smoothed-over cord-impressed sherds and fewer cord-impressed sherds in cluster 3, and for the opposite pattern in cluster 1. These trends are based, however, on only slight variations in proportions.

Some spatial patterning is present when cord impressions are subdivided into the types of cord used on the vessel exteriors (Table 8.7a). The majority of sherds with coarse cord impressions (80.2%) occur in levels 6–7 and 8–9, whereas the sherds impressed by the finer types of cord are concentrated in levels 4–5 and 6–7 (79.1%). Medium cord parallels the distribution of fine cord (73.6%) recovered in levels 4 through 7. Although finer cord is the dominant cord type for all levels, the proportion of sherds impressed by fine cord decreases with depth. The ceramic concentrations can also be distin-

TABLE 8.15
Paste Type by Level and Cluster

Level	Cluster	Paste Type (1)	(2)	(3)	(4)	(5)	(6)
Levels 4-5:	(1)	168 76.7 63.6	15 6.8 46.9	6 2.7 60.0	8 3.7 61.5	5 2.3 100.0	18 5.3 94.4
	(2)	63 81.8	9 11.7	2 2.6	3 3.9	0	0
	(3)	31 72.1 11.7	8 18.6 25.0	1 2.3 10.0	2 4.7 15.4	0	1 2.3 5.6
	(4)	2 66.7 .8	0	1 33.3 10.0	0	0	0
Levels 6-7:	(1)	133 76.9 57.1	17 9.8 12.2	4 2.3 19.0	9 5.2 29.0	2 1.2 66.7	8 4.6 100.0
	(2)	34 72.3 14.6	7 14.9 5.0	3 6.4 14.3	3 6.4 9.7	0	0
	(3)	63 30.3 27.0	112 53.8 80.6	14 6.7 66.7	18 8.7 58.1	1 .5 33.3	0
	(4)	3 42.9 1.3	3 42.9 2.2	0	1 14.3 3.2	0	0
Levels 8-9:	(1)	68 80.0 68.0	10 11.8 23.3	5 5.9 100.0	2 2.4 13.3		
	(2)	7 63.6 7.0	1 9.1 2.3	0	3 27.3 20.0		
	(3)	19 36.5 19.0	27 51.9 62.8	0	6 11.5 40.0		
	(4)	6 40.0 6.0	5 33.3 11.6	0	4 26.7 26.7		

Cells include count/row %/column %

guished by the type of cord. Fine cord dominates clusters 1 (59.5%, N = 204), 2 (50.5%, N = 49) and 4 (50%, N = 13). Cluster 3 has proportionately fewer sherds impressed with fine cord (27%, N = 64) and proportionately more sherds with coarse cord (27.4%, N = 65) in contrast to the other concentrations. As a matter of fact, 79.3% of the sherds impressed with coarse cord are located in cluster 3. This differential distribution of cord types begins in level 4–5 and becomes even more marked in levels 6–7 and 8–9.

Interior surface treatments show little patterning by cluster, an expected result considering the lack of patterning of this attribute in the formal analysis. There is a slight tendency for a larger proportion of sherds with rougher interiors to occur in clusters 2 and 3, and proportionately more sherds with smooth interiors in clusters 1 and 4, probably the result of the differential distribution of paste types by cluster. The distribution of sherds with striated interiors pose the only exception to this general lack of patterning. Nearly two-thirds (70.6%, N = 12) of the sherds with striated interiors are found in cluster 3.

Summary

Two sources of data provide information on the degree of dispersion and clustering of the ceramics: (1) the relative locations of matched vessel fragments horizontally and vertically; and (2) the differential distribution of the body sherds along the same dimensions. The majority of vessel fits occur less than 3 meters apart, although some vessel fragments are distributed up to 9 meters apart. By depth, most related vessel fragments are found within 20 to 40 cm of each other. Only two vessels have characteristics so unique that body sherds could be assigned to these vessels and maps of the locations could be made. Most of the associated body sherds were found within 9 meters of each other. These data suggest a moderate degree of dispersion and mixing at the site.

The density distribution of body sherds by weight reveals some spatial patterning within the deposits. The density of vessel fragments in levels 4–7 and the south-to-north downward shift of ceramic densities suggest a sloping surface in the northern portion of the excavation block. The ceramics are not distributed evenly across the site, but are concentrated in three fairly discrete clusters. Cluster 1 in the southern portion of the main block contains more ceramics than the other clusters. This cluster is more broadly distributed by depth than the other clusters, extending throughout all the levels at the site. The second cluster, immediately north of cluster 1, is heavily concentrated in level 4–5 with lower frequencies of pottery in levels 2–3 and 6–7. Cluster 3, the second largest cluster, begins at a lower level than the other two clusters and is heavily concentrated in level 6–7. Cluster 4 is a catchall category that encompasses the thin scattered deposits in the northern portion of the site.

The discreteness of these ceramic clusters strongly suggests that they were formed by shifts in the locus and nature of prehistoric occupations rather than by fortuitous postdepositional processes. To test the possibility that these clusters represent temporally discrete occupations at the site, the distribution of diagnostic vessel fragments and chronologically sensitive body sherd attributes were analyzed. Level 2–3 contains few ceramics and has probably been subject to historic disturbances so that little can be said about the chronological context of these deposits. This level is dominated by early Late Woodland and late Late Woodland vessels, with several probable Middle Woodland vessels also recovered.

In level 4–5, the ceramic concentrations begin to emerge. Cluster 1 contains the heaviest concentration of pottery. All the clusters in this level are dominated by early Late Woodland vessels, although every other Woodland period at the site is represented in this level. In particular, cluster 1 contains the widest temporal variety, including an Early Woodland vessel. In level 6–7, clusters 1, 2 and 4 continue to be dominated by early Late Woodland vessels. The striking increase of ceramics in cluster 3 is accompanied by an increase in Transitional vessels, although all other periods are also represented. It was suggested previously that the concentration of ceramics in this cluster may reflect overlapping occupations from numerous time periods, with some possible spatial concentrations of Transitional phase ceramics within the cluster, as suggested by the maps of the diagnostic ceramics.

By level 8–9, clusters 2 and 3 thin out, with only a few early Late Woodland vessels present. In contrast, cluster 1 does not change as much in terms of either ceramic densities or diagnostic vessels (i.e., early Late Woodland vessels continue to dominate the assemblage in this cluster). Cluster 4 contains the most diagnostic sherds in level 10–11, primarily Middle Woodland ceramics with a possible Transitional vessel.

The distribution of vessels shows that the different occupations of the Bridgeport site cannot easily be separated out spatially. The southern half of the site was occupied primarily in the later portion of the Woodland sequence, although all proveniences have some degree of mixing from different time periods. Cluster 3 contains materials from a number of different occupations that have been concentrated into a zone that is 20–40 cm thick. There may be a general trend of increasing age with depth in clusters 3 and 4, as suggested by the presence of primarily Middle Woodland vessels in level 10–11 of cluster 4 and by changes in body sherd attributes. As expected, the vessel data reveal no spatially discrete components; there are, however, differences across the site in the degree of overlap and mixing which may permit some separation of components.

The distribution of chronologically sensitive body sherd attributes provides a potentially independent means of sorting out occupations at the Bridgeport site. First, the data were analyzed for any patterning by depth, independent of lateral variation across the site. Arraying the values of thickness and paste against depth points to some interesting changes, particularly between levels 4–5 and 6–7. In level 4–5 and above, the deposits are dominated by thin, paste 1 sherds, with some increase in the variety of paste types present by level 4–5. The range and variation in thickness values changes dramatically in level 6–7. A bimodal distribution of thickness values appears with an increase in the sample's average thickness. These trends continue throughout the lower levels. Although paste 1 dominates the ceramics in all levels, there is a marked decrease in the proportion of paste 1 sherds relative to paste 2 in level 6–7. Furthermore, the majority of paste 3 and 4 sherds are found in these levels.

These shifts between levels 4–5 and 6–7 are paralleled by the other temporally sensitive attributes such as coil breaks, cord type and modelled interiors. The majority of coil breaks and modelled interiors are found in level 6–7 and below. Also, no sherds with incised or striated interiors occur above level 6–7. Although fine cord dominates all levels, the majority of sherds impressed with coarse cord are found in level 6–7 and below. These shifts in the proportions or presence of attributes imply that there may be a general change in the temporal affiliation of the ceramic deposits between levels 4–5 and 6–7.

The distribution of body sherd attributes was also considered by cluster. Clusters 1 and 2 are heavily dominated by thin, paste 1 sherds with a somewhat broader range of thickness values for sherds in cluster 2 than cluster 1. Furthermore, the majority of fabric-impressed sherds are located in clusters 1 and 2. Cluster 3 contains thicker sherds on average with a bimodal distribution of thickness values. There are proportionately fewer paste 1 and more paste 2 sherds in this cluster than in cluster 1 and 2. Also, the majority of sherds with incised interiors occur in cluster 3. Nearly half of the sherds assigned to pastes 3 and 4 are found in cluster 3. Clusters 1 and 3 can also be contrasted on the basis of slight differences in exterior surface treatment, as smoothed-over cord-impressed sherds are more frequent in cluster 3 than cluster 1 and cord-impressed sherds are more frequent in cluster 1 than 3.

If the temporal meaning assigned to these differences in exterior surface treatment, and paste and thickness attributes in the formal analysis is correct, cluster 3 would encompass a wider range of time periods, with the earlier portions of the Woodland sequence more represented in this cluster than in clusters 1 and 2. The evidence also suggests that clusters 1 and 2 are dominated by Late Woodland ceramics. This conclusion not only matches the results of the vessel distributions, but also the concentration of coil breaks and modelled interiors in cluster 3.

When both horizontal and vertical dimensions are considered, conclusions concerning chronological context, based on vessel distributions, are supported. The attributes of the ceramics in cluster 1 change less with depth than those in cluster 3, reaffirming the interpretation of cluster 1 as being the result of occupation over a shorter span of time than cluster 3. The dominance of thin, paste 1 sherds, regardless of level, and the lack of coil breaks and modelled interiors point to a Late Woodland occupation. In contrast, trends in cluster 3 of increasing thicknesses, proportions of pastes 2, 3 and 4, frequencies of coil breaks, coarse cord impressions and modelled interiors with depth, all suggest that a number of components are contained in this cluster, and that there is a larger earlier Woodland component toward its base than is found in the other clusters.

Miscellaneous Proveniences

Three proveniences separated from the main excavation block provide additional, albeit small, samples of body sherds (Table 8.16). Lloyd Bowen excavated a feature that yielded a rich faunal assemblage, as well as a handful of lithics and ceramics. The ceramics from this feature are very different from the UMMA-excavated samples. Only two rim fragments were recovered. One is too fragmentary for a chronological assessment (vessel 60). The second rim appears to be a portion of a Late Woodland Macomb Linear-corded vessel (vessel 62) and according to Fitting (1965) may date to around A.D. 1000.

In addition, eight body sherds were recovered from the Bowen feature. The placement of the ceramics within the feature is unknown. Of these eight sherds, three were categorized as paste 2 and five as paste 1. However, most of the sherds categorized as paste 1 contained more grit temper than most paste 1 sherds in the Bridgeport ceramic assemblage, suggesting that this small sample represents something different in cultural-historical terms. The identification of the Late Woodland Macomb Linear-corded vessel tends to confirm this observation. None of the body sherds show evidence of coil manufacture, although two sherds have modelled interiors and one has residue concretions. Only three body sherds have intact exterior surfaces, two of which are smoothed-over medium cord-impressed and one is impressed with a cord-wrapped object. Of the four sherds with interior surfaces, smooth, brushed and striated treatments are present. Only two sherds could be measured, yielding thicknesses between 5.0 and 11.0 mm.

Small samples of sherds were also recovered from 104N/81W ($N = 17$) and 104N/91W ($N = 20$) located east of the main excavation block (Table 8.16). For both units, the ceramic samples are too small to make any inferences about vertical distribution within the units. The majority of the body sherds in 104N/81W are thin paste 1 sherds that have been cord impressed.

TABLE 8.16
Miscellaneous Proveniences

Parameters	Bowen Feature	104N/81W	104N/91W
Number of large sherds	8	17	20
Paste	(1) 5 (2) 3	(1) 13 (2) 1 (4) 2	(1) 6 (2) 9 (3) 4 (4) 1
Coil	0	1	6
Residue	1	0	0
Exterior	smoothed over: 2 brushed: 1	smooth: 2 smoothed-over: 5 cord impressed: 4	smooth 1 smoothed-over: 5 cord impressed: 9 cord-wrapped cord: 2
Modelled	2	1	1
Interior	smooth: 2 brushed: 1 incised: 1	smooth: 7 less smooth: 3 brushed: 2 cord impressed: 1	smooth: 6 less smooth: 4 rough: 3 brushed: 1
Thickness	5.0–7.5 mm: 1 7.5–11.0 mm: 1	3.0–5.0 mm: 2 5.0–7.5 mm: 6 11.0–14.52: 1	3.0–5.0 mm: 2 5.0–7.5 mm: 3 7.5–11.0 mm: 5 11.0–14.52: 1
Cord	medium: 2	fine: 4 medium: 3 undetermined: 3	fine: 6 coarse: 3 undetermined: 4

There are also minor amounts of sherds that are thicker and that are impressed with coarse cord. Only one coil break was recorded, as well as one example of modelled interiors. Unit 104N/81W yielded six rim fragments and one decorated sherd. Two of the represented vessels date to the early Late Woodland (vessels 67 and 68) and one belongs to the Middle Woodland Green Point ware (vessel 69). One of the most intriguing vessel fragments from this provenience is a rim sherd that is practically identical in terms of motif, paste, and thickness to a sherd found in unit 103N/102W in the main excavation block. I have used these sherds to define vessel 59, but the processes that deposited these two sherds, if they are indeed from the same vessel, in such distant proveniences cannot be easily inferred.

Unit 104N/91W yielded 20 body sherds but no diagnostic ceramics. However, the attributes of these body sherds suggest a different kind of assemblage from 104N/81W. A high percentage (30%) of these sherds have coil breaks relative to the main excavation block at Bridgeport. Body sherds tend to be thick and almost half are categorized as paste 2 sherds (45%) with an additional five sherds categorized as paste 3 or 4. The combination of these attributes suggests that an earlier, pre-Late Woodland component is present in this unit, although a portion of these sherds are thin paste 1 types marked by fine cord impressions, which may point to another later component. The lack of diagnostic sherds renders these conclusions highly tentative.

Lloyd Bowen also collected and restored portions of several vessels from the Bridgeport site from contexts other than the feature mentioned above. The largest vessel segment recovered from the Bridgeport site (Plate 8.6) appears to be a Late Woodland vessel with similarities to some Late Woodland vessels from the Bussinger site (Halsey 1976). The use of a linear decorative motif over a cord-impressed exterior and the decorative attention to the lip points to a Late Woodland age, perhaps a later Wayne Decorated variant (Brashler 1981). However, the motif may also demonstrate a relationship to the southeastern Younge Tradition types. Although it is difficult to ascertain the kind of tool used to make the motif on the exterior of the vessel from the photograph, it appears to be a cord-wrapped object which was used to place impressions in a band well below the lip. Lines of punctations are placed above and below this band at opposed angles. This tool has also been used on the lip surface and for punctations placed in a row on the rim's interior. A second vessel in Bowen's collection is characterized by a smoothed-over cord-wrapped exterior with the paddle applied more than once at different angles on a portion of the exterior. Since there is no associated rim or decorated fragments, only a general Late Woodland affiliation can be suggested.

In photographs of the Bowen collection (Plate 8.7), three fragments of apparently different vessels are pictured. Fragment *a* is a decorated body sherd. The decoration on this sherd seems to have been applied with a wedge-shaped tool and may form a motif similar to that on the exterior of vessel 31 from the UMMA excavations. Sherd *b* has at least four rows of unidentified tool impressions on a smooth surface. Finally, 8.7*c*, the rim sherd, is a portion of a probable Late Woodland vessel. The intact lip is decorated with a cord-wrapped object placed perpendicular across the lip surface, resulting in a scalloped appearance. Similar lip decoration is found on vessel 18 from the UMMA assemblage and on rims identified as Wayne by Brashler (1981:285). However, it also suggests affiliation to the northwestern part of the state where such lip treatment is more frequent in Late Woodland sites (Cleland n.d.; Lovis 1973). In either case, this vessel is probably a Late Woodland type, although temporal placement within the Late Woodland cannot be made on present evidence.

OTHER CERAMIC OBJECTS

In addition to vessel fragments, several other ceramic objects were recovered from the Bridgeport site. Because of the fragmentary nature of these objects and the lack of comprehensive studies of chronologically significant variability in these classes of artifacts, the pipes and miniature vessels do not provide additional information on the chronology of the Bridgeport site. Two possible fragments of miniature pinch pots were found in unit 116N/103W (level 6–7). These two rims represent a very thin ware (4.46 mm at 0.8–1.0 cm below lip surface) with smooth surfaces and little to no temper. They have straight expanding rims which are very uneven. The curvature at the lip suggests that these fragments are portions of small pots rather than pipe bowls.

The Bridgeport deposits also yielded five pipe fragments, all characterized by an absence of temper and a compact paste. A total of three stem fragments were recovered from units 108N/102W (level 5–6) and 104N/81W (level 5–6). One is a roughly circular mouth piece. A second stem fragment comes from a pipe that is flattened on one surface, and a third fragment does not show any flattening of the stem. Two rims from pipe bowls were recovered from 110N/101W (level 6) and 109N/103W (level 5). Both bowl fragments have minimal decoration on the rims. The lip on one bowl is slightly thickened and sharply beveled to the exterior with thin incised lines that are perpendicular to the lip surface. The second bowl is characterized by a slightly outflaring rim and a roughly square lip marked by very faint, irregular slash marks. There is also a hint of thin discontinuous lines drawn on the rim exterior parallel to the lip surface (one immediately below the lip surface and a second one 0.5 mm below the lip surface).

DISCUSSION

A primary goal of the 20SA620 ceramic analysis is to place the site in a regional spatial and temporal framework. Through the analysis of diverse vessels and temporally sensitive body sherd attributes, a series of occupations within the Woodland sequence has been defined at the site. The ceramic inventory suggests that the initial Woodland occupation of the site occurred in the late Early Woodland, identified by the presence of Shiawassee ware diagnostic rims and body sherds. On the basis of the Schultz site Shiawassee wares, Fitting (1972) assigns a 400–100 B.C. timespan to such components in the Saginaw Valley. The Bridgeport site was reoccupied during the Middle Woodland, based on the presence of Tittabawassee and Green Point vessels. Fischer (1972) assigns dates of 100 B.C.-A.D. 300 to Tittabawassee and A.D. 300–500 to Green Point ware use.

The site continued to be a locus of occupational activity during the transitional late Middle Woodland/early Late Woodland phase and the subsequent early Late Woodland periods. The former poorly defined phase may fall in the A.D. 500–700 time range, with the Wayne occupation dating from A.D. 700 to 1000 (although Brashler [1981] suggests that the Wayne Tradition may have extended as late as A.D. 1200 in the Saginaw Valley region). There is further evidence of site use dating to the latter portion of the early Late Woodland based on the presence of Riviere au Vase type vessels. A later occupation during the late Late Woodland may have also occurred at the site, although the ceramic evidence is vague at best.

Another important focus of this study that has not been explicitly addressed is variation in the intensity of occupation during the different Woodland periods represented at 20SA620. This issue is not easy to resolve because of the difficulty of defining and measuring differences in intensity between components. Shifts in the function of a site within a settlement-subsistence system and the cultural reliance on ceramics hamper the comparability of quantities of artifacts between occupations and conclusions about occupation intensity. Differences in the length of occupation can also generate marked differences in ceramic deposition between occupations. Differences in the sampling of sites or components (particularly if the spatial loci of occupations within a site shifts over time) further limits inferences about change over time. Thus, the concept of occupation intensity potentially incorporates a number of temporal, spatial and functional factors that cannot easily be distinguished.

With these caveats in mind, dramatic differences in occupational intensity are suggested for the ceramic deposits at 20SA620. In general, changes in the number of vessels and the degree of dispersal of deposits have been used to differentiate components in terms of intensity of use. The early Late Woodland occupation at 20SA620 clearly contributed the vast majority of vessels (see Table 8.2). The high frequencies of cord-impressed surfaces and thin paste 1 body sherds lend support to this observation. Second in contribution to the ceramic deposits is the Transitional phase. The remaining time periods have provided such small samples that there is no way to differentiate between them further in terms of occupation intensity.

Observations about body sherd attributes known to vary by time period confirm the apparently lower levels of activity at the site during these time periods. For instance, low frequencies of smooth exteriors and coil breaks point to a low level of occupation during the Middle Woodland. The relative infrequency of sherds with modelled interiors and with thicknesses comparable to known Early Woodland ware thicknesses, and the small number of Early Woodland vessels recovered at the site, point to a similar low level of occupation during the Early Woodland. Thus, no long-term trends in occupation intensity can be shown. Only a dramatic increase in occupation intensity during the early Late Woodland, perhaps beginning immediately prior to the early Late Woodland, can be supported.

The spatial and functional data from the site may allow the elucidation of the processes behind these observed shifts in occupation intensity. Unfortunately, there are few direct indicators of vessel function in this assemblage. The vessel fragments are too small to allow consideration of changes in vessel sizes and shapes and, therefore, functions. Variations in vessel wall thicknesses and previous observations about changes over time in vessel dimensions suggest that there are changes in the use of ceramics during the Woodland periods. For instance, the large size and heavy ware of Early Woodland ceramics imply that these vessels were used in tasks that did not require transportation, perhaps in storage or on-site food processing. At least some of the later Woodland vessels were used in cooking, indicated by the presence of residue on a small number of predominantly thin, fine cord-impressed, paste 1 sherds. This ceramic assemblage, however, provides little additional information with which to study ceramic function and therefore site activities during the Woodland period.

The spatial evidence offers some insight to differences in ceramic deposition and thus occupation intensity at the site. All but the Transitional and early Late Woodland phases are represented by a small number of scattered vessels with some shifts in the general locus of deposition of these vessels through time. Such shifts may have resulted in a biased representation of different periods. The presence of later Late Woodland vessels in contexts outside of the main excavation block, such as the Bowen feature, may point to a dispersed but more substantial post-A.D. 1000 Late Woodland occupation at the site than can be inferred from the UMMA excavated samples. Despite this possible sampling bias, there is little evidence that the site was ever used as intensively as it was in the early Late Woodland. The concentrated early Late Woodland ceramic deposits point to an early Late Woodland occupation either characterized by larger population units, spanning a longer period of time, or involving tasks utilizing more ceramic vessels in contrast to all other time periods.

The only other episode of concentrated ceramic deposition occurred during the Transitional phase in a portion of the site somewhat removed from the main early Late Woodland occupation. A series of vessels are tentatively assigned to the Transition, based on the blending of chronologically distinctive traits and on observations by other researchers of the probable existence of this period (Holman 1984; Lovis and Davis 1986; Fischer 1972; Lovis and Holman 1976). The concentrated distribution of these vessels provides further support for the identification of a component temporally separate from the early Late Woodland. However, confirmation of this interpretation requires additional comparative samples in stratigraphically discrete contexts.

Changes in occupation intensity at 20SA620, as indicated by the ceramic assemblage, in some degree parallel trends noted at other occupations in the Saginaw Valley. Of course, as Lovis and Davis (1986:226) have noted, problems of disparities in ceramic description and typology as well as variable assemblage sizes hamper intersite comparisons. Sites with late Early Woodland Shiawassee components such as Bussinger and Schultz, like 20SA620, contained small numbers of Early Woodland vessels (11–22, 9, and 3–6 respectively). Garland notes that the majority of Early Woodland components with ceramics in Michigan have yielded a small number of vessels. Furthermore, these components generally occur in mixed, multicomponent sites (Garland 1986:47). Similarly, the recent Bay City excavations (20BY77 and 20BY79), previous excavations at Kantzler, Bussinger and Fletcher, and now 20SA620, have produced minor amounts of Tittabawassee ware vessels. Unlike the Bay City sites, there is no apparent increase in occupation intensity at 20SA620 during the later Middle Woodland Green Point phase.

An increase in the variety of site types as measured by variation in ceramic densities seems to occur during the Transitional and early Late Woodland periods in the Saginaw Valley. Reductions in ceramic densities occurred at Schultz and Kantzler, whereas other sites such as Fletcher produced intensive early Late Woodland occupations. Although there is a dramatic increase in ceramic densities at 20SA620 at this time period in contrast to the other components, ceramic deposits at the site still reflect a relatively small early Late Woodland occupation relative to other sites in the region. A sharp decline in ceramic deposition after A.D. 1000 at 20SA620 parallels similar trends at many sites in the region (Brashler and Holman 1985; Lovis and Davis 1986).

Finally, a constant though minor occurrence of ceramics that show stylistic affinities to localities beyond the Saginaw Valley (perhaps indicating a nonlocal origin) has been noted at numerous Late Woodland sites in the Saginaw Valley (Brashler 1981; Wobst 1968; Lovis and Davis 1986). Several vessels from 20SA620 show similarities to Allegan (Rogers 1972) and later wares from the west and Mackinac types from the north (McPherron 1967). The mechanisms responsible for these shared traits are unknown at present.

The analysis of the ceramic assemblage from 20SA620 has provided new data on Woodland occupations in the Saginaw Valley. On the intrasite level, chronologically distinct components were recognized on the basis of the study of diagnostic rims and decorated sherds. Differences in the spatial distribution of and the degree of occupation intensity between components were identified. Because of the close proximity of a number of components and the difficulty of observing attributes on small sherds, the body sherds could not easily be assigned to particular vessels or ware categories. Furthermore, the diagnostic sherds were often assigned only tentative chronological affiliation because of the highly fragmentary nature of the assemblage. However, it was demonstrated that the study of temporally sensitive body sherd attributes and patterns of covariation between such attributes could provide additional insight into the spatial-temporal context of sites that lack visible stratigraphy. On the intersite level, 20SA620 was compared and contrasted to other Woodland period sites in the Saginaw Valley and beyond. This study, in conjunction with the growing body of data on other small-scale Woodland occupations, will eventually provide the data base with which to expand our understanding of Woodland adaptations in the Saginaw Valley and to evaluate the roles of sites such as 20SA620 within these changing adaptive systems.

9
Faunal Remains from 20SA620

Karen Mudar
Museum of Anthropology, University of Michigan

METHODS

This chapter discusses the Bridgeport Township site's faunal remains from two contexts: midden deposits and features. This fauna is of particular interest, as it complements a growing body of data from other Woodland sites in the Saginaw Valley, and adds to our knowledge of animal exploitation during this time period.

Faunal remains from a sample of Woodland unit levels and features were submitted for analysis, including a Late Woodland feature excavated by Lloyd Bowen of the Michigan Archaeological Society. The assemblage consisted of a series of samples from five features and twelve levels of four excavation units. The units are a five percent sample of the total number of excavated units, and were systematically chosen equidistant from each other along the long axis of the excavation. Each sample consisted of bones from two 10 cm levels. Both screened material and material extracted from flotation samples were examined. Initial sorting was done in the Archaeozoology Range of the Museum of Anthropology, University of Michigan. Identifications were made using collections in the Fish, Herpetology, and Mammal Divisions of the Museum of Zoology, University of Michigan.[1]

The material from the midden contexts was quite fragmentary and extensively calcined. All the material was placed into one of four categories: fish; bird-small mammal; medium-large mammal; and turtle. The flotation samples were sorted under 25× magnification using a binocular microscope. Tables 9.1–9.4 present the weights of bone by each category for flotation and excavated samples combined. The small sizes of many of the bones pre-

[1]I wish to thank the curators of these divisions, Jerry Smith, R. Kluge, P. Myers, and their collections managers, Doug Nelson, and Greig Schneider, for access to collections and assistance in identifications.

cluded a meaningful count, and presentation of weights was thought to be more useful. Where possible, burned and unburned material was weighed separately. In all, 407.83 grams of bones were examined.

Several taxa of fish, specifically dogfish (*Amia calva*), gar (*Lepisosteus osseus*), and catfish and bullheads (Ictaluridae), were identified on the basis of distinctive surface texture of the bones. Since they can be identified from extremely small fragments, these species are probably over-represented in the identified samples. Therefore, I have noted their presence (see Table 9.4), but have not quantified the identifications.

The material from the Bowen Feature, in comparison to the rest of the sample, was composed of larger bone fragments which had not been subjected to burning. This unusual preservation of the Bowen Feature allowed for identification of a large number of individual elements and taxa. Therefore the identified mammal elements were weighed individually and counted, and the identified fish were weighed and counted by taxa (see Tables 9.5, 9.6). The calculation of minimum number of individuals (MNI) for mammals was modified to reflect the presence of both mature and immature animals. MNI for fish was based on inspection of dentaries. These elements were also used to compute an estimate of the live weight of a number of the individuals.

Estimates of the live weight of fish derived from a three-step process, and should be viewed with caution. First, the dentary was compared to a similar sized dentary from a comparative specimen, and the standard length (SL) of the comparative specimen recorded. Next, this measurement was converted to total length (TL) using conversion ratios (Carlander 1969, 1977). Weight estimates were derived by comparison of TL to TL-weight charts, or by computation of regression equations for each taxon. There are at least three possible sources of error in this method: length may not be perfectly correlated with size of dentary, the ratio of SL to TL may not be appropriate, and the TL to weight correlations used may not be appropriate for this sample. This provides a very approximate estimate of the size ranges of some of the species recovered from this feature.

Density ratios, the number or weight of bones per excavated volume, provide a standard measure of excavation materials and facilitate comparison with assemblages from other sites. Because volumes of units were all equal, and bones were rare from features, density ratios for this assemblage were not calculated. However, we provide flotation volumes here for future reference. Excavation volumes are listed elsewhere in this report. Except where noted elsewhere, the volumes of the flotation samples from the units are 10 liters, and the volumes for the features are: 5 liters (feature 2), 25 liters (feature 7), 8 liters (feature 9), and 22 liters (feature 10). No volume is available for the Bowen Feature.

RESULTS

Faunal remains occurred in levels 2 through 13 but were concentrated in levels 5 and 6 (Table 9.1). Unit N104/W81 contained the largest amount of material. The features, except for the Bowen Feature, contained almost no faunal remains. Bone density decreased from south to north across the site.

Mammals

Few mammals were identified to taxa in the assemblage from the midden. *Odocoileus virginianus*, white-tailed deer, was represented by several unburned fragments from unit N104/W81, levels 7 and 8. These elements, a distal humerus fragment, acetabular fragment, proximal metatarsal fragment, and petrus temporal, weighed a total of 15.58 grams. Levels 11 and 12 of the same unit yielded a proximal humerus fragment, unburned, and a burned carpal, sesamoid, and distal metapodial condyle fragment. These weighed 14.8 grams. A metapodial fragment and a tooth fragment were also recovered from N104/W101, level 5, weighing 0.7 grams.

The only identified small mammal present in the assemblage was muskrat (*Ondatra zibethicus*). Two elements were recovered from N104/W101, levels 4 and 5; both were astragali weighing 0.2 grams apiece. A *Microtus* tooth was recovered from feature 4; this was almost certainly intrusive.

The identifiable mammalian material from the Bowen Feature was more extensive (Table 9.6). At least two white-tailed deer are present, one adult and one immature. Nonmeat-bearing bones, such as carpals and metapodials, were predominant in the sample. At least three muskrat are represented in the assemblage; one is a subadult. At least one woodchuck is present, represented by several long bones. The distal, nonmeat-bearing portions of these bones are calcined. Unidentified mammal bone weights and counts from this feature are listed in Table 9.6.

Turtles

In this assemblage, turtles are the only reptiles represented. No turtle elements were recovered from features 4 through 10, but fragments were recovered from levels 3 through 9 of the midden. Turtles were present in the site, but could not be identified to species (Table 9.3).

Judging from the range of sizes represented in the bones, at least three turtles were recovered from the Bowen Feature (Table 9.6). Only fragments of the carapace of a Blandings turtle (*Emydoidea blandingi*) could be identified to species. The inside of the carapace was cut, removing a ridge along the margin, and the fragment had been burned. An unburned left humerus of a larger individual than the Blandings turtle was also recovered. In addition, several fragments of burned carapace and pectoral girdle from at least

TABLE 9.1
Unidentified Mammal Bones from 20SA620

Level	N104 W81	N104 W101	N114 W101	N126 W103	Fea. 4	Fea. 7	Fea. 9	Fea. 10	Total
2			.44						.44
3		17.45	1.35						18.80
4		5.68	17.00						22.68
5	23.44 (3.25)[2]	20.86	47.42		2.51				97.48
6		2.57	1.27						3.84
7	9.37 (11.70)	21.28	13.02	.30					55.67
8		23.41	4.07	.85					28.33
9	50.95 (14.20)	.33	1.43	1.44					68.35
10		.43		.58					1.01
11	49.67 (6.96)			.45		2.74 (.25)		.84	60.91
12		.30							.30
13							.81		.81
TOTAL	178.54	92.31	86.00	3.62	2.51	2.99	.81	.84	358.18

Weights are given in grams; weights in parentheses refer to unburned bones.

TABLE 9.2
Bird-Small Mammal Bones from 20SA620

Level	N104 W81	N104 W101	N114 W101	N126 W103	Fea. 4	Fea. 7	Fea. 9	Fea. 10	Total
3		.13							.90
4		.97 *Ondatra*							
5	1.77	.32 *Ondatra*							2.03
6		.13	.01						
7									.02
8				.02					
9		.01							.01
10									
11	.30					.10			.40
TOTAL	2.07	1.16	.01	.02		.10			3.36

Weights given in grams.

TABLE 9.3
Unidentified Turtle Bones from 20SA620

Level	N104 W81	N104 W101	N114 W101	N126 W103	Fea. 4	Fea. 7	Fea. 9	Fea. 10	Total
3		.25							.25
4		.28	.14						
5			.63						1.05
6		.11							
7	.35	.50							.96
8									
9	.13	.24		.10					.47
TOTAL	.48	1.15	.77	.10					

Weights given in grams.

one individual smaller than the Blandings turtle were present in the assemblage. All of these fragments had been burned. It was not possible to identify them to taxa.

Fish

The sample from the midden and feature 7 contained a number of fish bones which could be identified to family or specific level. At least seven species were represented: bowfin, catfish or bullhead, drumfish, gar, walleye pike, northern pike, and a member of the perch family (Table 9.4). The three taxa with characteristic bone surface texture, catfish, bowfin, and gar, were identified most frequently, and no species predominated. The other four taxa were identified only once or twice. This pattern is clearly a function of the ease of recognition of the taxa more frequently identified, and not due to greater representation of catfish, bowfin, or gar.

The Bowen Feature contained remains of at least 15 species of fish (see Table 9.5), identified primarily from dentaries. Bowfin, catfish, and pike were the most common, each represented by an MNI of 10 or more. Note that catfish from the Bowen Feature are identified to species level; catfish from the midden context were identified only to family level. The high proportion of walleye and low proportion of gar from the Bowen Feature may not indicate a subsistence shift between this and the earlier occupation represented by the midden sample. It may be due to preservation and sample size. Exposure to trampling and natural elements will fragment bones rapidly, and bones easily identified from small fragments will be over-represented in the identified portion of the sample, even though the actual proportion of this taxa may be small in the total assemblage. Likewise, taxa that are difficult to identify from small fragments, such as walleye, will be under-represented.

Most of the other species were represented by one to three specimens. All body parts were represented, including skull elements, vertebrae, ribs, spines, and scales.

Although very rough estimates, the projected weights indicate that most of the fish would have weighed roughly 0.5 kilograms. Several taxa, such as buffalo, bowfin, channel catfish, northern and walleye pike, and drumfish, can attain weights in excess of 0.5 kilograms. At least two specimens in this assemblage, a bowfin and a buffalo fish, are estimated to have weighed over a kilogram. Fish of this size could make substantial contributions to the diet.

Molluscs

Apart from the Bowen Feature, there was only one mollusc present in this assemblage (6.73 g). This was identified as a *Quadrula pustulosa* from N104/W81, level 8. It is possible that the absence of mussel shells in the assemblage is due to poor preservation rather than lack of exploitation.

TABLE 9.4
Fish Bones from 20SA620

Level	N104 W81	N104 W101	N114 W101	N126 W103	Fea. 4	Fea. 7	Totals
3		.06 *Ictalurus*					.06
4		.19	.36 *Amia* *Ictalurus*	.04 *Lepisosteus*			.59
5	.34 *Ictalurus* *Esox*	.51 *Lepisosteus* *Amia* *Ictalurus*	.62 *Ictalurus* *Stizostedion*		.05 *Amia*		1.52
6		.09	.35 *Lepisosteus* *Amia* Catastomidae *Ictalurus*				.45
7	2.29 *Lepisosteus* *Amia* *Stizostedion*	.18 *Amia* *Ictalurus*	.31 *Lepisosteus* *Amia* *Ictalurus* Percidae			3.45	6.23

8		.51 *Lepisosteus* *Amia* *Ictalurus*		.16 *Lepisosteus* *Amia* *Aplodinotus*			.68
9	1.19 *Amia* *Stizostedion*	.01 *Ictalurus*	.15 *Lepisosteus* *Ictalurus*	.07 *Lepisosteus*		1.51	2.94
10		.06 *Lepisosteus* *Amia* *Ictalurus*		.03 *Lepisosteus*			.09
11	.11					.07	.18
TOTAL	3.93	1.61	1.79	.30	.05	5.03	

Weights given in grams.

TABLE 9.5
Bowen Feature Fish Remains

Species	Number of Bones	Weight of Bones	MNI	Estimated SL (mm)	Estimated Weight (g)
Lepisosteus osseus Long-nosed gar	10	.79	1	–	–
Amia calva Bowfin	276	50.89	8	409	910
			1	491	1640
			1	357	595
Ictiobus sp. (cf. *cyprinellus*) Red-mouth Buffalo	2	1.3	1	353	1366
Catastomus commersoni Common sucker	1	1.01	1	282	425
Catastomidae	7	.58	–	–	–
Ictalurus punctatus Channel catfish	3	4.15	1	–	–
I. natalis Yellow bullhead	15	1.58	2	217	–
			1	285	–
			1	180	–
I. nebulosus Speckled bullhead	8	1.2	1	284	418
			1	315	574
			1	240	249

I. melas	7	1.61	2	211	281
Black bullhead			1	179	211
Ictaluridae	234	66.93	–	–	–
Esox lucius	35	2.17	10	–	–
Common pike					
Pomoxis nigromaculatus	2	.33	1	–	–
Black croppie					
Pomoxis sp.	3	.09	–	–	–
Ambloplites rupestris	8	.39	1	133	–
Rock bass			1	153	–
Lepomis sp. (cf. *gibbosus*)	18	.99	2	198	–
Sunfish			2	–	–
			1	170	–
Micropterus sp.	12	3.42	3	–	–
Stizostedion vitreum	8	4.21	1	412	–
Walleye pike			2	450	–
Aplodinotus grunniens	10	11.58	2	–	–
Drumfish					
Unidentified fish					
Skull parts	227	27.17	–	–	–
Scales	–	6.04	–	–	–
Vertebrae	–	105.35	–	–	–
Spines, Rays, Ribs	–	55.01	–	–	–

TABLE 9.6
Bowen Feature Faunal Remains (Excluding Fish)

Species	Element	Number of Bones	Weight of Bones	MNI
Odocoileus virginianus White-tailed deer	1st phalanx	4	7.3	
	2nd phalanx	5	6.3	
	3rd phalanx	2	2.8	
	metapodial	10	9.0	
	calcaneum	1	7.8	
	distal radius	2	9.3	
	carpals	5	5.0	
	mandible ramus	1	2.2	
	molar	1	2.8	
	deciduous pm4	1	1.3	
	deciduous pm3	2	.9	
	burned tooth fragments	–	.7	
TOTAL		**34**	**55.4**	
Large mammal				
	vertebrae	24	20.2	
	ribs	16	6.5	
	longbones	40	22.7	
	(burned)	7	4.0	
	cranium	4	2.3	
TOTAL		**91**	**55.7**	
Ondatra zibithecus Muskrat	femur	1		
	tibia	1		
	scapula	1		
	humerus	1		
	radius	2		
	mandible	4		
TOTAL		**9**	**7.3**	**3**
Marmota monax Woodchuck	mandible	1		
	femur	1		
	tarsel	1		
	distal tibia burned	1		
	distal radius burned	1		
TOTAL		**5**	**3.4**	**1**
Medium mammal	longbones	10	.7	
	vertebrae	4	.6	
Small mammal-bird		15	.3	
Bird		9	2.2	
Turtle	carapace	4		
	humerus	1		
	scapula	1		
	unidentified	1		
TOTAL		**7**	**5.1**	**3**

TABLE 9.7.
Comparison of Fish Taxa from Three Late Woodland Contexts in the Saginaw Valley

Taxon	Kantzler	Schultz[a]	Schultz[b]	Bridgeport
Acipinser fulvescens	X	X	X	–
Lepisosteus sp.	–	–	X	X
Amia calva	–	–	X	X
Stizostedion vitreum	X	X	X	X
S. canadense	X	–	–	–
Perca flavecens	X	–	X	–
Esox lucius	–	–	X	X
Ictalurus punctatus	X	X	X	X
I. natalas or melas	–	–	X	X
Micropterus sp.	–	–	X	X
Catastomidae	–	–	X	X
Salvelinus	–	–	X	–
Aplodinotus grunniuns	X	X	X	X
Sunfish	X	–	–	X

[a]Cleland
[b]Luxenburg

TABLE 9.8
A Stratigraphic Comparison of Classes of Bone Fragments from Selected Excavation Units at 20SA620

Class	Levels 2–7		Levels 8–13	
	%	N	N	%
Unidentified mammal	93%	198.91	159.71	81%
Identified mammal			30.38	15%
Small mammal	1%	2.95	.41	
Turtle	1%	2.26	.47	
Fish	4%	8.85	3.89	2%
TOTAL	100%	212.97	194.86	100%

Burned mussel shells would probably disintegrate quickly. The unburned mussel shells from the Bowen Feature (44.65 g), which is otherwise well preserved, are extremely soft, and the characteristic teeth on the hinges are, for the most part, eroded. It was possible, however, to identify two species, *Ellipto dilatatus* (one individual) and *Amblema costata* (two individuals). All three species may be found in the shallow waters of large rivers, and could have come from the Cass River.

DISCUSSION

The composition of this faunal assemblage has been strongly influenced by the context of deposition. The excavation units sampled midden, which appears to have accumulated slowly. Dense bones, such as deer teeth and carpals, and burned fish bone, seem to have resisted fragmentation most successfully. Although bone material was recovered from features, the low density suggests that their inclusion was accidental.

Seasonality is indicated only by the presence of turtle and one mussel shell. The presence of nonmigratory spawning fish is not considered to be an indication of seasonality, as it is possible that these taxa were available on a year-round basis. Therefore, it is suggested that the site was occupied during the summer, but perhaps at other times of the year as well.

One unusual feature of this portion of the assemblage is the presence of very small fish bone. The fragments were calcined, indicating human manipulation and not accidental inclusion in the site. The fish are probably too small to have been caught very efficiently with hook and line or by gill netting. They may have been caught by seining. Although basket traps are not known ethnographically from this area (Kinietz 1940), Becker (1983) notes that *Ictalurus* can be caught in this fashion.

As there are few bones identified to taxa in this sample, it is inadvisable to draw conclusions from comparisons of this assemblage to others in the Saginaw Basin. However, the few taxa that have been noted here, deer, muskrat, turtle, and several species of fish, are not incompatible with faunal assemblages from the Fletcher (Lovis 1985) and Schultz sites (Palsgaard, in Ozker 1982). The Fletcher site, which is also thought to be a late spring/summer occupation, although located in wetlands closer to the Lake Huron shoreline, was similar to this assemblage in its absence of sturgeon. However, northern pike and gar, present in this assemblage, were absent from the Fletcher site assemblage.

Comparing the four classes of material (medium-large mammal, small mammal-bird, turtle, and fish) from levels 2–7 and 8–13, we see there is no significant shift in the proportions of each class between the two major occupations of the site (see Table 9.8). This suggests that there was little change either in depositional context or subsistence practices through time.

The Bowen Feature

The depositional circumstances for this feature appear to be quite different than those for the units and features 4–10. The bones were less fragmented, delicate bones were more frequently recovered, and fewer bones were burned. The presence of such a large number of fish, and inclusion of all parts of the body (vertebrae, cranial elements, scales, and ribs and spines) suggests that the Bowen Feature is a cache of some sort, but the additional presence of fragmented mammalian and turtle bone, and mussel shells argues for an interpretation of the feature as being a trash pit.

The inclusion of all body parts of fish may indicate that the specimens were perhaps boiled or fileted, and refuse deposited in the feature. It should also be noted that the distal, nonmeat-bearing portions of the woodchuck (*Marmota monax*) were burned, suggesting that the meat had been prepared over an open fire while still attached to the bone.

The faunal remains from this feature suggest that formation occurred during a spring-summer occupation of the site. The lack of spring-spawning fish in the assemblage, such as sturgeon and suckers, indicates the latter rather than the former. However, Luxenberg (1972) argues that suckers are more common now than at the time of occupation, and the absence of this taxa cannot be taken as an indication of non-spring occupation. The presence of pike has also been used to indicate a spring occupation, but Becker (1983) suggests that a river such as the Cass might have supported these species on a year-round basis. Scales are available from the Bowen Feature. They were examined for indications of season of capture, but the results were inconclusive. Inclusion of shellfish suggests that formation occurred during summer, rather than the high water times of spring. Baker (1983) states that fawns in this region of the state are born in late May-early June. The presence of an immature deer in the assemblage also supports the suggestion of summer feature formation.

The fish fauna from the Bowen Feature were compared to two other Late Woodland sites in the Saginaw Valley (Table 9.7). As all sites are in the same drainage, it is not surprising that they should contain the same range of species. However, two species which are present at one or both of the other sites, sturgeon (*Asipenser fulvescens*) and lake trout (*Salvelinus* sp.), are absent from the Bridgeport assemblage. The absence of sturgeon may be a function of preservation, as the bones are cartilaginous, but one would expect to recover the characteristic scales if the species were present. It is also possible that the absence of these species is a function of seasonality. Sturgeon move up rivers to spawn in the spring, and are most accessible at this time. Lake trout, as their name implies, are found primarily in deep, large, lakes. They move into river systems to spawn in the fall, from mid-October to early December (Becker 1983:324). If feature formation occurred in the summer, it is possible that neither of these species were available for exploitation. The only taxon which was present at the Bridgeport site but not utilized as extensively as the others considered here are sunfish (Centrarchidae).

CONCLUSIONS

A sample of faunal material from the Bridgeport site is discussed here. The material was recovered from three contexts: a general midden, unspecified hearths or pits, which produced small bone fragments that had been burned, and the Bowen Feature, which produced large fragments of unburned bone. Both midden deposits and the Bowen Feature appear to have been formed in the summer. Occupation of the site at other seasons of the year as well is not contradicted by this data.

Identified taxa from the midden deposits consist of deer, muskrat, unidentified turtle, mussels, and several species of fish. The sample consisted of five percent of the total excavated area and included the contents from all features and selected samples of general midden. The species composition of the assemblage from the Bowen Feature is similar to that of the Late Woodland components of the Schultz site and the Kantzler site. In addition to the fourteen species of fish present, three species of mammals were identified, all common in the area today. One species of turtle was identified, and three species of mussel.

The brevity of conclusions presented here reflects the fragmentary nature of the faunal assemblage from the site. Mechanical and chemical weathering of bones from the open air midden context has made taxonomic identifications difficult. The small number of bones identified suggests that the sample may underrepresent the less common taxa in the total assemblage. Those interested in examining models of settlement-subsistence for Late Woodland occupations in the Saginaw Valley should recall that this sample is from five percent of the area excavated at the Bridgeport Township site. It is possible that analysis of a larger sample would provide addition information concerning the use of animal resources. Use of density ratios and determination of context should be considerations when making the detailed comparisons necessary to test models of resource utilization in this ecologically distinctive region.

10
Archaeobotanical Remains from 20SA620

Kathryn C. Egan
The Museum, Michigan State University

Archaeobotanical remains from the Bridgeport Township site provide information regarding the subsistence patterns and environment of the Late Archaic and Early, Middle, and Late Woodland occupants of the site and the Saginaw Valley. Collections from eight percent of the excavated units, features 4, 7, 9 and 10, and previously recovered archaeobotanical collections excavated by Bowen and Brunett were analyzed. Assuming that this sample is representative of the total archaeobotanical assemblage, generalizations regarding the Late Archaic and Woodland period subsistence activities, site seasonality, and environmental conditions can be made. Comparison of these results with other archaeobotanical assemblages from southern Michigan also clarifies broader trends in prehistoric subsistence patterns of southern Michigan and the Saginaw Valley in particular. In addition, these results can serve as an independent test of the models of Saginaw Valley subsistence developed from previously analyzed subsistence assemblages (e.g., Yarnell 1964; Allison 1972; Ozker 1982; Krakker 1983; Lovis 1985). Hence, these results contribute to our further understanding of resource use patterns in the valley.

ANALYTICAL METHODS

Charred plant remains collected during excavation using 1/16″ screens and from flotation samples are considered in this analysis. The collection and initial processing procedures used on the flotation samples are discussed in Chapter 4. In the laboratory, two methods of sorting were employed on these samples. Initially, wood and bark charcoal, nuts, and seeds were sorted out of the light and heavy fraction flotation samples without magnification.

These materials were then submitted to me for identification. It was immediately noted that the samples lacked the usual array of small (less than 2 mm) seeds commonly found in flotation samples from this region. Therefore, a second set of unsorted samples were submitted to the Flotation Laboratory of The Museum at Michigan State University, for sorting and analysis. Among these samples, light and heavy fraction materials were kept separate and run through a graduated series of geologic screens ranging in mesh diameter from 15 mm to 0.5 mm. Using low-power magnification (7×–30×) all wood and bark charcoal, carbonized nut and tuber remains, and seeds larger than 2 mm were collected. Carbonized seeds less than 2 mm were also sorted from the float matrix. The results of these two sorting procedures are presented in Tables 10.1 and 10.2.

Among the float samples sorted with magnification, the first twenty randomly selected wood charcoal fragments were identified to genus and species if possible, and otherwise to growth ring pattern if it could be determined. Additionally, randomly selected wood charcoal fragments from the field-collected materials (Table 10.3) and the flotation samples sorted without magnification were identified. Further, all seeds and nut fragments were identified to genus and otherwise, if possible, to family. Identifications were made with the aid of modern comparative collections and with identification keys (Koehler 1917; Martin and Barkley 1961; Montgomery 1977; Core, Cote and Day 1979).

Counts and weights of charcoal, tubers, and nuts, as well as seed counts, are standardized values expected from 10-liter float samples. These values were standardized to allow for intersite comparison.

Since the hand-sorted samples are biased against smaller plant materials, this analysis focused principally on samples that were sorted under magnification. The hand-sorted samples were cautiously used to supplement this analysis. For larger botanical remains, the two sample sets were statistically indistinguishable and both were employed in the analysis. For the purpose of standardized volumetric comparisons with other sites, however, only samples sorted under magnification were considered.

Although large quantities of uncarbonized plant remains were present within the samples, only the carbonized materials were collected and identified. This decision was based on the results of previous studies which indicate that uncarbonized materials are rarely preserved at open-air sites in temperate environments. Preservation of unburnt material can occasionally occur under unusual conditions such as anaerobic contexts, or in association with copper sulfates or high pH (Lopinot and Brussell 1982), conditions which were not present at 20SA620.

There are several ways to identify modern seed contamination. These include comparison of modern and reconstructed past vegetational patterns, and detailed anatomical studies (Keepax 1977:226–28). In this analysis, it was noted that uncarbonized seeds occurred in profusion and were predominantly ruderal species (e.g., *Chenopodium* spp., *Portulaca oleraceae*). These taxa often occur in disturbed environmental contexts such as the one surrounding the site during its excavation. Further, consideration of randomly selected seeds indicated that the epidermis of the seed coat (testa) was in many cases at least partially represented or that the embryo was moist and generally fresh in appearance. These characteristics of the uncarbonized seed assemblage indicate that the uncarbonized seeds are the result of recent contamination. Such contamination may be accounted for by recent disturbance of the archaeological deposits, natural seed rain introduced during excavation or processing of the flotation samples, and/or introduction through other natural agents such as rodent or earthworm activity (Keepax 1977; Minnis 1981; Stein 1983).

RESULTS AND INTERPRETATION

At the outset, it should be noted that the archaeobotanical remains discussed below represent only a small sample of the resources used prehistorically because of differences in the cultural formation and postdepositional processes that affected them. The relative percentages of different classes of plant remains do, however, provide a generalized view of their use when compared with other archaeological assemblages (Asch and Asch 1986). Consideration of the variations in preservation of different classes of plant remains can also aid in understanding archaeobotantical assemblages (see also Munson, Parmelee and Yarnell 1971). These factors have been taken into consideration in this analysis.

The floral assemblage from 20SA620 exhibits use of a variety of resources. Field collection and processing of 308 liters of float soil resulted in the recovery of wood and bark charcoal, nutshell and cotyledon fragments, seeds of wild and cultivated taxa, terrestrial and aquatic tuber fragments, stem/root fragments, and buds. In all, a total of 49.6 g of wood charcoal, 3.3 g of bark charcoal, 7.8 g of nut, 0.3 g of tuber, 0.2 g of stem/root, and negligible weights of seeds and buds were recovered from the samples considered in this analysis. Each class of archaeobotanical material will be described separately and conclusions regarding temporal changes in their use will be discussed. Because of the lack of clear stratification in the deposits at 20SA620, temporally diagnostic ceramics and their associated flora are used to establish a chronological framework for interpreting the archaeobotanical record (see Chapter 8).

TABLE 10.1—PART 1
Plant Remains Collected without Magnification from 20SA620 Flotation Samples

	104N/81W				104N/101W						
	lev 5-6	lev 7-8	lev 9-10	lev 11-12	lev 4	lev 5	lev 6	lev 7	lev 8	lev 9	lev 10
Total vol. of samples in liters	8	4	8	8	4	4	8	8	8	8	4
CHARCOAL											
Total wt	(0.8)	(0.5)	(0.9)	(0.5)	(0.1)	(0.2)	(0.1)	(0.1)	(1.8)	(<0.1)	(0.0)
Total # frags. recovered	56	25	44	20	15	21	12	23	147	6	0
Identified taxa											
Ash (*Fraxinus* spp.)	—	—	—	1	—	—	—	—	—	—	—
Beech (*Fagus grandifolia*)	—	—	—	—	—	—	—	—	—	—	—
Birch (*Betula* spp.)	—	—	2	—	—	—	—	—	—	—	—
Elm (*Ulmus* spp.)	—	1	—	—	—	—	1	—	2	—	—
Hickory (*Carya* spp.)	1	—	—	2	—	—	—	—	—	—	—
Maple (*Acer* spp.)	—	—	—	—	—	—	—	3	—	—	—
Oak (*Quercus* spp.)	—	—	—	—	1	—	—	—	—	—	—
Oak—white group	8	4	9	1	1	2	2	—	3	—	—
Pine (*Pinus cf. strobus*)	—	—	—	—	—	—	1	—	—	—	—
Diffuse porous	—	1	—	2	—	—	—	—	—	—	—
Ring porous	1	6	4	3	3	8	—	9	7	3	—
Unidentifiable	—	13	5	10	10	10	4	8	8	3	—
Total # of frags. identified	10	25	20	19	15	20	8	20	20	6	0
BARK (ct/wt)	—	5 (<0.1)	4 (0.1)	1 (<0.1)	2 (<0.1)	1 (<0.1)	3 (<0.1)	6 (<0.1)	8 (0.2)	1 (<0.1)	

STEM/ROOT (ct/wt)	—	—	—	—	—	—	—	—	—	—	—
NUT (ct/wt)	1 (<0.1)	2 (<0.1)	0	5 (0.1)	5 (<0.1)	7 (<0.1)	2 (<0.1)	5 (<0.1)	32 (0.2)	0	0
Walnut/Hickory family (Juglandaceae)	—	2 (<0.1)	—	4 (<0.1)	3 (<0.1)	3 (<0.1)	1 (<0.1)	4 (<0.1)	16 (0.1)	—	—
Hickory (*Carya* spp.)	1 (<0.1)	—	—	1 (0.1)	2 (<0.1)	1 (<0.1)	1 (<0.1)	—	11 (0.1)	—	—
Oak (*Quercus* spp.)											
shell	—	—	—	—	—	3 (<0.1)	—	1 (<0.1)	5 (<0.1)	—	—
cotyledon	—	—	—	—	—	—	—	—	—	—	—
TUBER cf. aquatic	—	—	—	—	—	—	—	—	—	—	—
SEED (total recovered)	—	—	—	1	—	—	—	—	—	—	—
Hornbeam (*Carpinus caroliniana*)	—	—	—	1	—	—	—	—	—	—	—

Numbers in ( ) represent weight in grams.

TABLE 10.1--PART 2
Plant Remains Collected without Magnification from 20SA620 Flotation Samples

	114N/101W					126N/103W			Features				TOTALS
	lev 4	lev 6	lev 7	lev 8	lev 9	lev 8	lev 9	lev 10	4	7	9	10	
Total vol. of sample in liters	4	4	4	4	8	8	8	8	8	25	8	4	165
CHARCOAL													
Total wt	(0.2)	(0.3)	0.1)	(0.1)	(<0.1)	(0.2)	(0.3)	(0.2)	(1.1)	(1.3)	(1.0)	(<0.1)	(9.8)
Total # frags. recovered	36	27	20	7	5	33	43	31	128	75	81	6	864
Identified taxa													
Ash (*Fraxinus* spp.)	1	—	—	—	—	—	—	—	—	1	2	—	5
Beech (*Fagus grandifolia*)	—	—	—	—	—	—	—	—	—	4	2	—	6
Birch (*Betula* spp.)	—	—	—	—	—	—	—	—	—	—	—	—	2
Elm (*Ulmus* spp.)	—	—	—	—	—	—	—	—	—	—	1	—	5
Hickory (*Carya* spp.)	1	—	—	—	—	—	—	4	2	—	—	1	11
Maple (*Acer* spp.)	1	—	—	2	—	—	—	—	—	—	—	—	6
Oak (*Quercus* spp.)	—	1	—	1	—	3	3	—	3	—	1	—	7
Oak—white group	—	—	—	—	—	—,—	—	5	1	—	—	42	
Pine (*Pinus cf. strobus*)	—	—	—	—	—	—	—	—	—	—	3	—	4
Diffuse porous	—	1	—	—	3	6	3	—	—	11	2	1	30
Ring porous	11	11	1	3	—	2	6	8	9	3	3	1	102
Unidentifiable	6	8	7	1	2	9	8	8	1	—	6	3	130
Total # frags. identified	20	21	8	7	5	20	20	20	20	20	20	6	350
BARK (ct/wt)	—	—	—	2 (<0.1)	1 (<0.1)	1 (<0.1)	1 (<0.1)	4 (<0.1)	11 (0.1)	10 (0.1)	2 (<0.1)	2 (<0.1)	65 (0.5)

STEM/ROOT (ct/wt)	—	—	—	—	1 (<0.1)	—	1 (<0.1)	—	—	—	—	—	2 (<0.1)
NUT (ct/wt)	2 (0.3)	8 (0.1)	5 (<0.1)	8 (<0.1)	1 (0.1)	3 (<0.1)	1 (<0.1)	1 (<0.1)	2 (<0.1)	7 (<0.1)	27 (0.2)	3 (<0.1)	127 (1.0)
Walnut/Hickory family (Juglandaceae)	—	8 (0.1)	4 (<0.1)	2 (<0.1)	1 (0.1)	3 (<0.1)	1 (<0.1)	1 (<0.1)	—	3 (<0.1)	27 (0.2)	3 (<0.1)	86 (0.5)
Hickory (*Carya* spp.)	1 (0.1)	—	—	—	—	—	—	—	1 (<0.1)	—	—	—	19 (0.3)
Oak (*Quercus* spp.)													
shell	—	—	1 (<0.1)	6 (<0.1)	—	—	—	—	1 (<0.1)	4 (<0.1)	—	—	21 (<0.1)
cotyledon	1 (0.2)	—	—	—	—	—	—	—	—	—	—	—	1 (0.2)
TUBER cf. aquatic (ct/wt)	—	—	—	—	—	—	—	—	—	—	4 (0.1)	—	4 (0.1)
SEED (total recovered)	—	—	—	1	—	—	1	—	2	—	—	—	5
Hornbeam (*Carpinus caroliniana*)	—	—	—	—	—	—	—	—	—	—	—	—	1
Knotweed (*Polygonum* sp.)	—	—	—	—	—	—	1	—	—	—	—	—	1
Lamb's quarter (*Chenopodium* sp.)	—	—	—	1	—	—	—	—	—	—	—	—	1
Unidentifiable seed	—	—	—	—	—	—	—	—	1	—	—	—	1
Unidentifiable cotyledon	—	—	—	—	—	—	—	—	1	—	—	—	1

Numbers in ( ) represent weight in grams.

TABLE 10.2 — PART 1
Plant Remains Collected with Maghification from 20SA620 Flotation Samples

	110N/102W							114N/102W			
	lev 3	lev 4	lev 5	lev 6	lev 7	lev 8-9	lev 10-11	lev 5	lev 6-7	lev 8-9	lev 10-11
Total vol. of samples in liters	8	4	8	8	8	8	8	8	8	8	8
CHARCOAL											
Total wt	(0.4)	(1.1)	(0.9)	(0.7)	(0.9)	(0.6)	(0.3)	(2.9)	(0.4)	(0.7)	(0.5)
Total # frags. recovered	72	178	155	118	125	51	34	278	35	70	57
Identified taxa:											
Ash (*Fraxinus* spp.)	—	—	—	—	—	—	—	—	—	—	—
Beech (*Fagus grandifolia*)	—	—	—	—	—	—	—	—	2	2	—
Birch (*Betula* spp.)	—	—	—	—	—	—	—	—	—	—	—
Elm (*Ulmus* spp.)	—	—	—	—	—	3	1	1	—	—	—
Hickory (*Carya* spp.)	—	1	1	—	—	—	—	—	—	1	1
Maple (*Acer* spp.)	1	—	—	—	1	1	—	1	—	—	—
Oak (*Quercus* spp.)	—	—	—	3	—	—	—	—	—	—	—
Oak—white group	12	4	12	4	8	1	2	19	6	—	1
Walnut (*Juglans* spp.)	—	—	—	1	—	—	—	—	—	—	—
Diffuse porous	4	—	—	—	1	1	1	1	7	2	5
Ring porous	—	—	5	6	8	6	6	3	4	14	5
Unidentifiable	3	5	3	6	2	7	10	1	2	6	7
Total # frags. identified	20	10	21	20	20	19	20	26	21	25	19
BARK (ct/wt)	1 (<0.1)	8 (0.1)	5 (0.2)	4 (<0.1)	5 (<0.1)	1 (0.1)	— —	6 (0.2)	3 (<0.1)	6 (<0.1)	3 (<0.1)

STEM/ROOT (ct/wt)	—	—	1 (0.1)	—	—	—	—	1 (<0.1)	1 (<0.1)	—	—
NUT (ct/wt)	3 (0.1)	6 (0.1)	11 (0.1)	6 (<0.1)	11 (<0.1)	10 (0.2)	6 (0.1)	4 (<0.1)	16 (0.1)	11 (<0.1)	19 (0.3)
Hickory (*Carya* spp.)	—	2 (<0.1)	10 (0.1)	6 (<0.1)	10 (<0.1)	7 (0.1)	5 (0.1)	—	—	—	—
Black Walnut (*Juglans nigra*)	—	—	—	—	—	—	—	—	—	—	1 (0.1)
Walnut/Hickory (Juglandaceae)	3 (<0.1)	4 (0.1)	1 (<0.1)	—	—	—	—	4 (<0.1)	15 (0.1)	10 (<0.1)	18 (0.2)
Oak (*Quercus* spp.)											
shell	—	—	—	—	1 (<0.1)	—	1 (<0.1)	—	1 (<0.1)	1 (<0.1)	—
cotyledon	—	—	—	—	—	3 (0.1)	—	—	—	—	—
TUBER cf. aquatic (ct/wt)	—	1 (<0.1)	—	—	—	—	—	—	—	—	—
SEED (total recovered)	1	—	3	1	2	—	—	2	1	—	—
Blackberry (*Rubus* spp.)	—	—	—	1	1	—	—	1	1	—	—
Grape (*Vitis* sp.)	—	—	—	—	—	—	—	—	—	—	—
Knotweed (*Polygonum* sp.)	—	—	—	—	1	—	—	—	—	—	—
Squash endosperm (*Cucurbita pepo*)	—	—	—	—	—	—	—	—	—	—	—
Pink family (Caryophyllaceae)	—	—	1	—	—	—	—	—	—	—	—
Grass family (Poaceae)	—	—	—	—	—	—	—	1	—	—	—
Rose family (Rosaceae)	1	—	1	—	—	—	—	—	—	—	—
Unidentifiable seed	—	—	1	—	—	—	—	—	—	—	—

Numbers in ( ) represent weight in grams.

TABLE 10.2—PART 2
Plant Remains Recovered with Magnification from 20SA620 Flotation Samples

	120N/101W					TOTALS
	lev 4	lev 5	lev 6-7	lev 8-9	lev 10-11	
Total vol.of samples in liters	8	8	8	8	8	124
CHARCOAL						
Total wt	(0.1)	(0.2)	(0.5)	(0.5)	(0.3)	(11.0)
Total # frags. recovered	6	49	64	49	43	1384
Identified taxa:						
Ash (*Fraxinus* spp.)	—	—	3	—	—	3
Beech (*Fagus grandifolia*)	—	—	—	—	—	4
Birch (*Betula* spp.)	—	—	1	—	—	1
Elm (*Ulmus* spp.)	—	—	—	2	2	9
Hickory (*Carya* spp.)	—	—	—	—	1	5
Maple (*Acer* spp.)	—	—	—	—	—	4
Oak (*Quercus* spp.)	—	1	—	—	—	4
Oak—white group	—	2	1	2	2	76
Pine (*Pinus strobus*)	—	—	—	—	1	1
Walnut (*Juglans* spp.)	—	—	—	—	—	1
Diffuse porous	—	3	1	2	2	30
Ring porous	2	4	7	1	4	75
Unidentifiable	4	10	4	12	7	89
Total # frags. identified	6	20	17	19	19	302
BARK (ct/wt)	—	5 (0.1)	—	1 (<0.1)	3 (<0.1)	51 (0.7)

STEM/ROOT (ct/wt)	—	4 (<0.1)	—	—	1 (<0.1)	8 (0.1)
NUT (ct/wt)	—	2 (<0.1)	—	14 (0.3)	10 (0.1)	129 (1.4)
Hickory (*Carya* spp.)	—	—	—	7 (0.2)	—	47 (0.5)
Black walnut (*Juglans nigra*)	—	—	—	—	—	1 0.1
Hickory/walnut (Juglandaceae)	—	2 (<0.1)	—	6 (0.1)	8 (0.1)	71 (0.6)
Oak (*Quercus* spp.)						
shell	—	—	—	1 (<0.1)	2 (<0.1)	7 (<0.1)
cotyledon	—	—	—	—	—	3 (0.1)
TUBER cf. aquatic (ct/wt)	—	1 (<0.1)	—	—	—	2 (<0.1)
SEEDS (total recovered)	1	2	5	—	1	19
Blackberry (*Rubus* spp.)	1	2	2	—	—	9
Grape (*Vitis* sp.)	—	—	1	—	—	1
Knotweed (*Polygonum* sp.)	—	—	—	—	—	1
Squash endosperm (*Cucurbita pepo*)	—	—	—	—	1	1
Pink family (Caryophyllaceae)	—	—	—	—	—	1
Grass family (Poaceae)	—	—	—	—	—	1
Rose family (Rosaceae)	—	—	—	—	—	2
Unidentifiable seed	—	—	2	—	—	3

Numbers in ( ) represent weight in grams.

TABLE 10.3—PART 1
Field Collected Flora from 20SA620

	104N/81W				104N/101W					
	lev 5-6	lev 7-8	lev 9-10	lev 11-12	lev 1	lev 3	lev 5	lev 7	lev 9	lev 10
CHARCOAL										
Total wt	(0.8)	(0.1)	(0.2)	(0.1)	(0.1)	(3.3)	(3.8)	(2.6)	(1.0)	(<0.1)
Total # frags. recovered	7	1	2	1	3	426	376	181	72	7
Identified taxa										
Ash (*Fraxinus* spp.)	—	—	1	—	1	1	—	—	—	—
Beech (*Fagus grandifolia*)	—	—	—	—	—	—	—	—	—	—
Elm (*Ulmus* spp.)	—	—	—	—	—	—	—	1	—	—
Hickory (*Carya* spp.)	—	—	—	—	—	—	3	—	—	—
Maple (*Acer* spp.)	—	—	—	—	1	—	—	—	—	—
Oak (*Quercus* spp.)	—	1	—	—	—	—	—	—	2	—
Oak—white group	6	—	—	—	—	7	3	3	1	—
Pine (*Pinus cf. strobus*)	—	—	—	—	—	—	—	—	—	—
Diffuse porous	—	—	—	—	1	—	1	3	—	—
Ring porous	1	—	—	—	—	10	8	8	2	4
Unidentifiable	—	—	1	—	—	2	5	5	14	3
Total # of frags. identified	7	1	2	0	3	20	20	20	19	7
BARK (ct/wt)	—	—	—	—	—	1 (<0.1)	38 (0.3)	15 (0.1)	8 (<0.1)	—

STEM/ROOT (ct/wt)	—	—	—	—	—	—	—	—	—	—
NUT (ct/wt)	—	—	—	—	—	17 (0.2)	46 (0.4)	26 (0.2)	15 (<0.1)	—
Walnut/Hickory (Juglandaceae)	—	—	—	—	—	6 (<0.1)	32 (0.2)	6 (<0.1)	12 (<0.1	—
Hickory (*Carya* spp.)	—	—	—	—	—	7 (0.1)	8 (0.1)	13 (0.1)	—	—
Black Walnut (*Juglans nigra*)	—	—	—	—	—	3 (0.1)	3 (0.1)	14 (0.1)	—	—
Oak (*Quercus* spp.) shell	—	—	—	—	—	1 (<0.1)	3 (<0.1)	3 (<0.1)	3 (<0.1)	—
cotyledon	—	—	—	—	—	—	—	—	—	—
Hazelnut (*Corylus americana*)	—	—	—	—	—	—	—	—	—	—
TUBER aquatic (ct/wt)	—	—	—	—	—	—	1 (<0.1)	—	1 (<0.1)	—
terrestrial (ct/wt)	—	—	—	—	—	—	—	—	—	—
SEED (total recovered)	—	—	—	—	—	1	2	—	—	—
Unidentiable cotyledon	—	—	—	—	—	1	2	—	—	—
BUD (ct)	—	—	—	—	—	1	—	—	—	—

Numbers in ( ) represent weight in grams.

TABLE 10.3—PART 2
Field Collected Flora from 20SA620

	114N/101W				126N/103W					TOTALS
	lev 4	lev 6	lev 7	lev 8	lev 3	lev 7	lev 8	lev 9	lev 10	
CHARCOAL										
Total wt	(5.9)	(1.8)	(3.1)	(2.3)	(1.1)	(0.2)	(0.7)	(1.3)	(0.5)	(28.9)
Total # frags. recovered	514	164	253	171	218	33	143	250	61	2883
Identified taxa										
Ash (*Fraxinus* spp.)	—	—	—	—	—	—	—	1	—	4
Beech (*Fagus grandifolia*)	—	1	4	—	—	—	—	1	—	6
Elm (*Ulmus* spp.)	—	—	—	—	1	—	—	—	—	2
Hickory (*Carya* spp.)	—	—	2	—	—	—	—	—	—	5
Maple (*Acer* spp.)	—	—	—	—	1	1	—	—	—	3
Oak (*Quercus* spp.)	—	—	—	—	—	—	—	—	—	3
Oak—white group	—	1	5	—	4	1	7	1	—	39
Pine (*Pinus cf. strobus*)	—	—	—	—	—	—	—	1	—	1
Diffuse porous	—	3	2	—	4	6	2	3	—	25
Ring porous	—	9	3	—	5	8	5	4	—	67
Unidentifiable	—	6	4	—	5	4	6	9	—	64
Total # of frags. identified	0	20	20	0	20	20	20	20	0	219
BARK (ct/wt)	58 (0.9)	12 (0.2)	18 (0.1)	6 (0.2)	3 (<0.1)	1 (<0.1)	14 (0.1)	7 (<0.1)	4 (<0.1)	185 (1.9)

STEM/ROOT (ct/wt)	1 (0.1)	—	—	—	1 (<0.1)	—	1 (<0.1)	—	—	4 (0.1)
NUT (ct/wt)	90 (0.3)	24 (0.4)	38 (0.5)	40 (0.5)	12 (<0.1)	2 (<0.1)	7 (<0.1)	17 (<0.1)	1 (<0.1)	335 (5.5)
Walnut/Hickory (Juglandaceae)	46 (0.6)	13 (0.1)	27 (0.2)	27 (0.2)	12 (<0.1)	2 (<0.1)	7 (<0.1)	15 (<0.1)	1 (<0.1)	206 (1.3)
Hickory (*Carya* spp.)	32 (1.2)	9 (0.3)	2 (0.1)	10 (0.3)	—	—	—	2 (<0.1)	—	83 (2.2)
Black Walnut (*Juglans nigra*)	4 (0.3)	—	1 (0.1)	—	—	—	—	—	—	25 (0.7)
Oak (*Quercus* spp.) shell	6 (<0.1)	2 (<0.1)	7 (<0.1)	3 (<0.1)	—	—	—	—	—	28 (<0.1)[a]
cotyledon	—	—	1 (0.1)	—	—	—	—	—	—	1 (0.1)
Hazelnut (*Corylus americana*)	2 (<0.1)	—	—	—	—	—	—	—	—	2 (<0.1)
TUBER										
cf. aquatic (ct/wt)	—	—	—	—	1 (<0.1)	—	1 (<0.1)	—	—	4 (<0.1)
terrestrial (ct/wt)	1 (<0.1)	—	—	—	—	—	—	—	—	1 (<0.1)
SEED (total recovered)	—	—	—	—	—	—	—	—	—	3
Unidentifiable cotyledon	—	—	—	—	—	—	—	—	—	3
BUD (ct)	—	—	—	—	—	—	1	2	—	4

Numbers in ( ) represent weight in grams.

[a]Total weight. Cumulative weight of fragments may be greater.

Wood Charcoal

Wood charcoal occurs in 98% of the provenience units considered in this analysis. It constitutes 81% of the carbonized flora by weight in the entire assemblage and 85% of the floated flora. Considering the flotation materials collected under magnification only, an average of 111.6 pieces per 10 liters, and 0.88 g per 10 liters of charcoal were recovered.

Among the identified wood taxa, white oak (*Quercus* spp.) occurs in greatest abundance, constituting 67.1% of the identifiable wood charcoal assemblage. Ash (*Fraxinus* spp.), beech (*Fagus grandifolia*), birch (*Betula* spp.), elm (*Ulmus* spp.), hickory (*Carya* spp.), maple (*Acer* spp.), white pine (*Pinus* cf. *strobus*) and walnut (*Juglans* spp.) occur in lesser quantities, each comprising less than 10% of the identified charcoal (Table 10.4). Although there is variability in the representation of wood taxa by unit and level, using temporally diagnostic ceramic associations to identify chronological differences, the forest type throughout the site's occupation appears to have been a mature, mixed, xeric forest. Oak predominates throughout the site's occupation, and hickory and walnut occur in association with both Late Woodland and Middle Woodland ceramics. Elm and maple are only found in association with Late Woodland ceramics, and ash and birch are present only in association with transitional Middle to Late Woodland ceramics.

The occurence of both southern- and northern-adapted genera at 20SA620 is a result of the geographic location of the site at the northern border of the Carolinian biotic province (C. Cleland 1966). In addition, the array of taxa represented indicates that the site location provided access to microenvironments associated with both upland and lowland floodplain habitats.

The General Land Office (GLO) survey records of the presettlement vegetation in the site vicinity report a similar range of northern- and southern-adapted taxa (see Chapter 3). In contrast to the archaeobotanical assemblage, the GLOs data suggest that a dry-mesic community occured within 1.5 km of the site and that no single taxon was dominant in the presettlement forest. The abundance of oak, especially white oak, in the archaeobotanical assemblage, therefore, suggests a cultural selection for high quality fuel wood rather than a major difference in forest type. Palynological data from the area do not reflect a major shift in vegetation or climate during the period of prehistoric occupation that could account for the dominance of southern, xeric taxa like white oak.

Bark Charcoal

Bark charcoal is present in 22% of the provenience units considered in this analysis. It represents 5% of all flora recovered, by weight, and 5% of the float recovered flora. Further, an average of 4.1 pieces per 10 liters and 0.06 g per 10 liters of the bark charcoal was recovered from float samples sorted

TABLE 10.4
Percentages of Wood Taxa by Count

Taxa	% of Total Wood Taxa	% of Identifiable Wood Taxa
Ash (*Fraxinus* spp.) (*N* = 12)	1.4%	4.6%
Beech (*Fagus grandifolia*) (*N* = 16)	1.8%	6.2%
Birch (*Betula* spp.) (*N* = 3)	0.3%	1.2%
Elm (*Ulmus* spp.) (*N* = 16)	1.8%	6.2%
Hickory (*Carya* spp.) (*N* = 21)	2.4%	8.1%
Maple (*Acer* spp.) (*N* = 13)	1.5%	5.0%
Oak (*Quercus* spp.) (*N* = 14)	1.6%	5.4%
Oak-white group (*Quercus* spp.) (*N* = 157)	18.0%	60.6%
Pine (*Pinus cf. strobus*) (*N* = 6)	0.7%	2.3%
Walnut (*Juglans* spp.) (*N* = 1)	0.1%	0.4%
Diffuse porous (*N* = 85)	9.8%	
Ring porous (*N* = 244)	28.0%	
Unidentifiable (*N* = 283)	32.5%	

with magnification. Hence, bark occurs in minor quantities that are consistently less than the quantities of wood charcoal. Its presence is probably a consequence of burning wood with bark or cambium rather than the intentional burning of bark for a specific purpose, such as preserving food and hides by smoking or keeping away insects.

Nuts

Nuts, including hickory (*Carya* spp.), black walnut (*Juglans nigra*), acorn (*Quercus* spp.) and hazelnut (*Corylus americana*), occur in 81% of the provenience units considered in this analysis. On the basis of weight, nut remains represent 12.7% of the total floral assemblage and 53% of the float-recovered flora. Among the float samples sorted with magnification, nut is present in quantities of 10.4 pieces per 10 liters and 0.1 g per 10 liters. All of the nut taxa represented were regularly used among Great Lakes Indians both prehistorically and historically (Yarnell 1964). Their presence in this assemblage suggests that they were used as food resources among the prehistoric inhabitants of the site.

The nut remains were extremely fragmented, making identification beyond the family level difficult in many instances. Consequently, 36% of the nut by weight and 61% by count are classified in the walnut-hickory family (Junglandaceae). Among the identified remains, hickory predominates, representing 25% by count and 45% by weight of all nut remains, and 65% by count and 71% by weight of the nut remains identified to genus. Lesser quantities of black walnut, acorn and hazelnut also occur (Table 10.5).

The hickory shell remains occur in greatest abundance in the southern portion of the excavation block in levels 4 through 11 (Tables 10.1–10.3). These remains occur in association with temporally diagnostic Middle and Late Woodland ceramics, and occur stratigraphically in proximity to the 3510 ± 80 b.p. date (see Chapter 5). Hence, it appears that hickory was exploited throughout the occupation of the site.

Black walnut shell represents 3% by count and 12% by weight of all recovered nut remains, and 7% by count and 19% by weight of the nut remains identified to genus. It is relatively restricted in its distribution, occurring only in the upper levels of 104N/101W and 114N/101W, and level 10–11 of 114N/102W (Tables 10.1 and 10.2). Larger quantities of black walnut are found in association with Late Woodland ceramics although the one specimen in 114N/102W is associated with Middle Woodland ceramics (see Chapter 8). This distribution indicates that black walnut was used during the Middle and Late Woodland periods and may have been more heavily exploited during the Late Woodland, a possibility discussed later in this chapter.

Acorn shell and cotyledon remains represent 10% by count and 6% by weight of all of the recovered nut remains, and 27% by count and 10% by weight of the nut remains identified to genus. They occur in the southern excavation units in levels 4 through 11 (Tables 10.1–10.3). These remains are associated with the Late Archaic through Late Woodland occupations of the site. Although the number of acorn fragments varies among the provenience units analyzed, there is no obvious pattern to the variation. Hence,

TABLE 10.5
Percentages of Nut Taxa

	% of Total		% of Identifiable Nut		% of Float Sorted with Magnification	
	wt	ct	wt	ct	ct	wt
Hickory (*Carya* spp.)	45%	25%	71%	65%	39%	36%
Black Walnut (*Juglans nigra*)	12%	3%	19%	7%	8%	< 1%
Walnut-Hickory family (Juglandaceae)	36%	61%	—	—	46%	55%
Oak shell (*Quercus* spp.)	< 1%	9%	< 1%	25%	< 1%	5%
Oak cotyledon (*Quercus* spp.)	6%	1%	10%	2%	8%	2%
Hazelnut (*Corylus americana*)	< 1%	< 1%	< 1%	< 1%	—	—

TABLE 10.6
Percentages of Nut Taxa by Weight and Count for Each of the Components at 20SA620

	Late Archaic Early Woodland[a]		Middle Woodland		Late Woodland	
	ct	wt	ct	wt	ct	wt
Walnut-hickory family (Juglandaceae)	80%	50%	65%	44%	54%	29%
Hickory (*Carya* spp.)			22%	33%	31%	46%
Black Walnut (Juglans nigra)			1%	11%	6%	18%
Acorn (*Quercus* spp.)	20%	50%	11%	11%	9%	7%
Hazelnut (*Corylus americana*)					1%	< 1%

[a]One provenience unit included in each calculation.

acorn, like hickory, appears to have been consistently exploited throughout the occupation of the site.

A single fragment of hazelnut was recovered (Table 10.3). It makes up less than 1% by count and weight of all recovered nut remains, both total and identifiable to genus. It occurs in association with other nut taxa suggesting that it was intentionally exploited rather than an incidental or natural inclusion to the assemblage. Its stratigraphic position suggests that it is associated with the Late Woodland occupation of the site.

While nuts were clearly exploited throughout the prehistoric occupation of the site, the contribution of each nut taxon to the subsistence pattern of each time period is unclear. It was, therefore, necessary to calculate the percentage representation of each taxa relative to the total amount of nut which could be attributed to any given time period. These percentages were calculated on the basis of both counts and weights (Table 10.6). For the purposes of taxonomic comparison counts are considered a more accurate measure because shell weights between taxa differ so dramatically (e.g., black walnut and acorn). Because of the small sample sizes these percentages are only estimates. Assuming they are representative, however, they suggest some general trends in nut exploitation patterns over time.

For the Late Archaic/Early Woodland component nut remains are sparse, occurring in only one context. It is not clear if this is a product of sampling error or whether nuts were of limited importance to this particular occupation. Nevertheless, Juglandaceae remains are more abundant by both count and weight than acorn (Table 10.6), indicating that hickory, walnut, or both, were more important resources.

The five samples of Middle Woodland nut remains (Table 10.6) suggests Juglandaceae continued to be an important resource. Further, the percentages suggest that during this occupation hickory was more important than black walnut. Acorn is also present in the Middle Woodland assemblage but appears to decrease in importance relative to hickory and black walnut, when compared with the Late Archaic/Early Woodland assemblage.

During the Late Woodland, a wide range of nut resources appear to have been exploited (Table 10.6). Juglandaceae taxa continue to predominate. While hickory is more abundant than black walnut, black walnut is relatively more abundant than in either the Late Archaic/Early Woodland or Middle Woodland occupations. Acorn is also present in this assemblage but appears to be decreasing in importance as hickory and walnut increase in importance. Hazelnut is also present in the Late Woodland assemblage although it is only a minor component.

It can be said, then, that nuts were clearly an important resource at 20SA620. Their presence suggests that from the Terminal Archaic to the Late Woodland period the site was occupied during the late summer to early autumn when nuts would be available. The range of nut taxa varies from one occupation the other (Tables 10.1–10.3) but small sample sizes make it difficult to determine whether this variation reflects changing exploitation patterns through time or if it is simply a product of sampling error.

Tubers

Both terrestrial and aquatic tubers are present in low frequencies. Overall, tubers constitute only 0.5% of the assemblage by weight. Terrestrial tubers occur in a single instance (114N/101W, level 4) in association with all of the nut taxa (Table 10.2), suggesting that its presence in the assemblage is due to intentional use. Aquatic tubers are more abundant and appear throughout the horizontal and vertical dimensions of the site (Table 10.1–10.3), in association with Middle and Late Woodland ceramics.

Tubers, unlike nuts, do not occur in all samples; their high water content greatly reduces their potential for preservation. Ethnographic references do, however, indicate that a variety of terrestrial and aquatic tubers including groundnut (*Apios americana*); pepperroot (*Dentaria laciniata*); Jerusalem artichoke (*Helianthus tuberosus*); American lotus (*Nelumbo lutea*); yellow pond-lily (*Nuphar luteum*); and arrowleaf (*Sagittaria latifolia*) were regularly exploited by historic Indians of the Great Lakes (Erichson-Brown 1979; King 1984).

Tubers are available year round, but during historic times were most commonly exploited in the spring and fall when their starch content is highest (King 1984:21). Hence, while their presence in the 20SA620 assemblage does not provide a definitive seasonal indicator, on the basis of analogy with historic practices the presence of tuber at 20SA620 suggests a spring and/or autumn occupation of the site for collection and/or processing of tubers.

Seeds, Root, Stem and Buds

Fragments of carbonized stem and root were sporadically present in the assemblage (Tables 10.1–10.3). None were identifiable. It is difficult to interpret their significance in this context. Although there are numerous ethnographic references to the use of roots and stems of many plants for food, medicinal, and technological purposes, their presence in this assemblage may as easily be a result of accidental carbonization as intentional utilization.

Seed remains from 20SA620 are sparse. A total of 27 seeds of nine identifiable taxa were recovered. Nineteen (70%) or 1.5 per 10 liters were recovered from the flotation samples sorted with magnification. (It is important to note that the minimal recovery of seeds from the field-collected [11%] and unmagnified flotation [19%] samples is most likely an artifact of the sorting method.) Yet, the ratio of 1.5 per 10 liters is comparable to or greater than that recovered from other Archaic and Early Woodland seasonal camps such as the Weber I site (Egan 1988) and sites in south-central Illinois (Johannessen 1984). Greater quantities have been recovered from Middle and Late Woodland agricultural sites in the Midwest because of the intensive use of starchy seeded annuals (e.g., maygrass, little barley, and lamb's quarter) and the intensity of the occupations (see for example Johannessen 1984).

The majority of the identifiable seed taxa at 20SA620, including smartweed (*Polygonum* sp.), lamb's quarter (*Chenopodium* sp.), pink family (Caryophyllaceae), and grass family (Poaceae), are ruderals, which are common to disturbed habitats such as human occupation sites and stream banks. Parts (root, stem, bark) of all of these taxa were used by Great Lakes Indian groups during historic times for medicinal and technological purposes (Densmore 1974; Huron Smith 1932, 1933; Erichson-Brown 1979; King 1984). *Chenopodium* (*berlandieri* ssp. *jonesianum*) and *Polygonum* (*erectum*) were domesticated prehistorically in Eastern North America (see B. Smith 1987 and Asch and Asch 1985, respectively). These domesticates possess distinctive morphological attributes that the specimens from 20SA620 do not possess. Further, all of the ruderal seeds occur singly throughout the units in this sample suggesting that they represent accidental inclusions in the archaeological record from natural seed rain.

Hornbeam (*Carpinus caroliniana*) is an arboreal species. There are no ethnographic references to the use of hornbeam seeds and the presence of them in this assemblage (Table 10.1) is likely due to natural seed rain from trees in the vicinity of the site. The absence of this taxa in the charcoal assemblage is not surprising, however, because the wood of this tree is extremely hard and the trees do not easily shed branches.

Three taxa of food plants (blackberry/*Rubus* spp.; grape/*Vitis* sp.; squash/*Cucurbita pepo*) and another possible food plant (Rosaceae) are also represented among the seeds in the assemblage. Blackberry seeds make up the bulk of the identifiable seed sample, with a general class of rose family (Rosaceae) being the next most prevalent taxa (Tables 10.1–10.3). Those seeds identified as Rosaceae may in fact be members of the *Rubus* genus but are smaller than the normal range for *Rubus*. They are, however, similar in form and surface reticulation. Further, it should be noted that the seeds identified as *Rubus* were consistently on the smaller end of the seed dimensions reported for this genus (ca. 2 mm) (Martin and Barkley 1961:166).

According to ethnographic references, several of the genera of Rosaceae and species of *Rubus* common to the Saginaw Valley (Voss 1985:336–444) were used by the Upper Great Lakes Indians (Erichson-Brown 1979; King 1984). With regard specifically to the genus *Rubus*, there are many ethnographic references to the use of berries, both fresh and dried, as well as uses of the bark and roots for medicinal purposes (e.g., Waugh 1916:145; Densmore 1974:358; Huron Smith 1923:50, 1928:243, 1932:385, 1933:79). *Rubus* and Rosaceae seeds are also commonly found in archaeological sites in this region. *Rubus* seeds have been found throughout southern Michigan in Archaic and Woodland contexts (Yarnell 1964; N. Cleland 1989; Egan 1988; Parachini 1984c). In some localities, such as the Crawford Lake site, a late prehistoric site in Ontario, large quantities of carbonized *Rubus* spp. seeds (N = 1,052, in 54.5% of the features) suggest intensive exploitation of this resource (McAndrews et al. 1974:3).

The blackberry and Rosaceae seeds from 20SA620 are distributed more widely over the excavated area and occur in association with other food plants. These seeds are ubiquitous and occur in relatively high percentages (blackberry, 33%; Rosaceae, 7%) in comparison to other seed taxa in the assemblage. The distribution of these seeds suggests regular exploitation of these resources although higher densities in the upper excavation levels of the site (Table 10.3) suggest greater exploitation during the Late Woodland occupation. Depending on the species, blackberry and rose fruits are available from July through September. Given the timing of availability of other resources in the assemblage it is likely that the blackberry and rose fruits were collected in the late summer. The type of use and processing—whether used fresh or dried over a fire—influences the potential for archaeological preservation through carbonization and may in part account for the variation observed.

The single grape seed (*Vitis* sp.) from level 6–7 of unit 120N/101W is of questionable economic significance. Grape's preference for stream margins, such as that adjacent to the site, makes its depositional origin suspect. We know, however, that grape was commonly used prehistorically, and ethnographic sources also document its use in historic times; so the association of the grape seed with other edible plant remains (i.e., blackberry seeds) suggests that its occurrence in this assemblage is due to cultural factors. Grapes ripen in September and would have been collected at that time.

Squash (*C. pepo*) is represented by a single carbonized seed endosperm (120N/101W, level 10–11) stratigraphically at or below Middle Woodland deposits and in association with nut remains (Juglandaceae and acorn). The pericarp is absent from this specimen and the identification is based on comparison of seed size and shape with modern and archaeological comparative collections. With regard to these attributes, the specimens compare well. In addition, there are few if any other taxa present in this geographic area with similar characteristics, so identification can be made with confidence (Richard Ford, personal communication). Squash is not native to this region. Therefore, its occurrence in this context clearly indicates cultural exploitation of this resource during the late summer when it could be harvested.

The only other identifiable carbonized flora recovered from the site are four buds. They occur at the northern and southern ends of the excavation trench (Table 10.1). They were not identifiable to family but are likely from a shrub or tree. Their cultural significance is unknown.

PREVIOUSLY RECOVERED FLORAL REMAINS

Testing of the site prior to the 1985 field season, resulted in the recovery of wood, acorn, grape, and squash remains. The locations and results of these excavations are discussed by Brunett (1983), and in Chapter 1.

Squash seeds, recovered during Brunett's testing of the site, are relatively abundant ($N = 9$) as compared with the other seed taxa, and they are uncarbonized. As discussed in the methods section of this chapter, uncarbonized seeds were considered modern in this analysis. In this case, the modern interpretation is supported by the fact that the squash seeds are similar in size and form to modern pumpkin seeds.

In addition to the squash seeds, 4.3 g of wood charcoal, 1.4 g of bark charcoal, one uncarbonized acorn and one grape seed were recovered by Bowen from a feature. The charcoal was considerably less dense and in much larger pieces than the charcoal recovered during the 1985 field season. Identifiable remains were red oak and ring-porous woods.

The uncarbonized grape and acorn are considered modern contaminants but the charcoal was submitted for radiocarbon dating and produced a date of 880 ± 80 b.p. (Chapter 5). The qualitative and quantitative differences between this charcoal and the specimens from the 1985 excavations are likely due to the differences in their depositional contexts. The materials collected in the 1985 excavations were deposited in a midden and were therefore subject to constant trampling and disturbance, while the charcoal recovered by Bowen was in a pit feature and therefore less likely to be crushed and fragmented by human activity.

This analysis suggests that the archaeobotanical remains recovered by Brunett are remains of modern agricultural activities. The feature excavated by Bowen clearly contains Late Woodland materials although there is evidence of disturbance that probably introduced the uncarbonized acorn and grape seed found in the feature.

INTERSITE COMPARISON

Comparing the 20SA620 archaeobotanical assemblage with the results of archaeobotanical analyses of other sites in southern Michigan aids in the interpretation of the 20SA620 subsistence pattern. In addition, such intersite comparisons contribute to our understanding of broader trends in prehistoric subsistence patterns in southern Michigan and the Saginaw Valley in particular.

The overall density of charcoal from 20SA620 (111.6 pieces; 0.88 g per 10 liters) is comparable to that recovered from the Late Archaic component at the Weber I site (99.9 pieces; 1.1 g per 10 liters) (Egan 1988). The charcoal from 20SA620, however, is primarily from midden contexts, while the majority of the charcoal from Occupation Zone I at the Weber I site is from feature contexts. Because features in occupied sites tend to have higher densities of charcoal than midden contexts, and both sites were occupied during the same season, the wood charcoal denisty from 20SA620 is likely the product of its long-term occupation.

The percentages of wood taxa from 20SA620 cannot be considered a quantitatively accurate reflection of the prehistoric forest composition because of the effects of cultural selection for firewood. However, it is significant that the 20SA620 assemblage contains a greater proportion of oak (67.1 %) than the Late Archaic assemblage from Weber I (57.0%). This difference may be due to one of two factors. First, it may simply be a reflection of phytogeographic differences between the two site locations, such that the 20SA620 locality possessed a greater abundance of oak. Although pollen data indicates that an essentially modern forest type was established in the Saginaw Valley as early as 5000 b.p. (Kapp 1977), remnant early postglacial communities persisted in the valley until a later date. For example, the Late Archaic component from the Weber I site, dating 2900–3000 b.p., contains a relatively high percentage (7.2%) of pine charcoal (Egan 1988: 22). An alternative explanation is that during Woodland times there was a preference for oak which burns at a more consistent temperature and is better for use with ceramics (Richard Ford, personal communication).

Considerable differences also exist among the types and quantities of nutshell represented at 20SA620 and other sites in southern Michigan. By weight, 20SA620 has a greater percentage (12.7%) of nut remains than several other sites in the area (Table 10.7). The sites with such low densities of nut remains have been interpreted as short-term occupations in which nut exploitation was not a major activity. The one exception to this pattern is the Wymer site (20BE122), a Late Archaic/Early Woodland occupation in Barrien County (Michigan) that has been interpreted as a spring and fall harvesting local for exploitation of nut as well as sturgeon and aquatic tuber (Parachini 1984d). In this instance, however, the quantity of nut is overshadowed by large quantities of charcoal and bark associated with smoking sturgeon and roasting aquatic tubers.

Three sites have greater quantities of nutshell than 20SA620. These sites are: the Rock Hearth site (20BE306), a Late Archaic and possible Middle or Late Woodland site in Berrien County; the Schultz site (20SA2), an Early through Late Woodland site in the Saginaw Valley; and Occupation Zone I from the Weber I site (20SA581), a Late Archaic occupation in the Saginaw Valley. At Rock Hearth, nutshell represented 14% of the weight of the floral assemblage. In this case, the majority of the nut remains appear to be associated with the Late Archaic component, and the site was probably a fall camp for harvesting black walnuts and butternut (Parachini 1984c). The entire

TABLE 10.7
Percentage by Weight of Nut Remains from Other Michigan Sites

	% of Nutshell[a]	Time Period	Reference
Schultz site (20SA2)	23%	Early Woodland Middle Woodland	Allison 1972
Home Depot site (20WA176)	1%	early Late Woodland	Egan 1987b
King site (20BE354)	0.3%	Late Archaic to Early Woodland Late Woodland	Parachini 1984a
Stover site (20BE307)	2%	Late Archaic to Early Woodland Late Woodland	Parachini 1984b
Rock Hearth site (20BE306)	14%	Late Archaic possible Middle or Late Woodland	Parachini 1984c
Wymer site (20BE132)	10%	Late Archaic to Early Woodland	Parachini 1984d
Eidson site (20BE122)	6%	Paleo Indian through Middle Woodland	Parachini 1984e
Weber I (20SA581)	48%	Late Archaic	Egan 1988

[a]To total floral weight.

floral assemblage from the Schultz site contained 23% nutshell by weight (Allison 1972), and the assemblage contained greater quantities of black walnut and butternut than does 20SA620. Allison (1972) reports that there was a decrease in nut use from the Early Woodland to the late Middle Woodland (dropping from 90% to 12% of the weight) and that nut continues to decrease in occurrence throughout the later occupation. Finally, the Late Archaic occupation (Occupation Zone I) at the Weber I site has an exceptionally high percentage (48%) of nut remains (Egan 1988). In this case exploitation of a variety of nut taxa (black walnut, hickory, Juglandaceae, and acorn) was clearly an important activity.

The pattern suggested by these sites is one of intensive exploitation of nut resources during the Late Archaic/Early Woodland and decreasing dependence on nuts during the Middle and Late Woodland periods. Such a decrease in nut use, however, is not apparent in the floral assemblage from 20SA620. Rather, nut exploitation appears to be more intensive and extensive during the Late Woodland at 20SA620. Interestingly, the archaeobotanical assemblage from the Birch Run Road site (20SA393), a Late Woodland site in the Saginaw Valley, also exhibits considerable variability in the types of nut exploited. One feature at the site contains large quantities of acorn, hickory, black walnut, butternut, and beech (Parker 1985). Hence, the Birch Run Road site and 20SA620 together suggest that a greater variety of nuts were exploited during the Late Woodland than during other time periods in the Saginaw Valley.

As is the case with 20SA620, tuber remains have occasionally been recovered from other archaeological sites in southern Michigan (e.g., Elam site [Parachini 1981; DeRoo and Parker 1989]; Schwerdt site [Cremin 1980; Walz 1989]; Eidson site [Parachini 1984e]; Wymer site [Parachini 1984d]; Birch Run Road site [Parker 1985]; Home Depot site [Egan 1987]). The regular occurrence of these easily decomposed plants indicates that tubers were commonly used during the Woodland period in southern Michigan. Furthermore, there is a marked increase in the occurrence of aquatic tubers in the Late Woodland. This increase may in part be related to increases in the availability of tubers during this time period because of fluctuations in lake levels and development of marshes in low areas (see also Lovis 1985; Larsen 1987). During the Woodland period, marshes would have provided a stable, high-yield resource to the occupants of the Saginaw Valley and the 20SA620 site, as well as other sites in southern Michigan.

The carbonized squash endosperm recovered during the 1985 excavation of 20SA620 is considered the only prehistoric domesticate in the assemblage; the squash seeds recovered by Brunett are considered modern. This domesticate is not native to the Saginaw Valley but rather it is a tropical cultigen that was, perhaps, introduced into the lower Illinois River valley as early as 7000 b.p. (Asch and Asch 1985). In the Saginaw Valley, squash is present in Early Woodland componenets of the Schultz and Green Point sites (Wright 1964; Ozker 1982; King 1985). At the Schultz site a clear impression of the pericarp is visible on a Schultz Thick ceramic vessel (Ozker 1982:38–40) and at the Green Point site *Cucurbit pepo* seeds ($N = 2$) were recovered beneath the Middle Woodland stratum (Wright 1964). The presence of a third specimen at 20SA620 helps to confirm the use of this resource by Early or Middle Woodland occupants of the Saginaw Valley.

While these isolated occurrences of squash represent only a small portion of these assemblages, the possibility that squash seeds or rind fragments will be preserved is extremely low. At the historic Zimmerman site in northern Illinois, for example, ethnographic accounts indicate that large numbers of pumpkins were grown and stored at the site, yet only two rind fragments were recovered from the archaeobotanical assemblage (Asch and Asch 1975).

Therefore, the economic role of squash in the Saginaw Valley is not yet clear. Ozker (1982) argues that they served as vessels for storing nut oils. While thin-fleshed squash rinds have often been used as containers, their seeds are also edible and highly nutritious (King 1985). Hence, squash may have served as containers and a food resource in the Saginaw Valley. Because squash is an adventive species, once introduced into a locale it can easily establish itself as a camp-follower. Fruit or squashes would be available for harvesting in the late summer or early fall (August through September) along with a variety of other fruits and nuts. Squash would require no more energy investment than any other naturally available resource and its collection could be carried out in conjunction with other gathering activities.

The differences between the 20SA620 archaeobotanical assemblage and those of other sites in southern Michigan may be due to several factors: changing subsistence patterns over time; differences in site function and seasonality; varying mast cycles among nut taxa; and differences in the availability of nut resources within any site catchment.

SUMMARY AND CONCLUSIONS

Initially, the transition from the Late Archaic to Woodland in the Saginaw Valley was thought to be part of a widespread change from hunting and gathering to a subsistence pattern based on agriculture (Yarnell 1964; C. Cleland 1966; Fitting 1969; Peebles 1978). More recent studies suggest, however, that a shift toward intensive agriculture did not occur until late in the prehistory of the area (Krakker 1983; Lovis 1985) and that hunting and gathering persisted throughout the earlier periods. The 20SA620 archaeobotanical assemblage supports this latter model.

On the basis of this assemblage and the intersite comparison it seems that nuts were an important resource in the Saginaw Valley from the Late Archaic through the Late Woodland. There is considerable variation in the overall quantity of nut and the representation of each taxa at sites in the valley. Therefore, the changing pattern of nut exploitation at 20SA620 does not characterize the overall subsistence pattern of the Saginaw Valley. Rather, the variation seems to be a result of differences in site function and nut availability. There is, however, a clear trend toward increasing use of aquatic tubers from the Middle Woodland through the Late Woodland in southern Michigan (Lovis 1985). The assemblage from 20SA620 fits this pattern well. In addition, the occurrence of squash in the Late Archaic/Early Woodland component at 20SA620 supports an early introduction of squash into this region (Ozker 1982). The absence of squash or other cultigens or domesticates in the later components of 20SA620 suggests, however, that agriculture was not a significant activity at the site until later in the Late Woodland period. Finally, the seeds recovered from 20SA620 indicate that fruits were gathered (especially *Rubus* spp.) but suggest that consumption and processing of berries were not major activities at the site.

11
Distributional Analysis

John M. O'Shea
Museum of Anthropology, University of Michigan

INTRODUCTION

Although the principal materials recovered from the Bridgeport Township site have been discussed in some detail, they have yet to be drawn together as parts of a single whole, in this instance as the coherent remains of prehistoric occupation at this site. The nature of the site makes this integration particularly difficult. As was noted in Chapter 4, the visual homogeneity of the archaeological deposit made the detection of distinct strata during excavation impossible. In addition, there has been extensive postdepositional modification of the site, including the disturbance of earlier layers by later prehistoric occupation, the extensive reworking of site deposits by small mammals, and more recently, the destruction of much of the site during land leveling. These disturbances have mixed or obscured the spatial and stratigraphic relationships that are the clues to understanding the nature of the prehistoric activities on the site. Nevertheless, the task of this chapter is to highlight the residual stratigraphic and spatial structure that is preserved in the site and to use this information to consider the character of the site's use through time.

To discover the remnant structure within the site, the density distribution of four categories of cultural material over the excavated site area was evaluated. It was expected that despite the considerable "noise" that has been introduced into the site by postdepositional disturbance, general trends in the stratigraphic and spatial distribution of materials would provide evidence for the location of specific occupation loci. The coherence of such loci, relative to the various categories of cultural material, may offer suggestions as to the degree of integrity of a given occupation surface, as well as clues to the kinds of activities that occurred in the immediate area. If such intact zones do exist within the site, they will represent only fragments of the occupation surface area, particularly when the lower levels of the site are considered. Of course, even when such surfaces are identified, they only represent a statistical generalization as distinct from a truly intact and undisturbed deposit. For this reason, the occurrence of specific diagnostic artifacts may or may not date to the same period as other objects on the surface. These limitations will be discussed in more detail in the final section of this chapter.

In this chapter, the discussion of site patterning proceeds in several steps. First the profile distribution of fire-cracked rock (FCR) is considered to provide a stratigraphic view of occupational intensity within the site that was not visible during excavation. This is followed by a description of the plan distribution of four categories of cultural material—FCR, daub, ceramic material, and lithic material—over the the entire site. Following the discussion of these distributions, the presumed occupational surfaces, distinguished during the preceding analysis, will be considered from the perspective of the activities they may imply for the site. The distribution of recognized site features and of faunal and floral materials will also be considered relative to these inferred occupation surfaces.

PROCEDURES

Without a doubt, the most commonly occurring material recovered during the excavations at 20SA620 was fire-cracked-rock. More than 585 kg of FCR was recovered, representing an average density of nearly 10 kg/m^3 of site deposit. FCR was not uniformly distributed throughout the site, however, and the character of its distribution can provide a useful guide for understanding both the stratigraphic character of the site, which was not obvious during excavation, and the spatial separation of activities over the site.

Counts and weights for FCR were recorded for each provenience unit excavated, with stone greater than, and less than, 16 mm in diameter recorded separately. As the distributional analysis of FCR began, it was immediately apparent that the total weight of FCR for each provenience unit was the most informative, and least spurious, value for analysis, and so it is on this value that the present results are based. The density contours plotted on both the plan and profile maps reflect gradations of one kilogram.

In five instances, complete weights were not available for a given square level due either to loss in the field or to processing error in the lab. In these cases a value for the missing level was estimated by interpolating between the values in the levels adjacent to the missing one. Values were interpolated for 104N/101W level 2–3; 105N/101W level 4–5; 114N/104W level 4–5; 114N/103W level 6–7; and 117N/103W level 6–7.

Daub—untempered fired clay—was represented at the Bridgeport Township site in the form of very small "crumbs" of irregular shape, with a maximum dimension rarely exceeding 1 cm. The largest single specimen of daub was recovered from square 111N/102W, level 8–9. It weighs 6.4 g and has a maximium dimension of 2.6 cm. The total quantity of daub recovered was 245 g, occurring in 92 of the 299 possible site levels. This represents an average occurrence over the entire site of 0.8 g/square level, and 2.7 g/square level average in those where daub was present.

The daub recovered from the site does not appear to be architectural in nature. Rather, it generally occurs in irregular forms, occasionally with small impressions suggestive of twigs or small woody plant stems. Overall, the daub is similar to that reported at the Schultz site by Ozker (1982). Although there is no direct evidence for the function of daub at Bridgeport, the pattern of spatial occurrence, particularly its regular proximity to hearth features, may support the assertion by Ozker (1982:154) that it was used in food preparation.

The third category is ceramic material. Two aspects of the ceramic distribution are considered: the distribution of sherds over the site; and the location of diagnostic rims when they are present. Sherd density by weight was considered separately for sherds greater than, and less than 2 cm in size. (Although only those greater than 2 cm are illustrated in this report.) For additional information concerning the distribution of specific kinds of body sherds or sherd attributes, see Chapter 8.

The final category is lithic material. Since the lithic material from the site has already been described in Chapter 7, consideration here is limited to an analysis of density distribution over the site. Unlike the other categories of material plotted, flakage values were plotted on the basis of counts, rather than weights.

Patterned stone tools, like rim sherds, also were plotted and included in the distributional analysis. In the plans that follow, tools are plotted in the center of the units in which they were found.

One problem that had to be resolved was how to maintain comparability between provenience units. Since many of the lower levels of the site were excavated in combined 20 cm levels, rather than the standard 10 cm level (see Chapter 4), a decision regarding comparability between such units was required. Two options were explored: to arbitrarily divide the 20 cm levels in half, assigning half the materials to the upper and half to the lower levels; or to combine all the standard 10 cm levels into 20 cm units. Although the first option seemed to retain the maximum existing stratigraphic definition for the distributions, much of this definition in the lower site levels would inevitably be spurious given the necessarily arbitrary division of levels. After some experimentation, the second option was adopted for all materials, since it provided the highest level of reliable comparability between the units. Fortunately during excavation the same pairs of 10 cm levels were combined, which facilitated the pairing process. For the purpose of analysis, the following levels were paired: levels 2–3, 4–5, 6–7, 8–9, 10–11 and 12–13. Although level 14 was excavated in a few squares, it was excluded from consideration for lack of sufficient comparable material. Similarly, because level 1 occurred in only five squares, (and often did not provide a full 10 cm depth due to variations in surface contour), it was not combined with any other level. Although the weights for FCR in these levels are presented in the profiles illustrated, the values do not figure in the analysis.

The weights for each material class (excepting lithic material, which was plotted by count) were coded by square and level and were processed by two small BASIC programs (PRO and PLAN), which produced profiles and plan views, respectively, over the site. These density maps were then contoured by hand. Squares in which the specific level did not exist or in which excavation was precluded by standing trees (see Chapter 4) are represented by hatching. North-south profiles of the site were constructed for transects 101W, 102W, and 103W (Figs. 11.1*a-c*). Plan views were drawn for each material class for levels 6–7, 8–9, and 10–11.

FCR PROFILE DISTRIBUTION

Since stratigraphic separation of occupation layers was not possible during excavation, the profile distribution of FCR, the most ubiquitous material present at the site, offered the potential of providing a provisional stratigraphy reflecting the intensity of activity at differing levels of the site. This information could then be used to assess the potential for stratigraphic separation of the archaeological components at the site.

The density of FCR was considered for north-south site transects at 101W, 102W, and 103W. Although different in detail, each transect exhibits the same basic pattern. The greatest density of FCR uniformly occurs in level 6–7. The main concentration appears to be located in the range 105N to 114N, with the precise locus of concentration shifting northward as one moves from transect 101W to 103W. This shift reflects the constricting shape of the unmodified landform, which progressively narrows to the west. Within this zone, two square levels exhibited particularly high densities: 106N/101W and 110N/102W. In both instances the FCR density was greater than 10 kg/0.2 m^3 (greater than 50 kg/m^3). In both instances, the FCR densities at lower levels of the same squares reveal similarly high values, suggesting they may both have been either hearths, or shallow basin-shaped features.

The levels below this primary occupation zone in level 6–7 exhibit high densities of FCR that for the most part mirror (but in reduced quantities) the densities observed in level 6–7. Although considerable vertical movement of cultural materials has taken place at the site, the relatively regular and horizontal distribution of FCR observed in these profiles suggests that much of this vertical mixing was on the scale of 10 to 20 cm. Although the pattern

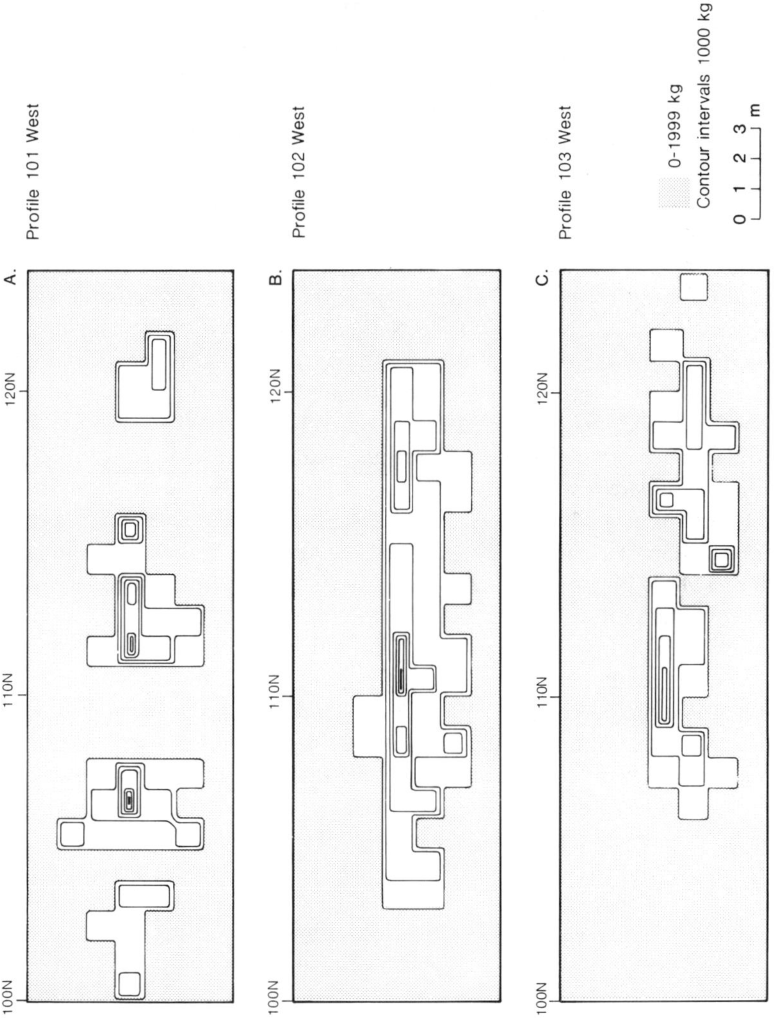

Figure 11.1. Profile density of FCR.

of FCR occurrence from level 6–7 is repeated virtually to the base of the cultural deposit in the southern portion of the site, this distribution probably reflects both the existence of features associated with the primary occupation that extended below the main living surface, as well as postdepositional movement of materials. We will return to this consideration after the distributions of other cultural materials are considered.

In addition to the main concentration of FCR in the southern half of the site in level 6–7, a series of smaller concentrations can be observed at lower levels in the northern half of the site that may represent distinct and potentially earlier occupation components. The most prominent of these occurs in level 8–9 from unit 118N to 121N. This locus of material extends uniformly east and west across the site and is in an area with much lower quantities of FCR in the upper levels. The greatest density of FCR within this region occurs in square 119N/103W, with a density of over 5 kg/0.2 m^3.

A third concentration of FCR occurs in level 10–11, from unit 114N to unit 116N. This concentration covers a smaller area than those already described, being visible primarily in transect 103W, and in only reduced form in transect 102W. Despite its limited distribution, the greatest density within the zone is again in the range of 5 kg/0.2 m^3 in 114N/103W.

A final concentration of FCR was encountered at the extreme north end of the site, in square 128N/103W. This concentration also occurred at level 10–11, and in a region with very little material in the layers above it. Although the absolute density, 2 kg/0.2 m^3, is not high, it is the only square north of 121N with a density in this range. Its isolated character and its depth make it worthy of note.

Overall, the profile distribution of FCR suggests that the principal site occupation is represented within the range of levels 6 through 9, with level 6–7 representing the main level of concentration and the closest approximation to an intact occupation surface. Below this occupation zone, traces of one and possibly two earlier occupation zones may be discerned in the northern half of the site, one focusing on level 8–9, and another at level 10–11. Although the main occupation appears to extend over much of the site, distinct occupations in the lower (earlier) levels may only be discernible in areas of limited later activity. A consideration of the plan distribution of FCR in these three levels will help clarify this assertion.

PLAN DISTRIBUTION OF CULTURAL MATERIALS

In this section the distribution of FCR is considered in plan view over the site for the three principal occupation levels noted in the preceding section, levels 6–7, 8–9, and 10–11. For each of these levels, the FCR distribution is briefly described and compared with equivalent patterns produced by daub, ceramics and lithics. In this manner both the existence and the potential character of remnant occupation surfaces can be explored.

Level 6–7

The plan view of FCR surface density for level 6–7 provides very clear patterning that is suggestive of the structure of a portion of the primary site component (Fig. 11.2*a*). The plan shows two areas of very high FCR concentrations that might be hearths in the southern end of the site, a broad scattering of FCR in a roughly circular fall-off pattern out from these features, and a possible second use zone in the central portion of the site. This second zone was not clearly discernible in the profile view of the site. These areas are designated surfaces 1 and 2 respectively. FCR concentration at this level clearly trails off as one moves further north on the site. The pattern of fall-off observed in FCR density also confirms that the primary occupation zone continued both west, into the area that was disturbed prior to excavation, and east, on the extension of the knoll feature beyond the township property line. As was noted in Chapter 5, the extreme southern end of the site was disturbed in modern times by the burial of a cow, and the densities of FCR in this zone are not considered meaningful. The apparent clarity of this plan view also tends to support the assertion made concerning the distribution of ceramic "fits" (Chapter 8): that relatively little lateral movement of materials has occurred on the site. The small lithic assemblage presents no definitive patterns in this respect.

The distribution of daub at this level, plotted by linking contiguous squares that produced daub, coincides very closely with the observed FCR concentrations (Fig. 11.3*a*), although in each case the daub scatter is offset from the point of densest FCR concentration. Only a small amount of daub was encountered in the northern two-thirds of the site at this level.

The distribution of ceramics within this level (Fig. 8.7*b*) exhibits a pattern that is very similar to the distribution of daub just described. There is a clear concentration of sherds in the southern third of the site that coincides with the two major concentrations of FCR in the area (surface 1). Like the daub, the areas of heavy sherd concentration are offset from the main points of FCR concentration. The density of pottery in the middle third of the site is extremely high, and is of a greater areal extent than the daub. This concentration of pottery coincides with surface 2, defined by the FCR distribution.

Sherds greater than and less then 2 cm are distributed in a nearly identical fashion over the site at this level. The one area of discordance is in the vicinity of squares 110N/102W and 109N/103W. In this region, which is very close to a possible hearth, a uniform, low density scatter of small sherds is contrasted with a dense concentration of larger sherds. A similar, although less marked, version of this pattern can be observed in the area of squares

118–120N/102W, again in the vicinity of a possible hearth. Given the likely depositional and postdepositional factors that determine the number of sherds of each size that survive to recovery, it is possible that these represent areas of less trampling during the site occupation. Alternatively, they simply may be areas of less postdepositional disturbance. The close agreement between the major densities of pottery and of FCR may also suggest a relatively expedient pattern of refuse discard, with vessels, whether functioning as receptacles for storage or food preparation, being discarded in the immediate vicinity of use and breakage. This pattern of discard will be considered again after all the level comparisons have been completed.

The distribution of flakage in level 6–7 (Fig. 11.4*a*) presents a pattern of scatter similar to all those discussed so far and is more directly comparable to the distribution of FCR than either the ceramics or daub. The areas of densest flake distribution in the southern third of the site coincide closely with the location of the two presumed hearths. Although the scattering of flakes is relatively uniform in this region of the site, it suggests the same northern boundary to surface 1 that was represented in all the other materials examined.

The central portion of the site in level 6–7 (surface 2) exhibits a more generalized scattering of flakage, in contrast to the very dense ceramic concentrations observed in the area of square 114N/103W. One square within surface 2 (117N/102W) did exhibit a relatively higher density ($N = 90$) of flakage than the surrounding squares. Interestingly, this square also had the highest density of FCR.

Although diagnostic rims were relatively rare at the Bridgeport Township site, it still is possible, particularly at this upper level, to compare their distribution with the density clusters already described (see Fig. 8.10*left*). The southern site concentration (surface 1), even with the potential mixing in the extreme southern squares (see Chapter 4), is overwhelmingly early Late Woodland in age. The consistency of this distribution of diagnostic rims supports the assertion that this area represents a largely intact living surface, associated with the main occupation episode at the site. The plotting of diagnostic rims also supports the reality of the second occupation surface (surface 2) in the central portion of the site. Somewhat unexpectedly, the diagnostics associated with this cluster seem to be primarily later Middle Woodland, although some mixing with both earlier and later materials is observed.

To summarize the distributions observed in level 6–7, all material classes examined support the existence of two relatively distinct and intact zones within the site: surface 1 in the southern third of the excavated area, and surface 2 in the center of the site. No doubt there is some significant mixing of these two occupation surfaces in the central portion of the site. The occurrence of diagnostic rims within these two identified regions suggests that the more southerly one is associated with an earlier Late Woodland occupation at the site, while the intact portion of the middle zone may be of transitional Middle/Late Woodland. It is unclear at this depth whether the deposits in the northern sector of the site represent simply sheet midden or slope wash from the slightly higher portions of the site to the south, or whether the lower quantities of materials, particularly FCR and daub, are indicative of some different form of site activity in this area.

Level 8–9

The plan view of FCR for level 8–9 (Fig. 11.2*b*) is less well defined than the previous levels described, and represents both the downward extension of site features from level 6–7, as well as remnants of an earlier occupation zone. In the entire southern half of the site, these two sources of FCR are indistinguishable. A potential third remnant of an occupation zone (surface 3) is also suggested in the north central portion of the site. Two points of relatively high concentration associated with this surface are squares 119N/103W and 123N/103W. The amount of disturbance which has affected this lower horizon, both cultural and animal, precludes a detailed description of the spatial structure of this component, however.

The distribution of daub within level 8–9 broadly fits with this model of site occupation (Fig. 11.3*b*). In the southern third of the site, scattered patches of daub underlay the early Late Woodland surface, and suggest stratigraphic continuity with it. The broad zone of daub that occurs in the central portion of the excavated area may similarly reflect the second living surface as described previously. The lack of spatial continuity between these two surfaces in the distribution of daub lends credence to their independent characters. In addition, the scattered pockets of daub that occur in the vicinity of 120N may in actuality be associated with a third habitation surface, suggested also by the FCR concentration focused on square 119N/103W (surface 3), and distinct from the more central surface 2. The effective absence of daub from the more northerly portions of the site suggests at this level, as seen previously, that either the character of use or of depositional context is in some manner different in this area of the site.

The distribution of ceramics at this level (see Fig. 8.8*a*) mirrors that of the FCR in all but the northern portion of the site. While small sherds are scattered uniformly over the southern two-thirds of the site, larger sherds reflect the two distinct concentrations noted previously (surfaces 1 and 2). The fit between the central scatter of larger sherds and daub is also very good, although both are offset to the south from the denser FCR concentrations at this level. The presence of a possible third site surface, in the vicinity of site area 120N, is only weakly supported by the distribution of ceramics which seems, rather, to suggest a degree of continuity into the more northerly area of the site. The

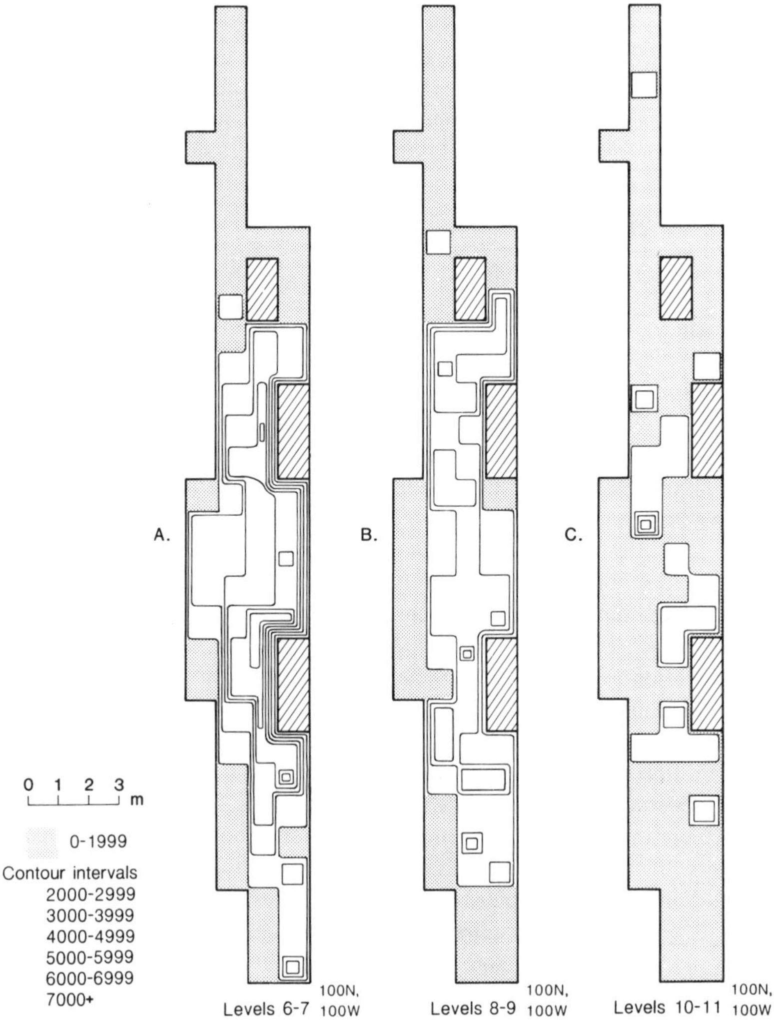

Figure 11.2. Plan density of FCR.

distribution of ceramics also continues into the far north of the excavated site area, with a relatively heavy concentration of sherds, particularly those less than 2 cm in size, in the vicinity of squares 124–125N/103W.

Lithic material is scattered more evenly across the site with only a very few areas of locally high concentration (Fig. 11.4*b*). One such location is found in square 104N/102W, which presumably is a downward continuation of the early Late Woodland occupation noted in level 6–7. A second concentration

Figure 11.3. Plan density of daub.

is found in square 117N/102W, which is in the vicinity of surface 2. In both of these instances there is a very close correspondence between areas of high FCR density and high flake counts. Several small pockets of higher flake counts are found, discontinuosly, in the area of the possible third occupation surface in the vicinity of site row 120N. The isolated character of these occurrences, however, makes them difficult to interpret. A final cluster of flakage that corresponds only to modest quantities of FCR occurs in the

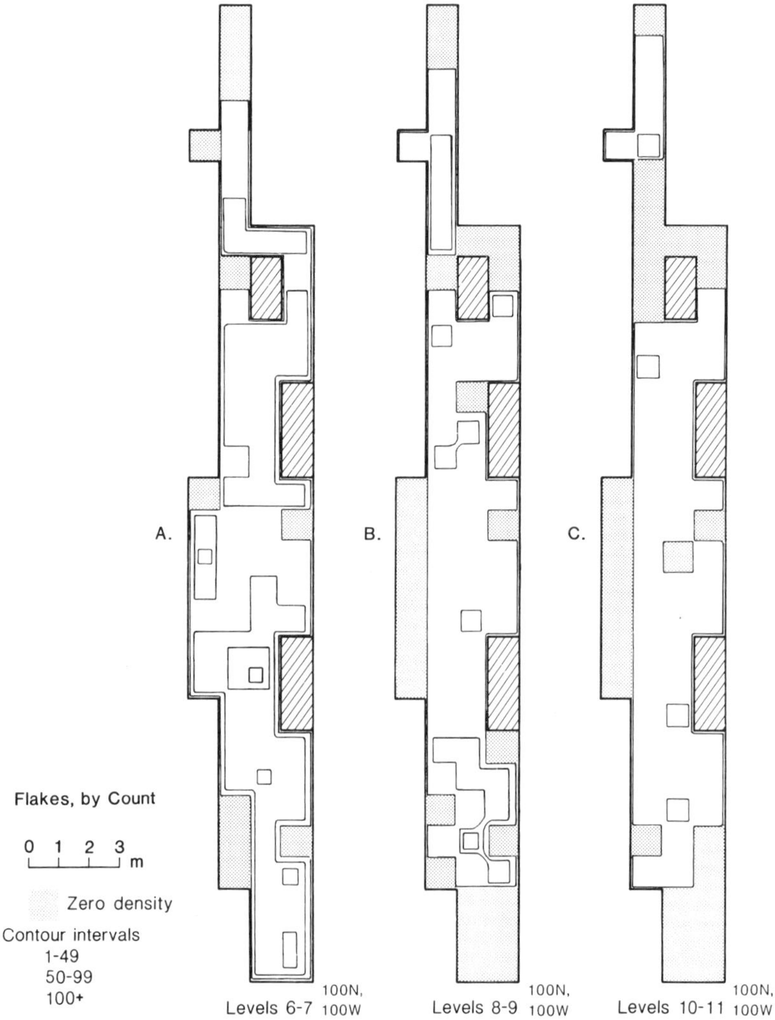

Figure 11.4. Plan density of lithic material.

northern portion of the site (surface 4). Here, as in level 6–7, ceramics and flakage occur in some abundance, with only modest concentrations of FCR and daub.

Overall, level 8–9 reveals a downward continuation of the two major occupation areas identified in level 6–7, along with possibly two additional fragments of living surface in the more northerly portion of the site. The information gleaned from these zones is limited, given the small number of diagnostic rims recovered here. Those present tend to confirm the downward impact of the main, early Late Woodland occupation, represented by surface 1, on level 8–9, and are unfortunately ambiguous regarding the age of the more northerly zones (surfaces 3 and 4) where both Wayne and Green Point vessels are represented. The plan distributions at this level also exhibit considerable consistency in their internal patterning with the preceding levels. The density of flakage and FCR continues to exhibit very similar patterns of spatial occurrence. Daub and ceramics also share a similar pattern of distribution across the site, and one in which the points of highest density generally coincide, although often a meter or two offset, with the major concentrations of FCR. The coincidence of flakage and ceramics in the northern portion of the site, labeled surface 4, is interesting since it argues for the existence of occupation surfaces associated with little FCR or daub. If similar zones existed in the more southerly portions of the site at this level, they would be undetectable due to the preponderance of materials associated with the later occupation in that area.

Level 10–11

Level 10–11 is the final plan view of the site that will be considered here. The plan view of level 10–11 presents what is effectively the base of the cultural deposit in most squares. For the southern half of the site, the densities still seem to reflect the continued influence of surfaces 1 and 2 from level 6–7 (Fig. 11.2*c*). In the central portion of the site, two basal features are worthy of note. There is the suggestion of the downward extension of the earlier occupation zone noted in level 8–9 (surface 3). The isolated character of this downward extension of FCR is largely limited to square 118N/103W, and may suggest the location of another hearth basin. An isolated concentration of FCR that was noted in the previous level (surface 4) is located in the extreme north end of the site. Although it, again, is represented only by modest quantities of FCR, the lack of high FCR densities in the levels above it and its isolated character, may suggest that it represents the remnant of an intact feature. Finally, the surprisingly high density of FCR in square 114N/103W may suggest the existence of a yet deeper hearth, and potentially a fifth occupation surface (represented by modest densities of FCR).

These interpretations of level 10–11 are strongly supported by the distribution of other cultural materials. Only scattered pockets of daub were observed in the southern half of the site (Fig. 11.3*c*). Indeed, the only continuous spread of daub recognized at this level occurs in the squares surrounding 119N/102W. This spread of daub seems to be associated with surface 3, as it is scattered around the area of densest FCR concentration associated with this surface. It is interesting that the sheet distribution of daub associated with this surface is visible only at this depth, and not at level 8–9, where the surface was first identified by a concentration of FCR. This may argue that the occupation is more directly associated with level 10–11, and that the FCR higher up is displaced. Although such an interpretation may seem contraintuitive, it seems difficult to otherwise explain the very distinct level differences in the distribution of daub in this area. No daub was observed north of this zone at this level.

The sherds smaller than 2 cm in diameter were distributed more or less evenly over the site at this level, but several concentrations were observed in the larger size category. The more southerly group of these seems to be a remnant of surface 2, while the northerly one might be associated, though offset as discussed previously, with the FCR concentrations of surfaces 3 and 5. Lithic material also was uniformly distributed in this level (Fig. 11.4*c*), with only four squares producing 50 or more flakes. Two of these, both located in the southern quarter of the site, probably still relate to surface 1. The remaining two are in the area of surfaces 3 and 5, mirroring again the distribution of FCR.

This final level of the site provides good evidence both for the continued downward effect of later occupations on the site deposit, particularly from surfaces 1 and 2, and for the increased definition of surfaces 3 and 4. The broad scatter of daub associated with surface 3 at this level, unprecedented in higher levels, may suggest that surface 3 is primarily associated with this, rather than higher levels. By contrast, the appearance of an FCR concentration associated with surface 4, may simply reflect the "subsurface" nature of the hearth or oven responsible for this feature, arguing that the surface, proper, may more accurately be associated with level 8–9, although it continues to a greater depth.

The final surface that is suggested at this level, termed surface 5, was defined on the basis of an unexpectedly high concentration of FCR (indeed the highest density figure for FCR in level 10–11). Its distinctness should be questioned, however, given its close proximity to surface 3 and the absence of other cultural material distributions to confirm the existence of a separate occupation. As such, it probably is most reasonable to consider the high concentration of FCR in square 114N/103W, as representing a downward extension or subsurface feature, such as a hearth or oven, associated with surface 3.

Unfortunately, only three diagnostic rims were recovered from this level, and the conclusions that can be drawn from them are tenuous. The one rim associated with surface 4 at this depth is Middle Woodland Tittabawassee ware, while a rim in the central portion of the site (surface 3) is also Middle Woodland in age. The third rim, representing vessel 17, is either of Middle Woodland or later Late Woodland age. The consistency of these dates lends credence to the supposition that these lower surfaces represent Middle Woodland occupations. However, since there is considerable vertical displacement of materials in the site, only limited confidence can be placed in this assertion. Furthermore, the surfaces that are represented in this level are, at best, intact fragments of actual occupation surfaces.

This consideration of the plan distribution of cultural materials at 20SA620 suggests that despite considerable postdepositional disturbance, and the relatively restricted area in which investigations could take place, a degree of spatial structuring may nonetheless be discerned. This result is particularly encouraging given the uniformity of soil conditions observed during excavation, which precluded the recognition of internal stratigraphy within the site.

DISCUSSION OF RECONSTRUCTED OCCUPATION SURFACES

Assuming that these portions of the site just identified do, indeed, represent fragments of more-or-less intact occupation surfaces, a consideration of their internal organization may provide insight into the character of the site occupations, while contrasts between the different surfaces may equally suggest the degree to which the character of use changed over the three millennia represented at the site.

Before undertaking such a consideration, however, it is important that the limitations inherent to such comparisons be clearly stated. Few aspects of the archaeological record are more susceptible to distortion than spatial relationships within a deposit. Such distortion derives from the nature of human activities on the site, the depositional pathways of cultural materials, subsequent postdepositional processes, and from the character of archaeological recognition and recovery (see Clarke 1973). The distortions introduced by these factors are particularly marked at the Bridgeport Township site. Yet, the existence of such distortion does not mean that the analysis of spatial patterning is futile or impossible, only that the nature of the bias that is likely to be present must be clearly recognized and controlled.

The most serious distortion of the archaeological deposits at this site is the lateral and vertical displacement of materials brought about by burrowing small mammals and later human occupation. In most, but not all, cases this kind of distortion obscures patterning that might exist within the site. Vertical displacement particularly obscures it by mixing materials between levels. In some instances, however, it can create spurious patterns (as in the case of the concentration of materials within a burrow). In effect, then, lateral and vertical re-working of the deposit introduces noise into any order that might have existed in the site distributions. To minimize the effects of this noise, emphasis in the search for spatial patterning has concentrated on the differential quantities of frequently occurring materials, and not on the more common approach of plotting diagnostic pieces. The logic of this approach is that while the location of specific diagnostic pieces may be subject to considerable displacement, which would result in seriously misleading results, the distribution of very broadly and frequently occurring materials will be least affected by re-working, as movement will tend to even itself out stochastically.

Two additional kinds of postdepositional disturbance will have a more direct impact on an assessment of intact living surfaces. The first can be termed marginal disturbance, and reflects the uncertainty surrounding the identification of boundaries of intact areas within the site. The second disturbance type may be termed "swiss-cheese" distortion, which occurs when a coherent feature from an upper stratigraphic level cuts through a lower occupation surface, in effect, punching holes in the occupation floor. What these two categories of distortion have in common, apart from the more general effects of re-working, is their systematic character. Because of this systematic character, they are not subject to the "evening out" that occurs from multiple small-scaled disturbances. Under normal circumstances, marginal distortion is almost always a problem, but "swiss cheese" distortion can often be identified stratigraphically, i.e., the intrusive pit or feature can be clearly recognized and its effect accounted for on the lower levels of the site. However, due to the lack of color or texture contrasts in the Bridgeport Township site deposits, such recognition was not possible. Indeed, in at least one instance (see below) the presence of such a pit feature is inferred based on the occurrence of an obvious hole in an occupation surface. Yet, the effects of both kinds of distortion can be predicted and so, at least partially, controlled for. Despite their systemic character, neither of these categories is likely to add spurious patterning to the archaeological deposit. Their effects will more likely obscure the patterning that is present.

A final source of bias in the analysis of spatial order on the site is the result of the limitations of archaeological recovery. The inability to detect clear stratigraphic separations within the deposit is one obvious source of bias, and one that removes the potential for an independent check on the spatial patterning suggested by the distribution of material culture. A second bias results from the arbitrary limits that were imposed on the areas that were archaeologically investigated. Since the north and south boundaries of excavation largely reflect the natural edges of the original landform, they probably do not seriously distort the main limits of human activity. The completely arbitrary nature of the east and west boundaries of excavation, the east being the township property line, and the west delineated by land-leveling prior to archaeological investigation (providing only a very narrow transect across a much more extensive living area) is a serious bias. The result of this bias is to remove any hope of estimating the size or extent of any of the occupation surfaces. Therfore any attempt to compare the size of living areas to other sites is futile.

Although this assessment of the biases inherent to any consideration of spatial organization at the Bridgeport Township site may seem hopelessly bleak, the hopeful aspect should not be overlooked. These processes, overwhelmingly, have the effect of removing pattern or coherence, such that if patterning is detected, there is good reason to believe it is principally the result of past human activity and not the result of spurious postdepositional influences. So, within the limits of caution, an exploratory consideration and comparison of the identified site surfaces at 20SA620 can be undertaken.

Surface 1

Surface 1 is the best preserved and most extensive occupation surface encountered at the Bridgeport Township site. The surface, as reconstructed within the excavated portion of the site (Fig. 11.5), covers roughly a nine by four meter area on level 6–7. The dominant structure within this surface is a pair of hearths. The presence of these hearths is inferred from the very dense concentrations of FCR in the two squares. In addition, the northern hearth lies directly under feature 4, a circular area of burned earth that was observed in the base of level 5 during excavation (see Chapter 5).

The distribution of other cultural materials around these two hearths is nearly identical. Both are surrounded by a scattering of daub, and both have associated concentrations of ceramic and lithic debris. The northern hearth has a large scatter of flakage and a more limited distribution of ceramics, while the southern hearth has a broader spread of ceramics and a small, but dense, concentration of lithic material. Chipped stone tools exhibit a distribution pattern peripheral to both possible hearths. Three bifaces are situated on the northern margin of the north hearth, along with a bipolar core and a spherical object (FS 620, described in Chapter 7). Only one of the bifaces is diagnostic and it agrees with the inferred Late Woodland affiliation of the floor. In similar fashion, three bifaces and a bipolar core flank the south hearth on surface 1. Of these bifaces, the only diagnostic is a definite Late Archaic Satchell biface. This specimen is clearly out of context on a Late Woodland floor and probably was redeposited by the processes described in Chapter 5. A possible unfinished slate gorget also occurs in the vicinity of the southern hearth. One potentially noteworthy observation relative to surface 1 is that no unifacial tools were found in association. At least eleven distinct early Late Woodland vessels can be directly associated with this surface. These vessels, as represented by distinguishable rims (see Chapter 8), tend to occur a meter or two back from the hearths, as opposed to the closer associations of flakage and daub. What is at least suggestive about these distributions is the contrast between the symmetrical scatter of daub (and FCR) around the hearths, and the asymmetrical scattering of flakage and sherds.

These patterns of distribution suggest small hearths with the bulk of activity occurring within the six to nine square meters surrounding the hearths.

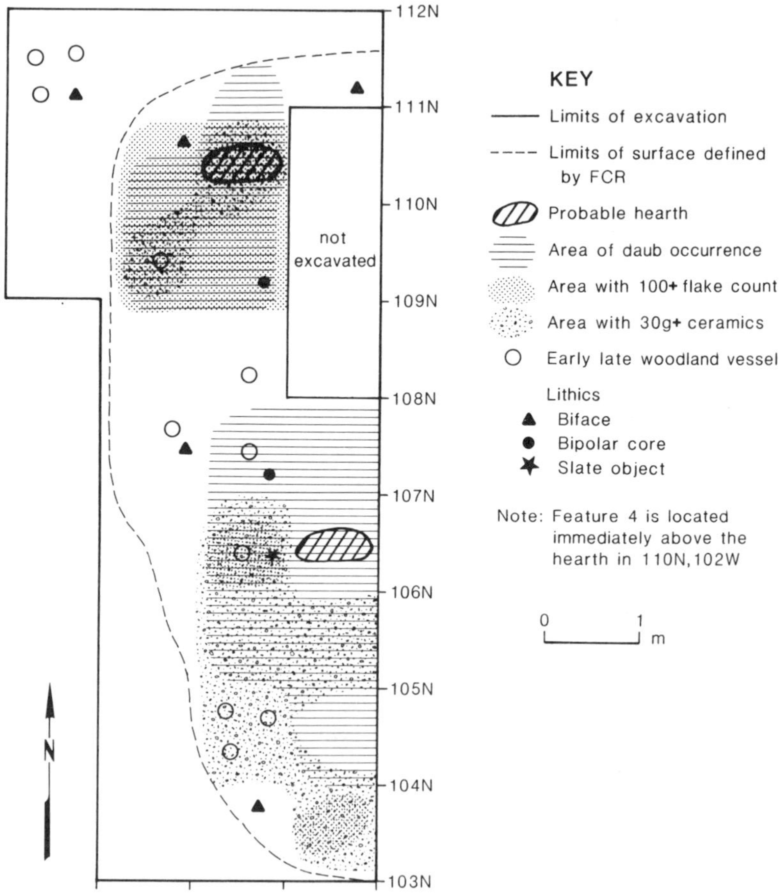

Figure 11.5. Composite plan of surface 1, level 6–7.

The one site feature associated with this surface, feature 4, yielded only limited faunal remains, but those present included dogfish, other fish, and quantities of unidentifiable bone, all heavily calcined (Chapter 9).

Overall, the pattern suggested by surface 1 is a series of hearths of small size and with little postdepositional disturbance of the surface. The limited area of the inferred hearth activity may suggest they were used by small groups of people, either families or small task groups, while the close proximity of the hearths may argue for their contemporaneous use. This suggestion is based both on their proximity, their relative lack of disturbance (no evidence of differential scattering or scavenging of stone) and the distinctness of each deposit. The clarity of patterning and lack of serious lateral displacement may also suggest that the hearths were not used for a long period of time, and that they presumably represent only a single occupation episode. This is not to suggest that the entire early Late Woodland component of the site is the result of a single occupation, but that the deposits forming surface 1 may well represent such a single occurrence. Unfortunately, the original spread of the habitation level associated with this, or any, surface cannot be determined due to the various disturbances of the site already discussed. Yet, the evidence that is available from surface 1 is consistent with a seasonal camp occupied by a small number of family groups.

Surface 2

Surface 2, although in the same broad stratigraphic range as surface 1, appears most likely to date to a transitional Middle/Late Woodland period (see Chapter 8). The surface also lacks the very clear spatial structure visible at surface 1, although it exhibits a similar pattern of material and spatial organization.

One and possibly two hearths (Fig. 11.6) are apparent on surface 2. The main hearth, in square 117N/102W, coincides with a very dense concentration of flakage. A broad, but less dense, scatter of flakage surrounds the hearth area and covers the entire northern and central portion of the intact surface. Also associated with this hearth is a dense distribution of ceramics, with a very dense cluster of large sherds occurring two meters to the southwest of the hearth. Eight Middle Woodland vessels are associated with this surface. These rims, interestingly, are not concentrated in the area of dense sherds, but are offset to the north and west of the hearth. Unlike the hearths of surface 1, daub is not closely associated with this hearth. A broad scattering of daub occurs two meters south of the hearth; although the three squares due east of the hearth could not be excavated, it is possible that daub may have extended into these squares, and in that way more closely approximate the surface 1 pattern.

In contrast to surface 1 (and 3, see below), chipped stone tools are abundant on surface 2. However, with few exceptions they are confined to the northern margin of the surface. Several, including a biface and two unifaces are situated amidst a dense cluster of transitional Middle/Late Woodland vessels in the northwest corner of the surface. In addition, a Middle or Late Woodland biface, FS 786, was found in unit 119N/101W. As expected, however, the chronological association of stone tools with the surface is not perfect, as two Early Woodland bifaces and three Late Woodland bifaces also occur within the range of surface 2. Unlike surface 1, surface 2 includes five unifacial tools along with the bifaces and a modest bipolar core assemblage.

A dense concentration of FCR in square 113N/101W originally was thought

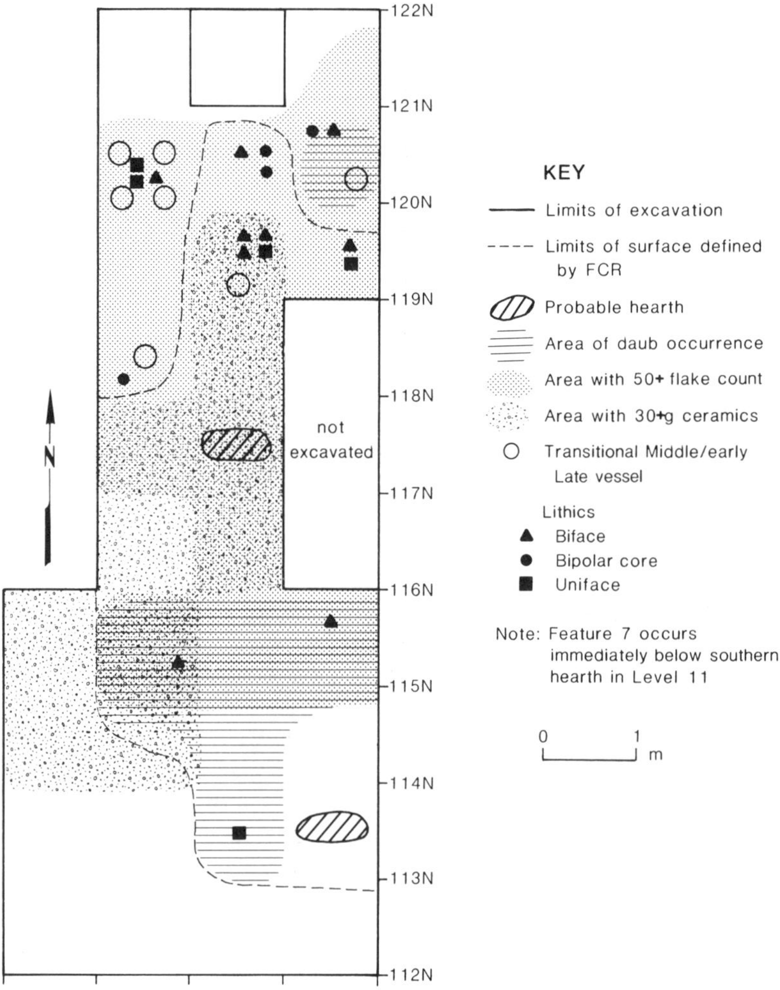

Figure 11.6. Composite plan of surface 2, level 6–7.

to be a second hearth, but it is equally likely to be associated with an intrusive pit that extends down from level 6 (or above) and continues to the base of level 11, where it becomes visible as feature 7. This interpretation is based on the close line-up between the FCR concentration and the lower feature (which only became visible when contrasted against the sterile yellow sands at the base of the site deposit (Chapter 5), and the apparent truncation of both the daub and lithic scatter on the occupation surface at this square in level 6–7. Arguing against this interpretation is the absence of any continuous downward deposition of FCR corresponding to a pit that is visible in the FCR profile of the site.

In general terms, this surface is directly comparable to the organization observed in surface 1, and suggests a similar kind of site occupation, both in terms of the integral group size and the duration of occupation. The significance of the differences in deposition pattern of daub, the very high densities of ceramic refuse and the greater number of chipped stone tools, particularly unifaces, is not clear. Possibly the greater densities of broken pottery, and the lesser quantities of flakage but greater number of stone tools, are due to a difference in site usage, perhaps one more focused on plant gathering and processing and one with less emphasis on mammal or fish procurement. Or possibly the differences between the two surfaces may reflect only stochastic variation in the discard of common materials, implying little or no difference in the underlying site activities producing the debris. Indeed, similar differences in the relative occurrence in ceramic and flakage debris were observed between the two hearths in surface 1. If feature 7 is in fact associated with surface 2, the greater quantities of of fish and bird remains and of calcined bone might suggest some difference in subsistence focus or in the duration of stay at the site for surface 2 compared with surface 1.

Surface 3

Surface 3 (Fig. 11.7) as was noted previously, has probably suffered more vertical disturbance than either surfaces 1 or 2. Despite the obvious disturbance, a relatively clear pattern of spatial relationships, centering on a presumed hearth in square 119N/103W, is apparent. This hearth corresponds closely with feature 10 (Chapter 5), which may represent either a hearth basin, or a small basin-shaped pit located next to the hearth. Like the hearths in surface 1, daub is closely associated with this hearth, although its distribution is broader and more continuous than in surface 1. The broader spread of daub, however, may simply be the result of lateral displacement by small mammals. Dense concentrations of both pottery and flakage occur in the immediate vicinity of the hearth. Yet, unlike the daub, very little scatter is noted for either of these categories of material. A second potential hearth is visible in square 113N/103W. This hearth has associated with it a small amount of daub and a very localized concentration of pottery. Only two identified vessels, both Middle Woodland, were associated with this surface, one adjacent to each hearth. No diagnostic stone tools are included in surface 3. Only three tools—two bifaces and a uniface—were recovered here. This small assemblage does not permit a meaningful distributional analysis.

Excluding the broad distribution of daub, the spatial pattern of material on this surface differs from the others described in the very limited spread

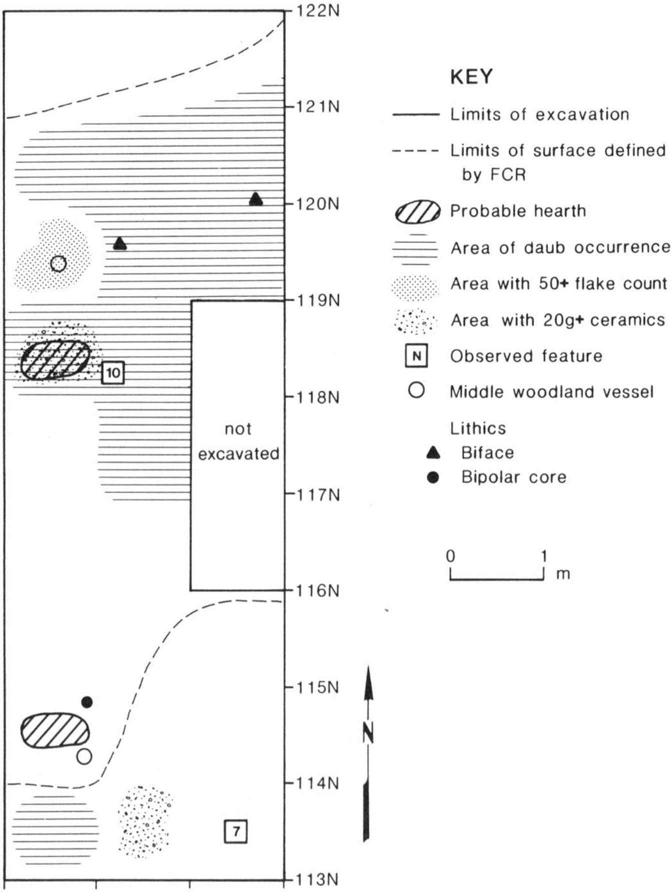

Figure 11.7. Composite plan of surface 3, level 10–11.

of material away from the hearths. If it accurately represents the pattern of deposition at the site, it could suggest a very brief occupation by a very small group of individuals. Unlike surface 1, there is nothing in the spatial distribution of materials to suggest that the two potential hearths were occupied at the same time, although both appear attributable to the Middle Woodland period. At the other extreme, it may simply reflect the extensive vertical movement of materials, leaving an extremely "swiss cheesed" fragment of a site surface. The one site feature that seems definitely associated with this surface, feature 10, contained calcined bone which, unfortunately, could not be reliably identified.

Overall, it is probably stretching the limits of exploratory speculation to draw conclusions from the disturbed remains of this surface. Nevertheless, if conclusions were to be drawn, the most plausible inference would be that the hearths represent distinct occupational episodes that were of very short duration and involved very small groups of people. Most consistent with such a model would be brief visits or collecting forays to the site by individual families.

Surface 4

Due to the limited area excavated in the vicinity of surface 4, little can be said concerning its spatial structure, or indeed its status as an occupation surface as opposed to slope midden. The area was first identified by the increased density of ceramic and lithic debris in the absence of FCR. At lower levels, modest concentrations of FCR became apparent. Although it is tempting to view surface 4 as a site activity area not associated with a hearth, it probably represents a midden deposit that formed on the northern slope of the narrow knoll feature on which the main site occupation occurred.

As a final point of comparison among the assemblages of the three primary site surfaces just described, cumulative percentage distributions by size class were calculated for the lithic debris components for each surface. Only slight differences are found in the flat platform flake distributions. However, surface 2 exhibits substantial differences in its faceted platform distribution when compared to the other surfaces. The surface 2 distribution is dominated by the larger size classes, especially the 8 mm fraction. Apparently, the occupation of surface 2 involved a greater degree of early stage lithic reduction than did surfaces 1 and 3. Smaller fractions characteristic of tool resharpening dominate those assemblages. Although the data are limited, to say the least, the surface 2 flake size distributions are consistent with the fuller range of activities, and suggest that surface 2 may have been the locus of a longer term residential occupation.

12 Conclusions

John M. O'Shea
Museum of Anthropology, University of Michigan

As previous chapters have described, the Bridgeport Township site was occupied intermittently over a long span of time, from Late Archaic Satchell times up to the late prehistoric period. Yet, it probably was never occupied for long at any one point in time, and indeed, it probably was never a major locus of occupation. Instead, over its entire history, it appears to have functioned as a temporary camp that small groups of people visited for a brief time in the later summer and early autumn. And, indeed, with the exception of slight shifts in emphasis during the Middle Woodland, the activities conducted at the site, both in terms of the resources exploited and the makeup of the social group present, appear to have remained unchanged.

The sandy knoll was effectively unoccupied from the time of its formation following the Lake Algoma stage up through the end of the Late Archaic period. The first substantial occupation of the site occurred during the later half of the Early Woodland period. This occupation, like those that follow it in later periods, suggests a summer to early autumn season of use. The Early Woodland occupation seems to have been of short duration and to have involved a very small number of people, perhaps only an extended family, as suggested by surface 3 (see Chapter 11). It is unclear from present evidence how frequently people returned to the location during the Early Woodland, but the quantity of materials attributable to the time period suggests multiple occupation episodes. The limited range of tools associated with these occupations, along with the apparent shortness of each stay, suggests that the people who occupied 20SA620 probably were associated with a more permanent residential base located elsewhere in the valley. Although the squash found at the site may have been grown locally, it is equally plausible that it was cultivated elsewhere and transported to the site. Given the emphasis on foraging activities at the site, it is unlikely that horticulture was more than a sideline to the inhabitants.

One potentially anomalous finding concerns the dating of the Early Woodland occupation. Although the ceramics overwhelmingly date to the later portion of the Early Woodland period, the diagnostic lithics, such as the Kramer points, argue for an occupation dating to the earlier portion of the period. It is possible, of course, that these data reflect two different kinds of occupations at 20SA620 during this time period.

Although scattered Middle Woodland ceramics were recovered from the site, the next intact traces of occupation date to the end of the Middle Woodland period. The transitional Middle/Late Woodland occupation at 20SA620, as represented by surface 2 (see Chapter 11), is indicative of a site use very similar to that already described for the Early Woodland. The site appears to have been occupied during the same season of the year, and to have been used by a relatively small group of people, although possibly larger than that suggested for the Early Woodland. The broader array of stone tools present, along with the evidence for a greater range of lithic reduction stages, suggests that this occupation may have been more broadly focused than the Early Woodland and perhaps represents a very short term residential base camp. The apparent association of burials with this occupation, although by no means a formal cemetery, would also support such a conclusion.

The early Late Woodland occupation at 20SA620 is both the most extensive and the best preserved. As represented by surface 1 (see Chapter 11), its appearance is very similar to the transitional late Middle Woodland surface (surface 2), yet the composition of its lithic assemblage suggests more similarity to the Early Woodland occupation. It is difficult to quantify occupational intensity between chronological periods and this is particularly true at 20SA620, where only a limited sample of the site area was available for examination. Yet, it seems inescapable that the intensity of site use was greater during the early Late Woodland period than at any prior time. Whether this occurred as a function of a larger group of people using the site at any one time, or whether it reflects more frequent visits to the site during the period is very difficult to determine. In all probability it was a combination of the two factors. Since the season of occupation does not appear to change with the early Late Woodland period, this intensified use is probably indicative of the site being visited with greater frequency on an inter-annual basis, such as every year or every second year, as opposed to less frequent intervals such as once in five or once in ten years.

Although the evidence for such an assertion is indirect, if true, it would suggest an intensification of the local foraging system within the Saginaw Valley that might well be linked to a continuing increase in the regional population during the early Late Woodland period. Such an intensification of foraging activities would suggest a minimal role for agriculture at this time, either in producing or accommodating population growth.

The late prehistoric use of the site seems qualitatively different from all that had gone before with the possible exception of the earlier portion of the Early Woodland. Camp debris and ceramics become scarce during this final period of use, while hunting refuse, including the greatest quantity of diagnostic projectile points and rubbish pits with expediently processed local foods, suggests a very ephemeral hunting camp. The intensity of site use and the size and composition of the groups using the location both appear to decrease radically from earlier times. From the scant evidence available, the season of use seems to remain the same, but with perhaps greater emphasis on summer and less on early autumn. This shift in the use of the site most probably relates to the large scale adoption of maize agriculture in the Saginaw Valley, and the resulting reorientation of the regional settlement system.

Given this occupation history at 20SA620, what, if anything, can be said about the the more general organization of society in the Saginaw Valley? Perhaps the most obvious thing to be gleaned from the present investigation is how little real change occurred in the basic structure of foraging activities during the Woodland period. This can be attributed to the unique geographical and ecological setting of the Saginaw Valley and the relatively constant influence it exerted on forager settlement and subsistence.

Major changes in the character of settlement at 20SA620 that might have had regional significance can be found only at the beginning and end of the occupation sequence. Although some Late Archaic material was encountered at 20SA620 in the form of Satchell Complex material in secondary context, it is surprising that Dustin material was not found, particularly since Dustin sites are ubiquitous in the locality and, indeed, occur within a couple hundred meters of 20SA620. The absence of materials attributable to Meadowood is similarly noteworthy. Whatever the specific role of the site locality during the Late Archaic, it may have carried over into the beginning of the Early Woodland, where hunting debris occurs but without early ceramics or other diagnostic artifacts.

The second major change in the use of 20SA620 occurs after the early Late Woodland occupation. The change associated with this latest phase of prehistoric settlement at 20SA620 brings us full circle, and appears, archaeologically, very similar to the earliest occupations at the site during the Early Woodland. Although little evidence for late prehistoric occupation is represented in the ceramic inventory, the relative abundance of diagnostic projectile points and the contents of the Bowen Feature make it clear that the site was used during this time, albeit in a substantially different manner than previously. Even the depositional context is different, with the hearth/midden areas of earlier Woodland occupations being replaced by subterranean trash pits filled with expediently processed fishbone and roasted small animal remains. The greater emphasis on summer use, and the corresponding de-emphasis of early autumn, and the more ephemeral character of site use in general, both fit well with the expected reorganization of the seasonal settlement system that would accompany the serious adoption of maize agriculture within the Saginaw Valley.

In the end, the significance of 20SA620 for understanding the Woodland period in the Saginaw Valley lies in its very insignificance as a major locus of occupation in the past. Because of this insignificance, it does not contain the elaborate structures of the Schultz site or the impressive arrays of storage facilities and burials of the Bussinger site. Yet its modest character serves to underline the fundamental unity of Woodland social and economic systems in the Saginaw Valley. It likewise emphasizes the qualitatively different character of the Archaic and late prehistoric patterns of land use from this core Woodland pattern. Without a doubt, our understanding of Woodland society would be seriously diminished were sites such as Schultz not investigated. The detailed study of 20SA620, however, serves to remind us of the limited nature of our knowledge, both of the organization of Woodland settlement systems in the Saginaw Valley, and, more specifically, of the smaller, more temporary, sites at which the Woodland inhabitants spent most of the days of their lives.

Bibliography

Albert, Dennis A., Shirley R. Denton, and Burton V. Barnes
1986 Regional Landscape Ecosystems of Michigan. School of Natural Resources, University of Michigan. Ann Arbor.

Allison, April
1972 Plant remains. In: The Schultz site at Green Point: A Stratified Occupation Area in the Saginaw Valley of Michigan, ed. James Fitting, pp. 77–85. University of Michigan Museum of Anthropology, Memoirs, 4. Ann Arbor.

Asch, David, and Nancy Asch
1985 Prehistoric plant cultivation in west-central Illinois. In: Prehistoric Food Production, ed. Richard I. Ford, pp. 149–203. University of Michigan Museum of Anthropology, Anthropological Papers, 75. Ann Arbor.

Asch, Nancy, and David Asch
1975 Plant remains from the Zimmerman site—grid A: A quantitative perspective. In: The Zimmerman Site: Further Excavations at the Grand Village of the Kaskaskia, by Margaret K. Brown, pp. 116–20. Illinois State Museum, Report of Investigations, 35.
1986 Woodland period archeobotany of the Napoleon Hollow site. In: Woodland Period Occupations of the Napoleon Hollow Site in the Lower Illinois Valley, pp. 427–512. Kampsville Arcaheological Center Research Series, Vol. 6. Center for American Archaeology. Kampsville, IL.

Baker, R. H.
1983 Michigan Mammals. Michigan State University Press. East Lansing.

Bailey, H. P.
1960 A method of determining the warmth and temperateness of climate. Geografiska Annaler, 43:1–16.

Becker., G. C.
1983 Fishes of Wisconsin. University of Wisconsin Press. Madison.

Beld, S. G.
1985 The Conservation Park site (20-GR-33) Gratiot County, Michigan. In: Radiocarbon Dating in Gratiot County-S84–194, ed. J. T. Luke, pp. 1–203. Alma College. Alma, Michigan.

Bigony, B.
1970 Late Woodland occupations of the Saginaw Valley. Michigan Archaeologist, 16:115–214.

Binford, L. R.
1980 Willow smoke and dogs' tails: Hunter-gatherer settlement systems and archaeological site formation. American Antiquity, 45:4–20.

Binford, L. R., and G. I. Quimby
1963 Indian sites and chipped stone materials in the northern Lake Michigan area. Fieldiana: Anthropology, 36:277–307.

Brashler, Janet G.
1981 Early Late Woodland boundaries and interaction: Indian ceramics of southern lower Michigan. Michigan State University Anthropological Series, 3(3). East Lansing.

Brashler, Janet G., and Margaret B. Holman
1985 Late Woodland continuity and change in the Saginaw Valley of Michigan. Arctic Anthropology, 22(2):141–52.

Brose, D.
1966 The Valley Sweets site, 20SA24, Saginaw, Michigan. Michigan Archaeologist, 12(1):1–21.

Brunett, F. V.
1981 A cultural resource reconnaissance for flood control study on the Tittabawassee River at Midland, Michigan. Saginaw Archaeological Commission Report No. 101381.
1982 An archaeological survey of a portion of section 17, T11N/R5E, Bridgeport Township, Saginaw County, Michigan. Saginaw Archaeological Commission.
1983 Additional work at 20SA620, Bridgeport Township, Saginaw County, Michigan. Saginaw Archaeological Commission.

Burton, T. M.
1985 The effects of water level fluctuations on Great Lakes coastal marshes. In: Coastal Wetlands, H. Prince and F. D'Itri (eds.), pp. 3–13. Chelsea, MI: Lewis Publishers.

Carlander, K. D.
1969 Handbook of Freshwater Fishery Biology. Vol. 1. Iowa State University Press.
1977 Handbook of Freshwater Fishery Biology. Vol. 2. Iowa State University Press.

Carskadden, J., and J. Morton
1974 Late Woodland projectile points. Ohio Archaeologist, 24(2):18–22.

Clarke, C. P.
1979 The Birch Run Road site, 20SA393. Saginaw Archaeological Commission Report No. 7324.

Clark, D. L.
1973 Archaeology: The loss of innocence. Antiquity, 47: 6–18.

Cleland, Charles E.
n.d. The Skegemog Point site: A Late Woodland village in Grand Traverse County, Michigan. Manuscript on file at the Michigan State University Museum, East Lansing.
1966 The Prehistoric Animal Ecology and Ethnozoology of the Upper Great Lakes Region. University of Michigan Museum of Anthropology, Anthropological Papers, 29. Ann Arbor.
1982 The inland shore fishery of the northern Great Lakes: Its development and importance in prehistory. American Antiquity, 47:761–84.

Cleland, Nancy
1989 An analysis of the botanical remains and paleoenvironment of the Weber I site. In: Archaeological Investigations at the Weber I and Weber II Sites, Frankenmuth Township, Saginaw County, Michigan, ed. William Lovis, pp. 175–89. Michigan Cultural Resource Investigation Series, I. Lansing.

Core, H. W., W. A. Cote, and A. C. Day
1979 Wood Structure and Identification. Second edition. Syracuse University Press. Syracuse.

Cowan, C. Wesley, and Tristine L. Smart
1981 Plant remains from the Hart site and Kretz site: 1978 excavation. University of Michigan, Museum of Anthropology, Ethnobotanical Report 521. Ann Arbor.

Cowardin, L. M., V. Carter, F. C. Golet, and E. T. LaRoe
1979 Classification of wetlands and deepwater habitats of the United States. Office of Biological Services, U.S. Fish and Wildlife Service. Washington, D.C.

Crabtree, D. E.
1972 An introduction to flintworking. Occasional Papers, Idaho State University Museum, 28. Pocatello.

Crabtree, D. E., and B. R. Butler
1964 Notes on experiments in flintknapping I: Heat treatment of silica materials. Tebiwa, 7:1–16.

Crane, H., and J. Griffin
1968 University of Michigan radiocarbon dates, XII. Radiocarbon, 10:61–114.

Cronon, William
1983 Changes in the land: Indians, colonists and the ecology of New England. New York: Hill and Wang.

Crumley, Carol S.
1973 The Kantzler site (20BY30): A multicomponent Woodland site in Bay County, Michigan. Michigan Archaeologist, 19:3–4; 19:183–291.

Curtis, John T.
1978 Vegetation of Wisconsin. The University of Wisconsin Press. Madison.

Densmore, Frances
1974 How Indians Use Wild Plants for Food, Medicine, and Crafts. New York: Dover.

DeRoo, Bryan, and Kathryn E. Parker
1989 Botanical remains from the Late Woodland component of the Elam site, a multicomponent Woodland campsite in southwestern Michigan. Paper presented at the 34th Annual Midwest Archaeological Conference, Iowa City.

Dice, L. R.
1943 The Biotic Provinces of North America. University of Michigan Press. Ann Arbor.

Dorr, John A., and Donald F. Eschman
1971 Geology of Michigan. University of Michigan Press. Ann Arbor.

Dorwin, J. T., and K. M. Weikel
1985 Cultural resource survey of the Shiawassee Flats Levee Project (Flint and Cass rivers), in Saginaw County, Michigan. Resource Analysts, Inc. Report RAI-1558. Bloomington, Indiana.

Dustin, F.
1915 Saginaw County as a center of aboriginal population. Michigan Pioneer and Historical Collections, 39:251–60.
1930 Some ancient Indian villages in Saginaw County, Michigan. Papers of the Michigan Academy of Science, Arts and Letters, 12:75–93.

Egan, Kathryn C.
1988 Middle and Late Archaic phytogeography and floral exploitation in the Upper Great Lakes. Midcontinental Journal of Archaeology, 13(1):81–107.
1987 Floral analysis. In: Archaeological Excavations at 0WA176, ed. Margaret Holman. Michigan Archaeologist, 33(1–2):83–89.
1988 Game theory and hunter-gatherer diet reconstruction. Paper presented at the 53rd annual meeting of the Society of American Archaeology. Phoenix, AZ.

Erichson-Brown, Charlotte.
1979 Use of Plants: For the Past 500 Years. Breezy Creeks Press. Ontario.

Farrand, W. R.
1982 Quaternary Geology of Southern Michigan. Map, 1:500,000. State of Michigan, Dept. of Natural Resources, Geological Survey Division, Lansing.
1988 Glacial Lakes around Michigan. Michigan Department of Natural Resources. Geological Survey Division, Bulletin 4 (revised). Lansing.

Fairchild, J. D.
1977 The Schmidt site: A pre-Nipissing village in the Saginaw Valley. Unpublished Master's thesis, Western Michigan University. Kalamazoo.

Fisher, F. W.
1972 Schultz site ceramics. In: The Schultz Site at Green Point, ed. James E. Fitting. University of Michigan Museum of Anthropology, Memoirs, 14:137–90.

Fitting, James E.
1965 Late Woodland cultures of southeastern Michigan. University of Michigan Museum of Anthropology, Anthropological Papers, 24.
1966 Radiocarbon dating the Younge tradition. American Antiquity, 31:738.
1968 Saginaw Valley archaeology. Michigan Archaeologist, 14:1–130.
1971 Scheduling in a shared environment: Late period land use patterns in the Saginaw Valley of Michigan. Ontario Archaeology, 17:35–41.
1972 The Schultz Site at Green Point: A Stratified Occupation Area in the Saginaw Valley of Michigan. University of Michigan Museum of Anthropology, Memoirs, 4.
1975a The Archaeology of Michigan. Cranbrook Institute of Science. Bloomfield Hills, MI.
1975b Field school at the Young site (20SA209), Saginaw County, Michigan. Michigan Archaeologist, 21:113–52.

Fitzgerald, W. R.
1982 Lest the beaver run loose: The early seventeenth century Christianson Site and trends in Historic Neutral archaeology. Archaeological Survey of Canada, Paper 111. Ottawa.

Flenniken, J. J.
1981 Replicative systems analysis: A model applied to the vein quartz artifacts from the Hoko River site. Washington State University Laboratory of Anthropology, Report of Investigations, 59. Pullman.

Fox, W. A.
1980 Of projectile points and politics. Arch Notes 80–2:5–3.

Frostic, F. W.
1918 Floods of the Saginaw Valley: Their causes and effects. Papers of the Michigan Academy of Science, Arts, and Letters, 20:67–81.

Garland, Elizabeth B.
1984 Archaeological investigations in the lower St. Joesph Valley, Berrien County, Michigan. Completion Report, US-31, Archaeological Mitigation Project. Michigan Department of Transportation.

1986 Early Woodland occupations in Michigan: A lower St. Joseph valley perspective. In: Early Woodland Archaeology, ed. Kenneth Farnsworth and Thomas E. Emerson, pp. 47–83. Center for American Archaeology, Kampsville Seminars in ARchaeology, Vol. 2. Kampsville, Illinois.

General Land Office Survey
1821 Description of T11N, R5E, Saginaw County, Michigan. Notebook on file at the State of Michigan Archives, Lansing.

Gilliam, Jeanne A., Ronald O. Kapp, and Robert D. Bogue
1967 A post-Wisconsin pollen sequence from Vestaburg Bog, Montcalm County, Michigan. Papers of the Michigan Academy of Science, Arts, and Letters, 52:3–17.

Gilmore, Melvin R.
1933 Some Chippewa Uses of Plants. Papers of the Michigan Academy of Science, Arts, and Letters, 17:119–143.

GLO Survey (see General Land Office Survey)

Goodyear, A. C.
1982 Toolkit entropy and bipolar reduction: A study of interassemblage lithic variability among Paleo-Indian sites in the northeastern United States. Unpublished manuscript.

Gosselink, J. G., and R. E. Turner
1978 The role of hydrology in freshwater wetland ecosystems. In: Freshwater Wetlands: Ecological Processes and Management Potential, R. Good, D. Whigham and R. Simpson (eds.), pp. 63–78. New York: Academic.

Halsey, John R.
1976 The Bussinger site: a multicomponent site in the Saginaw Valley of Michigan with a review of early Late Woodland mortuary complexes in the northeastern woodlands. Unpublished Ph.D. dissertation, University of North Carolina. Chapel Hill.
1968 The Springwells Mound group of Wayne County, Michigan. Contributions to Michigan Archaeology, ed. James Fitting, John R. Halsey and H. M. Wobst, pp. 79–159. University of Michigan Museum of Anthropology, Anthropological Papers, 32. Ann Arbor.

Hammond, R., and P. S. McCullagh
1982 Quantitative Techniques in Geography: An Introduction. Oxford University Press.

Harrison, S.
1966 The Schmidt site (20SA192), Saginaw County, Michigan. Michigan Archaeologist, 12:49–70.

Hayden, B.
1980 Confusion in the bipolar world: Bashed pebbles and splintered pieces. Lithic Technology, 9:2–7.

Heidenreich, C.
1971 Huronia: A History and Geography of the Huron Indians 1600–1650. Toronto: McClelland and Stewart.

Henry, D. O., C. V. Haynes, and B. Bradley
1976 Quantitative variations in flaked stone debitage. Plains Anthropologist, 21:57–61.

Hitchcock, R. K., and J. I. Ebert
1984 Foraging and food production among Kalahari hunter-gatherers. In: From Hunters to Farmers: The Causes and Consequences of Food Production in Africa, J. D. Clark and S. Brandt (eds.), pp. 329–48. The University of California, Berkeley.

Holman, Margaret
n.d. Notes on the artifact inventory of 20SA620. Unpublished notes. The Museum, Michigan State University. East Lansing.
1984 Pine River ware: Evidence for the in situ development of the Late Woodland in the Straits of Mackinac region. The Wisconsin Archaeologist, 65(1):32–48.

Hough, J. L.
1958 Geology of the Great Lakes. The University of Illinois Press. Urbana.

Hushen, Timothy W., Ronald O. Kapp, Robert D. Bogue, and John T. Worthington
1966 Presettlement forest patterns in Montcalm Country, Michigan. Michigan Botanist, 5(4):192–211.

Jackson, L. J.
1980 Dawson Creek: An Early Woodland site in south-central Ontario. Ontario Archaeology, 33:13–32.
1986 New evidence for Early Woodland seasonal adaptation from southern Ontario, Canada. American Antiquity, 51:389–401.

Jaworski, E., C. Raphael, P. Mansfield, and B. Williamson
1979 Impact of Great Lakes water level fluctuations on coastal wetlands. Institute of Water Resources, Michigan State University. East Lansing.

Johannessen, Sissel
1983 Plant remains from the Cement Hollow phase. In: The Mund Site, Andrew Fortier et al. (eds.), pp. 94–104. American Bottom Archaeology, FAI 270 Site Reports, 5. The University of Illinois Press. Urbana.
1984 Archaeobotany. In: American Bottom Archaeology: A Summary of the FAI 270 Project Contribution of the Culture History of the Mississippi River Valley, Charles J. Bareis and James W. Porter (eds.), pp. 197–214. The University of Illinois Press. Urbana.

Keeley, L. H.
1980 Experimental Determination of Stone Tool Uses: A Microwear Analysis. University of Chicago Press.

Keene, Arthur S.
1979 Prehistoric hunter-gatherers of the deciduous forest: A linear programming approach to Late Archaic subsistence in the Saginaw Valley (Michigan). Unpublished Ph.D. dissertation, University of Michigan. Ann Arbor.

Keepax, Carol
1977 Contamination of archaeological deposits by seeds of modern origin with particular reference to the use of flotation machines. Journal of Archaeological Science, 4:221–229.

Kelly, R. L.
1983 Hunter-gatherer mobility strategies. Journal of Anthropological Research, 39:277–307.

Kenyon, I. T.
1980 The George Davidson site: An Archaic "Broadpoint" component in southwestern Ontario. Archaeology of Eastern Northern America, 8:11–28.

King, Frances B.
1984 Plants, People and Paleoecology. Illinois State Museum Scientific Papers, 20. Springfield.
1985 Early cultivated cucurbits in eastern North America. In: Prehistoric Food Production, ed. Richard I. Ford, pp. 73–99. University of Michigan Museum of Anthropology, Anthropological Papers, 75. Ann Arbor.

Kinietz, W. Vernon
1940 The Indians of the Western Great Lakes 1615–1760. University of Michigan Museum of Anthropology, Occasional Contributions, 4.

Koehler, A.
1917 Guidebook for the Identification of Woods Used For Ties and Timbers. USDA Miscellaneous R.L. 1.

Krakker, J. K.
1983 Changing sociocultural systems during the late prehistoric period in southeastern Michigan. Unpublished Ph.D. dissertation, University of Michigan. Ann Arbor.
1984 Investigations of a small Late Prehistoric site in St. Clair County, Michigan. Michigan Archaeologist, 30:86–123.

Krakker, James K., and Michael J. Shott
1984 Report of Phase II archaeological investigation of the Huron Valley Wastewater Control System, Wayne County, Michigan. On file at the University of Michigan Museum of Anthropology.

Larsen, C. E.
1985 Geoarchaeological interpretation of Great Lakes coastal environments. In: Archaeological Sediments in Context, J. Stein and W. Farrand (eds.), pp. 91–110. Institute of Quaternary Studies. University of Maine. Orono.
n.d. Geologic history of Algonquin and the upper Great Lakes. Manuscript on file at University of Michigan Museum of Anthropology.

Leonhardi, T.
1985 Unpublished notes on catch summary, Cass River fish census. Michigan Department of Natural Resources, Fisheries Division. Lansing.

Leverett, Frank, and F. B. Taylor
1915 The Pleistocene of Indiana and Michigan, and the history of the Great Lakes. United States Geological Survey Monograph, 53. Washington, DC.

Lewis, C. F.
1969 Late Quaternary history of lake levels in the Huron and Erie basins. Proceedings of the 12th Conference on Great Lakes Research, pp. 250–70. International Association for Great Lakes Research. Ann Arbor.

Lewis, H. T.
1986 Hunter-gatherer, cowboy, ranger: The evolution and devolution of fire in northern Australia. Paper presented at the Conference on Ecology and Cultural Evolution in the Tropics. The University of Michigan. Ann Arbor

Limp, W. F., and V. A. Reidhead
1979 An economic evaluation of the potential of fish utilization in riverine environments. American Antiquity, 44:70–78.

Lopinot, Neil, and D. E. Brussell
1982 Assessing uncarbonized seeds from open-air sites in mesic environments: An example from southern Illinois. Journal of Archaeological Science, 9(1):95–108.

Lovejoy, C. O.
1985 Dental wear in the Libben population: Its functional pattern and role in the determination of adult skeletal age at death. American Journal of Physical Anthropology, 68:47–56.

Lovis, William A.
1973 Late Woodland culture dynamics in the northern lower peninsula of Michigan. Unpublished Ph.D. dissertation, Michigan State University.
1979 The archaeology and physical anthropology of 20LP98. Michigan Archaeologist, 25:1–69.
1981 Holocene lake level fluctuations and the Late Archaic of the Saginaw Valley. Paper presented at the 46th annual meeting of the Society for American Archaeology.
1985 Seasonal settlement dynamics and the role of the Fletcher site in the Woodland adaptations of the Saginaw drainage basin. Arctic Anthropology 22:153–70.

Lovis, William A. (ed.)
1986 Archaeological investigations at sites 20BY77, 20BY78, and 20BY79, at the Third-Street Bridge Replacment, Bay City, Michigan. Report submitted to City of Bay City, Michigan Department of Transportation, Michigan Department of State, Federal Highway Administration, and the U.S. Department of Transportation.
1989 Archaeological investigation at the Weber I and Weber II sites, Frankenmuth Township, Saginaw County, Michigan. Michigan Cultural Resource Investigation Series, I. Lansing.

Lovis, William A., and R. M. Davis
1986 The ceramic assemblage from sites 20BY77 and 20BY79, Bay City, Michigan. In: Archaeological investigations at sites 20BY77, 20BY78, and 20BY79, at the Third-Street Bridge Replacment, Bay City, Michigan, ed. W. Lovis, pp. 120–53. Report submitted to City of Bay City, Michigan Department of Transportation, Michigan Department of State, Federal Highway Administration, and the U.S. Department of Transportation.

Lovis, William A., and Margaret Holman
1976 Subsistence strategies and population: A hypothetical model for the development of Late Woodland in the Mackinac Straits-Sault Ste. Marie area. Michigan Academician, 8(3):267–76.

Lovis, William A., and J. A. Robertson
1989 The Archaic of Saginaw Valley: The view from Weber I. In: Archaeological Investigations at the Weber I and Weber II Sites, Frankenmuth Township, Saginaw County, Michigan, ed. W. A. Lovis, pp. 217–26. Michigan Cultural Resource Investigation Series, I.

Lovis, William A., K. C. Egan, G. W. Monaghan, B. A. Smith and E. J. Prahl
1989 Environment and subsistence at the Marquette Viaduct Locale of the Fletcher site. Manuscript on file at The Museum, Michigan State University. East Lansing.

Luedtke, B. E.
1976 Lithic material distributions and interaction patterns during the Late Woodland period in Michigan. Unpublished Ph.D. dissertation, University of Michigan.
1978 Late Woodland projectile points in Michigan. Michigan Archaeologist, 24:5–10.

Luxenberg, B.
1972 Faunal Remains. In: The Schultz Site at Green Point, ed. James Fitting. University of Michigan Museum of Anthropology, Memoirs, 4.

Mahjoory, R., and E. Whiteside
1976 Soils of Saginaw County, Michigan, 1976. College of Agriculture and Natural Resources, Michigan State University. East Lansing.

Mainfort, R. C.
1979 Indian social dynamics in the period of European contact: Fletcher site cemetery, Bay County, Michigan. Michigan State University Anthropological Series 1(4). East Lansing.

Martin, Alexander, and William Barkley
1961 Seed Identification Manual. University of California Press. Berkeley.

Martin, L. V.
1982 A history of the Michigan Archaeological Society. Michigan Archaeologist, 28:1–51.

Masao, F. T.
1982 On possible use of unshaped flakes: An ethno-historic approach from Central Tanzania. Ethnos, 47:262–70.

Mason, R. J.
1986 Rock Island: Historic Indian archaeology in the northern Lake Michigan basin. Midcontinental Journal of Archaeology Special Paper, 6.

Mayer-Oakes, W. J.
1955 Prehistory of the upper Ohio Valley. Annals of the Carnegie Museum, 34. Pittsburgh.

McAndrews, J. H., R. T. Byrne, and N. D. Rinlyson
1974 Report of the investigation at Crawford Lake. Canada Council Grant, Royal Ontario Museum. Toronto.

McCormick, W. R.
1881 Mounds and mound builders of the Saginaw Valley. Michigan Pioneer and Historical Collections, 4:379–83.

McMurray, M., G. Kloos, R. Kapp, and K. Sullivan
1978 Paleoecology of Crystal Marsh, Montcalm County, based on macrofossil and pollen analysis. Michigan Academician, 10:403–17.

McPherron, Alan L.
1967 The Juntunen Site and the Late Woodland Prehistory of the Upper Great Lakes Area. University of Michigan Museum of Anthropology, Anthropological Papers, 30.

Minnis, Paul E.
1981 Seeds in archaeological sites: Sources and some interpretive problems. American Antiquity, 46(1):143–52.

Mokma, D. L., and N. W. Stroesenreuther.
1982 Classification of Michigan Soils. Michigan Cooperative Soil Survey, Department of Crop and Soil Science, Michigan State University. East Lansing.

Monaghan, G. W., and L. Faye
1989 The geology of the Weber I site. In: Archaeological Investigations at the Weber I and Weber II sites, Frankenmuth Township, Saginaw County Michigan, ed. W. Lovis, pp. 41–50. Michigan Cultural Resource Investigation Series, I.

Monaghan, G. W., L. Faye, and W. Lovis
1986 Nipissing transition in the Saginaw Bay region, Michigan. Canadian Journal of Earth Sciences, 23(11):1851–54.

Montgomery, F. H.
1977 Seeds and Fruits of Eastern Canada and Northeastern United States. University of Toronto Press.

Munson, P. J.
1971 An archaeological survey of the American Bottoms and Wood River Terrace, Part I. Illinois State Museum Report of Investigations, 21. Springfield.

Munson, P. J., P. W. Parmalee, and R. A. Yarnell
1971 Subsistence ecology of Scovill, a terminal Middle Woodland village. American Antiquity, 36(4):410–31.

Odum, E. P.
1971 Fundamentals of Ecology. Philadelphia: Saunders.

Ozker, Doreen B.
1976a The Naugle site 20MD30, Midland County, Michigan: Early Late Woodland and Late Archaic components on a Pine River site. Michigan Archaeologist, 22:315–56.
1976b Heat treatment of Bayport chert. Michigan Archaeologist, 22:357–68.
1982 An Early Woodland Community at the Schultz Site 20SA2 in the Saginaw Valley and the Nature of the Early Woodland Adaptation in the Great Lakes Region. University of Michigan Museum of Anthropology, Anthropological Papers, 70. Ann Arbor.

Papworth, M. L.
1967 Cultural Traditions in the Lake Forest Region During the Late High-water Stages of the Post-glacial Great Lakes. Unpublished Ph.D. dissertation, University of Michigan. Ann Arbor.
n.d. The Vogelaar site, 20-SA-133. Unpublished manuscript, on file at the University of Michigan Museum of Anthropology. Ann Arbor.

Parachini, Kathryn
1984a Botanical remains (King site). In: Archaeological Investigations in the St. Joseph River Valley, Berrien County, Michigan, ed. Elizabeth Garland, p. 275. Report submitted to the Michigan Department of Transportation, Michigan Department of State, and the U.S. Department of Transportation Federal Highway Administration.
1984b Botanical remains (Stover site). In: Archaeological Investigations in the St. Joseph River Valley, Berrien County, Michigan, ed. Elizabeth Garland, pp. 346–54. Report submitted to the Michigan Department of Transportation, Michigan Department of State, and the U.S. Department of Transportation Federal Highway Administration.
1984c Botanical remains (Rock Hearth site). In: Archaeological Investigations in the St. Joseph River Valley, Berrien County, Michigan, ed. Elizabeth Garland, pp. 409–16. Report submitted to the Michigan Department of Transportation, Michigan Department of State, and the U.S. Department of Transportation Federal Highway Administration.
1984d Botanical remains (Wymer site). In: Archaeological Investigations in the St. Joseph River Valley, Berrien County, Michigan, ed. Elizabeth Garland, pp. 538–37. Report submitted to the Michigan Department of Transportation, Michigan Department of State, and the U.S. Department of Transportation Federal Highway Administration.
1984e Botanical remains (Eidson site). In: Archaeological Investigations in the St. Joseph River Valley, Berrien County, Michigan, ed. Elizabeth Garland, pp. 757–86. Report submitted to the Michigan Department of Transportation, Michigan Department of State, and the U.S. Department of Transportation Federal Highway Administration.

Parker, Kathryn
1985 Botanical remains from the Birch Run Road site. In: The Prehistory of the Birch Run Road Site, Saginaw County, Michigan, by Caven P. Clark. Master's thesis, Western Michigan University. Kalamazoo.

Patterson, L. W., and J. B. Sollberger
1978 Replication and classification of small size lithic debitage. Plains Anthropologist, 23:103–12.

Peebles, C. S.
1978 Of archaeology and archaeologists in Saginaw County, Michigan. Michigan Archaeologist, 24:83–129.

Peske, G. R.
1963 A preliminary point classification and temporal placement from surface materials. Papers of the Michigan Academy of Science, Arts, and Letters, 48:557–66.

Potzger, James E.
1948 A pollen study in the tension zone of Lower Michigan. Butler University Botanical Study, 8:161–77.

Prahl, E. J.
1970 The Middle Woodland period of the lower Muskegon Valley and the northern Hopewell frontier. Unpublished Ph.D. dissertation, University of Michigan. Ann Arbor.

Prufer, O. H.
1981 Raven Rocks: A specialized Late Woodland rockshelter occupation in Belmont County, Ohio. Kent State University Research Papers in Archaeology, 1. Kent, Ohio.

Rhoades, R. E.
1978 Archaeological use and abuse of ecological concepts and studies: The ecotone example. American Antiquity, 43:608–14.

Ritchie, W. A.
1961 A typology and nomenclature for New York projectile points. New York State Museum and Science Service Bulletin, 384. Albany.

Robertson, J. A.
1989 The lithic assemblage of 20SA581: description and analysis. In: Archaeological Investigations at the Weber I and Weber II Sites, Frankenmuth Township, Saginaw County, Michigan, ed. W. A. Lovis, pp. 51–138. Michigan Cultural Resource Investigation Series, I.

Rogers, Margaret B.
1972 The 46th Street site and the occurence of Allegan Ware in southwestern Michigan. Michigan Archaeologist, 18(2):47–108.

Roosa, W. B.
1966 The Warner School site. Michigan Archaeologist, 12:25–34.

Ruffner, J. A.
1980 Climates of the States. Volume 1. Detroit: Gale Research.

Shott, Michael, and Paul Welch
1984 Archaeological resources of the Thumb Area of Michigan. Michigan Archaeologist, 30:1–79.

Simons, D. B.
1971 Radiocarbon date from a Michigan Satchell-Type site. Michigan Archaeologist, 18:209–14.

Smith, Bruce

1987 The independent domestication of indigenous seed-bearing plants in Eastern North America. In: Emergent Horticultural Economies of the Eastern Woodlands, ed. W. F. Keegan. Occasional Paper, No. 7. Center for Archaeological Investigations. Carbondale, Illinois.

Smith, Huron

1923 Ethnobotany of the Menomini Indians. Bulletin of the Public Museum of Milwaukee, 4(1):1–174.

1928 Ethnobotany of the Meskwaki Indians. Bulletin of the Public Museum of Milwaukee, 4(2):175–326.

1932 Ethnobotany of the Ojibwe Indians. Bulletin of the Public Museum of Milwaukee, 4(3):327–525.

1933 Ethnobotany of the Forest Potawotomi Indians. Bulletin of the Public Museum of Milwaukee, 7(1):1–230.

Smith, H. I.

1901 Summary of the archaeology of the Saginaw Valley, Michigan, II. American Anthropologist, 3:501–12.

Speth, John A.

1972 Geology of the Schulz site. In: The Schultz Site at Green Point: A Stratified Occupation Area in the Saginaw Valley of Michigan, ed. James Fitting, pp. 77–85. University of Michigan Museum of Anthropology, Memoir 4. Ann Arbor.

Stahle, D. W., and J. E. Dunn

1982 An analysis and application of the size distribution of waste flakes from the manufacture of bifacial stone tools. World Archaeology, 14:84–97.

Stein, J. K.

1974 The Schmidt site: A geologic report. Unpublished manuscript. The Honors' College, Western Michigan University. Kalamazoo.

1983 Earthworm activity: A source of potential disturbance of archaeological sediments. American Antiquity, 48(2):277–89.

Stothers, D. M.

1977 The Princess Point Complex. Archaeological Survey of Canada Paper, 58. National Museum of Man, Mercury Series. Ottawa.

1983 The Satchell Complex: Tool kit or culture? Arch Notes, 83(3):25–27.

Taggart, D. W.

n.d. The Feeheley site: A Late Archaic site in the Saginaw Valley. Unpublished manuscript, on file at the University of Michigan Museum of Anthropology. Ann Arbor.

1967 Seasonal patterns in settlement, subsistence and industries in the Saginaw Late Archaic. Michigan Archaeologist, 13:153–70.

1981 The Leach site: The Donald W. Foster Collection. Paper presented at the annual meeting of the Michigan Academy of Science, Arts, and Letters. Ann Arbor.

USDA (United States Department of Agriculture)

1970 Saginaw County Soil Survey.

1988 Soils of Saginaw County, Michigan. Map on file at the USDA Soil Survey Office, Saginaw, Michigan.

Veatch, J. O.

1959 Presettlement Forest of Michigan. (Map.) Department of Resource Development, Michigan State University. East Lansing.

Voss, E. G.
1985 Michigan Flora, Part II. Cranbrook Institute of Science Bulletin, 59 and University of Michigan Herbarium.

Walz, Gregory
1989 Preliminary analysis of macroplant remains from Schwerdt, an early 15th-century encampment in the lower Kalamazoo River Valley. Paper presented at the 34th Annual Midwest Archaeological Conference, Iowa City.

Waugh, F. W.
1916 Iroquois foods and food preparation. Memoir 86, Anthropological Series 12. Canada Department of Mines. Ottawa.

White, A. M.
1968 The lithic industries of the Illinois Valley in the Early and Middle Woodland period. University of Michigan Museum of Anthropology, Anthropological Papers, 35. Ann Arbor.

White, J. P.
1969 Fabricators, outils écaillés or scalar cores? Mankind, 6:658–66.

Whittaker, R. H.
1970 Communities and ecosystems. London: MacMillan.

Williamson, B. B.
1979 The wetlands of Dickinson Island, St. Clair County, Michigan. Unpublished Master's thesis, Eastern Michigan University. Ypsilanti.

Winterhalder, B.
1980 Environmental analysis in human evolution and adaptation research. Human Ecology, 8:135–70.

Wobst, H. Martin
1968 The Butterfield site, 20BY29, Bay County, Michigan. In: Contributions to Michigan Archaeology, ed. James Fitting, John R. Halsay and H. M. Wobst, pp. 173–274. University of Michigan Museum of Anthropology Anthropological Papers, 32. Ann Arbor.

Wright, G. A.
1972 Historic floods in the Saginaw Basin. In: The Schultz Site at Green Point: A Stratified Occupation Area in the Saginaw Valley of Michigan, James Fitting, pp. 43–52. Memoirs of the Museum of Anthropology, University of Michigan, 4. Ann Arbor.

Wright, Henry T.
n.d. The geological sequence of the Schultz site, Saginaw County, Michigan. Unpublished manuscript on file at the University of Michigan Museum of Anthropology. Ann Arbor.
1964 A transitional Archaic campsite at Green Point (20SA1). Michigan Archaeologist, 10:17–22.

Wright, Henry T., and R. E. Morlan
1964 The Hart site: A Dustin complex fishing camp on the Shiawassee Embayment. Michigan Archaeologist, 10:49–53.

Yarnell, Richard A.
1964 Aboriginal Relationships between Culture and Plant Life in the Upper Great Lakes Region. University of Michigan Museum of Anthropology, Anthropological Papers, 23. Ann Arbor.

Yellen, J.
1977 Archaeological Approaches to the Present: Models for Reconstructing the Past. New York: Academic Press.

Appendix to Chapter 8

Vessel Descriptions

Vessel 1
Provenience:
100N/101W, level 3
101N/101W, level 3
Exterior surface treatment—fine fabric impressions
Interior surface treatment—smoothed by brushing
Lip decoration—oblique cord-wrapped cord, spaced very closely (4.14 mm apart)
Exterior decoration—undetermined
Interior decoration—shallow cord-wrapped cord-impressed parallel to lip surface beginning at lip margin, spaced closely (1.58 mm apart)
Lip shape—externally beveled, flat surface, slightly thickened
Rim shape—undetermined
Lip thickness—7.22 mm
Rim thickness—6.10 mm immediately below lip
Paste—compact, laminar, grit temper of medium to light density and small to large particle size
Manufacture—undetermined
Weight—2.4 grams
Number of fragments—3
Chronology—because vessel is so fragmentary, it is impossible to assign this vessel to the early Late Woodland or a Middle Woodland phase. Both of these alternatives are suggested by the use of cord-wrapped stick or cord decoration. However, the Middle Woodland Tittabawassee wares tend to have flat lips and sandier paste, and few have cord-impressed exteriors like this vessel. Therefore, it is more likely an early Late Woodland vessel.

Vessel 2
Provenience—100N/101W, level 3
Exterior surface treatment—smoothed-over fine cord impressions, oriented vertically and extends to edge of lip surface decoration
Interior surface treatment—grainy
Lip decoration—cord-wrapped object impressed obliquely across lip surface, leaving high thin ridges between impressions
Exterior decoration—undetermined
Interior decoration—cord-wrapped object impressed obliquely across interior lip margin, and continues at same angle with same decorative tool as on lip surface; leaves a high thin ridge where lip surface impression and interior impression meet; width of impression—5.94 mm
Lip shape—externally beveled, slightly thickened
Rim shape—everted
Lip thickness—7.13 mm
Rim thickness—6.46 mm immediately below lip thickening
Paste—poorly consolidated, laminar, grit temper of medium density and small to medium particle size
Manufacture—undetermined weight—5.0 grams
Number of fragments—1
Chronology—early Late Woodland affiliation suggested by lip morphology and exterior treatment, although the paste is not as hard and compact as the classic local Wayne wares (Plate 8.2*c*)

Vessel 3
Provenience:
103N/102W, level 4
101N/101W, level 3
100N/101W, level 3
Exterior surface treatment—medium cord impressions, oriented vertically and extends to base of lip
Interior surface treatment—smooth
Lip decoration—cord knot leaving deep circular impressions into surface; diameter of impressions—4.86 mm; distance between impressions—7.82 mm
Exterior decoration—undetermined
Interior decoration—small unidentified tool impressions in at least 2 rows; tool pulled

out at slight angle; tool may be a reed because of striations left by tool; impressions are 5.45 mm apart and rows of impressions are 7.98 mm apart
Lip shape—flat surface, slightly externally beveled, rolled and thickened lip
Rim shape—everted lip thickness—7.64 mm
Rim thickness—3.54 mm immediately below lip
Paste—compact, laminar, grit temper of medium density and small particle size
Manufacture—undetermined
Weight—2.0
Number of fragments—3
Chronology—probably early Late Woodland based on lip thickening, exterior treatment and lip decoration, although it is suggestive more of the northern Mackinac wares than the Wayne wares (Plate 8.2*f*)

Vessel 4
Provenience—101N/101W, level 3
Exterior surface treatment—smoothed-over fine cord impressions, oriented vertically and extends up to the lip margin
Interior surface treatment—smooth
Lip decoration—smoothed-over cord impressions, probably paddle
Exterior decoration—undetermined
Interior decoration-
Lip shape—flat surface, slightly thickening due to application of cordwrapped paddle surface
Rim shape—straight to slightly inverted*
Lip thickness—5.42 mm
Rim thickness—4.81 mm immediately below lip, thickens to 5.76 mm at 16.16 mm below lip surface
Paste—compact, laminar, grit temper of light density and small to medium particle size
Manufacture—undetermined
Weight—1.4 grams
Number of fragments—1
Chronology—early Late Woodland based on cord-impressed exterior, paste and lip morphology and treatment, probable Wayne or Saginaw Thin affiliation.

Vessel 5
Provenience—101N/101W, level 3
Exterior surface treatment—smoothed-over fine cord impressions at slightly oblique angle to lip surface; visible brush marks from smoothing
Interior surface treatment—smoothed by brushing
Lip decoration—smoothed-over cord impressions
Exterior decoration—undetermined
Interior decoration—undetermined
Lip shape—rounded
Rim shape—straight expanding*
Lip thickness—3.14 mm
Rim thickness—4.04 mm immediately below lip, to 5.55 mm at 14.28 mm below lip surface
Paste—compact, laminar, grit temper of medium density and small particle size
Manufacture—undetermined
Weight—1.3 grams
Number of fragments—1
Chronology—probably early Late Woodland suggested by exterior treatment and thinness of ware, but fragmentary and heavily eroded

---

Vessel 6
Provenience—102N/101W, level 3
Exterior surface treatment—smoothed-over fine cord impressions, oriented vertically and extends to bulge of lip
Interior surface treatment—smooth though slightly grainy
Lip surface—irregularly smoothed-over cord impressions at oblique angle across lip
Exterior decoration—undetermined
Interior decoration—undetermined
Lip shape—square, slight bulge along exterior lip margin
Rim shape—everted
Lip thickness—5.56 mm
Rim thickness—4.87 mm immediately below lip
Paste—compact, laminar, grit tempter of light density and small particle size
Manufacture—undetermined
Weight—1.5 grams
Number of fragments—1
Chronology—early Late Woodland suggested by rim eversion, thinness of ware and cord-mpressed exterior, but too fragmentary and heavily eroded to be certain

---

Vessel 7
Provenience—102N/101W, level 3
Exterior surface treatment—smoothed-over

*Based on a very small segment of the rim.

fine cord impressions, probably paddle, oriented vertically; more smoothed along external lip margin
Interior surface treatment—smooth
Lip decoration—smoothed-over cord impressions
Exterior decoration—undetermined
Interior decoration—undetermined
Lip shape—square
Rim shape—straight
Lip thickness—3.30 mm
Rim thickness—4.20 mm at 10.00 mm below lip surface
Paste—hard, compact, grit temper of very light density and small particle size
Manufacture—undetermined
Weight—0.9 grams
Number of fragments—1
Chronology—early Late Woodland by thinness of ware, paste, cord-impressed exterior and rim morphology; probably Saginaw Thin

---

Vessel 8
Provenience—103N/101W, level 3
Exterior surface treatment—very fine fabric impressions, only slightly smoothed-over, extends on to lip margin with wider fiber vertically oriented
Interior surface treatment—smoothed by brushing
Lip decoration—slightly smoothed-over cord or fabric impressions
Exterior decoration—undetermined
Interior decoration—undetermined
Lip shape—square
Rim shape—straight
Lip thickness—3.40 mm
Rim thickness—3.78 mm at 10.0 mm below lip surface
Paste—hard, compact, grit temper of light density and small particle size
Manufacture—undetermined
Weight—2.3 grams
Number of fragments—1
Chronology—early Late Woodland, a Wayne ware based on paste, cord-impressed exterior and rim-lip morphology

---

Vessel 9
Provenience:
103N/101W, level 5
104N/102W, level 4
Exterior surface treatment—medium cord impressions, extends up to lip margin and oriented vertically
Interior surface treatment—undetermined
Lip decoration—smoothed-over cord impressions
Exterior decoration—associated body sherd with irregularly distributed shallow circular impressions, with diameter of 4.40 mm, made with unidentified round end tool; can not determine precise location of impressions but curvature of sherd suggests located on gradual curving neck
Interior decoration—undetermined
Lip shape—square
Rim shape—straight
Lip thickness—undetermined
Rim thickness—undetermined
Paste—hard, compact, grit temper of light density and small particle size
Manufacture—undetermined
Weight—6.4 grams
Number of fragments—2
Chronology—early Late Woodland, probably Wayne from paste, cord-impressed exterior and multiple rows of punctates (Plate 8.1*f*)

Vessel 10
Provenience:
105N/101W, level 5
103N/101W, level 4
Exterior surface treatment—fine fabric impressions, oriented vertically
Interior surface treatment—brushed-on clay layer with larger temper particles poking through and numerous brush marks
Lip decoration—probably fabric impressions as on exterior surface
Exterior decoration—undetermined
Interior decoration—undetermined
Lip shape—square, though irregular surface due to impressions
Rim shape—straight
Lip thickness—3.93 mm
Rim thickness—5.80 mm at neck inflection at 14.74 mm below lip surface
Paste—hard, compact, laminar, grit temper of medium density and small to large particle size
Manufacture—undetermined
Weight—17.4 grams
Number of fragments—3
Chronology—early Late Woodland, Saginaw Thin based on exterior treatment, rim and lip morphology and paste characteristics

(see decorated sherd 7 for possible evidence of exterior decoration on this vessel) (Plate 8.1*i*)

Vessel 11
Provenience—105N/101W, level 5
Exterior surface treatment—smoothed-over fine cord impressions, oriented vertically and extends up to lip margin
Interior surface treatment—smooth though slightly grainy
Lip decoration—fine cord impressions, vertical to lip surface placed obliquely across lip surface
Exterior decoration—undetermined
Interior decoration—undetermined
Lip shape—square
Rim shape—straight*
Lip thickness—6.40 mm
Rim thickness—6.84 mm at 14.6 mm below lip surface, thickening slightly from lip
Paste—laminar, grit temper of medium to heavy density and small to medium particle size
Manufacture—undetermined
Weight—2.3 grams
Number of fragments—1
Chronology—though slightly thicker and more temper than classic Wayne ware, rim and lip morphology and exterior treatment suggests early Late Woodland, sharing paste and lip characteristics with southwestern Michigan early Late Woodland Allegan types

---

Vessel 12
Provenience—102N/101W, level 3
Exterior surface treatment—fine cord impressions oriented vertically and extending up to but not on bulging lip margin
Interior surface treatment—smooth
Lip decoration—shallow cord impressions on externally beveled lip surface and on interior lip margin, resulting in slightly rippled lip
Exterior decoration—undetermined
Interior decoration—undetermined
Lip shape—slightly thickened and externally beveled
Rim shape—undetermined
Lip thickness—5.22 mm
Rim thickness—4.26 mm immediately below lip
Paste—compact, laminar, grit temper of light density and small particle size
Manufacture—undetermined
Weight—0.5 grams
Number of fragments—1
Chronology—probably early Late Woodland, based on paste and slightly rolled lip, though very fragmentary evidence

---

Vessel 13
Provenience—102N/101W, level 3
Exterior surface treatment—smoothed, hint of previous impressions but too smoothed and fragmentary to discern
Interior surface treatment—smooth
Lip decoration—deeply impressed cord-wrapped cord in very complex pattern
Exterior decoration—shallower cord-wrapped stick,impressions in indistinguishable pattern
Interior decoration—cord-wrapped stick decoration continues to extend past lip margin
Lip shape—thickened, heavily decorated
Rim shape—undetermined
Lip thickness—11.32 mm
Rim thickness—undetermined
Paste—laminar, poorly consolidated, grit temper of heavy density and medium to large particle size
Manufacture—undetermined
Weight—4.3 grams
Number of fragments—2
Chronology—undetermined but probably Late Woodland based on thickness of lip and deep decoration on lip surface. Heavy temper points to Younge Tradition ware, but lack of exterior and interior surfaces limits any conclusive affiliation

---

Vessel 14
Provenience:
102N/101W, level 3
100–103N/100W, wall scraping
106N/101W, level 3
102N/102W, level 4
Exterior surface treatment—smoothed-over fine cord impressions, impressed up to lip margin and oriented vertically
Interior surface treatment—smoothed with larger temper poking through
Lip decoration—smoothed-over fine cord impressions

Exterior decoration—cord-wrapped cord-impressed oblique across exterior lip margin, offset from interior lip margin elements, forming a wavy pattern
Interior decoration—cord-wrapped cord-impressed oblique across interior lip margin
Lip shape—square, lip slightly thinner than rim
Rim shape—straight
Lip thickness—6.12 mm
Rim thickness—8.3 mm at 20 mm below lip surface
Paste—compact, friable, grit temper of medium to heavy density and medium particle size
Manufacture—undetermined
Weight—16.5 grams
Number of fragments—4
Chronology—undetermined but rim shape, decorative treatment limited to lip margins and ware thickness suggests a late Middle Woodland affiliation; ware type unique for assemblage and may point to later in the Late Woodland (Plates 8.3*g* and 8.4*g*)

Vessel 15
Provenience—103N/101W, level 3
Exterior surface treatment—fine cord impressions, oriented vertically and extends up to lip margin
Interior surface treatment—undetermined
Lip decoration—very smooth, with slight indications of some kind of surface treatment before smoothing
Exterior decoration—undetermined
Interior decoration—undetermined
Lip shape—square, with slight lipping on exterior margin
Rim shape—undetermined
Lip thickness—undetermined
Rim thickness—undetermined
Paste—hard, compact, grit temper of light density and small particle size
Manufacture—undetermined
Weight—0.3 grams
Number of fragments—1
Chronology—probably early Late Woodland based on exterior treatment and lip morphology, but very fragmentary so tentative assessment

---

Vessel 16
Provenience—101N/101W, level 3
Exterior surface treatment—probable cord impressions
Interior surface treatment—undetermined
Lip decoration—faint cord impressions parallel to lip axis
Exterior decoration—undetermined
Interior decoration—undetermined
Lip shape—square
Rim shape—undetermined
Lip thickness—undetermined
Rim thickness—undetermined
Paste—hard, compact, grit temper of light density and small particle size
Manufacture—undetermined
Weight—0.4 grams
Number of fragments—1
Chronology—probably early Late Woodland based on paste and exterior treatment, but very fragmentary, so any assessment is extremely tentative

---

Vessel 17
Provenience—105N/101W, level 3
Exterior surface treatment—cord impressions which extend to immediately below smoothed and flattened exterior lip margin
Interior surface treatment—smooth
Lip decoration—cord-wrapped cord-impressed perpendicular to lip axis; undetermined periodicity of decorative elements, smoothed-on exterior lip margin
Exterior decoration—undetermined
Interior decoration—undetermined
Lip shape—square, possibly rippled along lip axis due to cord-wrapped cord impressions, but too fragmentary to tell
Rim shape—undetermined
Lip thickness—6.36 mm
Rim thickness—5.50 mm immediately below lip
Paste—hard, compact, grit temper of small particle size
Manufacture—undetermined
Weight—1.1 grams
Number of fragments—1
Chronology—two affiliations suggested: (1) may be later in Late Woodland because of cord-wrapped cord impressions across the lip, resulting in an undulating lip surface and cord impressed exterior; (2) use of cord-wrapped cord or stick indicative of Tittabawassee Middle Woodland ware, and Fischer suggests that a minor amount of Tittabawassee had cord-impressed exteriors.

However, the paste is more suggestive of the later period. Furthermore, Fischer admits that the Tittabawassee ware is ill-defined and may subsume unrelated vessels.

Vessel 18
Provenience—105N/101W, level 3
Exterior surface treatment—smoothed-over fine cord impressions, oriented vertically and extends up to edge of lip
Interior surface treatment—smooth
Lip decoration—cord-wrapped stick-impressed perpendicular to lip surface; width of impression is 6.70 mm
Exterior decoration—undetermined interior decoration, undetermined lip shape, slightly externally beveled
Rim shape—undetermined
Lip thickness—6.40 mm
Rim thickness—6.68 mm at 8.0 mm below lip surface
Paste—compact, laminar, grit temper of light density and small particle size
Manufacture—undetermined
Weight—1.0 grams
Number of fragments—1
Chronology—probably late Late Woodland based on deep and wide cord-wrapped cord impression placed across lip producing an undulating surface, but based on a very small fragment, so affiliation is tentative

---

Vessel 19
Provenience:
100N/101W, level 4
104N/101W, level 2
104N/101W, level 3
Exterior surface treatment—although hard to discern due to pre-dominance of decorative motif, indication of smoothed-over fine cord impressions
Interior surface treatment—undetermined
Lip decoration—undetermined
Exterior decoration—medium cord or unidentified tool impressions in a complex pattern with faint striations crossing the pattern in some places
Interior decoration—undetermined
Lip shape—undetermined
Rim shape—undetermined
Lip thickness—undetermined
Rim thickness—undetermined
Paste—poorly consolidated, laminar, paste, grit temper of very heavy density and small to medium particle size
Manufacture—undetermined
Weight—14.0 grams
Number of fragments—3
Chronology—undetermined; lack of evidence for coil manufacture and heavy density of grit temper is suggestive of late Late Woodland, perhaps Younge Tradition, but without a fragment of the rim, these conclusions are highly speculative. A very distinctive ware from rest of the ceramic assemblage, both the early Late Woodland and Early Woodland. (Because of distinctiveness of temper, related body sherds were coded separately as paste 6.)

Vessel 20
Provenience:
103N/101W, level 3
104N/102W, level 4
Exterior surface treatment—fine cord impressions, irregularly smoothed, oriented vertically and extends up to lip margin
Interior surface treatment—smoothed by brushing leaving horizontal striations
Lip decoration—cord-wrapped cord elements impressed obliquely across lip surface, 14.1 mm apart
Exterior decoration—undetermined
Interior decoration—same cord-wrapped cord elements as on lip surface extending from lip edge, placed at opposite oblique angle from exterior decorative elements and offset from lip surface decoration
Lip shape—externally beveled, due to application of impressions
Rim shape—everted with thickened collar base at 22.4 mm below lip surface
Lip thickness—6.25 mm
Rim thickness—5.32 mm at base of collar
Paste—laminar, moderately compact, grit temper of light to medium density and small to medium particle size
Manufacture—undetermined
Weight—23.2 grams
Number of fragments—2
Chronology—early Late Woodland Wayne ware based on type of paste and cord-impressed exterior, probably later in the Wayne sequence because of the presence of a collar (post-A.D. 1000)

Vessel 21
Provenience—110N/101W, level 3
Exterior surface treatment—medium cord impressions, oriented vertically, irregular pattern
Interior surface treatment—smoothed by brushing with larger grit temper particles poking through
Lip decoration—shallow irregular cord impressions placed perpendicular across lip surface
Exterior decoration—at least four thin incised lines, placed roughly parallel to lip surface, at 5.50 mm apart
Interior decoration—circular, unidentified tool impression at interior of upper lip possibly indicates a row of such impressions; diameter of impressions is 5.92 mm
Lip shape—rounded
Rim shape—straight, with slight ridge marking where lip coil was placed on the rim
Lip thickness—7.44 mm
Rim thickness—9.96 mm at 13.53 mm below lip surface, where lip coil meets rim
Paste—sandy, coarse, with grit temper of light density and medium to large particle size
Manufacture—coil
Weight—9.8 grams
Number of fragments—1
Chronology—two possible interpretations: (1) late Early Woodland Shiawassee ware based on paste characteristics, coil manufacture type of exterior treatment and thickness; (2) late Middle Woodland-early Late Woodland temporal placement suggested by rounded lip and coil manufacture with cord-impressed exterior.

Vessel 22
Provenience—103N/101W, level 3
Exterior surface treatment—undetermined
Interior surface treatment—smooth
Lip decoration—cord-wrapped object impressed vertically on the interior edge, extending onto lip surface; 7.94 mm between impressions
Exterior decoration—undetermined
Interior decoration—undetermined
Lip shape—undetermined
Rim shape—undetermined
Lip thickness—undetermined
Rim thickness—undetermined
Paste—compact, laminar, grit temper of medium density and small particle size
Manufacture—undetermined
Weight—0.7 grams
Number of fragments—1
Chronology—undetermined; paste and decoration on interior of lip suggests early Late Woodland, but too fragmentary to be certain

---

Vessel 23
Provenience—114N/101W, level 2
Exterior surface treatment—medium cord impressions oriented vertically and extends part way up rolled lip exterior margin
Interior surface treatment—smoothed by brushing
Lip decoration—cord impressions placed slightly obliquely across front half of lip surface, 5.10 mm apart
Exterior decoration—undetermined
Interior decoration—slash marks, probably made with a thin cord, placed irregularly across lip margin at roughly 4.11 mm intervals and extending down the interior of rim 6.57 mm
Lip shape—thickened and rolled to exterior, then flattened by cord impressions, like those on exterior surface, making the lip externally beveled
Rim shape—everted
Lip thickness—6.32 mm
Rim thickness—5.68 mm immediately below thickened lip
Paste—laminar, appears sandy due to heavy erosion, grit temper of very light density and small particle size
Manufacture—undetermined
Weight—2.3 grams
Number of fragments—1
Chronology—early Late Woodland, based on thickening of lip, rim eversion and decorative treatment on lip; probable variant of Mackinac ware (Plate 8.2*e*)

Vessel 24
Provenience—120N/101W, level 4
Exterior surface treatment—medium cord impressions, placed at slight oblique angle to lip surface, extending up to small exterior lip margin fold
Interior surface treatment—smoothed by brushing near lip, with striations from a reedlike tool farther down the interior,

placed irregularly at slight angles or parallel to lip surface, at irregular intervals
Lip decoration—cord impressions placed obliquely across lip surface, pushing lip forward making a small roll overhang at exterior lip margin
Exterior decoration—undetermined
Interior decoration—see interior surface treatment
Lip shape—rounded with lip surface slightly flattened by cord impressions
Rim shape—straight expanding
Lip thickness—5.65 mm
Rim thickness—9.27 mm at 18.32 mm below lip surface
Paste—silty chunky, grit temper of light density and medium to large particle size
Manufacture—undetermined
Weight—6.5 grams
Number of fragments—1
Chronology—possibly transitional late Middle Woodland/early Late Woodland. It is coarser ware than early Late Woodland; lip and rim shape, exterior cord impressions and striated interior points to the relatively unknown Transitional period (see vessels 41, 43, 35 and 44) (Plates 8.3*c* and 8.4*c*)

Vessel 25
Provenience:
111N/101W, level 3
112N/101W, level 2
Exterior surface treatment—undetermined
Interior surface treatment—undetermined
Lip decoration—cord-wrapped cord elements placed slightly obliquely across lip interior 2.86 mm apart, with same decorative elements placed on lip surface at the opposite oblique angle
Exterior decoration—undetermined
Interior decoration—undetermined
Lip shape—undetermined, though probably thickened
Rim shape—undetermined
Lip thickness—undetermined
Rim thickness—undetermined
Paste—laminar, compact, grit temper of light density and small particle size
Manufacture—undetermined
Weight—13.0 grams
Number of fragments—2
Chronology—hard to defend any temporal attribution with such a tiny fragment; Tittabawassee Middle Woodland or early Late Woodland suggested by lip decoration. Latter more likely, based on paste characteristics and hint of lip thickening

---

Vessel 26
Provenience—102N/102W, level 4
Exterior surface treatment—smoothed-over fine cord impressions, oriented vertically and extends to immediately below lip
Interior surface treatment—smoothed with larger particles poking through
Lip decoration—wedge-shaped tool deeply cut perpendicular across lip surface, elements 5.21 mm apart and offset from interior margin decorative element
Exterior decoration—row of slightly deeper cord impressions irregularly at 12.0 mm below lip; possibly made by edge of paddle in placing a new panel of impressions, rather than intentional row of decorative elements
Interior decoration—smoothed-over tool impressions, possibly a cord with knot at one end, leaving an oblique element across interior lip margin 5.26 mm apart and extending on to interior surface by 6.40 mm
Lip shape—heavily impressed with decorations, rounded between deep impressions
Rim shape—everted
Lip thickness—5.94 mm
Rim thickness—5.63 mm at neck inflection below lip, 11.0 mm below lip surface
Paste—laminar, poorly consolidated, grit temper of medium to heavy density and small to medium particle size
Manufacture—undetermined
Weight—6.5 grams
Number of fragments—4
Chronology—early Late Woodland, Wayne or Saginaw Thin based on thinness of ware, slight rim eversion and decorated lip area, although heavier amount of temper not as characteristic of this ware (Plate 8.2*b*)

Vessel 27
Provenience:
118N/102W, level 4
126N/103W, level 6
Exterior surface treatment—smoothed by brushing, grainy
Interior surface treatment—smoothed by brushing, grainy
Lip decoration—none

Exterior decoration—unknown number of horizontal lines of cord-wrapped stick impressions separated, in one case, by 9.06 mm of untreated space; some smoothing after cord-wrapped object applied
Interior decoration—oblique lines of cord-wrapped stick impressions starting at lip, extending 11.38 mm down interior of rim and placed close together, 5.36 mm apart; smoothed-over after applied; thin incised line placed about 1 cm below base of oblique elements
Lip shape—rounded
Rim shape—straight expanding
Lip thickness—3.44 mm
Rim thickness—7.92 mm at 24.0 mm below lip surface
Paste—sandy, coarse, grit temper of medium density and small to medium particle size
Manufacture—coil
Weight—27.5 grams
Number of fragments—5
Chronology—Middle Woodland, probably Tittabawassee type, based on use of oblique lines of decoration on interior and paste characteristics (Plate 8.4*g-i*)

Vessel 28
Provenience—118N/102W, level 4
Exterior surface treatment—smoothed-over fine cord impressions placed at oblique angle to lip surface and extending to to exterior lip margin
Interior surface treatment—smoothed by brushing with larger temper particles poking through
Lip decoration—cord impressions as on exterior surface applied at oblique angle and cutting into interior lip margin, causing lip margin to appear rippled
Exterior decoration—undetermined
Interior decoration—undetermined
Lip shape—square
Rim shape—straight
Lip thickness—4.72 mm
Rim thickness—5.92 mm at 10.0 mm below lip surface
Paste—compact, laminar, grit temper of light density and small to large particle size
Manufacture—undetermined
Weight—4.8 grams
Number of fragments—1
Chronology—early Late Woodland, probably Wayne ware, based on lip shape, cord-impressed exterior and thinness of ware (Plate 8.1*b*)

Vessel 29
Provenience—106N/102W, level 3
Exterior surface treatment—fine fabric impressions, with predominant direction of weave running parallel to lip surface
Interior surface treatment—smoothed by brushing leaving clear brushing marks parallel to lip surface
Lip decoration—very smoothed surface with very faint fabric or cord impressions visible on interior edge of lip surface
Exterior decoration—undetermined
Interior decoration—undetermined
Lip shape—externally beveled
Rim shape—straight*
Lip thickness—3.20 mm
Rim thickness—5.06 mm at 8.0 mm below lip surface
Paste—compact, laminar, grit temper of light density and small to medium particle size
Manufacture—undetermined
Weight—1.0 grams
Number of fragments—2 (glued together)
Chronology—probably early Late Woodland, based on paste and thinness of ware, a textile- or fabric-impressed variant of Wayne ware; striated interior may suggest a slightly earlier affiliation, the late Middle Woodland/early Late Woodland transition, but most of the vessels in this assemblage which may come from this phase (vessels 35, 41, 43 and 44) have coarser paste. One named type from this time period based on sherds from the Schultz site, Ruben Linear Cord-impressed, has a finer, more compact paste like this vessel

---

Vessel 30
Provenience—106N/102W, level 3
Exterior surface treatment—fine cord impressions placed slightly obliquely to lip surface and up to lip margin
Interior surface treatment—irregularly smoothed interior
Lip decoration—smoothed with some linear marks parallel to lip axis near interior and exterior lip edges
Exterior decoration—undetermined
Interior decoration—undetermined
Lip shape—square

Rim shape—straight
Lip thickness—5.50 mm
Rim thickness—5.12 mm at 6.80 mm below lip surface
Paste—compact, laminar grit temper of medium to heavy density and medium particle size
Manufacture—undetermined
Weight—1.9 grams
Number of fragments—1
Chronology—early Late Woodland, a Wayne ware vessel by paste, exterior treatment and thinness of ware; some similarities, the smoothed flat lip, to southwestern Michigan Allegan wares (Plate 8.1*c*)

Vessel 31
Provenience:
104N/102W, level 3
103N/102W, level 3
102N/102W, level 4
Exterior surface treatment—smoothed-over fine cord impressions, oriented vertically and extending over entire lip
Interior surface treatment—undetermined
Lip decoration—cord-wrapped tool impressions placed obliquely across lip surface, spaced very closely leaving little lip surface intact
Exterior decoration—at least 3 rows of deep wedge-shaped tool impressions with impressions place closely vertically and horizontally; impressions 6.36 mm in maximum length and 3.42 mm in maximum width
Interior decoration—cord impressions on upper interior which was flattened, probably with a cord-wrapped paddle; remaining interior missing
Lip shape—narrow externally beveled surfaced with wider flattened interior surface, thickened lip
Rim shape—everted
Lip thickness—5.22 mm
Rim thickness—undetermined
Paste—compact, laminar, grit temper of light density and small particle size
Manufacture—undetermined
Weight—3.4 grams
Number of fragments—3
Chronology—Late Woodland based on thickened lip, everted rim and paste; lack of collar and presence of rolled thickened lip suggests early in Late Woodland sequence, but unusual tool type used on exterior suggestive of a southeastern relationship, such as Riviere au Vase phase (Plate 8.1*g*)

Vessel 32
Provenience:
102N/102W, level 3
107N/102W, level 3
110N/102W, level 3
Exterior surface treatment—medium cord impressions, oriented vertically and extends up to roll of lip
Interior surface treatment—smooth
Lip decoration—exterior and interior lip margin cut with deep oblique tool incisions, irregularly horizontal spacing but on average 4.00 mm apart; line impressed parallel to lip axis down the middle of the lip surface, probably made by a thin cord or thin striated object used for brushing on pots in this assemblage
Exterior decoration—undetermined
Interior decoration—at least one row of very small impressions, made by cord or cord knots, 9.14 mm below lip surface, 5.58 mm between each impression; rim broken along this row
Lip shape—square, thickened
Rim shape—everted
Lip thickness—7.32 mm
Rim thickness—6.28 mm immediately below lip
Paste—laminar, compact, grit temper of light to medium density and small medium particle size
Manufacture—undetermined
Weight—4.4 grams
Number of fragments—3
Chronology—early Late Woodland based on eversion of rim, thickened lip and cord impressed exterior, although paste not the classic hard compact characteristic of Wayne ware (Plate 8.2*d*)

Vessel 33
Provenience—110N/102W, level 5
Exterior surface treatment—smoothed-over fine cord impressions, oriented vertically and extends up to lip margin
Interior surface treatment—undetermined
Lip decoration—smoothed-over cord impressions with tiny cord-wrapped cord cutting obliquely across exterior lip margin, 7.26 mm between these decorative elements

Exterior decoration—one impression, probably made with cord, at 13.54 mm below lip surface, which may represent a row of impressions
Interior decoration—undetermined
Lip shape—square
Rim shape—straight
Lip thickness—undetermined
Rim thickness—undetermined
Paste—hard, compact, grit temper of very light density and small particle size
Manufacture—undetermined
Weight—0.9 grams
Number of fragments—1
Chronology—early Late Woodland from rim and lip morphology and compact paste, probably Wayne ware/Saginaw Thin

---

Vessel 34
Provenience—109N/103W, level 4
Exterior surface treatment—smoothed-over undetermined surface treatment
Interior surface treatment—smooth
Lip decoration—smoothed-over undetermined treatment
Exterior decoration—undetermined
Interior decoration—undetermined
Lip shape—square
Rim shape—straight
Lip thickness—7.67 mm
Rim thickness—11.72 mm at 13.6 mm below lip surface
Paste—sandy/silty, chunky, grit temper (distinctive dark crystalline temper) of light to medium density and medium particle size
Manufacture—coil
Weight—3.1 grams
Number of fragments—1
Chronology—Shiawassee Ware, a late Early Woodland ware, which is characterized by coil manufacture, a distinctive temper, sandy/silty paste

---

Vessel 35
Provenience—113N/103W, level 4
Exterior surface treatment—coarse cord impressions placed parallel to lip surface
Interior surface treatment—smooth
Lip decoration—thin cord or incised lines cut perpendicular across lip surface at irregular intervals
Exterior decoration—undetermined
Interior decoration—horizontal lines of coarse incising
Lip shape—square to slightly externally beveled
Rim shape—straight
Lip thickness—7.78 mm
Rim thickness—9.44 mm at 13.0 mm below lip surface
Paste—sandy/silty, chunky, grit temper of medium density and medium to large particle size
Manufacture—coil
Weight—4.5 grams
Number of fragments—1
Chronology—undetermined but may fall into the late Middle Woodland/early Late Woodland phase, based on the striated interior, oblique exterior cord impressions and rim-lip shape (see vessels 41, 42, 43, and 44)

Vessel 36
Provenience—109N/103W, level 4
Exterior surface treatment—smoothed-over fine cord impressions oriented vertically surface and extends up to lip margin
Interior surface treatment—smooth
Lip decoration—cord-wrapped cord oblique elements deeply cut across lip surface, 6.90 mm between elements, cutting into exterior lip margin
Exterior decoration—undetermined
Interior decoration—7.76 mm-wide band of oblique lines of thin cord or carved paddle over a loosely woven fine weave textile
Lip shape—rounded
Rim shape—straight*
Lip thickness—5.66 mm
Rim thickness—5.44 mm at 10.0 mm below lip surface
Paste—compact, laminar, grit temper of light density and small to medium particle size
Manufacture—undetermined
Weight—1.5 grams
Number of fragments—1
Chronology—undetermined; cord-impressed exterior, paste attributes and thinness of ware suggests early Late Woodland, but too fragmentary

---

Vessel 37
Provenience—119N/103W, level 3
Exterior surface treatment—smoothed-over

coarse cord impressions placed at slight angle to lip surface
Interior surface treatment—smoothed by brushing, modelled interior
Lip decoration—brushing marks over grainy surface
Exterior decoration—undetermined
Interior decoration—undetermined
Lip shape—rounded with slight interior beveling
Rim shape—straight
Lip thickness—10.28 mm
Rim thickness—11.25 mm at 17.0 mm below lip surface
Paste—sandy, coarse, grit temper of medium to heavy density and small to medium particle size
Manufacture—coil
Weight—8.6 grams
Number of fragments—2
Chronology—Early Woodland, based on thickness, temper density and size coarseness of ware; most likely late Early Woodland Shiawassee ware

---

Vessel 38
Provenience:
115N/103W, level 5
114N/104W, level 4
Exterior surface treatment—smoothed-over coarse cord impressions placed at angle to lip surface
Interior surface treatment—smooth, grainy where eroded
Lip decoration—same smoothed-over coarse cord impressions as on exterior surface
Exterior decoration—undetermined
Interior decoration—undetermined
Lip shape—flat surface, slightly externally beveled
Rim shape—straight*
Lip thickness—8.03 mm
Rim thickness—5.16 mm at 15.0 mm from lip surface
Paste—silty/sandy, chunky, grit temper of medium density and small to medium particle size
Manufacture—coil
Weight—5.1 grams
Number of fragments—2
Chronology—undetermined; coarse paste, thickness and coil manufacture point to a pre-early Late Woodland time period

---

Vessel 39
Provenience—112N/101W, level 2
Exterior surface treatment—smooth
Interior surface treatment—undetermined
Lip decoration—smoothed with a round impression, possibly a cord knot, poked into lip surface, causing surface to look undulating
Exterior decoration—undetermined
Interior decoration—undetermined
Lip shape—thickened and roughly rounded
Rim shape—undetermined
Lip thickness—7.11 mm
Rim thickness—undetermined
Paste—sandy, coarse, grit temper of light density and small to medium particle size
Manufacture—undetermined
Weight—2.0 grams
Number of fragments—1
Chronology—undulating lip surface suggestive of Late Woodland, but rim heavily eroded; attribution to Late Woodland uncertain because of sandy, coarse paste; possibly a Tittabawassee variant similar to one example of this ware from the Schultz site

---

Vessel 40
Provenience—117N/103W, level 4
Exterior surface treatment—widely spaced medium cord impressions with shallower thin fibers between, probably a multi-layered paddle, at slight oblique angle to lip surface
Interior surface treatment—smoothed by brushing
Lip decoration—thin cord cut irregularly at oblique angle to lip axis
Exterior decoration—see exterior surface treatment
Interior decoration—irregular, generally deep incised lines, placed roughly parallel to lip surface, which does not extend below neck inflection
Lip shape—square
Rim shape—straight expanding, neck inflection 15 mm below lip surface
Lip thickness—6.22 mm
Rim thickness—9.91 mm at neck inflection at 15 mm below lip surface
Paste—sandy, coarse, grit temper of medium density and small to very large particle size
Manufacture—undetermined
Weight—12.9 grams
Number of fragments—1

Chronology—late Early Woodland Shiawassee by paste, irregular loosely twisted cord on exterior which appears to be Shiawassee when compared to Schultz; however, may be from ill-defined late Middle Woodland to early Late Woodland transition, because of interior striations/wiping, although very different in paste from the Transitional type defined at Shultz, Ruben Linear Cord-impressed (Plate 8.5*b*)

Vessel 41
Provenience—120N/103W, level 4
Exterior surface treatment—heavy fabric impression, with thicker fibers applied vertically
Interior surface treatment—smoothed by brushing
Lip decoration—fabric impression applied obliquely to lip surface
Exterior decoration—11.86 mm wide band of fabric applied obliquely adjacent to lip across previously applied vertically oriented fabric impressions, possibly for decorative effect
Interior decoration—undetermined
Lip shape—square
Rim shape—straight
Lip thickness—5.17 mm
Rim thickness—6.68 mm at 14.0 mm below lip surface
Paste—compact, laminar, grit temper of light density and medium to large particle size
Manufacture—undetermined
Weight—5.2 grams
Number of fragments—1
Chronology—possible early Late Woodland based on rim-lip morphology, exterior surface treatment and paste, although striated interior may suggest placement in the late Middle Woodland to early Late Woodland transition (see vessels 35, 42, 43 and 44) (Plates 8.3*d* and 8.4*d*)

Vessel 42
Provenience—120N/103W, level 4
Exterior surface treatment—medium cord impressions, impressed deeply with intervening ridges smoothed-over and oriented vertically
Interior surface treatment—smoothed by brushing
Lip decoration—smoothed on interior margin, cord impressions half-way up exterior margin, surface cord-impressed
Exterior decoration—undetermined
Interior decoration—undetermined
Lip shape—flattened top, rounded interior and exterior margins, with uneven indentation on interior below lip, thickened
Rim shape—straight with slight incurving
Lip thickness—7.89 mm
Rim thickness—6.12 mm immediately below lip; body then thickens to 7.90 mm at 25.0 mm below lip surface, resulting in incurving of rim
Paste—silty-sandy, compact, grit temper of light density and small to medium particle size
Manufacture—undetermined
Weight—7.0 grams
Number of fragments—1
Chronology—medium thin compact ware with exterior cord impressions suggests early Late Woodland, but lip-rim morphology may point to late Middle/early Late Woodland affiliation

---

Vessel 43
Provenience—120N/103W, level 4
Exterior surface treatment—large cord impressions over a layer of of finer cord impressions, suggests a multilayered cord-wrapped paddle, at slight oblique angle to lip surface
Interior surface treatment—smoothed
Lip decoration—smoothed-over cord impressions
Exterior decoration—see exterior surface treatment
Interior decoration—very light irregularly spaced incised lines, possibly striations left from brushing surface
Lip shape—slightly rounded
Rim shape—straight expanding
Lip thickness—6.32 mm
Rim thickness—12.28 mm at 9.0 mm below lip surface
Paste—silty, very chunky, grit temper of light density and small to very large particle size
Manufacture—undetermined
Weight—6.7 grams
Number of fragments—1
Chronology—undetermined; oblique cord exterior treatment, rim-lip shape and interior striations suggest transitional late Middle Woodland/early Late Woodland, but thickness and paste characteristics slightly

differentiate this vessel from other vessels of this time period (see vessels 35, 41, 42 and 44, Plates 8.3*b* and 8.4*b*)

Vessel 44
Provenience—120N/103W, level 4
Exterior surface treatment—medium cord impressions placed at least twice across surface at different angles, leaving a hatched appearance
Interior surface treatment—smoothed
Lip decoration—smoothed-over cord impressions
Exterior decoration—see exterior surface treatment
Interior decoration—band of incised lines or striations of varying depths and widths at slight angle to lip surface
Lip shape—square
Rim shape—straight expanding
Lip thickness—5.80 mm
Rim thickness—9.02 mm at 17.0 mm below lip surface
Paste—silty/sandy, chunky, grit temper of medium density and small to large particle size
Manufacture—undetermined
Weight—6.2 grams
Number of fragments—1
Chronology—probable late Middle Woodland/early Late Woodland transition, based on exterior treatment, rim-lip shape and interior striations (see vessels 35, 41, 42 and 43, Plates 8.3*a* and 8.4*a*)

Vessel 45
Provenience—105N/102W (slump)
Exterior surface treatment—see exterior decoration
Interior surface treatment—smooth
Lip decoration—undetermined
Exterior decoration—medium cord impressions at oblique angle to axis of collar base, with vertical fine cord impressions below the base
Interior decoration—undetermined
Lip shape—undetermined
Rim shape—slight collar*
Lip thickness—undetermined
Rim thickness—4.25 mm at base of collar
Paste—hard, compact, grit temper of medium density and small particle size
Manufacture—undetermined
Weight—1.8 grams
Number of fragments—1
Chronology—probably early Late Woodland Wayne ware, based on thin compact ware attributes, cord-impressed exterior; may be late in the Wayne sequence because of hint of a slight collar; cannot be definite without portion of upper rim

---

Vessel 46
Provenience—122N/103W, level 3
Exterior surface treatment—smoothed-over widely spaced medium cord impressions, oriented vertically and extends to lip margin
Interior surface treatment—undetermined
Lip decoration—smoothed-over cord impressions placed perpendicular to lip axis
Exterior decoration—undetermined
Interior decoration—undetermined
Lip shape—square
Rim shape—straight
Lip thickness—undetermined
Rim thickness—undetermined
Paste—compact, laminar, grit temper of light density and small particle size
Manufacture—undetermined
Weight—3.4 grams
Number of fragments—1
Chronology—early Late Woodland; Wayne Cordmarked/Saginaw Thin by compact paste, rim-lip morphology and surface treatment (Plate 8.1*a*)

Vessel 47
Provenience—123N/103W, level 4
Exterior surface treatment—fine cord impressions placed at oblique angle to lip surface
Interior surface treatment—undetermined
Lip decoration—smoothed-over cord impressions on lip surface, with deep unidentified tool impressions cut perpendicular across interior lip margin (7.50 mm apart), obliquely across exterior lip margin (6.80 mm apart)
Exterior decoration—undetermined
Interior decoration—undetermined
Lip shape—thickened, square
Rim shape—straight*
Lip thickness—7.36 mm
Rim thickness—5.12 mm immediately below lip

Paste—porous, laminar, grit temper of light density and small particle size
Manufacture—undetermined
Weight—2.6 grams
Number of fragments—1
Chronology—probable early Late Woodland from thickened lip, lip margin decoration, paste, cord-impressed exterior, but no direct type relationship drawn (Plate 8.2*a*)

Vessel 48
Provenience—127N/103W, level 5
Exterior surface treatment—smoothed-over fine cord impressions
Interior surface treatment—smooth
Lip decoration—smoothed-over cord impressions
Exterior decoration—at least 2 rows of tiny impressions or holes placed 4.23 mm apart, with holes within rows 4.54 mm apart
Interior decoration—undetermined
Lip shape—peaked
Rim shape—straight expanding*
Lip thickness—4.30 mm
Rim thickness—6.72 mm at 16.0 mm below lip in midst of rows of decoration
Paste—sandy, coarse, grit temper of medium density and small to large particle size
Manufacture—undetermined
Weight—1.9 grams
Number of fragments—1
Chronology—undetermined; paste does not suggest Late Woodland and thickness does not suggest Early Woodland. Too fragmentary to make any other claims.

Vessel 49
Provenience—114N/104W, level 4
Exterior surface treatment—fine fabric impression oriented vertically
Interior surface treatment—smooth
Lip decoration—smoothed-over fabric impressions
Exterior decoration—undetermined
Interior decoration—undetermined
Lip shape—square
Rim shape—straight
Lip thickness—3.48 mm
Rim thickness—3.58 mm at 13.0 mm below lip surface where incurving begins
Paste—hard, compact, grit temper of very light density and small particle size
Manufacture—undetermined
Weight—2.0 grams
Number of fragments—1
Chronology—early Late Woodland Saginaw Thin Cord-marked, by paste, thinness, vertical rim shape and slight rim thickening from compression from smoothing (Fischer 1972) (Plate 8.1*d*)

Vessel 50
Provenience—111N/104W, level 4
Exterior surface treatment—smoothed-over fine cord impressions, oriented vertically
Interior surface treatment—smoothed by brushing, with larger grit particles poking through
Lip decoration—smoothed-over cord impressions
Exterior decoration—a single deep cord impression along edge of exterior lip margin, with a second deep impression by a thin, tool placed parallel to and 7.33 mm below lip surface
Interior decoration—undetermined
Lip shape—slightly externally beveled, flat surface
Rim shape—straight
Lip thickness—4.58 mm
Rim thickness—4.71 mm at 14.0 mm below lip surface
Paste—compact, laminar, grit temper of medium density and small to medium particle size
Manufacture—undetermined
Weight—1.7 grams
Number of fragments—1
Chronology—probable early Late Woodland by thinness, paste and cord-impressed exterior; Wayne or Allegan-like, based on the smoothed lip (Plate 8.1*e*)

Vessel 51
Provenience—104N/102–103W (slump)
Exterior surface treatment—smooth
Interior surface treatment—smooth
Lip decoration—undetermined
Exterior decoration—lines of tight cord-wrapped cord placed at oblique angle to lip surface, 2.92 mm apart
Interior decoration—same tool impressed at opposite oblique angle from elements on exterior, 4.80 mm apart
Lip shape—undetermined
Rim shape—straight*

Lip thickness—undetermined
Rim thickness—4.37 mm
Paste—compact, laminar, grit temper of medium density and small particle size
Manufacture—undetermined
Weight—0.7 grams
Number of fragments—1
Chronology—undetermined. Not Early Woodland because of thinness of fragment and kind of decoration; use of tight cord-wrapped cord might suggest Tittabawassee ware, but not borne out by paste and thinness; tentatively may be a Late Woodland vessel, but very fragmentary.

Vessel 52
Provenience:
107N/103W, level 4
107N/103W, level 5
Exterior surface treatment—smoothed-over fine cord impressions, oriented vertically
Interior surface treatment—undetermined
Lip decoration—thickened exterior margin impressed with same cord impression as rest of exterior surface, lip surface broken off
Exterior decoration—row of small, unidentified tool impressions placed at inflection of neck 6.40 mm apart (rim fragment broken off at punctates)
Interior decoration—undetermined
Lip shape—slightly thickened, front of lip flattened
Rim shape—undetermined
Lip thickness—4.74 mm
Rim thickness—undetermined
Paste—compact, laminar, grit temper of medium density and small particle size
Manufacture—undetermined
Weight—1.6 grams
Number of fragments—2
Chronology—early Late Woodland Wayne ware or Saginaw Thin; very fragmentary but exterior cord impressions, evidence of a row of punctates on exterior and thickened lip suggests this temporal placement

---

Vessel 53
Provenience—103N (slump)
Exterior surface treatment—large coarse cord impression, oriented vertically
Interior surface treatment—smooth
Lip decoration—fine cords wrapped obliquely from flat interior surface across beveled lip surface, following same angle; cords irregularly 2.48 mm apart
Exterior decoration—undetermined
Interior decoration—undetermined
Lip shape—externally beveled, thickened then flattened on exterior
Rim shape—straight*
Lip thickness—6.85 mm
Rim thickness—4.76 mm immediately below thickened lip
Paste—exfoliated, grit temper of small to medium particles (heavily rolled)
Manufacture—undetermined
Weight—1.6 grams
Number of fragments—1
Chronology—extremely water rolled; possible cord-impressed exterior and rolled lip suggests early Late Woodland, but very tentative

---

Vessel 54
Provenience—106N/102W, level 3
Exterior surface treatment—undetermined
Interior surface treatment—smooth with large grit particles poking through
Lip decoration—smoothed-over cord impressions
Exterior decoration—undetermined
Interior decoration—undetermined
Lip shape—square
Rim shape—undetermined
Lip thickness—undetermined
Rim thickness—undetermined
Paste—sandy, coarse, grit temper of heavy density and small to large particle size
Manufacture—undetermined
Weight—0.5 grams
Number of fragments—1
Chronology—possible late Early Woodland; tiny fragment but paste characteristics reminiscent of Shiawassee ware

---

Vessel 55
Provenience—104N/102W, level 5
Exterior surface treatment—smoothed-over cord impressions
Interior surface treatment—smooth with larger grit particles poking through
Lip decoration—shallow small incised lines or cord marks placed slightly obliquely across lip surface
Exterior decoration—deep, thin incised line cut vertically from exterior lip margin,

extending down 7.81 mm; probably a series of such notches along lip exterior margin
Interior decoration—undetermined
Lip shape—slightly rounded
Rim shape—straight*
Lip thickness—4.74 mm
Rim thickness—expanding to 6.40 mm at 10.0 mm below lip surface
Paste—sandy, coarse, grit temper of heavy density and small to large particle size
Manufacture—undetermined
Weight—0.9 grams
Number of fragments—1
Chronology—undetermined; notched exterior lip and rounded lip suggest Middle Woodland affiliation, but too small and fragmentary to defend

---

Vessel 56
Provenience—107N/102W, level 4
Exterior surface treatment—fine cord impressions, oriented vertically
Interior surface treatment—undetermined
Lip decoration—fine cord impressions placed parallel to lip axis, with additional impressions on front of thickened lip
Exterior decoration—undetermined
Interior decoration—undetermined
Lip shape—thickened
Rim shape—everted*
Lip thickness—undetermined
Rim thickness—undetermined
Paste—compact, laminar, grit temper of light density and small to medium particle size
Manufacture—undetermined
Weight—0.9 grams
Number of fragments—1
Chronology—probably Late Woodland from exterior cord impressions and thickened lip; too fragmentary to tell more

---

Vessel 57
Provenience—100N/101W, level 3
Exterior surface treatment—smoothed-over cord impressions
Interior surface treatment—smooth
Lip decoration—smoothed-over cord impressions
Exterior decoration—undetermined
Interior decoration—undetermined
Lip shape—rounded
Rim shape—straight*
Lip thickness—4.88 mm
Rim thickness—4.34 mm at 10.0 mm below lip surface
Paste—poorly consolidated, laminar, grit temper of medium density and small to medium particle size
Manufacture—undetermined
Weight—0.9 grams
Number of fragments—1
Chronology—undetermined; very thin ware, so not Early Woodland

---

Vessel 58
Provenience—115N/103W, level 4
Exterior surface treatment—smoothed-over fine cord impressions
Interior surface treatment—undetermined
Lip decoration—cord-wrapped cord at oblique angle across lip
Exterior decoration—undetermined
Interior decoration—undetermined
Lip shape—flat
Rim shape—undetermined
Lip thickness—undetermined
Rim thickness—undetermined
Paste—compact, laminar, grit temper of small to medium particles
Manufacture—undetermined
Weight—0.5 grams
Number of fragments—1
Chronology—possibly early Late Woodland, because of cord-impressed exterior, paste and cord-wrapped cord impressions on lip surface, although latter decoration may also point to Tittabawassee Middle Woodland; paste characterisics more in line with early Late Woodland

---

Vessel 59
Provenience:
103N/102W, level 3
104N/81W (slump)
105N/102W (slump)
Exterior surface treatment—obscured by decoration
Interior surface treatment—smoothed-over cord impressions
Lip decoration—undetermined
Exterior decoration—linear impressions possibly made by a carved paddle in two bands, one parallel to the lip and one at an oblique angle to and being truncated by the first band (see photograph)
Interior decoration—undetermined

Lip shape—undetermined
Rim shape—undetermined
Lip thickness—undetermined
Rim thickness—5.91 mm at neck
Paste—poorly consolidated, laminar, grit temper of medium to heavy density and medium particle size
Manufacture—undetermined
Weight—19.2 grams
Number of fragments—3 (Note: one of the sherds is from a provenience 21 meters away from the other two, but by all characteristics, appears to be from the same pot)
Chronology—Late Woodland. This is a highly unusual vessel for this ceramic assemblage because of the cord impressions on the interior and the decorative motif on exterior; this kind of ware with the diagonal motif points to later in Late Woodland, but no known relationship (Plates 8.3 and 8.4*e-f*)

Vessel 60
Provenience—Bowen Feature
Exterior surface treatment—undetermined
Interior surface treatment—smoothed by brushing
Lip decoration—smoothed
Exterior decoration—undetermined
Interior decoration—undetermined
Lip shape—square
Rim shape—undetermined
Lip thickness—8.41 mm
Rim thickness—undetermined
Paste—laminar, grit temper of heavy density and small to medium particle size
Manufacture—undetermined
Weight—0.6 grams
Number of fragments—1
Chronology—undetermined; too fragmentary

Vessel 61
Provenience—104N/102W, level 4
Exterior surface treatment—fine fabric impressions
Interior surface treatment—heavily brushed over a thin clay layer with only large grit particles poking through
Lip decoration—undetermined
Exterior decoration—field of vertically oriented fabric impressions truncated by a single cord impression, above which is another field of cord impressions
Interior decoration—undetermined
Lip shape—undetermined
Rim shape—undetermined; curvature of fragment and body thickening where single cord impression is placed indicates fragment most likely from neck-rim juncture
Lip thickness—undetermined
Rim thickness—4.47 mm at maximum width
Paste—hard, compact, grit temper of medium density and small to medium particle size
Manufacture—undetermined
Weight—2.3 grams
Number of fragments—1
Chronology—Late Woodland, probably early Late Woodland based on cord-impressed exterior, thinness of ware, and compact ware like classic Wayne-Saginaw wares

---

Vessel 62
Provenience—Bowen Feature
Exterior surface treatment—smooth
Interior surface treatment—smoothed by heavy brushing, leaving horizontal brushing marks
Lip decoration—cord impressions parallel to axis of lip
Exterior decoration—loosely twisted cord impressions parallel to each other and oblique to lip surface, 4.34 mm apart
Interior decoration—undetermined
Lip shape—square
Rim shape—castellated (not enough of rim to determine presence of a collar)
Lip thickness—6.15 mm
Rim thickness—7.52 mm at 10.0 mm below lip surface
Paste—exfoliated, grit temper of medium density and small to large particles
Manufacture—undetermined
Weight—2.1 grams
Number of fragments—1
Chronology—Late Woodland Macomb Linear-corded, based on presence of castellation and decorative motif; Fitting (1965) suggests an A.D. 800 to 1000 age for this southeastern Michigan ceramic type; this vessel probably occurs later in this time range, because of the presence of castellations (Plate 8.5*d*)

Vessel 63
Provenience—115N/103W, level 4
Exterior surface treatment—smoothed-over

medium cord impressions, vertically oriented and extends to lip margin
Interior surface treatment—smoothed by brushing, with larger grit particles poking through, modelled interior
Lip decoration—irregular cord impressions and incisions over previously heavily brushed surface
Exterior decoration—undetermined
Interior decoration—undetermined
Lip shape—flat surface, internally beveled
Rim shape—straight
Lip thickness—11.8 mm
Rim thickness—12.87 mm at 20 mm below lip surface
Paste—sandy/silty, chunky, heavily eroded, grit temper (dark crystalline temper) of light density and small to very large particle size
Manufacture—coil
Weight—9.1 grams
Number of fragments—1
Chronology—late Early Woodland Shiawassee Ware based on thickness, coarse and chalky paste, type of temper and surface treatment (Plate 8.5*a*)

Vessel 64
Provenience—123N/103W, level 5
Exterior surface treatment—heavily smoothed, producing a distinctive sheen
Interior surface treatment—smoothed by brushing, modelled interior
Lip decoration—undetermined, hint of smoothed-over cord impressions on fragmentary lip surface
Exterior decoration—3 very shallow unidentified tool marks in a row; marks are 3.22 mm long and spaced 4.54 mm apart
Interior decoration—undetermined
Lip shape—undetermined
Rim shape—undetermined
Lip thickness—undetermined
Rim thickness—undetermined
Paste—silty, chunky, grit temper of light density and small to medium particle size
Manufacture—coil
Weight—12.5 grams
Number of fragments—2 (Fragments consist of a very fragmentary lip interior and a large body sherd. Although no exact fit can be demonstrated, the distinctive paste and surface treatment and the location of these sherds in the same provenience unit isolated from other vessel fragments strongly suggest that they are from the same vessel.)
Chronology—Middle Woodland based on smooth exterior and type of punctates in neck-shoulder area; punctates suggest Green Point, not Tittabawassee, but too fragmentary to pinpoint which period within the Saginaw Valley Middle Woodland sequence (Plate 8.5*e*)

Vessel 65
Provenience—114N/101W, level 2
Exterior surface treatment—smoothed-over fine cord impressions, placed slightly obliquely to the lip surface
Interior surface treatment—undetermined
Lip decoration—heavily eroded slightly oblique unidentified tool slashes across externally beveled surface, similar slightly oblique marks aross interior of lip
Exterior decoration—undetermined
Interior decoration—undetermined
Lip shape—thickened, rolled forward, external beveling
Rim shape—everted
Lip thickness—7.34
Rim thickness—undetermined
Paste—compact, laminar, grit temper of very light density and small particles
Manufacture—undetermined
Weight—1.6 grams
Number of fragments—1
Chronology—early Late Woodland, based on cord-impressed exterior, paste, thickened lip and everted rim; Wayne ware although rolled and thickened lip suggest northern Mackinac type

---

Vessel 66
Provenience—104N/101W, level 2
Exterior surface treatment—smoothed-over fine cord impressions, vertically oriented and extends up to lip margin
Interior surface treatment—smooth
Lip decoration—none, smooth surface
Exterior decoration—undetermined
Interior decoration—undetermined
Lip shape—square
Rim shape—straight expanding
Lip thickness—3.12 mm
Rim thickness—6.30 mm at 12.0 mm below lip surface
Paste—hard, compact, laminar, grit temper of light density and small particle size
Manufacture—undetermined

Weight—1.5 grams
Number of fragments—1
Vessel relationships—this rim fragment is very similar in most characteristics to vessel 7, which was found only 2 units away; however, vessel 7 appears to have a straighter rim profile and clear indications of cord impressions on the lip surface, so I have counted this rim fragment as a separate vessel
Chronology—early Late Woodland, based on thinness of ware, cord-impressed exterior, and paste; flat, smoothed lip suggests Allegan wares from southwestern Michigan although some Wayne wares have this kind of lip treatment

---

Vessel 67
Provenience—104N/81W, level 5-6
Exterior surface treatment—smoothed-over fine cord impressions, vertically oriented and extending on to front of the thickened lip
Interior surface treatment—undetermined
Lip decoration—very fine cord-wrapped cord impressions placed slightly obliquely across lip surface and cutting across interior lip margin, making the interior lip margin rippled; impressions placed 4.18 mm apart
Exterior decoration—undetermined
Interior decoration—undetermined
Lip shape—thickened and then flattened with cord-wrapped paddle
Rim shape—everted*
Lip thickness—3.16 mm
Rim thickness—undetermined
Paste—compact, laminar, grit temper of light density and small particles
Manufacture—undetermined
Weight—1.2 grams
Number of fragments—1
Chronology—early Late Woodland, probable Wayne ware, based on paste characteristics, cord-impressed exterior, lip decoration, and thickened rolled lip

---

Vessel 68
Provenience—104N/81W, level 5-6
Exterior surface treatment—fine to medium cord impressions, vertically oriented and extends to about 4.06 mm below lip surface
Interior surface treatment—smoothed by brushing
Lip decoration—smoothed-over cord impressions, with the smoothing extending on to the lip exterior margin
Exterior decoration—undetermined
Interior decoration—undetermined
Lip shape—square
Rim shape—straight*
Lip thickness—5.58 mm
Rim thickness—4.77 mm at 10.0 mm below lip surface
Paste—compact, laminar, grit temper of medium density and small to large particle size
Manufacture—undetermined
Weight—4.3 grams
Number of fragments—1
Chronology—probably early Late Woodland affiliation by cord impressed exterior, lip-rim morphology; paste not classic Wayne ware; can draw some relationships to western Allegan-Spring Creek wares

---

Vessel 69
Provenience—104N/81W, level 5-6
Exterior surface treatment—heavily smoothed
Interior surface treatment—smooth with larger grit particles poking through
Lip decoration—undetermined
Exterior decoration—row of oblique slash marks of variable length, from 9.04 to 11.95 mm long and about 3.6 mm apart, at what appears to be the neck of the vessel by the curvature of the sherd
Interior decoration—similar slash marks spaced 4.6 mm apart which appear to be on the interior of the upper rim, but the lip is missing
Lip shape—undetermined
Rim shape—undetermined
Lip thickness—undetermined
Rim thickness—undetermined
Paste—compact, laminar, grit temper of medium density and small to medium particle size
Manufacture—undetermined
Weight—5.7 grams
Number of fragments—2
Chronology—Middle Woodland Green Point Incised, based on smooth exterior and type of decoration (Plate 8.5*f*)

Vessel 70
Provenience—114N/81W, level 5-6
Exterior surface treatment—undetermined
Interior surface treatment—smooth
Lip decoration—unidentified tool cutting a deep wedge-shaped gash perpendicular across lip surface, with shallower cord impressions parallel to the deep gash
Exterior decoration—undetermined
Interior decoration—undetermined
Lip shape—slightly internally beveled
Rim shape—undetermined
Lip thickness—undetermined
Rim thickness—undetermined
Paste—compact, laminar, grit temper of medium density and small to medium particle size
Manufacture—undetermined
Weight—0.6 grams
Number of fragments—1
Vessel relationships—because of shared paste characteristics, in contrast to other vessel fragments in this isolated provenience unit, this rim may be related to Decorated Sherd 26.
Chronology—undetermined; too fragmentary and no distinctive characteristics

Decorated Sherds

Decorated 1
Provenience:
111N/101W, level 3
112N/102W, level 2
113N/103W, level 4
107N/101W, level 3
Exterior surface treatment—medium cord impressions, partially smoothed
Interior surface treatment—smoothed by brushing with larger grit particles poking through
Decoration—columns of unidentified tool impressions, leaving oblong oblique (relative to direction of surface treatment) impressions with flat sides and wedgelike end that was pulled out of clay consistently in one direction leaving a short trail; variable number of impressions, from 5 to 7 impressions in 3.1 cm; average length of impression is 5.79 mm and average width is 2.18 mm
Placement on vessel—fragments are straight with little hint of curvature, suggesting a very straight rim profile and/or gradual shoulder
Thickness—7.65 mm
Paste—compact, laminar, grit temper of light density and small to large particle size
Manufacture—undetermined
Weight—28.0 grams
Number of fragments—4
Vessel relationships—No direct association with a rim can demonstrated, particularly no link with rim fragments located near Decorated 1. Count as an additional vessel in Maximum Vessel Count.
Chronology—Late Woodland Younge Phase of the Younge Tradition, probably from a Vase Tool-impressed vessel, suggested by oblique tool marks (Fitting 1965) (Plate 8.5*c*)

Decorated 2
Provenience—105N/103W, level 3
Exterior surface treatment—smoothed-over fine cord impressions
Interior surface treatment—undetermined
Decoration—radiating, thin, shallow incised lines cutting through cord impressed surface
Placement on vessel—undetermined
Thickness—undetermined
Paste—compact, laminar, grit temper of medium density and small to large particle size
Manufacture—unknown
Weight—1.5 grams
Number of fragments—1
Vessel relationships—in close proximity to vessels 17 and 18 and could possibly be related, but it is not conclusive. Counted as an additional vessel in Maximum Vessel Count.
Chronology—Possibly early Late Woodland Wayne Crosshatched because of crosshatched motif over cord-impressed surface, but based on very fragmentary sherd

---

Decorated 3
Provenience—118N/103W, level 4
Exterior surface treatment—smoothed-over cord impressions
Interior surface treatment—smoothed by brushing
Decoration—single fine cord impression with 2 parallel thin incised lines cut perpendicular across cord impression
Placement on vessel—undetermined
Thickness—11.69 mm
Paste—sandy/silty, coarse, grit temper of medium density and small to very large particle size
Manufacture—coil
Weight—6.1 grams
Number of fragments—1
Vessel relationships—most similar in paste-temper, thickness and manufacture technique to vessel 37, which is located at the same depth and within 1 unit of Decorated 3. However, this body sherd could be a thicker segment of a vessel like vessel 44, located at the same level 2 units away. Although a direct relationship with

another vessel cannot be demonstrated, there are numerous vessels in the vicinity to which it could be related. Therefore, this fragment will not be counted as an additional vessel.
Chronology—late Early Woodland Shiawassee ware vessel based on thickness, paste and crude crosshatching on exterior (Halsey 1976)

Decorated 4
Provenience—105N/102W, level 3
Exterior surface treatment—heavily smoothed-over cord impressions
Interior surface treatment—smooth
Decoration—a fragment of a curving relatively deeply incised line
Placement on vessel—undetermined
Thickness—5.3 mm
Paste—compact, laminar, grit temper of light density and small particle size
Manufacture—undetermined
Weight—00.9 grams
Number of fragments—1
Vessel relationships—no vessel shares the same surface treatment or paste characteristics, particularly those vessels in close proximity. However, this is a tiny fragment upon which to designate an additional vessel. Will do so only for the Maximum Vessel Count.
Chronology—undetermined

Decorated 5
Provenience—105N/102W (slump)
Exterior surface treatment—smoothed-over cord impressions
Interior surface treatment—undetermined
Decoration—panel of twisted fiber or carved paddle impressions placing at least 3 parallel lines across cord impressions
Placement on vessel—undetermined
Thickness—undetermined
Paste—compact, laminar, grit temper of medium to heavy density and small to large particle size
Manufacture—undetermined
Weight—1.7 grams
Number of fragments—1
Vessel relationships—same tool type is used on vessel 59, which is located within 2 units. Although a direct relationship cannot be demonstrated, this sherd will not be counted as an additional vessel.
Chronology—see vessel 59

Decorated 6
Provenience—107N/102W, level 3
Exterior surface treatment—smoothed-over fine cord impressions
Interior surface treatment—obscured by decoration
Decoration—unidentified wide tool, possibly carved paddle, cutting at least three 3.90 mm wide lines into surface, leaving high thin ridges of clay between impressions
Placement on vessel—curvature suggests that decoration is on the interior; otherwise, can not locate fragment on vessel
Thickness—3.8 mm
Paste—compact, laminar, grit temper of light density and small to medium particle size
Manufacture—undetermined
Weight—0.9 grams
Number of vessels—1
Vessel relationships—no connection can be drawn to any vessel, but this sherd is located in an area where numerous fragmented vessels are represented. Shows the closest similarity to vessel 56 which is located in the underlying level of the same unit. Because the connection cannot be demonstrated and no sherd or vessel shows the same decoration as present on this sherd, an additional vessel will be counted in the Maximum Vessel count.
Chronology—undetermined; thinness of ware and paste points to non-Early Woodland affiliation, but no other conclusions possible based on such fragmentary evidence

---

Decorated 7
Provenience—104N/102W, level 4
Exterior surface treatment—fine fabric impressions
Interior surface treatment—smoothed with larger grit particles poking through
Decoration—a row of slightly oblique cord impressions broken in half, so cannot determine whether or not it is a cord-wrapped cord impression; impressions are 7.33 mm apart
Placement on vessel—appears to be located

at the neck from curvature of fragment, or farther down on shoulder, if it is a fragment of vessel 10 (see Vessel Relationships)
Thickness—5.60 mm
Paste—hard, compact, laminar, grit temper of light to medium density and small to medium particle size
Manufacture—undetermined
Weight—9.8 grams
Number of fragments—1
Vessel relationships—probably related to vessel 10 which is located in close proximity. Interior and exterior surface treatments and paste characteristics are similar. There may be a fit with vessel 10, which if accepted, places the row of small impressions on the shoulder rather than the neck. Because of the strong similarities to, and possible fit with, vessel 10, this sherd will not be counted as an additional vessel.
Chronology—early Late Woodland, see vessel 10

Decorated 8
Provenience:
112N/101W, level 3
110N/101W, level 3
111N/101W, level 3
Exterior surface treatment—smoothed-over fine cord impressions
Interior surface treatment—undetermined
Decoration—at least 2 rows of cord-wrapped cord impressions 10.8 mm apart and rows 11.00 mm apart
Placement on vessel—undetermined
Thickness—undetermined
Paste—compact, laminar, grit temper of light density and small to large particle size
Manufacture—undetermined
Weight—10.0 grams
Number of fragments—5
Vessel relationships—possibly related to vessel 25, which is located in close proximity. The same tool and paste characteristics suggest a relationship. Vessel 25 is also one of only 2 vessels (with vessel 23) found in the vicinity of these decorated sherds and the only one with similar characteristics. Although a direct relationship cannot be demonstrated, the possibility that this set of sherds may be from vessel 25 removes them from the count as an additional vessel.
Chronology—early Late Woodland, probable Wayne Decorated variant, based on paste, cord-impressed exterior and multiple rows of punctates (Plate 8.1*h*)

Decorated 9
Provenience—114N/103W, level 6
Exterior surface treatment—smoothed-over medium cord impressions
Interior surface treatment—very smooth
Decoration—a deep, annular tool, leaving interior core of 4.28 mm in diameter; tool diameter is 6.7 mm
Placement on vessel—undetermined
Thickness—7.65 mm
Paste—silty, chunky, grit temper of medium density and small to large particle size
Manufacture—undetermined
Weight—5.0 grams
Number of fragments—1
Vessel relationships—isolated relative to other vessels. Closest to vessels 38 and 39. However, decorated 9's paste is much siltier than these vessels. This sherd will be counted as an additional vessel in the Maximum Vessel Count.
Chronology—undetermined; possible Middle Woodland affiliation suggested by interior bosses and paste, but further placement undetermined

---

Decorated 10
Provenience—106N/103W, level 4
Exterior surface treatment—undetermined
Interior surface treatment—smoothed
Decoration—interior of a slightly thickened lip with some kind of decoration cutting across the lip interior
Placement on vessel—interior margin of a rim
Thickness—undetermined
Paste—compact, laminar, grit temper
Manufacture—undetermined
Weight—0.5 grams
Number of fragments—1
Vessel relationships—may be the interior of vessel 52's rim fragment but the evidence is not conclusive. Several other fragmented rims lack interior surfaces (vessels 12 and 15), but are located at some distance. Although no definite relationships can be demonstrated with other vessels, this sherd will not be counted as an additional vessel, because of the extremely fragmentary nature of this sherd and the possibility of relationships to other vessels.

Chronology—undetermined; not Early Woodland

Decorated 11
Provenience—102N/102W, level 3
Exterior surface treatment—undetermined, too eroded
Interior surface treatment—smooth, grainy
Decoration—a deep, small, annular tool impression; diameter of tool is 3.57 mm
Placement on vessel—undetermined
Thickness—6.14 mm
Paste—sandy, compact, grit temper of medium density and small to medium particle size
Manufacture—undetermined
Weight—0.9 grams
Number of fragments—1
Vessel relationships—no direct relationship drawn to any particular vessel; located in an area with numerous vessels. Since sherd so is fragmentary and eroded, it will not be counted as an additional vessel.
Chronology—undetermined; sandiness of ware suggests not early Late Woodland, and thinness suggests not Early Woodland

---

Decorated 12
Provenience—102N/102W (slump)
Exterior surface treatment—smoothed-over variable width cord impressions
Interior surface treatment—smooth with larger grit particles poking through
Decoration—deep circular flat-bottomed tool impressions, 4.10 mm in diameter, leaves a prominent boss on interior; 2 rows of these punctates suggested by placement of punctates relative to surface treatment; punctates are 10.97 mm apart
Placement on vessel—curvature suggests location on gradual neck to shoulder region
Thickness—5.57 mm
Paste—compact, laminar, grit temper of medium density and small to medium particle size
Manufacture—undetermined
Weight—2.5 grams
Number of fragments—1
Vessel relationship—no direct relationship to any vessel can be demonstrated, but shares similarities in paste and surface treatment to vessel 23, which was found in close proximity and vessel 23, found at a great distance. However, there is no direct evidence of a relationship, plus the tool used to make punctations on this sherd is not seen elsewhere in this assemblage, so this sherd will be counted in the Maximum Vessel Count.
Chronology—early Late Woodland, a Wayne Decorated variant, due to relative thinness of ware, cord-impressed exterior and use of punctates in multiple rows

---

Decorated 13
Provenience—103N (slump)
Exterior surface treatment—smoothed-over medium cord impressions
Interior surface treatment—undetermined
Decoration—deep unidentified tool or cord impression; squarish punctate about 3.54 mm on a side
Placement on vessel—undetermined
Thickness—undetermined
Paste—compact, laminar, grit temper of light density and small particle size
Manufacture—undetermined
Weight—1.0 grams
Number of fragments—1
Vessel relationships—could be related to a number of very tiny rim fragments which reflect similar paste and surface treatment characteristics, but the provenience is too vague to defend any such connection. This sherd also does not have the diagnostic characteristics to defend the attribution of an additional vessel based on its presence in the assemblage alone.
Chronology—undetermined; possibly early Late Woodland from compactness of paste and cord-impressed exterior

---

Decorated 14
Provenience—120N/102W, level 3
Exterior surface treatment—appears to be smoothed around decoration
Interior surface treatment—undetermined
Decoration—unidentified tool with striated sides dragged in clay, too fragmentary to describe resulting shape of impression
Placement on vessel—curvature suggests fragment may be a lip surface
Thickness—undetermined
Paste—compact, laminar
Manufacture—undetermined
Weight—0.3 grams

Number of fragments—1
Vessel relationships—no vessel relationships could be demonstrated. Found in an area with few vessels represented. Will count as an additional vessel.
Chronology—undetermined; from paste and type of decoration, can at least exclude an Early Woodland affiliation

---

Decorated 15
Provenience:
109N/102W, level 3
109N/103W, level 3
106N/102W, level 4
107N/102W, level 3
107N/102W, level 4
107N/101W, level 3
Exterior surface treatment—smoothed-over fine cord impressions
Interior surface treatment—undetermined
Decoration—3 to 5 lines of cord-wrapped cord placed perpendicular to direction of surface treatment, spaced 2.64 mm apart
Placement on vessel—curvature and placement of decoration relative to direction of surface treatment suggests that these decorative lines are located on the neck of a vessel with a gradual sloping shoulder
Thickness—undetermined
Paste—compact, laminar, grit temper of light density and small to medium particle size
Manufacture—undetermined
Weight—6.9 grams
Number of fragments—6 (These sherds have been lumped together because of similarity of decorative elements, paste characteristics and proximity of locations. It cannot be demonstrated conclusively that they are all from the same vessel.)
Vessel relationships—located in an area containing numerous vessels. Similarities of paste characteristics and surface treatment can be argued for vessels 30, 36 and 56. Vessel 36 is a strong candidate because of use of cord-wrapped cord on lip, but cannot prove relationship. Because of possible numerous associations, these sherds will not be counted as an additional vessel.
Chronology—possibly early Late Woodland, due to characteristics of paste, thinness of ware, cord-impressed exterior and use of cord-wrapped-object decorative elements; extensive use of cord-wrapped-object decorative elements on Middle Woodland Tittabawassee ware, but paste and thickness different

---

Decorated 16
Provenience:
(A) 124N/103W, level 5, 126N/103W, level 5
(B) 103N/101W, level 4
(C) 108N/102W, level 4, 107N/103W, level 5
(D) 111N/104W, level 4
(E) 117N/102W, level 3
Exterior surface treatment—smoothed-over fine cord impressions
Interior surface treatment—smooth with larger grit particles poking through
Decoration—cord-wrapped cord impressions placed at a regular angle leaving marks ranging from 5.7 mm to 4.34 mm in length, 3.0 mm wide, and 5.20 mm apart within the rows; at least 3 rows found on some fragments
Placement on vessel—undetermined
Thickness—5.22 mm
Paste—compact, laminar, grit temper of light density and small particle size
Manufacture—undetermined
Weight—(A) 2.5 grams (B) 1.1 grams (C) 1.4 grams (D) 0.8 grams (E) 0.6 grams
Number of fragments—(A) 4 (B) 2 (C) 2 (D) 1 (E) 1
Vessel relationships—these fragments have been lumped under one heading because of the similarity in all characteristics. Because of the dispersions of some of these fragments, it cannot be assumed that all of these sherds represent a single vessel. They have therefore been grouped into more plausible sets of fragments by location.
For sets A through D, there are plausible relationships with vessels located in their vicinity: (A) = vessel 47; (B) = vessel 12; (C) = vessels 36, 52, 56; and (D) = vessel 50. In none of these situations can relationships be demonstrated. Because no vessel relationships can be claimed for (E), one additional vessel will be counted in the Maximum Vessel Count. However, given the possible wide dispersions of vessel fragments at this site, if these fragments may all represent the same vessel.
Chronology—Wayne Decorated, punctate variety (corded), from thinness of ware,

paste type and similarity of decoration to Draper Park site Wayne ware examples (Brashler 1981:311)

Decorated 17
Provenience—118N/103W, level 6
Exterior surface treatment—undetermined
Interior surface treatment—very smooth
Decoration—irregularly distributed network of thin incised line covering interior of sherd
Placement on vessel—undetermined
Thickness—at least 7.28 mm
Paste—silty, chunky, grit temper of light density and small to large particle size
Manufacture—undetermined
Weight—4.0 grams
Number of fragments—1
Vessel relationships—distinctive paste characteristics and location indicate a relationship with vessels 41, 43 or 44. Therefore, this sherd will not be treated as a separate vessel.
Chronology—undetermined; coarse, silty ware does not point to a Late Woodland affiliation, and thinness and interior incising not suggest Early Woodland. If related to vessels 41, 43 or 44, may be transitional late Middle Woodland/Early Late Woodland

---

Decorated 18
Provenience—124N/103W, level 5
Exterior surface treatment—undetermined
Interior surface treatment—very smooth
Decoration—series of irregular incised lines, 2 parallel to each other and a third at an oblique angle to others, too fragmentary to discern a pattern
Placement on vessel—undetermined
Thickness—undetermined
Paste—silty, chunky, grit temper of low density and small particle size
Manufacture—undetermined
Weight—1.9 grams
Number of fragments—1
Vessel relationships—because of shared distinctive paste characteristics and provenience (which contains only one other clearly represented, and clearly unrelated, vessel), this sherd probably belongs to vessel 64 and therefore will not be counted as a separate vessel
Chronology—similar to decorated 17; does not appear to be Early Woodland or Late Woodland. If related to vessel 64, it is probably Middle Woodland.

Decorated 19
Provenience:
123N/103W, level 3
123N/103W, level 5
Exterior surface treatment—smoothed-over cord impressions
Interior surface treatment—smooth
Decoration—very thin, but well-defined incised lines, possibly radiating out of a fragmentary impression
Placement on vessel—undetermined
Thickness—4.73
Paste—compact, laminar, grit temper of light density and small to medium particle size
Manufacture—undetermined
Weight—1.0 grams
Number of fragments—2
Vessel relationships—no other vessel in close proximity shares paste characteristics, surface treatment, or evidence the same type of decoration. This sherd therefore represents an additional vessel in the Maximum Vessel Count. Note: although these two sherds were discovered about 30 cm apart vertically, it is clear that the two sherds fit and that the smaller fragment was dragged down by some postdepositional process.
Chronology—possibly Early Late Woodland Wayne Crosshatched because of crosshatching on cord-impressed surface and relative thinness of ware; too fragmentary to be conclusive

---

Decorated 20
Provenience—102N/101W, level 3
Exterior surface treatment—smoothed-over cord impressions
Interior surface treatment—undetermined
Decoration—a single small, deep punctate made with an unidentified blunt-ended cone shaped tool; blunt end is 2.42 mm in diameter
Placement on vessel—undetermined
Thickness—undetermined
Paste—hard, compact, grit temper
Manufacture—undetermined
Weight—0.4 grams

Number of fragments—1
Vessel relationships—although no direct link to a vessel can be demonstrated, this sherd is located in an area with numerous fragmented vessels with similar paste characteristics and surface treatment. The same provenience yields at least four vessels to which this sherd could belong: vessels 12, 13, 16 and 5. This sherd will not be counted as an additional vessel.
Chronology—possibly early Late Woodland, from paste, cord-impressed exterior and punctates, but it is an extremely small fragment upon which to base temporal affiliation

---

Decorated 21
Provenience—106N/103W, level 4
Exterior surface treatment—smoothed-over fine cord impressions
Interior surface treatment—smooth
Decoration—striated linear unidentified impression, blunt-ended, possibly made by a reed
Placement on vessel—undetermined
Thickness—5.9 mm
Paste—compact, laminar, grit temper of medium density and medium particle size
Manufacture—undetermined
Weight—0.9 grams
Number of fragments—1
Vessel relationships—found in area with several vessels represented. Although not clearly associated with any particular vessel, has some similarities in paste and thickness to vessel 30, which is located in close proximity. Therefore, although this relationship cannot be demonstrated, this sherd will not be counted as an additional vessel.
Chronology—undetermined; cord-impressed exterior and punctate suggests Late Woodland. Definitely not Early Woodland because of paste and thinness of ware.

Decorated 22
Provenience—103N/101W, level 3
Exterior surface treatment—smoothed-over cord impressions
Interior surface treatment—undetermined
Decoration—deep impression by round unidentified tool with striated sides, 4.10 mm in diameter; deeply impressed, but do not know if poked through vessel wall or left boss on interior because interior surface is missing
Placement on vessel—undetermined
Thickness—undetermined
Paste—compact, laminar, grit temper of light density and small particle size
Manufacture—undetermined
Weight—0.6 grams
Number of fragments—1
Vessel relationships—located on north edge of area with numerous vessels. No direct relationship can be demonstrated although located in close proximity to vessel 6 with which it shares paste characteristics as well as surface treatment. Will not count as a separate vessel.
Chronology—undetermined

Decorated 23
Provenience—102N/102W (slump)
Exterior surface treatment—smooth
Interior surface treatment—undetermined
Decoration—cord-wrapped cord leaving an elongated pattern in a row spaced 5.8 mm apart
Placement on vessel—difficult to determine if decoration is on interior or exterior of vessel; may be from interior of rim
Thickness—4.38 mm
Paste—hard, compact, grit temper of light density and small to large particle size
Manufacture—undetermined
Weight—0.9 grams
Number of fragments—1
Vessel relationships—provenience is too vague and the area too full of represented vessels to classify this sherd as an additional vessel. Shares paste characteristics with vessels 3 and 31, but the sherds are too fragmentary to draw a conclusive connection.
Chronology—undetermined; not Early Woodland based on paste, thinness and decorative motif

---

Decorated 24
Provenience:
(A) 112N/104W, level 4
(B) 119N/102W, level 3

(C) 102N/101W, level 3, 101N/101W, level 3, 105N/101W, level 3
Exterior surface treatment—smoothed-over fine cord impressions
Interior surface treatment—smooth
Decoration—thin cord-wrapped cord impressions in isolated lines (C, D) or in series of rows of impressions (A, B, D)
Placement on vessel—undetermined
Thickness—thin ware, ranging from 3.41 to 4.14 mm
Paste—compact, laminar, grit temper
Manufacture—undetermined
Weight—(A) 0.6 grams (B) 0.3 grams (C) 1.9 grams
Number of fragments—(A) 1 (B) 1 (C) 3
Vessel relationships—these fragments have been lumped together, because of similarity in decorative elements. Because of their dispersed locations, these do not represent one vessel. If grouped by proximity, plausible relationships to other vessels can be suggested, though none can be demonstrated: (A) is similar to vessel 49 in paste characteristics and thickness; (B) No relationship suggested, so count as an additional vessel in Maximum Vessel Count; (C) located in an area with numerous vessels; most plausible relationship to vessel 1 which uses cord-wrapped cord motif on the lip.
Chronology—undetermined; thinness of ware and paste suggest early Late Woodland rather than Middle Woodland, although share use of cord wrapped object. Definitely not Early Woodland.

Decorated 25
Provenience—100–103N/100W (wall scraping)
Exterior surface treatment—undetermined
Interior surface treatment—smooth
Decoration—cord-wrapped cord impressions at least 9.14 mm long, and spaced 7.2 mm apart
Placement on vessel—probably the interior surface of upper rim, as suggested by curvature
Thickness—undetermined
Paste—compact, laminar, grit temper of light density and small to medium particle size
Manufacture—undetermined
Weight—0.9 grams
Number of fragments—1
Vessel relationships—similar to decorated 23. Provenience is too vague and the area too full of fragmented vessels to claim that this sherd represents an additional vessel. Although no particular vessel in the vicinity appears to be related, the use of cord-wrapped-object impressions around the rim is a common decorative motif used at this site. No additional vessel will be counted.
Chronology—undetermined

Decorated 26
Provenience—104N/81W, level 5-6
Exterior surface treatment—smoothed-over impressions
Interior surface treatment—undetermined
Decoration—deep dentate-like unidentified tool impressions 10.3 mm long and 3.9 mm at maximum width arranged in uneven rows and columns of unknown number, with longest axis of impression probably arranged vertically on pot as suggested by slight curvature of sherd
Placement on vessel—undetermined
Thickness—undetermined
Paste—compact, laminar, grit temper of medium density and small particle size
Manufacture—undetermined
Weight—2.5 grams
Number of fragments—1
Vessel relationships—recovered from an isolated unit. May be a fragment from vessel 70 which comes from the same provenience and shares paste characteristics, but this relationship cannot be conclusively demonstrated. Will not be counted as an additonal vessel.
Chronology—not Early Woodland; otherwise, paste and other attributes not distinct enough to pinpoint temporal affiliation

UMMA Backlist

Four series of publications are available from the Publications Office of the University of Michigan Museum of Anthropology. The Occasional Contributions, published from 1932 through 1956, and the Anthropological Papers, begun in 1949, are two series of short monographs, while the Memoirs, first published in 1970, are longer, more detailed studies. The fourth series, Technical Reports, begun in 1971, are brief, highly technical discussions of recent advances in several areas of anthropological study. New subseries will be added to the Technical Reports from time to time. Contributions to all of the series are prepared by staff members, associates, and friends of the Museum and include descriptions of museum collections and field work, results of research in various anthropological fields, and discussions of field and museum techniques.

Henry T. Wright, Director
Museum of Anthropology

The books below may be ordered from the Museum of Anthropology, 4009 Museums, University of Michigan, Ann Arbor, MI 48109. Libraries and members of the Michigan Archaeological Society receive a 20% discount. Checks must be in U.S. funds drawn on a U.S. bank. Please include $2 postage for all orders less than $10. Prepayment is required.

Occasional Contributions

6. The Younge Site: An Archaeological Record from Michigan, by Emerson F. Greenman. 1937. Reprinted 1967. Pages 172, 33 plates, 9 figures, 10 maps. Price $3.00.
15. Araucanian Culture in Transition, by Mischa Titiev. 1951. Pages 164, 17 plates, 9 figures, 2 maps. Price $2.50.

Anthropological Papers

13. The Puerto Rican Population: A Study of Human Biology, by Frederick P. Thieme. 1959. Pages 156, 4 figures, 2 maps. Price $2.50.
14. Tell Toqaan: A Syrian Village, by Louise E. Sweet. 1960. Pages 280, 54 figures. Price $2.50.
34. The Prehistory of the Burnt Bluff Area, edited by James E. Fitting. 1968. Pages 140, 47 figures. Price $3.00.
39. Rules of Descent: Studies in the Sociology of Parentage, by Guy E. Swanson. 1969. Pages 108. 4 figures, 7 tables. Price $2.00.
41. The Archaeology of Summer Island: Changing Settlement Systems in Northern Lake Michigan, by David S. Brose. 1970. Pages 236, 31 tables, 17 figures, 35 plates. Price $3.00.
42. The Occupations of Migrants in Ghana, by Polly Hill. 1970. Pages 84, 11 tables. Price $2.00.
43. Prehistoric Biological Relationships in the Great Lakes Region, by Richard Guy Wilkinson. 1971. Pages 168, 40 tables, 33 figures, 2 plates. Price $3.50.
44. Property Control and Social Strategies: Settlers on a Middle Eastern Plain, by Barbara C. Aswad. 1971. Pages 180, 16 tables, 33 figures, 2 plates. Price $3.50.
48. The Wardell Buffalo Trap 48 SU 301: Communal Procurement in the Upper Green River Basin, Wyoming, by George C. Frison. 1973. Pages 111, 29 figures, 6 tables, 14 plates. Price $3.00.

50. Faction and Conversion in a Plural Society: Religious Alignments in the Hindu Kush, by Robert Leroy Canfield. 1973. Pages 142, 11 figures, 4 tables, 1 appendix. Pricce $3.00.
55. The Ait Ndhir of Morocco: A Study of the Social Transformation of a Berber Tribe, by Amal Rassam Vinogradov. 1974. Pages 128, 11 figures, 13 plates. Price $4.00.
59. An Analysis of Effigy Mound Complexes in Wisconsin, by William M. Hurley. 1975. Pages 466, 63 figures, 48 tables, 45 plates. Price $8.00.
60. Yerbas de la gente: A Study of Hispano-American Medicinal Plants, by Karen Cowan Ford. 1975. Pages 438, 1 figures. Price $5.00.
62. The Demography of the Semai Senoi, by Alan G. Fix. 1977. Pages 123, 17 figures, 38 tables. Price $5.00.
63. Economic and Social Organization of a Complex Chiefdom: The Halelea District, Kauai, Hawaii, by Timothy Earle. 1978. Pages 205, 27 figure, 7 tables, 6 plates. Price $6.00.
64. Wāsita in a Lebanese Context: Social Exchange Among Villagers and Outsiders, by Frederick Charles Huxley. 1978. Pages 174, 6 figures, 47 tables, 5 plates. Price $6.00.
65. Meadowood Phase Settlement Patterns in the Niagara Frontier Region of Western New York State, by Joseph E. Granger, Jr. 1978. Pages 403, 73 figures, 113 tables, 35 plates. Price $8.00.
66. The Snodgrass Site of the Powers Phase of Southeast Missouri, by James E. Price and James B. Griffin. 1979. Pages 189, 80 figures, 2 tables, 17 plates. Price $6.00.
67. The Nature and Status of Ethnobotany, edited by Richard I. Ford. 1978. Pages 428, 33 figures, 28 tables, 24 plates. Price $10.00.
68. The Biological and Social Analyses of a Mississippian Cemetery from Southeast Missouri: The Turner Site, 23BU21A, by Thomas K. Black III. 1979. Pages 170, 7 figures, 69 tables, 10 plates. Price $6.00.
69. The Ait Ayash of the High Molouuya Plain: Rural Social Organization in Moroco, by John Chiapuris. 1980. Pages 186, 15 figures 9 maps, 12 plates. Price $6.00.
70. An Early Woodland Community at the Schultz Site 20SA2 in the Saginaw Valley and the Nature of Early Woodland Adaptation in the Great Lakes Region, by Doreen Ozker. 1982. Pages 273, 27 tables, 33 figures, 15 plates. Price $10.00.
71. Persian Diary, 1939–1941, by Walter N. Koelz. 1983. Pages 227, 2 maps, 68 photos. Price $10.00.
72. Lulu Linear Punctated: Essays in Honor of George Irving Quimby, edited by Robert C. Dunnell and Donald K. Grayson. 1983. Pages 354, 39 figures, 19 plates, 20 tables. Price $12.00.
73. Paleoethnobotany of the Kameda Peninsula Jomon, by Gary W. Crawford. 1983. Pages 200, 27 figures, 12 tables, 23 plates. Price 48.00.
74. The Archaeology of the Sierra Blanca Region of Southeastern New Mexico, by Jane Holden Kelley. 1983. Pages 527, 85 figures, 10 maps, 41 tables, 87 plates. Price $15.00.
75. Prehistoric Food Production in North America, edited by Richard I. Ford. 1985. Pages 411, 39 figures, 22 tables. Price $15.00.
76. Primitive Polluters: Semang Impact on the Malaysian Tropical Rain Forest Ecosystem, by A. Terry Rambo. 1985. Pages 104, 5 figures, 5 tables, 16 plates. Price $8.00.
77. Jumano and Patarabueye: Relations at La Junta de los Rios, by J. Charles Kelley. 1986. Pages 180, 14 figures, 9 plates. Price $10.00.
78. Protohistoric Yamato: Archaeology of the First Japanese State, by Gina L. Barnes. 1988. Pages 473, 94 figures, 17 tables. Price $15.00.
79. The Foxie Otter Site: A Multicomponent Occupation North of Lake Huron, by Christopher C. Hanks. 1988. Pages 203, 21 figures, 14 tables. Price $12.00.

Memoirs

2. The Burial Complexes of the Knight and Norton Mounds in Illinois and Michigan, by James B. Griffin, Richard E. Flanders and Paul F. Titterington. 1970. Pages 216, 177 plates. Price $7.00.
3. Prehistoric Settlement Patterns in the Texcoco Region, Mexico, by Jeffrey R. Parsons. 1971. Pages 447, 8 tables, 14 maps, 88 figures, 57 plates. Price $8.00.
4. The Schultz Site at Green Point: A Stratified Occupation Area in the Saginaw Valley of Michigan, edited by James E. Fitting. 1972. Pages 317, 84 figures, 70 tables, 2 appendixes. Price $8.00.
7. Formative Mesoamerican Exchange Networks with Special Reference to the Valley of Oaxaca, by Jane W. Pires-Ferreira. Prehistory and Human Ecology of the Valley of Oaxaca, Vol. 3. Pages 111, 44 figures, 27 tables, 4 plates. Price $6.00.
8. Fábrica San José and Middle Formative Society in the Valley of Oaxaca, by Robert D. Drennan. Prehistory and Human Ecology of the Valley of Oaxaca, Vol. 4. 1975. Pages 300, 10 tables, 2 maps, 75 figures, 29 plates. Price $8.00.
9. Studies in the Archaeological History of the Deh Luran Plain, by Frank Hole. 1977. Pages 369, 94 tables, 119 illustrations, 55 plates. $10.00.
10. Part 1. The Vegetational History of the Oaxaca Valley, by C. Earle Smith, Jr. Pages 39, 1 table, 2 maps, 10 plates. Part 2. Zapotec Plant Knowledge: Classification, Uses, and Communication About Plants in Mitla, Oaxaca, Mexico, by Ellen Messer. Pages 149, 29 figures, 1 map, 10 plates. Prehistory and Human Ecology of the Valley of Oaxaca, Vol. 5. 1978. Price $8.00.
11. An Archaeological Survey of the Keban Reservoir Area of East-Central Turkey, by Robert E. Whallon. 1979. Pages 309, 211 figures, 20 tables, 2 plates. Price $10.00.
12. Excavations at Santo Domingo Tomaltepec: Evolution of a Formative Community in the Valley of Oaxaca, Mexico, by Michael E. Whalen. Prehistory and Human Ecology of the Valley of Oaxaca, Vol. 6. 1981. Pages 225, 38 tables, 58 figures, 73 plates. Price $13.00.
13. An Early Town on the Deh Luran Plain: Excavations at Tepe Farukhabad, edited by Henry T. Wright. 1981. Pages 462, 99 figures, 96 tables, 21 plates. Price $15.00.
14. Prehispanic Settlement Patterns in the Southern Valley of Mexico: The Chalco-Xochimilco Region, by Jeffrey R. Parsons, Elizabeth Brumfiel, Mary H. Parsons, and David J. Wilson. 1982. Pages 504, 128 figures, 115 tables, 40 maps, 31 plates. Price $16.00.
15. Monte Albán's Hinterland, Part 1: The Prehispanic Settlement Patterns of the Central and Southern Parts of the Valley of Oaxaca, Mexico, by Richard E. Blanton, Stephen Kowalewski, Gary Feinman, and Jill Appel. Prehistory and Human Ecology of the Valley of Oaxaca, Vol. 7. 1982. Pages 506, 43 tables, 139 figures. Price $20.00.
16. A Fuego y Sangre: Early Zapotec Imperialism in the Cuicatlán Cañada, Oaxaca, by Elsa M. Redmond. Studies in Latin American Ethnohistory and Archaeology, Vol 1. 1983. Pages 216, 75 figures, 46 tables, 42 plates. Price $15.00.
17. Irrigation and the Cuicatec Ecosystem: A Study of Agriculture and Civilization in North Central Oaxaca, by Joseph W. Hopkins, III. Studies in Latin American Ethnohistory and Archaeology, Vol. 2. 1984. Pages 148, 13 figures, 3 tables, 16 plates. Price $15.00.
18. Aztec City-States, by Mary G. Hodge. Studies in Latin American Ethnohistory and Archaeology, Vol. 3. 1984. Pages 166, 64 figures, 30 tables. Price $15.00.
19. Early Neolithic Settlement and Society at Olszanica, by Sarunas Milisauskas. 1986. Pages 319, 160 figures, 153 tables, 51 plates. Price $20.00.
20. Chipped Stone Tools in Formative Oaxaca, Mexico: Their Procurement, Production and Use, by William J. Parry. Prehistory and Human Ecology of the Valley of Oaxaca, Vol. 8. 1987. Pages 178, 42 tables, 52 figures, 20 plates. Price $18.00.
21. Conflicts Over Coca Fields in XVIth-Century Perú, by María Rostworowski de Diez Canseco. Studies in Latin American Ethnohistory and Archaeology, Vol. 4. 1988. Pages 314, 21 figures, 2 tables. Price $19.50.

22. Agricultural Intensification and Prehistoric Health in the Valley of Oaxaca, Mexico, by Denise C. Hodges. Prehistory and Human Ecology of the Valley of Oaxaca, Vol. 9. 1989. Pages 146, 6 figures, 42 tables, 4 appendices. Price $16.00.
23. Monte Albán's Hinterland, Part II: Prehispanic Settlement Patterns in Tlacolula, Etla and Ocotlán, the Valley of Oaxaca, Mexico, by Stephen Kowalewski, Gary Feinman, Laura Finsten, Richard Blanton and Linda Nicholas. 1989. Pages 1146 (in 2 vols.), 141 figures, 116 tables, 8 plates, 9 appendices. Price $40.00.

Technical Reports

2. LONGTERM and PEAKSCAN: Neutron Activation Analysis Computer Programs, by Thomas Meyers and Mark Denies. Contributions in Computer Applications to Archaeology, No. 2. 1972. Pages 76, 43 pages computer output, 2 figures. Price $1.00.
3. Data on the Abnormal Hemoglobins and Glucose-6-Phosphate Dehydrogenase Deficiency in Human Populations, by Frank B. Livingstone. Contributions in Human Biology, No. 1. 1973. Pages 289. Price $2.50.
4. An Arachaeological Investigation on the Loboi Plain, Baringo District, Kenya, by William R. Farrand, Richard W. Redding, Milford H. Wolpolff, and Henry T. Wright. Research Reports in Arcaeology, No. 1. 1976. Pages 59, 10 figures. Price $3.50.
5. Digging for Gold: Papers on Archaeology for Profit, edited by William K. Macdonald. Research Reports in Archaeology, No. 2. 1976. Pages 86. Price $3.50.
6. An Investigation of Ethnographic and Archaeological Specimens of Mescalbeans (*Sophora seconiflora)* in American Museums, by William L. Merrill. Research Reports in Ethnobotany, No. 1. 1977. Pages 167, 3 figures, 3 tables, 25 plates. Price $5.00.
7. Excavations at Quachilco: A Report on the 1977 Season of the Palo Blanco Project, by Robert D. Drennan. Research Reports in Archaeology, No. 3. Pages 81, 18 figures. Price $4.00.
10. Archaeological Investigations in Northeastern Xuzestan, 1976, edited by Henry T. Wright. Research Reports in Archaeology, No. 5. 1979. Pages 140, 52 figures, 20 tables. Price $6.00.
11. Prehistoric Social, Political, and Economic Development in the Area of the Tehuacan Valley: Some Results of the Palo Blanco Project, edited by Robert D. Drennan. Research Reports in Archaeology, No. 6. 1979. Pages 260, 46 figures, 26 tables. Price $6.50.
12. Late Prehistoric Bison Procurement in Southeastern New Mexico: The 1978 Season at the Garnsey Site, by John D. Speth and William J. Parry. Research Reports in Archaeology, No. 7. 1980. Pages 384, 39 figures, 32 tables, 34 plates. Price $9.00.
14. Archaeological Settlement Pattern Data from the Chalco, Xochimilco, Ixtapalapa, Texcoco and Zumpango Regions, Mexico, by Jeffrey R. Parson, Keith W. Kintigh, and Susan Gregg. Research Reports in Archaeology, No. 9. Pages 222. Price $8.00.
15. The Garnsey Spring Campsite: Late Prehistoric Occupation in Southeastern New MExico, by William J. Parry and John D. Speth. Research Reports in Archaeology, No. 10. Pages 228, 24 figures, 27 tables, 24 photos. Price $8.00.
16. Regional Archaeology in the Valle de la Plata, Colombia: A Preliminary Report on the 1984 Season of the Proyecto Arqueológico Valle de la Plata, edited by Robert D. Drennan. Research Reports in Archaeology, No. 11. 1985. Pages 195 (including complete Spanish translation), 43 figures, 16 tables. Price $8.00.
17. Zooarchaeology of Six Prehistoric Sites in the Sierra Blanca Region, New Mexico, by Jonathan C. Driver. Research Reports in Archaeology, No. 12. 1985. Pages 103, 29 tables, 8 figures, 1 appendix. Price $5.00.
18. The Henderson Site Burials: Glimpses of a Late Prehistoric Population in the Pecos Valley, by Thomas R. Rocek and John D. Speth. Research Reports in Archaeology, No. 13. 1986. Pages 348, 118 figures, 63 tables. Price $13.00.

19. Medicinal Plants of Native America, by Daniel E. Moerman. 1987. Pages 912 (in 2 vols.). Price $30.00.
20. Late Intermediate Occupation at Cerro Azul, Peru, by Joyce Marcus. 1987. Pages 112, 70 figures. Price $8.00.
21. The Inscriptions of Calakmul: Royal Marriage at a Maya City in Campeche, Mexico, by Joyce Marcus. 1987. Pages 205, 65 figures, 7 tables. Price $8.00.

Special Publications

The Williams Collection of Far Eastern Ceramics, Chinese, Siamese, and Annamese Ceramic Wares Selected from the Collection of Justice and Mrs. G. Mennen Williams in the University of Michigan Museum of Anthropology, by Kamer Aga-Oglu. 1972. Pages 73, 85 black and white photographs. Price $4.00.

The Williams Collection of Far Eastern Ceramics—Tonnancour Section, by Kamer Aga-Oglu. 1975. Pages 185, 183 black and white photographs, 18 color photographs. Price $8.00.